Social Physics
and a Theory
of Everything

Social Physics
and a Theory
of Everything

TIM DELANEY

McFarland & Company, Inc., Publishers
Jefferson, North Carolina

ISBN (print) 978-1-4766-9846-5
ISBN (ebook) 978-1-4766-5614-4

Library of Congress cataloging data are available

Library of Congress Control Number 2025017326

Front cover image: © pashabo/Shutterstock

Printed in the United States of America

*McFarland & Company, Inc., Publishers
Box 611, Jefferson, North Carolina 28640
www.mcfarlandpub.com*

To those who are inspired to pursue the answers
to life's most profound questions and present them
in the form of a coherent theory.

Acknowledgments

Special thanks to the fine folks at McFarland who work hard to publish informative, entertaining, educational and inspiring books that offer unique and innovative ideas and perspectives on the world and the universe we live in. I acknowledge my colleague Professor Tim Madigan for his initial review of the manuscript. And I acknowledge the relevant ideas of social thinkers, especially sociologists and physicists, that influenced the formation of the theory of everything proposed here.

Table of Contents

Preface

"Social physics" was the term that Auguste Comte first proposed in the early 1820s for his new academic discipline of "positive philosophy" that would eventually come to be known as sociology. It is too bad that he did not stick with social physics as it's a perfect description for his original idea of combining the rigor of the hard sciences, specifically, physics and mathematics, along with the scientific study of society and human behavior, sociology. The term "social physics" makes it clear that the study of social phenomena, societies, organizations, groups and human behavior is to be conducted scientifically. Furthermore, the terms "positivism" and "positive philosophy" have fallen out of favor with many contemporary sociologists. Alas, the term "social physics" had mostly disappeared from academic discourse as well. In *Social Physics and a Theory of Everything*, not only is the concept of "social physics" reintroduced to academic discourse, it is also applied to a topic area that few social thinkers, if any sociologists, have ever attempted to create, a "theory of everything."

A limited number of physicists have attempted to establish a "theory of everything" but they did not give equal value to the role of humanity and human behavior. Sociologists have certainly not attempted to create a "theory of everything" from a sociological perspective that incorporates the important aspects and contributions of physics. In this text there is a meshing of contributions from both of these academic disciplines, which makes it the very essence of a revised social physics. All of this and much more makes this book unusual. Its goals are to be informative, educational, inspiring, thought-provoking, and at times entertaining; to educate readers about the origins and development of physics, the origins and development of sociology, and the beauty of the concept of "social physics"; and to offer the most complete, well-rounded "theory of everything" yet written.

The book is divided into four parts, each with three chapters. In Part A ("From Early Science to Physics"), Chapter 1 describes the major early breakthroughs and discoveries in science including developments from the ancient Chinese, Egyptians, Babylonians, and the Indians; the Ancient Greeks; the early Common Era; the early modern era; and the modern era. The many examples of scientific breakthroughs and discoveries in physics will pave the way for our discussion in future chapters. Chapter 2 examines the history and development of physics; describes the basics of physics (something that will be very beneficial in the chapters that follow); and covers the branches of physics. Chapter 3 takes a closer look at the development of physics from the perspective of the major paradigms of thinking and the significant social thinkers and prevailing concepts associated with each theory that took shape over the years: classical mechanics, often called Newtonian mechanics; the development of quantum theory; the subsequent progression to quantum mechanics; and the move to the dominant way of thinking in physics now, string theory and superstring theory.

Part B ("From Early Social Thought to Social Physics to Sociology") introduces the reader to some of the earliest influences on sociological thought beginning with social thought prior to the official creation of sociology. In Chapter 4, we learn how the philosophical speculation of such social thinkers as Niccolo Machiavelli, Martin Luther, Thomas Hobbes, John Locke and Jean-Jacques Rousseau would play an important role in early sociological thought, and in most cases, remains an influence in contemporary sociological theory. The Age of Enlightenment, also known as the "Age of Reason," refers to a period of time (circa 1685–1815) where writers of this era were convinced that they were emerging from centuries of darkness and ignorance into a new age enlightened by reason, science, and a respect for humanity. Two significant political revolutions—the American and French revolutions—are both highlighted as the revolutionists sought to overthrow oppressive regimes and replace them with governments based on ideals of the rights of those governed. Perhaps the single most important event toward the end of the Enlightenment Era was the Industrial Revolution. The Industrial Revolution is a hugely significant event for sociologists, and as we shall see, it plays a role in the theory of everything as it marks a period in the time when humans began to completely and heavily rely on fossil fuels for their energy needs. A discussion on Claude-Henri Saint-Simon concludes the chapter as he has a direct impact on the thoughts of Auguste Comte. Chapter 5 is a very significant chapter as this is where we learn about the founder of sociology—Auguste Comte—and his creation of the concept of "social physics"—an important aspect of the theory of everything discussed in this book. Chapter 6 has three primary subject areas all designed to emphasize the idea that sociology is a science that is strongly connected to the idea of gaining knowledge through unbiased observations and discoveries and conducting data analysis in an attempt to support or disprove a theory.

Part C ("Physics: Theories of Everything") provides an in-depth look at three physicists and their attempt to create a "theory of everything." Chapter 7 describes, perhaps, the most famous attempt of a "theory of everything" by Albert Einstein who attempted to create a unified field theory (uniting the four fundamental forces of the Universe: the strong nuclear force, the weak nuclear force, gravitational force and electromagnetism). Unfortunately, by shunning the developments of his contemporaries in quantum mechanics, Einstein never did accomplish his goal. Chapter 8 covers Stephen Hawking's attempts to prove Einstein's theory of everything was possible by using more advanced methods of physics. He also tried to explain everything in the Universe. He was successful in discussing the origin of the Universe by writing about the "Big Bang" theory but his overall attempt at completing a theory of everything would also fall short. Chapter 9 is about contemporary physicist Michio Kaku's attempt to create a theory of everything, again trying to finish Einstein's theory, but by using superstring theory.

Part D ("A Theory of Everything from the Social Physics Perspective") represents the key material of this book. Attempting a "theory of everything" from the social physics perspective provides us with the advantage of utilizing the knowledge already gained from the field of physics on certain matters, such as the properties of the forces of Nature, without the unnecessary worry of trying to create a unified field theory, and from the field of sociology to incorporate the role of human behavior. This combined knowledge can be merged in order to create a "theory of everything" from the social physics perspective which is concerned with the evolutionary growth of human knowledge leading to the development of Artificial Intelligence; the fate of humanity; questions surrounding a possible afterlife; the fate of Earth; and the fate of the Universe. With this in mind, Chapter 10 describes social physics and its connection to a "theory of everything"; expands upon the stages of human progress by adding a fourth evolutionary stage, Artificial Intelligence (AI); describes the positives and negatives of this AI stage of human evolution; and warns of AI singularity. Chapter 11 describes the fate of humanity; specifically, is there a future for humanity? Chapter 11 also describes whether or not there is an afterlife and, if yes, what the possible scenarios are. Finally, in Chapter 12, the fate of Earth and the Universe are explained. The answers provided in these three chapters reveal the social physics theory of everything.

PART A

FROM EARLY SCIENCE TO PHYSICS

How do we attempt to explain "everything"? There are so many mysteries to ponder, including the origin of life, the elements that make up Nature, our role in the Universe, whether life exists on other planets and what happens when we die? Humans have contemplated such profound questions throughout millennia by utilizing various thought processes. Ultimately, there are four major paradigms of thought: tradition; faith; common sense; and rational, enlightened thinking. Rational and enlightened thought allows for scientific discovery and explanation. In addition to acknowledging the four major paradigms of thought, Chapter 1 takes a look at the early history of breakthroughs and discoveries in science that led to the development of physics. In Chapter 2, we will take a closer look at physics, including the history and development of physics, the basics of physics, and take a look at a number of significant branches of physics. In Chapter 3, we will examine classical mechanics, known also as Newtonian mechanics; major developments in quantum theory, including the key contributions from many brilliant physicists; quantum mechanics; and string theory.

1

Early Breakthroughs
and Discoveries in Science

Introduction

Have you ever heard of the adage, in one form, or another, "The more you learn, the more you realize how little you know?" A learned person and an academic certainly understands the meaning of the statement. Anyone learning a new profession, starting a new job, or becoming a parent for the first time can relate as well. When you find yourself starting a new job you discover that it is like an onion, once you comprehend one layer of responsibility you realize there is another layer, followed by another, and so on. The more difficult and challenging the position the more there is to learn and the more overwhelming it may seem. As a college professor, I often observe students begin to grasp course material only to be overwhelmed when they discover the depth of the subsequent steps in the course material.

In this chapter, there is a great deal of information on the major paradigms of thought and especially the brief history of breakthroughs and discoveries in science presented. Pertaining to the history of science specifically, it is likely that you have heard that no idea is truly unique as all ideas had a genesis from previous ideas. Consider, for example, most people believe that it was Galileo Galilei (1564–1643 CE) that first proved (in 1609) that the Sun was the center of the Universe and the planets rotated around it (the heliocentric system) but learned people would quickly point out he simply proved the Copernican model and that Nicolaus Copernicus (1473–1543 CE) had published such a fact in 1543. This is when knowledge of science becomes fun and interesting and frustrating all at once as Indian astronomer and mathematician Aryabhata (476–550 CE) created a heliocentric model in which the Earth was viewed to be spinning on its axis and the sun stationary and the center of the solar system nearly 1,000 years before Copernicus. To further add to this story, Aristarchus of Samos (310–230 BCE), a Greek astronomer proposed a heliocentric model of universe nearly 800 years prior to Aryabhata.

The examination of the early breakthroughs and discoveries in science will also reveal that (1) astronomy and mathematics led the way as the early sciences; (2) a great deal of science occurred prior to the Enlightenment Era, which is a critical aspect of the enlightened, rational thought paradigm; and (3) discoveries of particular importance will be dominated by physics in the most recent centuries.

The Major Paradigms of Thought

In previous publications, most significantly in *Common Sense as a Paradigm of Thought* (2019), I articulated upon the four major paradigms of thought. "A paradigm of thought is defined as a model of thinking and a way of viewing reality for a community of like-minded people and their associated behavioral patterns—especially in connection with social interaction" (Delaney 2019:11). The four major paradigms of thought are: tradition; faith; common sense; and enlightened, rational thought. It is enlightened rational thinking that gave rise to scientific discovery and explanation.

Tradition

Tradition refers to a way of thinking, behaving, or doing something that has been utilized by people of a particular grouping over a long period of time. At the societal level, it involves passing down elements of a culture from generation to generation, especially via oral communication—or as sociologists would explain, via the socialization process. Examples would include the manner in which a society's population celebrates national holidays; whether or not basic human rights are extended to all members of that society; the role of government over private citizens' everyday lives; and the political ideology of a nation with regard to the global community. In many past, as well as many current societies, the power of tradition as a paradigm of thought is overwhelming and citizens of a given society governed by a traditional way of thinking will face serious consequences for violating long-established doctrines (e.g., in some contemporary Islamic nations drinking alcohol is punishable by public flogging, fines and/or lengthy imprisonment) and nations that embrace the archaic concept of "royalty" believe in birth rights over merit with regard to attaining leadership positions. At the familial level, traditions vary from family to family. Each of us can examine the traditions of our family of orientation and our family of procreation and the families of friends of ours. The very notion of what constitutes a family may also vary and challenge long-held traditional beliefs.

Tradition is likely to be the first paradigm of thought as early humans were lacking in great intellectual contemplation and organized religious doctrines. The human species learned to survive via trial and error, behavioral reinforcement, modeling, observation, and in many cases because of luck. Their quest for daily survival left little or no time for philosophical or spiritual reflection (Delaney 2019). In reality, humans were barely more advanced than other animal species that were also incapable of comprehending the meaning of life from a philosophical or religious understanding. Based on the knowledge that we have today, the first humans can be traced to Africa's Great Rift Valley (an area that includes parts of present-day Ethiopia, Kenya and Tanzania), they began to migrate to other parts of the world generally for survival purposes (scarcity of food supplies and safe havens to inhabit) (Khan Academy 2017). Other research indicates that humans (Homo sapiens) likely developed in other areas of Africa around the same time (350,000 to 260,000 years ago) (Higham 2021; Handwerk 2021a). Each generation of survivors would pass on their knowledge to the next; thus, demonstrating the value of traditional wisdom. However, as humans evolved in their development (generally measured in terms of our primary means of subsistence) from hunter-gatherer (wild plants and animals), to pastoral (domesticated livestock), horticultural (cultivation of crops), agrarian (cultivation of crops with assistance from animals and/or machinery), industrial (mechanized manufacturing of goods), and post-industrial (service-oriented work) past traditions had to be replaced with new ones as the old customs became outdated and less functional.

As the first paradigm of thought, traditions have existed since the dawn of humanity and prior to written documentation. Making decisions based on tradition was a dominant way of thinking during ancient eras and they remain so in most instances in the contemporary era as well. It would be pointless (and it is not the focus of this book) to provide examples of traditional ways of thinking in the ancient and contemporary eras but suffice it to say, tradition has always been, and will remain, as a significant paradigm of thought.

Faith

Tradition has played a significant role in maintaining social order throughout the millennia and across the globe. In heavily traditional-based societies people are expected to behave a certain way in accordance to "the way things have always been." The ambiguity of which course(s) of action to take when presented with given situations is eliminated by simply choosing to do things the way they've always been done. Such a mode of thinking is obviously conservative and lacking in progressive thought and consequently does not lend itself to being capable of making quick behavioral modifications in the face of new societal challenges and changing values and norms among the masses. The faith centered paradigm of thought works much in the same manner as tradition in that adherents to a certain faith are taught to choose courses of action that abide by specific belief systems that have long been enacted. Faith-based thought systems are passed down from one generation to the next within the family, like-minded communities, and societies that often show little or no tolerance toward people who do not share the same belief system.

As the second paradigm of thought, faith involves putting complete trust or having confidence in someone or something. There are, in fact, different types of faith. We put faith in our relationship partners that they will remain loyal to us; we put faith in auto mechanics that they did properly repair the car brakes when we left the car in the shop; we put faith in the pilot of the plane we are flying in that they are competent and know how to fly; we put faith in our friend who promised to take us to the hospital for a medical procedure at a specific time; and so on.

When speaking of faith as a paradigm of thought, however, we are clearly talking about a belief system that involves religion. Many people use spirituality and religion interchangeably but that is a misnomer. Both spirituality and religion are aspects of faith. Religion generally involves spirituality as well. However, spirituality does not have to be associated with religion. Spirituality can be experienced by anyone, religious or non-religious persons as it involves feelings of awe, contentment, wonderment, peace and tranquility. Many people find communing with nature as a spiritual experience, they are not praying to a god or a religious entity of any sort, they are simply enjoying being a part of nature. Sitting on the beach and listening to the ocean waves crash on the shoreline while the sun sets can bring a great sense of spiritual well-being for some people. Spirituality involves aspects of one's inner sense of self, a set of beliefs and practices, their search for a purpose in life, and adapting to individual experiences through personal study and self-reflection (Scott 2019). Spirituality is a personalized experience that seeks individual goals compared with religion that seeks organization goals. Spirituality allows for individual interpretation of the meaning of life and the afterlife and moral codes of behavior, religion involves a predefined belief system with consequences for violations of certain rules and behavioral expectations. While nonreligious spiritual persons may not claim affiliation to an organized religion most religious persons claim to be spiritual believing that their faith is what drives their spirituality.

Religion is one of the oldest social institutions of humanity. It arose out of the human need to explain life's many mysteries and the eventual desire of powerful people to control the ignorant (defined as those lacking knowledge or awareness). Early humans were all very simple-minded and ignorant in their ability to explain straightforward natural phenomena such as eclipses, planetary revolution around the sun, gravity and so on. Lacking the proper intellect to comprehend planetary alignment as a cause of a temporary blockage of the sun or moon, certain community member leaders would attempt to infuse a religious-based explanation such as an angry god(s) wanting to punish certain community member members for violating some local custom or belief. Generally, some sort of religious ritualistic behavior (e.g., human sacrifice) would follow and, lo and behold, the sun (or moon) came back in full display, apparently because the gods were now pleased by the human offering of a sacrifice and prayer. Clearly, this thought process is flawed as those creating doctrines of religious principles based on a belief of an angry god being responsible for an eclipse were as clueless on how to provide a rational explanation for this natural occurrence as those who were willing to be believe such a tale. To this day, religious adherents are willing to believe tall tales that are written in holy books that supposedly represent God's will. In some religions, the writings can be traced to a religious leader but just because someone who is considered holy says something is true does not make it so. This is where faith comes into play. Followers are told to have faith because their religious leaders and religious teachings speak the truth, the absolute truth and such truth is not to be question even in the face of evidence to the contrary.

Historically, the paradigm of thought of faith has been used in the maintenance of social order. A faith-based system of social order presents a very specific manner in which people are supposed to behave and gives a very specific reason why they are to obey—because God (or some other entity) commands they do so. The religious hierarchy uses the fear of upsetting God as a primary way to motivate people into falling in line and acting as the specific doctrines dictate. The traditional authorities, such as monarchies and "royals," recognized the growing power of religion and how easily the masses were duped by such simple answers to life's complicated questions that they sought a way to combine their authority with that of the religious leaders. During the Middle Ages, for example, this led to the development of the concept of "divine rights of kings"—the idea that God preordained certain people to be rulers and the rest to be subjects. To challenge the rule of the kings was akin to challenging God. In this regard, both the religious leaders and monarchs centralized power. Many contemporary societies are dominated by such an antiquated ideal.

Faith and religion does have its positive aspects. In many cases it helps people to positively confront their daily challenges (e.g., coping with an illness or the loss of a loved one and helping to provide structure and a sense of meaning to their lives). The concern with the faith-based paradigm of thought rests with the realization that most of the things people believe to be true simply are not. Having a belief in something is not the same thing as having evidence of factual knowledge about something. Another concern with the faith-based paradigm is the realization that many adherents are so certain their beliefs are true they have to believe that other beliefs are false, and this often leads to intolerance and war. It also leads to a distrust in science. Religion is based on a system of beliefs that followers generally abide by without question. As a belief-based entity, religion is often at odds with science because it is an evidence-based entity. (We will see in later chapters, however, that many scientists maintain a belief in God even though they have a commitment to science.) As Plato explained long ago, there is a difference between knowledge and science and opinion and religious belief (Lindsay 1943). Science is grounded by a commitment in the empirical testing of theoretical postulates. Religion, on the other hand, is consumed by a faith-based structure centered on beliefs, dogmatic beliefs at that. Religious adherents are told to rely on their faith. Some religious people follow such tenets blindly and close their minds to enlightened, rational thought.

Common Sense

It certainly could be argued that a certain degree of common sense was a characteristic of early humans as it should be quite evident that a single hunter was no physical match for bears, saber tooth cats or any other large predator. Sole warrior-hunters that attempted to kill an animal with primitive weapons and in harsh environments would quickly lose such battles and stories of such defeats would spread to others who might have thought of such a heroic task in an attempt to feed the clan. Before long, such knowledge was transformed into common sense. And that's the primary lesson we must learn when it comes to "common sense"; that is to say, nothing is common sense until it is learned.

It is fairly ordinary to hear such expressions as "Use your common sense" or "Anyone with any common sense at all would've seen that coming." Seemingly, everyone whether liberal, moderate or conservative; religious or non-religious; highly educated or poorly educated; tend to promote the idea of using one's common sense. Consequently, we are all expected to use common sense and we expect others to also use common sense. It seems straight-forward enough that people would be better off utilizing common sense as opposed to not applying common sense in their life decisions, doesn't it? The prevalence of the popular notion that people should use their common sense is why we can treat common sense as a paradigm of thought. Unlike the concepts of tradition, faith and enlightened rational thought, "common sense" is quite vague. Ask someone, "What *is* common sense?" or ask them to define "common sense" and ask yourself these same questions. The answers to these and other related questions will vary quite significantly.

As previously mentioned, I wrote a book titled *Common Sense as a Paradigm of Thought* (2019). As common sense should dictate, I spent a great deal of time explaining the meaning of the term *common sense* and eventually came up with parameters to explain the concept. I looked at both dictionary and academic explanations. The *Merriam-Webster* dictionary defines common sense as "sound and prudent judgment based on a simple perception of the situation or facts." Among the problems with this definition are, we are not told how to ascertain "sound and prudent" judgment and it does not allow for the fact that people often perceive things differently from one another. *Dictionary.com* defines common sense as "sound judgment that is independent of specialized knowledge, training, or the like; normal native intelligence." This definition is equating common sense with a judgment call on what a practical course of action should be; but, it also introduces an important variable that common sense is normal native intelligence—which means it is something that people indigenous to a particular region should know (thus implying that non-native people, or those from a different culture, might not have the same knowledge and common sense notions about particular behaviors). *Cambridge Dictionary* defines common sense as "the basic level of practical knowledge and judgment that we all need to help us live in a reasonable and safe way." Once again, we have the important variable that we must have knowledge of the given situation but the definition does not explain what the basic level is or what is reasonable or safe. The *Urban Dictionary* has changed its definition from three years ago and now defines common sense as a "mythical force that is supposed to bestow knowledge of the obvious." While defining common sense is indeed problematic, it is not mythical nor is it knowledge that based on the obvious.

In my *Common Sense* book I have two chapters wherein I cite the research of many brilliant scholars and their research on common sense. The following is a sampling and a very short summary of their ideas. Thomas Reid (1710–1796), a Scottish philosopher, promoted the utilization of common sense as he felt that humans can acquire knowledge through empirical observations and experimentations. Reid (1764) argued that we can make common sense assumptions of the external world because our senses and capacity for memory allow us to share in a common life with others, thus giving the opportunity for repeated experiences that can come to be regarded as common sense in future situations. Reid states that the longer someone lives the more common sense knowledge they should develop. Furthermore, Reid put forth the idea that common-sense knowledge is not innate, it is learned. Thomas Paine (1737–1809) was born in England but became famous after moving to the United States and following his publication *Common Sense* (1997 [1776]). In this publication, Paine directly advocated the colonists' right to declare their independence based on a number of "common sense" notions including moral and political, human dignity, the right for self-determination, and the belief that people should not be taxed without representation. Paine did not describe how common sense arises or debate its merits as a concept but rather he assumed that common sense was a real thing. G.E. Moore (1873–1958), a British philosopher believed that a number of behaviors can come to be seen as acts of common sense as they are routine, ordinary, and practical, and treated as common sense by those involved (Moore 1925).

Early sociologists (i.e., Charles Horton Cooley, George Herbert Mead, Herbert Blumer and Erving Goffman), especially those who examined the sociology of everyday life (e.g., symbolic interactionism, phenomenology, dramaturgy, and ethnomethodology) examined the role of behavior from the standpoint of habits (rather than instincts), the impact of the environment on modifying human behavior, the ability to interpret repeated symbols (e.g., gestures and language) during social interactions with others, the study of the behaviors between individuals, pragmatic behavior, social acts, the development of self, impulses, and the meanings behind behaviors, all critical elements in common sense notions. Alfred Schutz (1899–1959), an Austria-born phenomenologist wrote that people have a "stock of knowledge" which is like a recipe of conceptions of appropriate behavior that enable individuals to think of the world as made up of "types" or things (e.g., categories of sports, movies, emojis, and automobiles). In his *Phenomenology of the Social World* (1967 [1932]), Schutz wrote that a stock of knowledge is determined by individuals' life experiences and education. Harold Garfinkel (1917–2011), an American ethnomethodologist wrote specifically about a taken-for-granted world, accounts and the commonsense world. Garfinkel conducted breaching experiments in an attempt prove his primary point that people want to live in a "taken-for-granted" world and that they will make accounts for the behaviors of others when they violate common sense notions of behavior. Few social thinkers so specifically discussed common sense as a concept. He used the term "the commonsense world" to expand upon the idea of the taken-for-granted world (Garfinkel 1967).

When one wants to explain human behavior, the best discipline to turn to is sociology as sociology involves the scientific study of human behavior in the social context of groups, organizations, social institutions, and society, and in terms of how social forces affect behavior. Human behavior is a product of interaction with others. As for common sense specifically, it is important to realize that anything labeled as common sense is actually learned behavior; that is to say, any knowledge we have is the result of interactions with others. These interactions include the notions of experience, observation, reason, and the socialization process. Thus, anything labeled as "common sense" is really learned behavior. That people have different notions as to what constitutes as common sense is reflected by the socialization process, observations and life experiences.

Enlightened, Rational Thought

Throughout most of human history, tradition and faith have been the two dominant paradigms of thought that have primarily shaped the idea of how social order should be structured. In many instances, these two forces have formed a symbiotic relationship (e.g., the "divine rights of kings" concept) in an attempt to keep the masses subordinate to those in power. These two paradigms of thought are rife with shortcomings and certainly not conducive in explaining the big questions that confront humanity, the planet and the cosmos. The notion of common sense also falls short as the ultimate system of knowledge. This leaves us with enlightened, rational thought, the fourth paradigm of thought.

The tradition- and faith-based forms of thought are generally conservative in design because they look to maintain the status quo and keep those in power (this includes the notion of keeping God or other religious figures in power) and to keep the oppressed, subjugated. The enlightened, rational thought paradigm promotes liberal ideas such as equality, freedom, liberty, individualism and the pursuit of happiness while also promoting science and technology as the means of gaining knowledge. The tradition- and faith-based doctrines recognize that workers need to be educated to the point that they can help the economic system increase productivity in order to keep the rich in power but the enlightened, rational thought paradigm promotes higher education for the purpose of educating the masses so that they may challenge those who would attempt to keep them powerless in addition to helping them become productive members of society. Remember this fact whenever you hear someone make the irrational claim of "university indoctrination," something that is usually directed toward the social sciences that try to enlighten students of different modes of thinking. The fact is, by the time most children attend school they have been fully indoctrinated in a belief system by their parents and in many cases religious figures and single-focused community leaders. When these children are finally introduced to rational, scientific facts and different modes of looking at the world it may be shock to both them and their parents. The fault here lies not with the schools and teachers and colleges and professors that are trying to enlighten students but with the closed-minded indoctrination that many students had to endure while they were being raised. Unable to handle such realities rationally, many parents lash out at schools and teachers, ironically, for trying to indoctrinate their children. Sadly, some students will attend an indoctrination-based college (e.g., a religious school) and never receive the education they so desperately need in order to be tolerant and accepting of others and open-minded enough to learn about other modes of thinking. It is at college and university where many indoctrinated students first meet very diverse groups people and are exposed to ideas and evidence that run contrary to the stereotypes and closed-minded way of thinking they were exposed to by their parents and most local-level schools where school boards are dominated not by qualified educators but by parents and zealots who want certain traditional and/or faith-based curriculum taught. (We learned during the COVID-19 pandemic that many irrational parents did not even want to keep their children safe by having them wear masks in school or by having them get vaccinated.) Is it any wonder that so many students that entered college following the Covid era were ill-prepared for enlightened, rational thought-based courses? Or, that many students will never attend college because they do not see the value of enlightened, progressive thinking? With the increasing influence of irrational conservative thinking it is certainly no surprise the United States, a nation that once led the way in democratic principles, progressive thinking and valued higher education, is falling so far behind other nations of the world.

Enlightened, rational thought, as a paradigm of thinking, is responsible for bringing about numerous advancements that have benefited humanity. These benefits extend to the realms of medicine, communication, travel, higher education, exploration, invention and innovation, DNA fingerprinting, a wide variety of houseware products, improvements in food production, industrial improvements, developments in family planning, fuel energy production, and so on. It was the "Age of Enlightenment," a collective term used to describe the trends and writings in Europe and the American colonies during the eighteenth century that helped to propel societies from centuries of darkness and ignorance into a new age of enlightenment by means of reason, science, and a respect for humanity. The Enlightenment was a period of dramatic intellectual development and change in philosophical thought. A number of long-standing ideas and beliefs were being abandoned and replaced during the Enlightenment era (Ritzer 2000).

The Enlightenment thinkers kept a close eye of the social arrangements of society and offered an alternative to the existing social arrangements. The Church and its secular allies in the monarchy kept a close eye on free thinkers and freedom of inquiry and diversity of thought were not tolerated. Those who promoted diverse ideas were often tortured and executed (Garner 2000). Enlightened thinkers "central interest was the attainment of human social perfectibility in the here and now rather than in some heavenly future. They considered education and scientific understanding of self and society the routes to all human social progress" (Adams and Sydie 2001:11). Enlightenment thinkers believed progress was possible because humans held the capacity for reason. They did not want reason constrained by tradition, religion or sovereign power. The Age of Enlightenment was characterized by the promotion of "liberal individualism" as it was a movement that emphasized the individual's possession of critical reason, and it was opposed to traditional authority in society and the primacy of religion as the bearers of knowledge (Hadden 1997). According to Seidman (1983), liberalism arose as a reaction against static hierarchical and absolutist order, which suppressed individual freedom. Social thinkers of this era were impressed by Isaac Newton's discovery of universal gravitation as it led them to believe that if humanity could so unlock the laws of the universe, "God's own laws," why could they not also discover the laws underlying all of nature and society? Scientists came to assume that through a rigorous use of reason, an unending progress would be possible—progress in knowledge, in technical achievement, and even in moral values. Another core belief of the enlightened thinkers is a notion similar to that of the common sense paradigm that knowledge is not innate but comes only from experience and observation but in this case, guided by reason. Not surprisingly, the enlightenment thinkers promoted education. Through education, humanity itself could be altered, its nature changed for the better as truth could be discovered through observation of nature, rather than through the study of authoritative sources such as holy books (e.g., Bible and Koran) and societal rulers (e.g., monarchs). It is important to note that just like most scientists in the contemporary era, the Enlightenment thinkers did not renounce the idea of God completely; instead, they saw God as a Prime Mover, a motivator of sorts (Garner 2000).

A Brief History of Breakthroughs and Discoveries in Science

The paradigm of enlightened and rational thought began in earnest during the Enlightenment era. Among the key aspects of this paradigm of thought is the promotion of knowledge through rationality, reason, critical thinking and science.

Science itself did not begin with the Enlightenment; in fact, there were scientific breakthroughs well before this era. The exact timeline for a history of science is a matter of debate and one that will not be attempted to be resolved here. Instead, some key historical moments in the development of science will be highlighted below.

Developments from the Chinese, Egyptians, Babylonians, and the Indians

The term "science" has been used a number of times already and perhaps part of the confusion in establishing a clear timeline of science is defining the concept of science in the first place. Definitions of the term "science" generally include such criteria as having attained knowledge through the scientific method. The "scientific method" is defined as the pursuit of knowledge involving the stating of a problem, the collection of facts through observation and (perhaps) experimentation, and the testing of ideas (hypotheses) to determine whether they appear to be "valid" or "invalid." Just as the natural scientists, social scientists employ the scientific method as they maintain a strong commitment to testing their theories through statistical and/or systematic analysis. The key aspect of any claim of being a science, or engaging in scientific study, is a commitment to the systematic study of a natural or social phenomenon or behavior and the goal of attaining "facts." Unlike the other three paradigms of thought, science is not afraid to modify its claims of knowledge when presented when new and overwhelming data and information that runs contrary to earlier beliefs. Thus, from a historic perspective, established laws of science can be replaced by new ones as in the case of Ptolemaic and Copernican astronomy (Crump 2001). The Ptolemaic model had the Earth as the center of the universe and everything in the universe revolving around the Earth but the Copernican model (1543) correctly pointed out that the center of the universe and the majority of the bodies in the universe revolve around the sun.

If we start with the rudiments of science, that is to say, that it is based on that which is observable, the earliest science would be limited to human experience complied from the five senses. As time went on, humans developed devices (e.g., microscopes, telescopes, thermometers, accelerators, semiconductors, microprocessors) to observe items found in the natural world that were otherwise undetected by the senses. If a human had not seen something with their own eyes it was likely hard to believe in the truth spoken by strangers of creatures and adventures of foreign lands; and yet, all this information would develop into a growing body of knowledge.

Where does science begin? Many historians point to the combination of religion and astronomy as a fundamental early start of the history of science as astronomy is often looked upon as the first science. Did science begin with Stonehenge (constructed about 5,000 years ago) and the other megalithic structures that seem to have combined religious and astronomical purposes? "Stonehenge is shaped in a circle, but some of the other megalithic structures are egg-shaped and, apparently, constructed on mathematical principles that require at least practical knowledge of the Pythagorean Theorem that the square of the hypotenuse of a right triangle is equal to the sum of the squares of the other two sides. This theorem, or at least the Pythagorean numbers that can be generated by it, seems to have been known throughout Asia, the Middle East, and Neolithic Europe two millennia before the birth of Pythagoras" (Williams 2022). The late Neolithic period occurred about 2500 BCE and Pythagoras was born about 570 BCE on the island of Samos.

Astronomy developed in many parts of the world many thousands of years ago and with its close relationship to religion it generally had a ritualistic dimension that stimulated the growth of mathematics (Williams 2022). Early Chinese *savants* (people of learning), for example, had devised a calendar and methods of plotting the positions of stellar constellations from the very dawn of the Chinese state in the 2nd millennium BCE. The Chinese government used the knowledge of the universe not to create gods and demons whose arbitrary wills determined events but rather established orderly events for humans to figure out via the scientific method. This line of thinking led to the development of chemistry (or, rather alchemy), medicine, geology, geography and technology that were encouraged by the state (Williams 2022). British archaeology experts, however, discovered what they believed to be the world's oldest "calendar" created by hunter-gatherer societies and dating back to around 8,000 BCE. "The Mesolithic monument was originally excavated in Aberdeenshire, Scotland, by the National Trust for Scotland in 2004. New analysis by a team led by the University of Birmingham [published in 2013 in the journal *Internet Archaeology*] sheds remarkable new light on the luni-solar device, which pre-dates the first formal time-measuring devices known to Man, found in the Near East, by nearly 5,000 years" (University of Birmingham 2013). Around the same time as the development of the calendar in China was the creation of the Babylonian Calendar in an area where the first cities were formed between the Tigris and Euphrates rivers that originated in the Taurus Mountains of southeastern Turkey (what is now modern Iraq). The Babylonian calendar was likely developed during the height of its Empire from around 1896 BCE to 539 BCE (Calendar 2022). Historians debate the origin date of this calendar but seem to agree that Egyptian calendars date back to 3,000 BCE, which would coincide with the same 5,000 years ago timeline (Calendar 2022). The civilizations of Babylon, Egypt, and Mesopotamia developed mathematical formulas that allowed for measurement and arithmetic, algebra, geometry and trigonometry. The Mesopotamians developed major public works, like canals, dams, and irrigation systems, in an attempt to avert massive starvation when the forces of nature were unkind to the region (Williams 2022). The sciences of mathematics and astronomy were strong during this period. Astronomy was also studied in India for calendrical purposes to set the times for both practical and religious tasks. As in other regions, astronomy and the creation of a calendar, would spirit the development of mathematics (Williams 2022). Ancient India also developed measuring devices such as rulers, protractors and weighing scales.

Developments from the Ancient Greeks

Building on the contributions from the Chinese, Egyptians, Babylonians, and the ancient Greeks, with such figures as Thales of Miletus, Pythagoras, and Aristotle, developed ideas in mathematics, astronomy, and logic that would influence Western thought, science, and philosophy for centuries to come (Violatti 2013; Weinberg 2015). According to Violatti (2013), "Aristotle was the first philosopher who developed a systematic study of logic, an early form of evolution was taught by such figures of Greek philosophy as Anaximander and Empedocles, and Pythagoras' mathematical theorem is still used today." While giving credit to the Greeks for their great achievements, Violatti argues that Greek science had its flaws. "Observation was undervalued by the Greeks in favor of the deductive process, where knowledge is built by means of pure thought. This method is key in mathematics, and the Greeks put such an emphasis on it that they falsely believed that deduction was the way to obtain the highest knowledge" (Violatti 2013). Weinberg (2015) counters, "Nevertheless, it was from Greece that Europe drew its model and its inspiration, and it was in Europe that modern science began, so the Greeks played a special role in the discovery of science" (Weinberg 2015:1). The contributions to science and mathematics from the Greeks would not be significantly surpassed until the scientific revolution of the sixteenth and seventeenth centuries in Europe (Weinberg 2015).

There is some debate as to why the Greek civilization advanced to the point that it became a leader in scientific achievement but one explanation resides with the realization that by the sixth century BCE the western coast of what is now Turkey had for some time been settled by Greeks, primarily speaking Ionian dialect. The richest and most powerful of the Ionian cities was Miletus. In Miletus, for over a century before the time of Socrates, the Greeks began to speculate about the fundamental substance of which the world is made (Weinberg 2015). The local inhabitants of Miletus, the Milesians had been referred to as "physicists" although they had little in common with modern physicists. The first Milesian of whom anything is truly known was Thales, who lived about two centuries before the time of Plato. Thales receives credit for having predicted a solar eclipse that occurred in 585 BCE (Weinberg 2015). Thales developed the idea that the world can be explained without resorting to supernatural explanations. "It is likely that the astronomical knowledge that Thales got from Egyptian and Babylonian astronomy allowed him to predict a solar eclipse which took place on 28 May 585 BCE" (Violatti 2013). Thales also described magnetism after observing the attraction of iron by the mineral magnetite.

A few other ideas from the Ancient Greeks include the concept of humans evolving from animals. Anaximander, an Ionian, argued that since human infants are helpless at birth, if the first human had somehow appeared on earth as an infant, it would not have survived. Anaximander reasoned that people must, therefore, have evolved from other animals whose young are hardier. It was Empedocles who first taught an early form of evolution and survival of the fittest (Violatti 2013). Empedocles is believed to be the first to teach that all matter is composed of four elements: water, air, earth, and fire (Weinberg 2015). Pythagoras helped to expand the knowledge of mathematics with his 3:4:5 triangle principle. He took this concept and stretched it to its limit by deducting a mathematical theorem that bears his name: that in a right triangle, the square of the opposite side of the right angle (the hypotenuse) is equal to the sum of the squares on the other two sides. This theorem was not only true for the 3:4:5 triangle but applicable to any other right triangle, regardless of its dimensions (Violatti 2013). It was Aristarchus of Samos (310–230 BCE), a Greek astronomer who first proposed a heliocentric model of the universe in which the sun, not the earth was at the center (Mark 2022). His theory was noted by other thinkers of his time but it was rejected as implausible and the geocentric model was retained for 1,700 years afterward (Mark 2022).

With Socrates, in the late fifth century BCE, and Plato, some forty years later, the center of the stage for Greek intellectual life moved to Athens, one of the few cities of Ionian Greeks on the Greek mainland (Weinberg 2015). Socrates is admired for his integrity, profound philosophical insight, and his great argumentative skill. Socrates is known as a "moral philosopher." Most of what we know about Socrates is from the works of Plato. Plato is most famous for his work the *Republic*, which describes a society run by a philosopher. Aristotle is considered one of the most brilliant thinkers of all time. He developed a systematic study of logic. His framework for thinking would become an authority in deductive reasoning for over two thousand years. He did emphasize the importance of induction but he prioritized deduction as a means of building knowledge. His doctrine of syllogism is his most influential contribution to logic Violatti (2013). While Aristotle called the earlier Greek philosophers *physiologi*, and this sometimes translated as "physicists," the term is misleading as the word *physiologi* simply means students of nature (*physis*), and the early Greeks had very little in common with today's physicists (Weinberg 2015). "Many important scholars have blamed Plato and Aristotle for delaying scientific progress, since their ideas were turned into dogmas and, especially during medieval times, nobody could challenge their work while keeping their reputation intact. It is highly likely that science would have reached its modern state a lot earlier if these ideas had been open to review, but this by no means questions the genius of these two talented Greeks" (Violatti 2013). The counter point is that it is not the fault of Plato and Aristotle that people in the Middle Ages treated their works so dogmatically.

Early Common Era Developments and Discoveries in Science

In India, developments of mathematical formulas, *linguistics* (the scientific study of language and its structure, including syntax, phonetics and semantics), studies in biology and anatomy that began during the Iron Age (circa 1200 BCE–600 BCE) continued to expand 2,000 to 1,500 years ago. "The mathematical genius of the ancient Indians was mainly computational and let to spectacular achievements in arithmetic and algebra. But the basis and inspiration for the whole of Indian mathematics is geometry" (Amma 1999:1). Indian geometry after the dawn of the Christian era can pertinently be termed chord-geometry. "It was studied for the sake of astronomy and along with the rest of mathematics, forms part of astronomical treatises" (Amma 1999:2). In the early third century CE, Chinese arithmetic acknowledges negative numbers and establishes laws to establish their use in formulas (Hodgkin 2005). The Chinese used red rods to represent positive numbers and black rods to symbolize negative numbers (Rogers 2008). Negative numbers would not gain acceptance, however, until the sixteenth century when English mathematician John Wallis (1616–1703) used them. While Johannes Gutenberg generally receives credit for developing the first printing press (1450 CE)—his invention of metal movable type has been described as "an invention that changed the world" (Museum of the Bible 2017)—Chinese monks actually invented the first printing presses around 600 CE and were further developed during the reign of the Tang Dynasty in China and Korea and Japan. Eventually, the printing press invention made its way to Europe, where Gutenberg printed 180 copies of the Bible, cemented his place in history, and helped to flame the Protestant Reformation of the sixteenth century (Gordon 2019; Museum of the Bible 2017).

Within the realm of early physics, strides were made in the first six centuries of the CE era that included calculations in latitudes and day lengths and elliptical orbits of planets and eclipse timings. Claudius Ptolemy (87–150 CE), a mathematician and astronomer published a number of then-significant books including a major work *Geography* in which he attempted to map the known world by giving coordinates of the major locations in terms of latitude and longitude (although his maps were quite inaccurate because of questionable sources). It was his publication of *Optics* that endured for many centuries as he discussed visual perception, reflection, and refraction of light, including the first known table of refractive angles (Davidson 2022). "Ptolemy applied the cathetus principle as a regulative means for explaining qualitative effects related to visual perception in concave spherical mirror" (Zik and Hon 2019:1). (Note: In a right triangle, a catheus, commonly known as a leg, is either of the sides that are adjacent to the right angle; the side opposite the right angle is the hypotenuse.) Indian astronomer and mathematician Aryabhata (476–550 CE) created a heliocentric model in which the Earth was viewed to be spinning on its axis and the sun was stationary and the center of the solar system. Centuries later the Copernican model would also propose that the orbits of the planets to be circular when they were actually elliptical.

Varāhamihir (505–587 CE), also called Varaha or Mihira, an Indian philosopher, astronomer, and mathematician, produced a monumental amount of work on astronomy giving complete Ptolemaic mathematical charts and tables and described a large number of comets in the Brihat Samhita (an encyclopedia) in 550 CE, hundreds of years before English astronomer, geophysicist, and physicist, Edmond Halley; and he predicted water existed on Mars. John Philoponus (490–570 CE), a Christian philosopher made many contributions to science including the celebrated theory of impetus, "which is commonly regarded as a decisive step away from an Aristotelian dynamics towards a modern theory based on the notion of inertia" (*Stanford Encyclopedia of Philosophy* 2018). Despite the fact that Philoponus had created a theory that discredited Aristotle's notion of how motion works it was Aristotle's theory that remained in vogue. Philoponus' theory would also be proven erroneous more than a thousand years later but it represented an achievement in science. Ibn Sahl (940–1000 CE), a Persian mathematician and physicist of the

Islamic Gold Age, studied Ptolemy's *Optics* and came up with the optical properties of curved mirrors and lenses that are critical aspects of Snell's law (also known as Snell-Descartes law) of refraction—an equation that determines the angle at which a ray or beam of light is refracted when a visible light enters a transparent material such as glass at an angle (Kurtus 2022). Snell's Law (1621), named after the Dutch scientist Willebrord Snell also addressed the quantitative variable of how much the light ray refracts. The Law of Refraction indicates that when light travels from one medium to another, it generally bends, or refracts (caused by the change in speed). Snell's law gives us a way of predicting the amount of bend. His Law is expressed in terms of the ratio of the sine of the angle of incidence to the sine of the angle of refraction is a constant for a given color of light and for a given pair of media. Snell's Law is important for optical devices, such as fiber optics, which are particularly important in modern telecommunication services (e.g., the internet).

Early Modern Developments and Discoveries in Science

Jumping ahead in time we come to Nicolaus Copernicus (1473–1543 CE) who developed a heliocentric astronomical model in which the Earth and planets revolve around the Sun as had been proposed by Aryabhata roughly 1,000 years earlier and even much earlier than that by Aristarchus of Samos (as early as the third century BCE). Copernicus's theory would have a profound impact on such major figures as Galileo, Kepler, Descartes and Newton. Danish nobleman Tycho Brahe (1546–1601 CE) made contributions on the study of comets (that they were astronomical and not atmospheric) by utilizing the most precise instruments available of his era before the invention of the telescope and came up with the idea of supernova (new stars). His extensive data on the planet Mars would later prove crucial to Kepler in his formation of the laws of planetary motion. Kepler's Laws of Planetary Motion are: The First Law, Planets move in ellipses with the Sun at one focus (1605); The Second Law, The radius vector describes equal areas in equal times (1609); and his Third Law, The squares of the periodic times are to each other as the cubes of the mean distances (1618) (NASA 2022a).

In 1600, Englishman William Gilbert (1544–1603 CE) published *De Magnete*, considered the first work of experimental physics wherein he was largely responsible for creating the science of magnetism (Tilley and Pumfrey 2003). Gilbert demonstrated in his experimentations that magnetic forces often produce circular motion, which led him to develop the idea of an Earth as akin to a great magnet. In 1608, Dutch spectacle-maker (eye glasses) Hans Lippershey (1570–1619 CE) (or Lipperhey) created the first optical telescope, an invention that would prove to be invaluable to Galileo Galilei (1564–1642 CE). His invention was so popular and word of it spread so quickly that he was not granted a patent and was thus, more or less, lost in history, especially once Galileo came along and constructed his own and increased the magnification to a factor of 20 with the ability to spot mountains and craters on the Moon, see that the Milky Way was composed of stars, and discover the four largest moons of Jupiter (Greene 2019). Lippershey continued his work with optics and invented the compound microscope (Green 2019). Galileo, as he is known, is an

Italian natural philosopher, astronomer and mathematician who made many contributions to science including those in the area of motion, astronomy, strength of materials and the development of the scientific method. "His formulation of (circular) inertia, the law of falling bodies, and parabolic trajectories marked the beginning of a fundamental change in the study of motion. His insistence that the book of nature was written in the language of mathematics changed natural philosophy from a verbal, qualitative account to a mathematical one in which experimentation became a recognized method for discovering the facts of nature. Finally, his discoveries with the telescope revolutionized astronomy and paved the way for the acceptance of the Copernican heliocentric system, but his advocacy of that system eventually resulted in an Inquisition process against him" (Van Helden 2022). Galileo was very popular among his patrons but also drew the ire of his academic colleagues as he had challenged and abandoned the long-held Aristotelian notions about motion and instead embraced the Archimedean approach (Van Helden 2022). He used empiricism by actually testing the laws of motion rather than just repeating Aristotle's claims, which he disproved. It was his use of the telescope starting in 1609 that led to his greatest achievements and greatest condemnation (from the Church) as he proved the Copernican model and disproved the Church's teachings of the Earth as the center of the universe (see the book that made his reputation, *Sidereus Nuncius*).

Seventeenth-century mathematics and physics played witness to many significant achievements including John Napier's use of logarithms for calculations. John Napier (1550–1617), nicknamed "Marvellous Merchiston," a famous Scottish mathematician, physicist and astronomer who is best known for his invention of logarithms (see *Mirifici Logarithmorum Canonis Descriptio*, 1614) and mathematical calculations of spherical trigonometry. He is also credited with bringing the decimal point into common use. Rene Descartes (1596–1650), a mathematician, scientific thinker and an original metaphysician, developed the techniques that made possible algebraic (or "analytic") geometry. He was a co-framer of the sine law of refraction, developer of an important empirical account of the rainbow, and provided a naturalistic account of the formation of the earth and planets (a precursor to the nebular hypothesis) (Hatfield 2014). It was in his work on metaphysics that he designed his ideas on the principles of physics, especially the nature of matter, the activity of God in creating and conserving the world, the nature of mind (the thinking substance of humans), mind-body union interaction, and the ontology of sensory qualities (Hatfield 2014). Such an ambitious ideal is much like a theory of everything. Descartes first presented his metaphysics in *Meditations* and then, to make it of a higher order, reformulated it in textbook-format in *Principles*. Another French mathematician and scientist as well as inventor and theologian is Blaise Pascal (1623–1662). In mathematics, Pascal was an early pioneer in the fields of game theory and probability theory; in philosophy, he was an early pioneer in existentialism (Simpson 2022). "Pascal made historic contributions to mathematics and to physical science, including both experimental and theoretical work on hydraulics, atmospheric pressure, and the existence and nature of the vacuum. As a scientist and philosopher of science, Pascal championed strict empirical observation and the use of controlled experiments;

he opposed the rationalism and logico-deductive method of the Cartesians; and he opposed the metaphysical speculations and reverence for authority of the theologians of the Middle Ages" (Simpson 2022).

One of the most accomplished early social thinkers in the history of science is English physicist and mathematician Isaac Newton (1642–1726). "His ideas about motion and gravity are fundamental to the science of physics and other fields. Newton also shares credit with Gottfried Wilhelm Leibniz of Germany for independently developing calculus in the 17th century" (Petruzzello 2022). Calculus is an advanced branch of mathematics that concerns itself mostly with rates of change and with problems such as determining areas or volumes within curved lines or surfaces. Newton's *Philosophiae Naturalis Principia Mathematica* (first published in 1687 with further edition in 1713 and 1726) is considered seminal in the development of modern physics and astronomy. With this publication it was clear that Newton had help to launch physics. Newton also conducted revolutionary research into optics using a prism with light in a series of experiments. His work led to such discoveries as explaining rainbows as a result of refraction due to light bending at different angles. (The rock band Pink Floyd made this prism with the rainbow color refraction popular with its 1973 album cover "Dark Side of the Moon" and subsequent sale of t-shirts which are still popular today.) His belief that chromatic aberration, or color distortion, would always be present in glass lenses led to his developing the first ever reflecting telescope. His observations, reported in his book *Opticks*, of the fundamental nature of light have been foundational in modern science (Petruzzello 2022). Newton's work on planetary motion and universal gravitation helped British astronomer Edmond Halley with his research on orbital dynamics. Newton's Laws of Motion (first published in 1687) remain, with a few exceptions, to be a mostly accurate account of nature (Petruzzello 2022). Newton's first law states that unless a body (such as a rubber ball, car, or planet), is acted upon by some force, is in motion, it will remain in motion and a body at rest tends to remain at rest (the law of inertia). The second law states that when an external force acts on a body, it produces acceleration (change in velocity) of the body in the direction of the force. This law is often simplified as force equals mass times acieration. This law is one of the most important in all of physics. Newton's third law states that when two bodies interact, they apply forces to one another that are equal in magnitude and opposite in direction. This is commonly stated as for every action, there is an equal and opposite reaction (Petruzzello 2022).

The seventeenth century was quite profound as it started with Galileo's "heretical" proof that the earth was not the center of the universe (as the Church had traditionally taught) and ended with the publication of Sir Isaac Newton's *Principia Mathematica* a book containing the foundations of mathematics including the basic laws of physics and symbolic logic (Kornblum 1994). Newton could be considered the first physicist and he certainly set the tone for modern physics.

Modern Era Breakthroughs and Discoveries in Science

Many other great scientific achievements would occur in the following centuries; many of which contributed to the field of physics. A few such highlights include:

Hans Christian Oersted, a Danish physicist and chemist who discovered in 1820 that electric current in a wire can deflect a magnetized compassed needle which inspired the development of electromagnetic theory; Thomas Johann Seebeck, a German physician, physicist and chemist who first observed the workings of semiconductors (1821); George Ohm, a German physicist, best known for his "Ohm's Law," which states that the current flow through a conductor is directly proportional to the potential difference (voltage) and inversely proportional to the resistance (1827); geologist Charles Lyell established the "Principle of Uniformitarianism" (a theory of evolution) in his *Principles of Geology* (1830 to 1833) wherein he described how species evolved over millions of years, a discover so influential it would impact Charles Darwin's (1859) theory of evolution by natural selection; Russian chemist Dmitri Mendeleev's establishment of the Periodic Table in 1869; Serbian American inventor Nikola Tesla received a patent on the electric transmission and application of power in 1888 and subsequently demonstrated alternating current electricity (the AC/DC current); and Polish and naturalized–French physicist Marie Curie discovered the elements radium and polonium (1898) and coined the term "radio-active," her pioneering achievements as a female in a male-dominated academic field earned her the distinction as "mother of physics."

Among the great scientific achievements from the twentieth century were those from such brilliant thinkers as Albert Einstein, who initially was ignored by the physics community except by Max Planck (see chapter 3 for more on Planck), the founder of quantum theory (Kaku 2022). Among Einstein's achievements were his theory of general relativity (1913), quantum theory of light, his theory of E=mc2 (demonstrating the link between mass and energy), Brownian Movement (motion) (the existence of atoms and molecules), his work on the Manhattan Project, and his contribution to inventing the refrigerator; chemist Walther Nernst, third law of thermodynamics (1906); physicist Ernest Rutherford's discovery of the nucleus of the atom in 1911; with his "Hubble Constant," American physicist and astronomer Edwin Hubble demonstrated that the Milky Way is just one of many galaxies; physicist, philosopher, and biologist Erwin Schrödinger proposes a quantum mechanical model of the atom, which treats electrons as matter waves, via the Schrödinger equation (1925); German physicist Werner Heisenberg proposed in his "uncertainty principle" or "indeterminacy principle" that we cannot know both the position and speed of a particle, such as a photon or electron, with perfect accuracy; one of the most significant theories about the origins of our very existence comes from Belgian astronomer, mathematician and priest Georges Lemaitre and his theory of the Big Bang (1927) which proposes that the observable universe began with the explosion of a single particle at a definite point in time; Scottish physician and microbiologist Alexander Fleming discovered penicillin (1929); Canadian-born Oswald Avery proved that DNA is the genetic material of the chromosome and thus lays the foundation for the new science of molecular genetics and immunochemistry; American virologist and medical researcher developed a vaccine against polio (1952); James Watson and Francis Crick's 1953 discovery of the double helix, the twisted-ladder structure of deoxyribonucleic acid (DNA); and in 1996 the Roslin Institute at the University of Edinburgh successfully cloned the first mammal from an adult cell, a sheep named Dolly.

At the early stages of the twenty-first century there have been many scientific breakthroughs here on Earth and explorations of other planets and distant galaxies, although not in-person by humans, as of this writing. The new millennium began with a major bang as the continuing work on the Human Genome Project led to the first draft publication by the International Human Genome Sequencing Consortium in 2001; Russian-born physicists Andre Geim and Konstantin Novoselov isolated graphene, a super-strong, super-light and highly-conductive material with countless commercial possibilities; in 2012, physicists at CERN, the world's largest particle physics research center, discovered the "holy grail" of physics—the so called "God particle," known as Higgs boson; in 2016, nearly 100 years after Einstein predicted the existence of gravitational waves (ripples in the fabric of space-time that are set off by extremely violent, cosmic cataclysms in the early universe) the LIGO Scientific Collaboration team directly observed gravitational waves from a black hole merger (the two massive black holes are 1.3 light years away) in an instrument on Earth; the LIGO/Virgo collaboration has produced additional recordings of gravitational waves since 2016; in 2019, the Event Horizon Telescope captured the first ever image of a black hole and it's in the center our own Milky Way galaxy; and, in 2020, NASA and SOFIA (Stratospheric Observatory for Infrared Astronomy) discovered about 12 ounces of surface water in the Clavius crater, one of the moon's largest visible craters. In 2022, NASA released the deepest images of the universe ever taken from its most technologically-advanced James Webb Space Telescope.

Many of the physicists and specific events (i.e., the Higgs boson discovery) referenced from the past one hundred years or so will be discussed in further detail in Chapters 2 and 3 when we shift our attention exclusively to specific subject matters in physics.

Summary

This chapter begins with a review of the four major paradigms of thought: tradition; faith; common sense; and enlightened, rational thought. A paradigm of thought is defined as a model of thinking and a way of viewing reality for a community of like-minded people and their associated behavioral patterns—especially in connection with social interaction. Tradition refers to a way of thinking, behaving, or doing something that has been utilized by people of a particular grouping over a long period of time. At the societal level, it involves passing down elements of a culture from generation to generation, especially via oral communication—or as sociologists would explain, via the socialization process. When speaking of faith as a paradigm of thought we are talking about a belief system that involves religion. Historically, the paradigm of thought of faith has been used in the maintenance of social order. A faith-based system of social order presents a very specific manner in which people are supposed to behave and gives a very specific reason why they are to obey—because God (or some other entity) commands they do so. It could be argued that a certain degree of common sense has been characteristic of humanity throughout history but it is important to realize that anything labeled as "common sense" is really learned behavior. That people have different notions as to what constitutes as common sense is reflected by the socialization process, observation and life experiences. As demonstrated in this chapter there have been many breakthroughs and scientific discoveries for multiple millenniums but the paradigm of enlightened rational thought did begin in earnest until the era of Enlightenment when reason, rationality, critical thinking and scientific facts began to dominate decision-making in matters of societal and personal behavior.

The description of the history of breakthroughs and discoveries in science is, in of and of itself, very enlightening as we learn that savants and learned people have made many fantastic contributions that would continue to inspire subsequent generations. The first inroads in science began with astronomy many thousands of years ago and that stimulated the growth of mathematics. Developments in science can be traced to the ancient civilizations of China, Egypt, Babylonia and India. The Ancient Greeks build upon their contributions and furthered the ideas of astronomy and mathematics and developed ideas in philosophy and logic that would influence Western thought. By the early CE era, developments of mathematical formulas stimulated linguistics and studies in geometry, biology and anatomy to newer heights. Early strides in physics were also evident and as the centuries progressed, that academic discipline would rise to the top as the respected science. The many examples of scientific breakthroughs and discoveries in physics will pave the way for our discussion in future chapters.

2

Physics

Introduction

Physics is a field of study that examines variables that can be precisely measured (Kuhn and Noschese 2020). These quantities would include such things as speed, distance, acceleration, motion, force and velocity. *Physics* is the branch of science that is concerned with elements of Nature and properties of matter and energy with a subject matter that includes mechanics, heat, light and other radiation, sound, electricity, magnetism and the structure of atoms. A *physicist* is a scientist who studies, and is trained, in the field of physics. Put another way, a physicist is a scientist who specializes in the field pf physics. Physicists cannot comprehend how to measure such variables as loyalty, honesty, trustworthiness and the countless other human characteristics. Physicists generally enjoy creating long and complicated formulas to explain occurrences that are often relatively simplistic to observe, for example, how does a ball roll? A physicist will inform you that things such as a change in its angular momentum, which requires a torque, which is provided by a frictional force acting on the ball, along with the instantaneous speed of the occurrence will cause the ball to roll. The physics of a ball rolling actually involves even more variables including gravity and this helps to explain why formulas become seemingly complicated. A toddler, meanwhile, can simply roll a ball without any calculations whatsoever. The ball will, of course, eventually stop rolling and there are formulas (going back to Newton's Laws of Motion) designed to explain that as well. A toddler will likely get frustrated with the ball when it stops rolling and will prefer a partner to roll it back to them; again, no formulas needed for enjoyment.

Creating formulas are important, however, for tasks that are more complicated than a child and caregiver rolling a ball to one another for simple enjoyment and the rudiments of hand-eye coordination and spatial awareness. Complicated formulas are very necessary in order to create automobiles that can accelerate at safe speeds and stop in short periods of time or to create rockets that can breach the atmosphere and explore outer space.

In this chapter a brief review of the history and development of physics will be presented; a number of the basic elements of physics will be described; and we will look at some of the branches of physics.

History and Development of Physics

The origin of the term "physics" is traced back to Ancient Greece to either *phusika* (natural things) from *phusis* (nature); *physikos* (all aspects of nature); or to the Greek philosopher Thales who believed the world consisted of one element (water) with many materials and developed his theories around Physis the Greek goddess of nature. Torretti (1999) interprets Aristotle as proclaiming philosophy the Greek quest to understand everything, while physics was the attempt to understand *physis* (nature). This connection to nature would lump physics together with such other academic disciplines as botany, zoology, astronomy and chemistry as "natural philosophy" until the nineteenth century when physicists would begin to use the term "experimental science" to distinguish themselves from philosophers. According to Roger C. Newton (2000), "To call physics *experimental* is to emphasize, as Isaac Newton did in his *hypotheses non fingo* that our theories are not fanciful speculation but they are capable of soaring as high as any poetic imagery and delving as deep as any philosophical thought" (p. 3). Walecka (2008) states that by the end of the nineteenth century, physicists took pride that their academic discipline had gained its independence, so to speak, from natural philosophy because of its established Newtonian mechanics, the statistical analysis of Boltzmann and Maxwell's equations for electromagnetism (to be discussed later in this chapter).

A number of select breakthroughs and discoveries in science were presented in Chapter 1 and some of them involved the realm of physics. The following pages will examine some of these same contributors to physics as well as other new ones. (Those physicists who made specific contributions to quantum mechanics or string theory will be discussed in Chapter 3.) Isaac Newton is often referred to as the first physicist, or at the very least, the scientist that set the tone for modern physics. He possessed knowledge in all the key areas of science that helped to develop physics: astronomy, mathematics (calculus), and optics. He established laws (e.g., universal law of gravitation and laws of motion) and he analyzed planetary motion. (See Chapter 1 for a further discussion of Newton.) Walecka (2008) describes James Clerk Maxwell's (1831–1879) equations for electromagnetism as being as significant as Newton's laws. McKie (2013) concurs and states, "In contrast to Newton and Einstein, Edinburgh-born Maxwell (1831–79) is virtually unknown to the general public. Yet his contribution to physics was every bit as significant, particularly his discovery of the theory of electromagnetism. This showed that electricity, magnetism and light are all manifestations of the same phenomenon, the electromagnetic field. The development of radio, TV and radar were the direct consequences. Maxwell also carried out pioneering work in optics and color vision." Austrian physicist and philosopher Ludwig Eduard Boltzmann (1844–1906) explained how irreversible macroscopic laws, in particular the second law of thermodynamics (the law of increasing entropy), originate in the time-reversible laws of microscopic physics (Goldstein 2001). "The basic notion of ergodic theory, in particular ergodicity and mixing, are widely believed to play a crucial role in the foundation of statistical mechanics" (Goldstein 2001:6–7). (Note: Ergodic theory is a branch of mathematics that studies statistical properties of deterministic and commutative dynamical systems.) Statistical mechanics itself, according to Gregersen (2022a), "explains and predicts how the properties of atoms (such as mass, charge, and structure) determine the visible properties of matter (such as viscosity, thermal conductivity, and diffusion)." Boltzmann worked out the general law for the distribution of energy (a probability distribution) among the various parts of a system at a specific temperature and derived the theorem of equipartition of energy, known as the Maxwell-Boltzmann distribution law (Gregersen 2022a).

Physicist Niels Bohr (1885–1962), born in Copenhagen, developed the modern idea of an atom, which has a nucleus at the center with electrons revolving around it (McKie 2013). Bohr, a Nobel Prize winner in Physics in 1922, found that when electrons move from one energy level to another, they emit discrete quanta of energy (McKie 2013). The Bohr model of the atom, a radical departure from earlier, classical descriptions, was the first that was incorporated in quantum theory and was the predecessor of wholly quantum-mechanical models (Tikkanen 2022). McKie (2013) provides us with some interesting sidebar information, "For his achievements, Carlsberg brewery gave Bohr a special gift: a house with a pipeline connected to its brewery next door, thus providing him with free beer for life."

Marie Curie (1867–1934) was mentioned in Chapter 1; she was the first woman to win a Nobel (in physics, with her husband, Pierre, in 1903, for discovering radioactivity) and the first person to win two separate Nobels. She was not allowed to participate in the keynote lectures winners give because she was a woman. After her husband died in a road accident in 1906, Marie won her second Nobel (in chemistry) in 1911 for discovering radium (McKie 2013). A bit of scandal stirred in the French press when it was revealed that Curie was involved with a married colleague, Paul Langevin, and there was an attempt to rescind her second Nobel (McKie 2013). Such is the pettiness of the social world when it attempts to interfere with the scientific world. Curie's research furthered the development of X-rays and the cause in fighting cancer. Unfortunately, she died in 1934 of aplastic anemia likely caused by exposure to radiation.

New Zealand–born Ernest Rutherford (1871–1937) is considered one the greatest of all experimental physicists; he discovered the idea of radioactive half-life and showed that radioactivity involved the transmutation of one chemical into another (McKie 2013). At the University of Manchester (England), Rutherford continued his work on the atom. "In 1912 Niels Bohr joined him at Manchester and he adapted Rutherford's nuclear structure to Max Planck's quantum theory and so obtained a theory of atomic structure which, with later improvements, mainly as a result of Heisenberg's concepts, remains valid to this day" (The Nobel Prize 2022a). Rutherford won the Nobel Prize in chemistry in 1908.

German-born, American naturalized, Albert Einstein (1879–1955) is synonymous with the ideal of genius and since his death his status is both of brilliant scientist and pop sensation (nearly every American can identify Einstein in the photo of him sticking out his tongue when asked by photographers to smile on the occasion of his 72nd birthday on March 14, 1951). Einstein was awarded the Nobel Prize for Physics in 1921 "for his services to Theoretical Physics, and especially for his discovery of the law of the photoelectric effect" (The Nobel Prize 2021). (Einstein received his Nobel one year later as there wasn't a ceremony in 1921.) A number of Einstein's achievements were highlighted in Chapter 1; noteworthy here is Einstein's scientific work designed to improve upon "the inadequacies of Newtonian mechanics and his special theory of relativity stemmed from an attempt to reconcile the laws of mechanics with the laws of the electromagnetic field" and his "work on the probabilistic interpretation of quantum theory" (The Nobel Prize 2021). "He contributed to statistical mechanics by his development of the quantum theory of a monatomic gas and he has also accomplished valuable work in connection with atomic transition probabilities and relativistic cosmology" (The Nobel Prize 2021). We will take a closer look at the achievements of Einstein, specifically his theory of everything, in Chapter 7.

As mentioned in Chapter 1, Georges Lemaitre proposed in 1927 that the very existence of our observable universe began with the explosion of a single particle at a definite point in time, an event known as the "Big Bang." Howell and May (2022) state that the Big Bang being described as an "explosion" is a misleading image as it conjures images of fragments flung about from a central point into a pre-existing space. Instead, Howell and May (2022) prefer the idea of the Big Bang as "an expansion of space itself—a concept that comes out of Einstein's equations of general relativity, but has no counterpart in the classical physics of everyday life. It means that all the distances in the universe are stretching out at the same rate." Explosion or expansion, and expansion does sound more reasonable, the theory states that "the universe as we know it started with an infinitely hot and dense single point that inflated and stretched—first at unimaginable speeds, and then at a more measurable rate—over 13.8 billion years to the still-expanding cosmos that we know today" (Howell and May 2022). Howell and May (2022) state that existing technology doesn't yet allow astronomers to literally peer back at the universe's birth so that we can truly understand about Big Bang origins. However, one of the many very exciting aspects of the James Webb Space Telescope (to be discussed later in this chapter) is the knowledge we are gaining of the universes, present and past. It is true that the majority of the astronomical community accepts the Big Bang theory while others have alternative explanations such as eternal inflation or an oscillating universe (Howell and May 2022). While the Big Bang theory cannot describe what the conditions were at the very beginning of the universe, it can help physicists describe the earliest moments after the start of the expansion (CERN 2022a).

When the explosive cosmic expansion began, it was a period of cosmic inflation that lasted mere fractions of a second and released a flood of matter and radiation, known as "reheating" and began populating our universe with particles, atoms and other items that become stars, galaxies, and so on (CERN 2022a; Howell and May 2022). "As the universe continued to expand and cool, things began to happen more slowly. It took 380,000 years for electrons to be trapped in orbits around nuclei, forming the first atoms. These were mainly helium and hydrogen, which are still the far most abundant elements in the universe. Present observations suggest that the first stars formed from clouds of gas around 150–200 million years after the Big Bang. Heavier atoms such as carbon, oxygen and iron, have since been continuously produced in the hearts of stars and catapulted throughout the universe in spectacular stellar explosions called supernovae" (CERN 2022a). Physicists, including those at CERN, the world's largest particle physics research center, note "An even more mysterious form of energy called 'dark energy' accounts for about 70% of the mass-energy content of the universe. Even less is known about it than dark matter. This idea stems from the observation that all galaxies seems to be receding from each other at an accelerating pace, implying that some invisible extra energy is at work" (CERN 2022a).

There are those who believe that Lemaitre's deeply-held religious beliefs might have led to the notion of a beginning of time, a specific starting point of the Universe, as the Judeo-Christian tradition propagates a similar idea in its teachings. But Lemaitre became alarmed when Pope Pius XII referred to the Big Bang theory as a scientific validation of the Catholic faith. Lemaitre clearly insisted that there was neither a connection nor a conflict between his religion and his science (American Museum of Natural History 2000). The beauty of the Big Bang theory is that its simplicity can be understood by anyone (Singh 2004). It helps us to begin to comprehend how the vastness of the universe—and it is vast, with over 100 billion galaxies, and each one contains roughly 100 billion stars—came about and gives us an indication of where it is headed (Singh 2004).

Lars Onsager (1903–1976), an American chemist born in Oslo, Norway, won a Nobel Prize in chemistry in 1968 "for the discovery of the reciprocal relations bearing his name, which are fundamental for the thermodynamics of irreversible processes" (The Nobel Prize 2022b). This pioneering work in nonequilibrium thermodynamics applied the laws of thermodynamics to systems that are not in equilibrium, such as systems in which differences in temperature, pressure, or other factors exist. "Onsager also was able to formulate a general mathematical expression about the behavior of nonreversible chemical processes that has been described as the 'fourth law of thermodynamics'" (The Editors of Encyclopædia Britannica 2022).

One of the twentieth century's most influential and colorful physicists is American Richard Feynman (1918–1988), a brilliant scientist and teacher who played a key role in the development of quantum electrodynamics, the theory that describes how light and matter interact, earning him a Nobel Prize in 1965 (McKie 2013). Feynman was actually co-awarded the Nobel for physics for his work "which tied together in an experimentally perfect package all varied phenomena at work in light, radio, electricity, and magnetism" (Gleick 2022). James Gleick (2022) describes Feynman glowingly stating that he was a "theoretical physicist who was widely regarded as the most brilliant, influential, and iconoclastic figure in his field in the post–World War II era." Speaking to his academic achievements, Feynman also contributed to the fields of quantum computing and nanotechnology and was a member of the Rogers Commission that lambasted NASA over the destruction of the space shuttle Challenger in 1986 (McKie 2013). Gleick (2022) states, "Feynman remade quantum electrodynamics—the theory of the interaction between light and matter—and thus altered the way science understands the nature of waves and particles." He translated Mayan hieroglyphics and, for better or worse, assisted in the development of the U.S. atomic bomb project at Princeton University (1941–1942) and then at the new secret laboratory at Los Alamos, New Mexico (1943–1945). As to his more colorful side, Feynman "was a keen drummer, experimented with drugs and often worked on physics problems in topless bars because he said they helped him concentrate" (McKie 2013). The Sheldon character on the television show *The Big Bang Theory* spoke of Feynman with admiration helping to keep his reputation alive in popular culture circles. It is worth noting that quantum computing—a multidisciplinary field comprising aspects of computer science, physics and mathematics that utilizes quantum mechanics to solve complex problems faster than "classical" computers—is on the verge of completely revolutionizing computing systems. Classical computers is a term used to describe the computers used by most people today. Quantum computers can compute multiple values at the same time via subatomic particles, such as electrons or photons. It is quantum bits, or qubits that allow these particles to exist in more than one state (e.g., 1 and 0) at the same time. Conversely, classical computers today employ a stream of electrical impulses (1 and 0) in a binary manner to encode information in bits. Quantum computing can solve problems in physics, engineering, chemistry, medicine and more and have practical applications in Artificial Intelligence, drug development, solar capture and so on.

The CERN organization has been mentioned briefly in both Chapters 1 and 2; CERN is the acronym for the French "Conseil Europeen la Recherché Nucleaire," or European Council for Nuclear Research. At the end of World War II, European science was no longer world-class and as a result a handful of visionary scientists imagined creating a European atomic physics laboratory and this resulted in the 1954 founding of the CERN laboratory astride the Franco-Swiss border near Geneva (CERN 2022b). According to its website the mission statement of CERN is to help uncover what the universe is made of and how it works and they do that by providing a unique range of particle accelerator facilities to researchers to advance the boundaries of human knowledge (CERN 2022b).

As mentioned in Chapter 1, physicists at CERN discovered the "holy grail" of physics—the so called "God particle," known as the Higgs boson. (Note: A boson is a subatomic particle.) "The Higgs boson has been the missing link in the standard model of physics all these years, the one that could describe the entire material world, the particle that gives mass to everything" (Amsterdamski 2014). So, just what is the Higgs boson and why was its discovery so important? The physicists at CERN explain: "You and everything around you are made of particles. But when the universe began, no particles had mass; they all sped around at the speed of light. Stars, planets and life could only emerge because particles gained their mass from a fundamental field associated with the Higgs boson. The existence of the mass-giving field was confirmed in 2012, when the Higgs boson particle was discovered at CERN" (CERN 2022c). Basic to our current description of Nature is the idea that every particle is a wave in a field. "The most familiar example of this light: light is simultaneously a wave in the electromagnetic field and a stream of particles called photons. In the Higgs boson's case, the field came first. The Higgs field was proposed in 1964 as a new kind of field that fills the entire Universe and gives mass to all elementary particles. The Higgs boson is a wave in the field. Its discovery confirms the existence of the Higgs field" (CERN 2022c). Because particles do not have mass of their own, they need to interact with the Higgs field and the stronger the particle interacts with the field, the heavier the particle ends up being. Electrons, quarks and bosons but not photons interact with the field and have a variety of masses. Through the use of supplicated equipment, mathematical formulas and data calculations, the Higgs boson was discovered in 2012 and reaffirmed in 2013. Such a discovery does not represent the conclusion of the CERN mission. In fact, in the ten years since, physicists have examined how strongly the Higgs boson interacts with other particles to see if this matches theoretical predictions. How exciting it must be for a physicist to be working at CERN.

Researchers from the Advanced Laser Interferometer Gravitational Wave Observatory (LIGO) and the Advanced Virgo Detector have collaborated on a number of projects and have made great advancements in not only substantiating Einstein's predicted existence of gravitational waves but have directly observed gravitational waves from a black hole merger using instruments on Earth. The merger of two black holes was observed in 2017 and involved one that was 30.5 times the mass of the sun with another 25.3 times the mass of the sun. The event occurred 540 megaparsecs from Earth, or about 1.8 billion light years away. The signal has been traveling for almost 2 billion years towards Earth and heralds a new era of multi-messenger gravitational wave astronomy (Voss 2017). For those interested, the LIGO Scientific Collaboration website publishes news and press releases of their continuous discoveries and advancements in gravitational wave research.

The collaboration between astronomy and physics continues to help unlock the mysteries of the universe and our very existence. Scientists at CERN have discovered the Higgs boson and researchers at LIGO/Virgo have observed gravitational waves. In 2019, astronomers at the Event Horizon Telescope (EHT) Collaboration unveiled the first image of the supermassive black hole at the center of our own Milky Way galaxy. Scientists had previously viewed stars orbiting around something invisible, compact, and very massive at the center of the Milky Way, but the 2019 images provides the first direct visual evidence of a black hole (Event Horizon Telescope 2022). The scientists could not actually see the black hole itself, because it is completely dark, but the glowing gas around it reveals a telltale signature: a dark central region (called a "shadow") surrounded by a bright ring-like structure. "The new view captures light bent by the powerful gravity of the black hole, which is four million times more massive than our Sun" (EHT 2022).

Previously, it was suggested that it must be exciting for a physicist to be working at CERN and the images provided by the EHT are impressive but imagine what it must be like to be a part of the team working with NASA's James Webb Space Telescope, especially as the images and data came rushing in during July 2022. On July 12, 2022, NASA Administrator Bill Nelson announced, "Today, we present humanity with a groundbreaking new view of the cosmos from the James Webb Space Telescope—a view the world has never seen before. These images, including the deepest infrared view of our universe that has ever been taken, show us how Webb will help to uncover the answers to questions we don't even yet know how to ask; questions that will help us better understand our universe and humanity's place with it" (NASA 2022b). NASA proclaimed on July 12, 2022, the dawn of a new era in astronomy as the world gets its first look at the full capabilities of James Webb Space Telescope (JWST).

As we know, the Universe was born into darkness 13.8 billion years ago, and even after the first stars and galaxies exploded or expanded into existence; they too stayed dark and their beginnings were inaccessible to every eye and instrument. That is, until July 12, 2022, when the James Webb Space Telescope, the most powerful space observatory yet built, offered a spectacular slide show of our previously invisible nascent cosmos (Overbye 2022). And the photos are indeed spectacular as the world has seen for themselves (via the traditional news and social media outlets).

The Telescope is a partnership between NASA, the European Space Agency (ESA) and the Canadian Space Agency (CSA) and is named after James E. Webb, who served as Undersecretary of State from 1949 to 1952, and ran the fledging NASA space agency from February 1961 to October 1968. The Webb Telescope's primary mirror is 6.5 meters in diameter, compared with the Hubble Space Telescope's, which is 2.4 meters, giving Webb about seven times as much light-gathering capacity and thus the ability to see further into the past. The Webb cameras and other instruments are equipped with cameras and other instruments sensitive to infrared, or "heat," radiation which allows it to pick up wavelengths invisible to human eyes (Overbye 2022). This is a key point as the Hubble Telescope provided outstanding images and glimpses of distant galaxies that were too difficult to capture; they appeared as a deep red in color, meaning they were farther away. Distant objects appear red and have longer wavelengths (lowest frequency and refracted the least) that are "stretched," this phenomenon is known as "redshift." (Closer stars and galaxies appear blue.) The JWST was specifically designed with infrared instruments for clarity in imagery and to gain access to more distant galaxies, perhaps dating back to the Big Bang itself. Launched in December 2021 from French Guiana, the Webb telescope is 1 million miles from Earth and like the Hubble it will orbit the Sun's second Lagrange point which keeps it in line with Earth as our planet revolves around the Sun. This solar orbit also allows the satellite's large sunshield to protect the telescope from the light and heat of the Sun, Earth and our Moon.

So concludes our brief look at the history and development of physics from its beginning to the present and glimpses of its very exciting future.

Basics of Physics

The reader is reminded, yet again, this is not a text on physics, and it does not pretend to exhaust everything one needs to know about physics in order to master the subject. Instead, the review provided here in Part A is a stepping stone to help pave the way for the information needed to understand, in particular, Chapters 3, 7, 8 and 9. So far, the reader has been exposed to many significant breakthroughs and discoveries in science in general, and in physics in particular.

As we have established, physics deals with quantities that can be measured. These quantities are among the basics of physics. A sampling of other basics of physics are presented below (their presentation is in no particular order). These concepts are either applicable to physics in general or specific branches of physics, a topic to follow this review.

1. Motion—Motion is the action of an object changing its location or position with respect to space and time. Motion can be measured in terms of displacement, distance, velocity, acceleration, speed and time. The general study of the relationships between motion, forces and energy is called *mechanics*. The study of motion without regard to the forces or energies involved is called *kinematics*; it is the simplest branch of mechanics. "The branch of mechanics that deals with both motion and forces together is called *dynamics* and the study of forces in the absence of changes in motion or energy is called *statics*" (*The Physics Hypertextbook* 2022a).

2. Force—A force may influence the motion of an object in a push or pull manner resulting from the object's interaction with another object; a force can cause an object with mass to change its distance, velocity, acceleration, speed and time. When the interaction between the two objects ceases, the two objects no longer experience the force. Force is a quantity that is measured using the standard metric unit known as the *Newton*; abbreviated by an "N."

3. Conservation of momentum and energy—The term conservation refers to something that doesn't move, the total energy of the object remains constant over time. Newton's First Law of Motion is applicable here as it states that unless a body/object is acted upon by some force it will remain motionless but if it is acted upon by some energy force it will move (as it has attained momentum). The Law of Momentum Conservation states that an object/system will not change unless acted upon by an external force.

4. Gravity—Understandably, gravity is a force of utmost importance in physics and for all objects, including humans and other species. Gravity is a force that has the ability to cause mutual attraction between all things with mass or energy and it can lock planets, stars and galaxies in their orbits. Gravity is measured by the acceleration that it gives to freely falling objects; on Earth, the acceleration rate is about 9.8 meters (32 feet) per second squared. Interestingly, gravity is assumed to be the same everywhere on Earth but it varies because the planet is not perfectly spherical or uniformly dense—it is weaker at the equator due to centrifugal forces produced by the planet's rotation. People also weigh less at higher altitudes (i.e., Mount Everest) because gravity is weaker farther from the Earth's center (Aron 2013).

5. Acceleration—The rate at which velocity changes with time, in terms of both speed and direction; acceleration is a vector quantity (because it has both a magnitude and a direction); an object is accelerating if it is changing its velocity. In physics, an object moving in a straight line has accelerated if it speeds up or slows down. Acceleration is defined as the change in the velocity vector in a time interval, divided by the time interval (Gregersen 2022b).

6. Atoms and Molecules—An atom is the smallest unit of ordinary matter that forms a chemical identity and consists of a heavy central nucleus with positive particles (protons) and neutral particles (neutrons) surrounded by a cloud of negatively charged particles called electrons. The number of protons is referred to as the atomic number and identifies the chemical element. A

molecule is a group of atoms (two or more) held together by an intricate chemical bonding between their electrons.

7. Gases, Liquids, Solids and Plasma (states of matter)—There are four natural states of matter: gases, liquids, solids and plasmas (although some classification schemes do not include plasma). A solid is a dense state of matter that retains its shape and density when not confined, it is characterized by particles arranged such that their shape and volume are relatively stable, and the particles are packed tightly together. In a liquid, the particles are more loosely packed (than a solid) and are able to flow around each other resulting in an indefinite shape; as a result, a liquid will conform to the shape of its container. A gas is a substance that does not have a definite volume (or fixed volume) or a definitive shape. While plasma is not a common state of matter here on Earth, it may be the most common state of matter in the universe. Plasma consists of highly charged particles with extremely high kinetic energy (Bagley and Dutfield 2021). The noble gases (helium, neon, argon, krypton, xenon and radon) are often used to make glowing signs by using electricity to ionize them to the plasma state (Bagley and Dutfield 2021). Other states of matter are in the works including the Bose-Einstein condensate (BEC), created by scientists in 1995. Using a combination of lasers and magnets scientists created the BEC to study quantum mechanics on a macroscopic level. "Light appears to slow down as it passes through a BEC, allowing scientists to study the particle/wave paradox. A BEC also has many of the properties of a superfluid, or a fluid that flows without friction. BECs are also used to simulate conditions that might exist in black holes" (Bagley and Dutfield 2021).

8. Temperature and Heat—The two concepts of temperature and heat are closely related. Temperature is a measure of the average kinetic energy of the atoms or molecules in the system. Heat is thermal energy transferred from a hotter system to a cooler system (a type of energy transfer that is caused by a temperature difference) that comes in contact with one another (Khan Academy 2022a). Heat, then, refers to the flow of energy from one object to another, and this flow of energy is caused by a difference in temperature.

9. Wavelength and Frequency—A wavelength is the distance from one crest to another; the crest is the highest point of the wave and the trough is the lowest. Frequency is the number of occurrences of a repeating event per unit time. Frequency and wavelength are inversely proportional to each other; thus, the wave with the greatest frequency has the shortest wavelength. Wavelength ratio is the inverse of the frequency ratio. With regard to energy, the shorter the wavelengths and the higher the frequency, the greater the energy.

10. Sound—Sound is created when an object vibrates and sends waves of energy (vibration) particles through a transmission medium such as a gas or a, liquid; sound cannot travel through a vacuum. The stronger the wave vibrations the louder the sound will be. There is no sound in outer space. As the tagline for the movie *Alien* put it, "In space, no one can hear your scream." Sound produces a variation in pressure: a region of increased pressure on a sound

wave is called a compression (or condensation), while a region of decreased pressure on a sound wave is called a rarefaction (or dilation).

11. Static electricity—All physical objects are made up of atoms which consist of protons, electrons and neutrons and therefore, all things are made up of charges. Opposite charges attract each other and like charges repel each other. Most of the time positive and negative charges are balanced in an object, which makes that object neutral. Static electricity is the result of an imbalance between negative and positive charges in objects. These charges can build up on the surface of an object until they find a way to be released or discharges. One way to discharge them is through a circuit. The rubbing of certain materials (e.g., if you rub your shoe on the carpet, your body collects extra electrons) against one another can transfer negative charges, or electrons. If you reach and pet your dog or cat, you may get a shock because of the surplus electrons being released from you to your unsuspecting pet (Library of Congress 2022).

12. Electric current—When describing an electric current in physics the adjective "electric" is implied by the context of the situation being described and thus, the term "current" is generally sufficient. In any event, an electric current is defined as the rate at which charge flows through a surface, such as a section of a wire. An electric current is a flow of charged particles, such as electrons or ions, moving in a circuit. The current is measured in coulombs per second with the most common unit for being the Ampere or amp.

13. Electrical Induction—Electrical induction, or just induction, is the result of the process of generating electrical current in a conductor by placing the conductor in a changing magnetic field. This produces Voltage or EMF (Electromotive Force) across the electrical conductor. The process is referred to as induction because the current is said to be induced in the conductor by the magnetic field. Units of Henry (H) are the measurement used with induction.

14. Electromagnetic Waves—Electromagnetic (EM) waves are waves that are created as a result of vibrations between an electric field and a magnetic field. In this regard, EM waves are composed of oscillating magnetic and electric fields. An EM wave can travel through anything—be it air, a solid material or vacuum. It does not need a medium to propagate or travel from one place to another. Conversely, mechanical waves (like sound waves or water waves), on the other hand, need a medium to travel. Examples of EM waves are radio waves, microwaves, infrared waves, X-rays, and gamma rays (*The Economic Times* 2022).

15. Light—Light is a transverse, EM wave that can be seen by the typical human. Light is produced by one of two methods: incandescence, the emission of light from "hot" matter, and luminescence, the emission of light when excited electrons fall to lower energy levels (in a matter that may or may not be "hot") (*The Physics Hypertextbook* 2022b). Among the characteristics of light is amplitude and frequency. The amplitude of light is related to its intensity (the absolute measure of a light wave's power density) and brightness

(relative to intensity as perceived by the average human eye). The frequency of a light wave is related to its color. Color is more complex and determined by monochromatic or polychromatic frequencies (*The Physics Hypertextbook* 2022b). Another important aspect of light is optics. We have already learned of the importance of optics in the development of physics. Optics remains as an important branch of physics as this is the field that assists in the construction of instruments used to detect light, especially ultraviolet and infrared light.

16. Color—As alluded to in the description of light, color is determined first by frequency and then by how these frequencies are combined or mixed when they reach the eye. Light reaches our receptor cells (called cones) at the back of the eye (the retina) and a signal is sent to the brain along a neural pathway called the optic nerve. This signal is processed by the part of the brain near the back of the skull (called the occipital lobe). Color, then, is a function of the human visual system, and is not an intrinsic property. Objects don't have color; they give off light that appears to be a color (*The Physics Hypertextbook* 2022c). The perception of light is a matter of physics, physiology, psychology and sociology as we sometimes see what we want to see. Color is described in terms of hue, brightness and saturation. In physics, color is associated specifically with electromagnetic radiation of a certain range of wavelengths visible to the human eye. Radiation of such wavelengths constitutes that portion of the electromagnetic spectrum known as the visible spectrum, e.g., light (Nassau 2022).

17. Reflection, Refraction and Dispersion—When light travels from one medium to another, there are three possible outcomes: reflection, refraction and dispersion. Reflection involves the light waves changing direction after they bounce off a medium. The Law of Reflection states that images can be reflected (e.g., such as in a home mirror or telescope). Refraction refers to the process of the light entering a medium, going through some changes, and then exiting the medium. (As described in Chapter 1, Snell's Law of Refraction is applicable here.) Dispersion refers to the spreading of white light into its full spectrum of wavelengths and was first quantified by Descartes and Newton (e.g., the analysis of a rainbow).

18. Thermal expansion—Thermal expansion refers to the increase of the size (length, area or volume) of a body due to a change in temperature, usually as a result in a rise of temperature. Higher temperatures imply greater distance between atoms resulting in expansion. Because materials have different bonding forces they also have different expansion coefficients. Contrastly, thermal contraction is the decrease in size due to a change in temperature, usually a decrease in temperature. In the case of thermal contraction, atoms and molecules move slower due to a decrease in their kinetic energies. Thermal stress can result if there is a change in the temperature of materials and/or if the size or volume of materials is constrained due to a change in temperature.

19. Archimedes' Principle of Buoyancy—The Archimedes' Principle states that "the upward buoyant force that is exerted on a body immersed in a fluid,

whether partially or fully submerged, is equal to the weight of the fluid that the body displaces and acts in the upward direction at the center of mass of the displaced fluid." This applied force reduces the net weight of the object submerged in a fluid (e.g., a boat in water). From this we have the Law of Buoyancy: The buoyant force is equal to the weight of the displaced fluid (*New World Encyclopedia* 2022a). This principle was first discovered by Greek mathematician, physicist, engineer, astronomer, and philosopher Archimedes (287 BCE–212 BCE) of Syracuse (now Sicily). He created the Archimedes Screw, a device which draws water up and was used to remove bilge water from ships (*New World Encyclopedia* 2022a). The exploits and discoveries of Archimedes are numerous and profound and "exceeded [that] of any other European mathematician prior to the European Renaissance" (*New World Encyclopedia* 2022a).

20. Stress—We may all suffer from stress and this is true for materials as well as stress refers to the force acting on a unit area of a material. Stress can cause deformation and therefore has a physical quantity. The effect of stress acting on a body is referred to as strain. Materials have a breaking point, a maximum amount of stress it can sustain, before the strain becomes too much and the material under tension reaches a breaking point.

Branches of Physics

As with any scientific field or academic disciple, physics has its distinct branches, or specialty interests. Below is a description of some of key branches of study in physics.

Thermodynamics

Thermodynamics is a branch of physics that is concerned with heat, temperature and other forms of energy. Simply stated, thermodynamics is the study of the different forms of energy and the conditions under which it can be transformed. To understand the study of thermodynamics it is helpful to review the Laws of Thermodynamics which have to do with energy (these laws were referenced earlier in this chapter). Van Ness (1969) states that the first two laws are of particular importance. The First Law says that energy is conserved and the Second Law invokes a quantity called entropy. Klein and Nellis (2012) describe the versatility of thermodynamics stating that it can be applied to any discipline, technology, application, or process and that it is used to understand the energy exchanges accompanying a wide range of mechanical, chemical, biological and nuclear processes. Agreeing with Van Ness, Klein and Nellis (2012) state that the first two Laws of Thermodynamics are always applicable to thermodynamics. As for the meaning of the term "thermodynamics" itself, "thermo" originates from a Greek word meaning warm or hot, which is related to temperature, and heat. "Dynamics" suggests motion or movement. Put together, thermodynamics may be loosely interpreted as "heat motion" (Klein and

Nellis 2012). Thermodynamics was developed originally to explain how heat, usually generating from combusting a fuel, can be provided to a machine in order to generate mechanical power or "motion" (Klein and Nellis 2012). This definition is far more limited that current interpretations of thermodynamics as a physical science that studies the relations and conversion of heat and other forms of energy (e.g., mechanical, electrical or chemical) from one form to another.

Acoustics

Acoustics is a branch of physics that examines sound and its way of propagating; vibration; ultrasound; infrasound; mechanical waves passing through different forms (e.g., gases, liquids and solids); and focuses on the production, control, transmission, reception and effects of sound and how it is absorbed. Acoustics physics is among the classical branches of the field and yet its applications are as modern as any other in the disciple (Randall 2005). The concepts of "sound" and "acoustics" are similar but distinct. As Randall (2005) indicates, "*sound* should be used only in connection with effects directly perceivable by the human ear" (p. 2). Sounds are the result of wave motion set up in the air by the vibration of material bodies with frequencies which are audible to the ear. "Acoustics," while still focused on what can be heard, is applied to a range of frequencies well outside the audible range, particularly in the ultrasonic (high-frequency) region (Randall 2005). A number of basic terms in physics previously discussed in this chapter are applicable to the study of acoustics physics including sound, vibrations, frequency, amplitude, mechanical waves and wavelengths. Practical applications of acoustic physics include the basics such as musical and architectural but it also expands to noise control, SONAR for submarine navigation, ultrasounds for medical imaging, thermoacoustic refrigeration, seismology, bioacoustics, and electroacoustic communication (Acoustics Research Group 2022).

Optics

It has been established that the field of optics has always been important in the development of physics and it certainly remains so today. Optics has as a primary focus of the study of light and its properties and behaviors, including its interactions with matter. Optics physics involves the construction of instruments (e.g., optoelectronics) that use or detect visible, ultraviolet and infrared light. Optics physics also incorporates such phenomena as reflections, refraction and interferences while studying the quantum mechanical properties of individual packets of lights known as photons (*Nature* 2022). The field of optics has been at the forefront for the development of lasers, fiber optics, nonlinear devices, semiconductor sources and detectors, and geometrical optics (or ray optics, a model of optics that describes light propagation in terms of rays).

The awe-inspiring images provided by the James Webb Space Telescope were the result of optic physics, specifically, the Optical Telescope Element (OTE). "The OTE gathers the light coming from space and provides it to the science instruments.

The OTE consists of the mirrors as well as structures and subsystems that support the optics" (NASA 2022c). The OTE consists of a 6.5 meter diameter primary mirror made of 18 hexagonal segments; a round 0.74 meter secondary mirror; a tertiary mirror and fine steering mirror, both of which are contained in the Aft Optics Subsystem; telescope structure, the secondary mirror support structure, and the deployable tower array; thermal management subsystem; aft deployable ISIM radiator (ADIR), and Wavelength sensing and control system (NASA 2022c). (Note: Webb's mirrors are covered in microscopically thin layer of gold, which optimizes them for reflecting infrared light, which is the primary wavelength of light this telescope will observe.) This contribution from optics physics helped to provide the most exciting images of outer space ever and may contribute to unlocking some of nature's grandest mysteries.

Electromagnetism

Equations and theories on electromagnetism were developed by Maxwell (and described earlier in this chapter). As Wald (2022) states, "The full development of the theory of electromagnetism in the nineteenth century stands as one of the greatest achievements in the history of physics. The theory of electromagnetism as formulated by Maxwell is a mathematically consistent theory that provides an excellent description of an extremely wide range of physical phenomena" (p. 1). Wald (2022) explains that while Maxwell's classical theory on electromagnetism cannot properly describe phenomena in which the quantum properties of the electromagnetic field play an important role, the development of quantum field theory of electromagnetic field is built upon his classical theory. Baird (2019) adds, "While Maxwell's equations describe how electromagnetic fields are generated and behave, the Lorentz force law describes how the fields interact with charged particles. This law states that an electric field exerts a forward or backward force on a charged particle and a magnetic field exerts a sideways force on a moving charged particle. Charged objects, electric currents, and magnets exert forces on each other through the electromagnetic field according to Maxwell's equations and the Lorentz force law." The Lorentz Force Law refers to the force on a charged particle due to electric and magnetic fields; a charged particle in an electric field will always feel a force due to this field.

Electromagnetism, then, refers to the study of the interaction among electrically charged particles in electric and magnetic fields and the propagation of electromagnetic waves through space. "The electromagnetic interaction is one of the four fundamental interactions of the universe. This interaction encompasses all physical phenomena related to electricity, magnetism, electromagnetic fields, light and atoms. As such, electromagnetism forms the fundamental basis for a wide variety of sciences, including solid-state physics, optics, chemistry, and molecular biology. All electromagnetic effects arise from the interaction of electrically charged particles, particles with an intrinsic magnetic moment, and the electromagnetic field" (Baird 2019). Described in another manner, electromagnetism is the science that deals with the phenomena associated with electric and magnetic fields and their interactions with each other and with electric charges and currents.

Relativity

The branch of physics of relativity is the brainchild of Albert Einstein. His theory of general relativity expanded upon his theory of special relativity that he had published 10 years earlier by adding the variable of gravity to the fabric of space-time. The theory of general relativity associates the force of gravity with the changing geometry of space-time; it also allows for mass of objects as mass influences the surrounding dimensions (space-time) in such a way that the object seems to act as if it can pull on other masses; it is as if matter creates a "curve" that causes other nearby matter to slide towards it (Science Alert 2022). Einstein's theories on relativity transformed theoretical physics and astronomy during the twentieth century and his brilliance is still marveled today.

Einstein has been referenced and discussed in both Chapters 1 and 2 but, it is his theory of relativity as a branch of physics that it relevant here. The theory of general relativity can be used to predict such things as the existence of black holes, light bending due to gravity and the behavior of planets in their orbits and thus, relativity physics has practical applications. For example, Einstein's theory of relativity has shown that the orbit of the planet Mercury is shifting very gradually and within a few billion years will likely collide with the Sun or another planet. "Gravitational Lensing" comes into play with regard to light bending. "Light bends around a massive object, such as a black hole, causing it to act as a lens for the things that lie behind it. Astronomers routinely use this method to study stars and galaxies behind massive objects" (Tillman, Bartels and Dutfield 2022). The Einstein Cross, a quasar in the Pegasus constellation, according to the European Space Agency (ESA), is a perfect example of gravitational lensing. "The quasar is seen as it was about 11 billion years ago; the galaxy that it sits behind is about 10 times close to Earth" (Tillman, Bartels and Dutfield 2022). Relativity physics has also provided inroads in frame-dragging of space-time around rotating bodies (i.e., NASA's Gravity Probe B was calibrated after it slightly drifted over time); gravitational redshift (as described earlier with the James Webb Space Telescope); gravitational waves (e.g., can be caused by such events as the collision of two black holes which create ripples in space-time); and observing neutron stars (Tillman, Bartels and Dutfield 2022).

Astrophysics

Astrophysics is the branch of physics that studies the physical nature of the motion of bodies and systems in space, such as stars, quasars, galaxies, radio telescopes and space probes; it also examines the application of the laws and theories of physics in its interpretation of astronomical observations. Cosmology and planetary science is closely associated with astrophysics. NASA's Science Mission Directorate for its Astrophysics Division has set goals of understanding the universe and our place it in. This Astrophysics Division is investigating the very moment of the creation of the universe and is close to learning the full history of stars and galaxies and how galaxies and environments hospitable for life develop (NASA Science 2022). Among the current programs for the Astrophysics Division at NASA: Physics of the

Cosmos; Cosmic Origins; Exoplanet Exploration; Astrophysics Explorer Program; and Astrophysics Research (NASA Science 2022).

The question of whether or not we are alone in the universe, or any galaxy, for that matter, is one that has longed puzzled humanity. Clearly, it would be naïve, at best, to think this is the only planet in the infinite number of planets and stars that exist to sustain life; such a notion is just ludicrous. There could be microscopic life on the moon or Mars let alone in some distant galaxy. If anything the images provided by the JWST make it clear that with the vastness of limitless galaxies something must exist "out there." Astrophysicist Frank Drake created an equation in 1961, known as the "Drake Equation," to calculate the very possibility of life outside of our planet. "The Drake equation has since gone on to achieve great fame and great notoriety. Whereas some scientists will laud it as one of the most important contributions to scientific inquiry, others have criticized it for its obvious uncertainties and conjectural nature" (Williams 2021). At the very least, the Drake equation has served as a significant starting point for astrophysicists who are attempting to explain whether life exists beyond Earth.

Nuclear Physics

Among the charges of nuclear physicists is explain the nature of matter; the quest to understand the properties of the nucleus of the atom—made up of protons, neutrons, and other particles—and the arrangement of these particles in the nucleus, the forces that hold them together, the way in which nuclei release energy in the form of natural radioactivity or due to fusion or fission reactions becomes of utmost importance. Experiments in nuclear physics use large accelerators that collide particles up to nearly the speed of light to study the structure of nuclei and also use low-energy, precision nuclear experiments, many enabled by new quantum sensors to search for a deeper understanding of fundamental symmetries and nuclear interactions (United States Department of Energy 2022). Experiments and studies of the reactions in which nuclei release energy is very important for practical reasons as nuclear power is used for power generation, nuclear weapons, magnetic resonance, imaging, medicines, industrial and agricultural isotopes.

A better understanding of how nuclear energy works is critical as it is a better alternative to burning fossil fuels. However, threats such as a core reactor meltdown, human error (i.e., the Chernobyl accident), concerns over how to safely transport and store nuclear radioactive waste, radioactivity (the phenomenon of the spontaneous disintegration of unstable atomic nuclei resulting in the release of unstable, subatomic particles) toxic exposure, and the threat of nuclear weapons—especially in the "wrong hands"—that may lead to nuclear war is a scary outlook for humanity. Such concerns would make moot are quest for knowledge of other universes and the origin of life.

This chapter concludes with the acknowledgment that all sciences include theoretical and experimental (testing and research) aspects. Theoretical physics involves the development of mathematical formulas and computational protocols; mathematical models; and constructs and abstractions based on observations of natural phenomena. Theory represents a starting point in the discovery of new knowledge. In science, theories must be supported by data. As Walter Fox Smith (2020) states, "Physics is an experimental science. That means, although we greatly value the insights of theorists, the determination of whether a new idea is true or not is done experimentally. In addition to this important role of checking theories, experimentalists also often discover exciting, unexpected phenomena" (p. 4). From this quote, we come to understand that experimental physicists seek to test hypotheses and theories, usually in a lab, in the hopes of making discoveries of new phenomena or to develop new applications of ideas. To accomplish this, experimental physicists may need to develop new strategies, technologies and equipment and tools. As Smith (2020) adds, "experimental physicists frequently make the first steps toward applying recent theoretical and experimental discoveries toward the creation of important new devices and technologies" (p. 4).

Finally, this chapter did not specially discuss quantum mechanics or string theory as they are the primary topics of Chapter 3.

Summary

This chapter discussed the history and development of physics. The word "physics" itself has origins that can be traced back to Ancient Greece. The review of the specific significant developments in physics began with Isaac Newton, often referred to as the first physicist, or at the very least, the scientist that set the tone for modern physics. Contributions from such physicists as James Clark Maxwell, Ludwig Boltzmann, Niels Bohr, Marie Curie, Ernest Rutherford, Albert Einstein, Georges Lemaitre, Lars Onsager, and Richard Feynman were discussed. Major scientific breakthroughs as a result of physics discussed include, a discussion on the "Big Bang Theory"; the discovery of the Higgs boson (the God particle); LIGO/Virgo's observation of the merger of two black holes; and the launch of two massive telescopes, the Hubble, and most significantly, the James Webb Space Telescope.

Twenty basic terms utilized in physics and that appeared in the works of many of the early physicists and reappear in application in the various branches of physics were outlined and detailed. A review of seven highly significant branches of physics was also included, these branches were: thermodynamics; acoustics, optics, electromagnetism, relativity, astrophysics, and nuclear physics.

3

Quantum Mechanics and String Theory

Introduction

In the "Tangerine Factor" episode (May 19, 2008) of the highly popular TV show *The Big Bang Theory* (2007–2019), the Penny character discusses with her next door neighbor Sheldon that his roommate Leonard has asked her out on a date but she is not sure whether or not to accept. She has become good friends with Leonard and does not want to risk losing the friendship if the date and possible relationship fail. Also, Leonard is not the typical type of guy that Penny dates. Sheldon, a theoretical physicist who is socially-inept, answers Penny in the best way he can, with an example from physics. The example he chooses is the Schrödinger's Cat experiment. Penny has not heard of Schrödinger or of his cat experiment so Sheldon attempts to explain it to her. He states that in 1935, Erwin Schrödinger in an attempt to explain the Copenhagen interpretation of quantum physics, proposed an experiment where a cat is placed in a box with a sealed vial of poison that will break open at a random point of time. Since no-one knows when or if the poison has been released the cat can be thought of as both alive and dead, until the box is opened. Penny is confused and frustrated and does not get the point. Sheldon elaborates and tells Penny that just like Schrödinger's cat, her potential relationship with Sheldon can have both positive and negative outcomes. It is only by opening the box (going on the date with Sheldon) that she'll find out which outcome will occur. Missing the point, Penny replied, "Okay, so you're saying I should go out with Leonard." That is not what Sheldon was saying. He becomes further frustrated with Penny and starts the story of Schrödinger's Cat over again.

What was actually happening, of course, is that while Sheldon was not specifically telling Penny what course of action to take, he did provide her with the incentive to proceed. Meanwhile, Leonard is very nervous about dating the younger and very attractive Penny and imagines all sorts of scenarios wherein the date will go horribly wrong. He is especially worried about how to handle the first date "good-night kiss" (something we can all relate to). When he goes to Penny's apartment to start the date he awkwardly asks, "Have you ever heard of Schrödinger's Cat?" Penny replies that she has heard far too much about "Schrödinger's Cat." Leonard replies, "Good." He then grabs her and kisses her passionately. Penny, impressed by the kiss responds, "Alright, the cat's alive, let's go to dinner."

The TV show *The Big Bang Theory* made many references to physics and understandably so, as three of the main characters were physicists and worked at the California Institute of Technology (commonly referred to as Caltech). The show took pride in making sure their references to physicists and physics were accurate. The Schrödinger Cat reference would appear a number of times in the long-running series and eventually to the point where Penny was explaining it to others.

In this chapter we will determine whether or not the description of Schrödinger's Cat by the fictional Sheldon matches up with reality. We will be introduced to classical mechanics in physics, learn about the major contributors that led to the development of quantum mechanics, learn about quantum mechanics itself, and then investigate string theory.

Classical Mechanics

Classical mechanics, often called Newtonian mechanics, is the branch of physics and an area of mathematics that involves the study of motion of macroscopic objects under the action of forces or displacements and the subsequent effects of the physical bodies on their environment; and the examination of bodies that remain at rest. Classical mechanics does not involve the study of situations in which objects move with a velocity of light or phenomena on the atomic scale. The description of atomic phenomena requires quantum mechanics. "Classical mechanics is used for describing the motion of macroscopic objects, from projectiles to parts of machinery, as well as astronomical objects, such as spacecraft, planets, stars, and galaxies. It produces very accurate results within these domains, and is one of the oldest and larges subjects in science, engineering and technology" (*New World Encyclopedia* 2022). In physics, mechanics has two major sub-fields, classical mechanics, which is concerned with the set of physical laws governing and mathematically describing the motions of bodies and aggregates of body; and quantum mechanics, which will be discussed later in this chapter.

Benacquista and Romano (2018) state, "Much of classical mechanics was developed to provide powerful mathematical tools for obtaining the equations of motion for systems of objects subject to external and internal forces. These include Newton's laws, the principle of virtual work, and Hamilton's principle." The tools provided by classical mechanics allow physicists to describe motion when observed from non-inertial reference frames, such as the rotating surface of the Earth. "A deeper study of these mathematical tools and how they respond to different transformations of the system (e.g., translations or rotations or the coordinates) leads to a better understanding of the nature of Newtonian mechanics, and points the way to the modern physics of quantum mechanics and special relativity" (Benacquista and Romano 2018). Irish mathematician William Hamilton, in 1834, stated that the motion of a dynamical system in a given time interval is such as to maximize or minimize the action integral, this is known as Hamilton's principle. Hamilton's Action Principle determines the path of the motion and the position of the path as a function of time. Newton's laws state that when bodies are at equilibrium there are equal forces of applied and constraint; this means that the virtual work of the constraint forces must also be in equilibrium, at zero, as well. One of the important applications of the idea of the virtual work principle arises in the study of static equilibrium of mechanical systems.

Newton's Laws of Motion are of particular relevance to classical mechanics. As we'll recall from Chapter 1, Newton's First Law describes the motion of an object with respect to an inertial reference frame: Unless acted on by an outside force the natural motion of an object is constant velocity. Newton's Second Law tells us how an applied force will alter this natural motion: The effect of an applied force "F" upon an object of mass "m" is to induce acceleration "A" such F=ma (Benacquista and Romano 2018). This formula assumes that the mass is constant, but we can include the effect of a varying mass by allowing for momentum. When there are multiple objects exchanging forces between themselves within a system, Newton's Third Law describes how the forces of interactions behave: If an object applies a force "F" on a second object, then the second object applies an equal and opposite force "-F" on the first object (Benacquista and Romano 2018).

According to Goldstein (2022), classical mechanics in physics in the science of action on material bodies and it forms a central part of all physical science and engineering. Of first concern in the problem of motion are the forces that bodies exert on one another. This leads to the study of such topics as gravity, electricity, and magnetism, based on the nature of the forces involved. "Given the forces, one can seek the manner in which bodies move under the action of forces; this is the subject matter of mechanics proper" (Goldstein 2022). Goldstein traces classical mechanics to Newton such as Benacquista and Romano and indicate that since the time of his laws of motion in the seventeenth century, the laws of motion have been modified and expanded by the theories of quantum mechanics and relativity. However, classical mechanics accurately represented the effects of forces under all conditions known in Newton's time. Goldstein (2022) adds that Newton's theory of motion can be divided into statics, the study of equilibrium, and dynamics, and the study of motion caused by forces.

As explained by Coolman (2014), in addition to Newtonian laws, there are other laws and principles at the core of classical mechanics: Newton's Law of Universal Gravitation, the pull of gravity between two objects will be proportional to the masses of the objects and inversely proportional to the square of the distance between their centers of mass; Law of Conservation of Energy, energy cannot be created nor destroyed, and instead changes from one form to another (e.g., from mechanical energy into heat energy); Law of Conservation of Momentum, in the absence of external forces such as friction, when objects collide, the total momentum before the collision is the same as the total momentum after the collision; and Bernoulli's Principle, within a continuous streamline of fluid flow, a fluid hydrostatic pressure will balance in contrast to its speed and elevation.

Development of Quantum Theory

The development of quantum theory represents a transformation from classic mechanics. Described in the following pages are significant contributors to this transformation.

Max Planck: The Founder of Quantum Theory

The brilliant Michio Kaku (2022) describes German physicist Max Planck (1858–1947) as the founder of quantum theory. Planck's earliest work was on the subject of thermodynamics; he published papers on entropy, on thermoelectricity and on the theory of dilute solutions. His attention shifted to the problem of the distribution of energy in the spectrum of full radiation. Planck's experimental observations on wavelength distribution of energy emitted by a black body as a function of temperature were at variance with the predictions of classical physics (The Nobel Prize 2022c). He also found that hot objects do not radiate a smooth, continuous range of energies as had been assumed in classical physics. Instead, he found that the energies radiated by hot objects have distinct values, with all the other values forbidden (Famous Scientists 2022). These discoveries were at variance with the prediction of classic physics leading him to a new direction in physics. In 1900, he published a paper demonstrating the relationship between energy and the frequency of radiation based on the revolutionary idea that the energy emitted by a resonator could only take on discrete values or quanta. The energy for a resonator of frequency is a universal constant, now called Planck's constant (The Nobel Prize 2022c). Planck's constant is a fundamental or universal constant that defines the quantum nature of energy and relates the energy of a photon to its frequency. Planck's groundbreaking work would change the course of physics as it represented a clear departure from classical mechanics to a new field that would come to be known as quantum theory. "Quantum theory revolutionized our understanding of atomic and subatomic processes, just as Albert Einstein's theories of relativity revolutionized our understanding of gravity, space and time. Together these theories constitute the most spectacular breakthroughs of twentieth-century physics" (Famous Scientists 2022). Planck won the Nobel Prize in Physics in 1918. It should be noted that Albert Einstein also played a significant role in the development of quantum theory and we will learn about that in Chapter 7.

Niels Bohr

Planck's new quantum theories were not immediately accepted within the scientific world but after the published works of Niels Bohr (1885–1962) in 1913 in which he calculated positions of spectral lines using the theory, quantum theories gained acceptance. But even Planck himself admitted that he did not truly understand the complexities of quantum theory as other physicists continued to expand on his original thoughts (Planck 1949). As for Bohr, recall that in Chapter 2, his contributions to the understanding of atoms representing a radical departure from classical mechanical physics represented a significant contribution to the development of quantum theory, was discussed. Bohr worked on the Manhattan Project but both during and after this assignment supported peaceful applications of atomic energy and openness between nations with regard to nuclear weapons (Atomic Heritage Foundation 2019a). Bohr adapted Rutherford's nuclear structure to Planck's quantum theory and created the Bohr model, the most widely accepted model of the atom. Bohr's contributions to quantum theory and mechanics remain impactful.

Ernest Rutherford

Ernest Rutherford (1871–1937), was also briefly discussed in Chapter 2, and like Planck and Bohr he is a Nobel Prize winner (in chemistry). Rutherford is often called the "father of nuclear physics." In 1907, Rutherford, Hans Geiger and Ernest Marsden conducted the Geiger-Marsden experiment where they observed alpha particles scattering backwards when fired at a gold foil. The surprising result led Rutherford to formulate his model of the atomic nucleus, a revolutionary development in nuclear physics (Atomic Heritage Foundation 2019b). In 1912, Bohr joined Rutherford wherein they adapted a nuclear structure to Planck's quantum theory and so obtained a theory of atomic structure which, with later improvements, mainly as a result of Heisenberg's concepts, remain valid to this day (The Nobel Prize 2022a). Rutherford also coined the term "proton" and theorized about the existence of neutrons, which were discovered by his colleague and former student James Chadwick in 1932 (Atomic Heritage Foundation 2019b). Particles named and characterized by Rutherford also include the alpha, beta, and gamma (Atomic Heritage Foundation 2022).

Erwin Schrödinger

Erwin Schrödinger (1887–1961), born in Vienna, was a physicist, philosopher and biologist and proposed a quantum mechanical model of that atom which treats electrons as matter waves leading to the "Schrödinger Equation" (Khan Academy 2022b). Schrödinger built upon Niels Bohr's theory of the atom, electrons absorb and emit radiation of fixed wavelengths when jumping between fixed orbits around a nucleus by assuming that matter (e.g., electrons) could be regarded as both particles and waves and consequently formulated a wave equation (in 1926) that accurately calculated energy levels of electrons in atoms (The Nobel Prize 2022d). Schrödinger won the Nobel Prize in Physics in 1933 and he helped to set the tone for wave mechanics.

As described in the chapter's introductory story, Schrödinger is associated, both scientifically and within the realm of popular culture, with the "Schrödinger's Cat" thought experiment. Designed in 1935, this thought experiment was designed to shine a spotlight on the difficulty with interpreting quantum theory. Unlike other forms of physics, quantum physics is not always definitive. Until the properties of a particular theory can be pinned down to specific mathematical formulas (preferably those that are applicable to this universe) there are a range of possible outcomes

(Howgego 2022). It was the Copenhagen interpretation, first proposed by Niels Bohr in 1920, that underscored the ambiguity with quantum mechanics. In the Copenhagen interpretation Bohr claimed that a quantum particle doesn't exist in one state or another, but in all of its possible states at once. Physicists at the time, and still today, debated the validity of the Copenhagen interpretation. Schrödinger created a "thought experiment" (he did not actually put the lives of cats at risk) wherein subjects could be asked about a scenario that involves a cat trapped in a box with poison that will be released if a radioactive atom decays. Radioactivity is a quantum process, so before the box is opened, the story goes, the atom has both decayed and not decayed, leaving the cat in limbo, a superposition between life and death (Merali 2020). That the cat can be both alive and dead until the box is opened is akin to the idea that a quantum particle can exist in any and all possible states at once.

Louis de Broglie

Louis de Broglie (1892–1987) was a French physicist who proposed that all particles could be treated as matter waves with a wavelength. Based on the work of Planck and Einstein that demonstrated how light waves could exhibit particle-like properties, de Broglie hypothesized that particles also have wavelight properties (Khan Academy. 2022b). In 1929, de Broglie was awarded the Nobel Prize for Physics for his discovery of the wave nature of electrons and for good reason as his research on matter waves was an essential development of quantum theory. That wave characteristics are only detectable at the atomic level represented a shift from classical mechanics (Newtonian) to quantum mechanics. UNESCO also awarded him the first Kalinga Prize (1952) for his efforts to explain aspects of modern physics to laypersons (his writings also including works on X-rays, gamma rays, atomic particles, optics and a history of the development of contemporary physics). In his Foreword to de Broglie's *Research on the Theory of Quanta*, Hirokazu Nishimura (2021) states that de Broglie made ground-breaking contributions to the burgeoning quantum theory by establishing the foundation of wave mechanics that would later be completed by Erwin Schrödinger. It was de Broglie's firm conviction that the wave-particle duality theory of matter, known as the *de Broglie hypothesis*, established that any moving particle had an associated wave. In the 1920s, de Broglie engaged in the "pilot wave model," a comprehensible quantum theory but he was persuaded to give up his model in favor of the then mainstream Copenhagen interpretation. David Bohm rediscovered de Broglie's pilot wave model in 1952 and the reformulated version is known as the *de Broglie-Bohm theory* (Nishimura 2021). "This theory is the first known example of a hidden variable theory, interpreting quantum mechanics as a deterministic theory and avoiding troublesome notions such as wave-particle duality, instantaneous wave function collapse and the paradox of Schrödinger's cat" (Nishimura 2021: vi–vii).

Werner Heisenberg: The Shift to Quantum Mechanics Begins

Werner Heisenberg (1901–1976) was a German physicist who developed a theory on quantum mechanics that, along with its applications, resulted in the discovery of allotropic forms of hydrogen and earned him the Nobel Prize in Physics in 1932 (The Nobel Prize 2022e). According to Lakshmibala (2004), Heisenberg is one of the founding fathers of quantum mechanics as opposed to previous theorists that worked in the "old" field of quantum theory and were the ones who originally broke from classical mechanics. Two of his concepts, the "Matrix equation" and the "Uncertainty Principle" will secure his name association with quantum mechanics forever.

Heisenberg disagreed with mechanical physics notions of atoms and particles being identified by ordinary numbers (e.g., such as their position and velocity) and instead argued for the utilization of abstract mathematical structures called "matrices" and as a result he formulated his new theory in terms of "matrix equations" (The Nobel Prize 2022e). In his Foreword to de Broglie's *Research on the Theory of Quanta*, Hirokazu Nishimura (2021) states, "Matrix mechanics is not easy to handle. Physicists succeeded in calculating the spectrum of a hydrogen atom by matrix mechanics, but they could not proceed to the next stage of calculating the spectrum of a helium atom. Then came wave mechanics, which gave physicists great joy because they could return from their unfamiliar discrete world to their continuous homeland" (p. v). Physicist Lakshmibala (2004) states that "the matrix formulation was built on the premise that all physical observables must be represented by matrices. The set of eigenvalues of the matrix representing an observable is the set of all possible values that could arise as outcomes of experiments conducted on a system to measure the observable" (pp. 48–49). However, "it was soon realized that the matrices representing the observables are really operators in an appropriate linear vector space, and that their eigenstates are column vectors in space. This space could even be infinite-dimensional" (Lakshmibala 2004: 49). Further uncertainties with the matrix equations and variable measuring problems subsequently led to what Heisenberg called the *Uncertainty Principle*.

The "uncertainty principle" or "indeterminacy principle" states that we cannot know both the position and momentum of a particle, such as a photon or electron, with perfect accuracy. We can determine the accuracy of one variable, however. As Heisenberg (2013/1949) explains, "The uncertainty principle refers to the degree of indeterminateness in the possible present knowledge of the simultaneous values of various quantities with which the quantum theory deals; it does not restrict, for example, the exactness of a position measurement alone or a velocity measurement alone. Thus suppose that the velocity of a free electron is precisely known, while the position is completely unknown." The principle states that every subsequent observation of the unknown variable is restricted by the uncertainty relation. In short, the *Uncertainty Principle* claims that we cannot know all things about a particle at any given time; this is contrary to Newtonian physics.

Paul Dirac

Paul Dirac (1902–1984) was born in Bristol, England, and won the Nobel Prize in Physics in 1933. Dirac followed in the footsteps of Heisenberg embracing the new quantum mechanics and independently produced a mathematical equivalent which consisted of a noncommutative algebra for calculating atomic properties. During the period of 1925 to 1926, Dirac worked on quantum theories that accurately described the energy levels of electrons in atoms. These equations were later adapted to Einstein's theory of relativity, however. In 1928, Dirac formulated a fully relativistic quantum theory. "The equation gave solutions that he interpreted as being caused by a particle equivalent to the electron, but with a positive charge. This particle, the positron, was later confirmed through experiments" (The Nobel Prize 2022f). Dirac's theory of holes (1930) states that, the continuum of negative energy states are filled with electrons and that the vacancies (holes) in the continuum are manifested as positrons with energy and momentum that are the negative of those of the state. The "hole theory" introduced a model for the vacuum, the lowest energy state of the system. Dirac's work on wave equation introduced special relativity into Schrödinger's equation. Dirac predicted the existence of antimatter, created some of quantum mechanics' key equations and laid the foundations for today's micro-electronics industry (McKie 2013).

J. Robert Oppenheimer

(Julius) Robert Oppenheimer (1904–1967) was born on April 22, 1904, in New York City and died on February 18, 1967, in Princeton, New Jersey. He was an American theoretical physicist, science administrator and the director of the Los Alamos Laboratory of the Manhattan Project. It was his outstanding work at Los Alamos that would earn him the title of "Father of the Atom Bomb." Oppenheimer earned his undergraduate degree (1925) at Harvard University where he excelled in Latin, Greek, physics, chemistry, poetry and Eastern philosophy (Rouzé 2023). He sailed to England to do research at the Cavendish Laboratory at the University of Cambridge where he studied under Ernest Rutherford (mentioned earlier in this chapter). Oppenheimer then attended the University of Göttingen (Germany), where he met other prominent physicists, such as Niels Bohr and Paul Dirac (also mentioned in this chapter) and Max Born, and where he would earn his doctorate in physics in just one year (1927) at the age of 22. He returned to the United States to teach physics at the University of California at Berkeley and the California Institute of Technology (Caltech) (Rouzé 2023). At this time, Oppenheimer was *the* authority on quantum mechanics in the United States as he had gained insights from the leading and cutting-edge theorists in the field and combined that with his immense intellect—which was always highly respected—and it did not take long for Oppenheimer to gain a reputation as *the* physicist of the United States. By 1929, he had made his name by publishing sixteen first-rate papers (Feldman 2007). He became a full professor of physics at UC Berkeley in 1936.

Oppenheimer was chosen by the U.S. Army to head a huge team of physicists to become the first nation to build a nuclear bomb. The project, known as the Manhattan Project, was carried out in Los Alamos, near Santa Fe, New Mexico. Under Oppenheimer's directorship they did build several atomic devices, one of which was used in the first nuclear test near Alamogordo, New Mexico (codenamed "Trinity") and two atom bombs that the U.S. military dropped Japan, one on Hiroshima

(August 6, 1945) and the other on Nagasaki (August 9, 1945). The devastation is well documented. While Oppenheimer was pleased with his scientific achievement he quickly came to realize the power that he had created with the atomic bomb. And, like his colleague Niels Bohr, he warned against using such a weapon again. He had hoped that by using the atomic bomb to end the war with Japan it would serve as deterrent to end of wars in the future. If only that was true.

Oppenheimer's work on the atom bomb overshadows his significant contributions to theoretical physics, including achievements in quantum mechanics and nuclear physics such as the Born-Oppenheimer (BO) approximation (the best-known mathematical approximation in molecular dynamics; and published as "On the Quantum Theory of Molecules") for molecular wave functions, work on the theory of electrons and positrons, the Oppenheimer-Phillips process in nuclear fusion, and early work on quantum tunneling. It was his work on what he then called a "dark star," or in today's terminology, a "black hole" that was, perhaps, most important. Building off of Einstein's theory of general relativity, Oppenheimer wrote a series of papers in the 1930s on the topic of black holes. In their 1939 paper, "On Continued Gravitational Contraction," Oppenheimer and Hartland Sweet Snyder proved that black holes were not merely mathematical quirks thought up by physicists but real astrophysical objects. The physicists showed how large stars would collapse to form black holes. In their abstract, Oppenheimer and Snyder (1939) state, "When all thermonuclear sources of energy are exhausted a sufficiently heavy star will collapse. Unless fission due to rotation, the radiation of mass, or the blowing off of a mass by radiation, reduce the star's mass to the order of that of the sun, this contraction will continue indefinitely" (p. 455).

Arguably, Oppenheimer should have been awarded a Nobel Prize for his pioneering work on black holes but he was not. When the first actual black hole was discovered decades later Oppenheimer should have received a share in a Nobel Prize, but that did not happen. He should have won a Nobel Prize for his work on the atom bomb but that did not happen either. So many of his brilliant colleagues received Nobels and yet this exceptional physicist did not. If you watched the blockbuster 2023 movie *Oppenheimer* you have an understanding of the politics that always lurked in the background on this man's life.

Julian Schwinger

Julian Schwinger (1918–1994), was an American theoretical physicist and in 1965 was awarded the Nobel Prize in Physics "for his fundamental work in quantum electrodynamics, with deep ploughing consequences for the physics of elementary particles" (Atomic Heritage Foundation 2019c). During the summer of 1943, Schwinger worked briefly on the development of the atomic bomb at the University of Chicago's Metallurgical Laboratory and later that year transferred to the Radiation Laboratory at MIT where he provided theoretical support for the development of radar. Schwinger's work on quantum electrodynamics is considered revolutionary and improved physicists' understanding of charged particles with electromagnetic fields. Schwinger formulated the "Schwinger model," the first example of a confining theory, with quantum electrodynamics in one space and one time dimension (Atomic Heritage Foundation 2019c).

In June 1947, Schwinger presented experimental data at a conference that contradicted the predictions of theoretical physicist Paul Dirac's relativistic quantum theory of the electron. "In particular, experimental data contradicted Dirac's prediction that certain hydrogen electron stationary states were degenerate (i.e., had the same energy as certain other states) as well as Dirac's prediction for value of the magnetic moment of the electron. Schwinger made a quantum electrodynamical calculation that made use of the notions of mass and charge renormalization, which brought agreement between theory and experimental data" (Schweber 2022). This would prove to be a critical breakthrough that initiated a new era in quantum field theory. Richard Feynman and Shin'ichiro Tomonaga independently carried out similar calculations as Schwinger and as a result, shared the 1965 Nobel with Schwinger.

Freeman Dyson

Freeman Dyson (1923–2020) was an English-American theoretical physicist and mathematician who unified the three versions of quantum electrodynamics by Schwinger, Feynman and Tomonaga. His work on unifying these theories would have earned him joint ownership of the 1965 Nobel but tradition held that just three people could share in it (Dijkgraaf 2020). By the late–1950s, Dyson worked on designing rockets (Project Orion) driven by nuclear explosions, a potent means of propulsion, with hopes of sending rockets to Saturn and eventually the nearest stars. He was disappointed by the limited ambition of visiting only the moon (Dijkgraaf 2020). Dyson envisioned eventual colonization of the cosmos by self-replicating robots or a "space ark" carrying the genetic material of all terrestrial organism, this became known as the "Dyson sphere" (Dijkgraaf 2020). Dyson returned to his work in physics and mathematics and subsequently worked on nuclear reactors, solid state physics, ferromagnetism, astrophysics and biology, looking to solve problems where his elegant mathematics could be usefully applied (Institute for Advanced Study 2022). He established the theory of random matrices—square arrays of numbers chosen randomly—to categorize the statistics of complex quantum systems. He continued to work on a problem in mathematics that had long bothered him, the behavior of the Riemann zeta function that captures the distribution of prime numbers. Working with mathematician Hugh Montgomery, Dyson's breakthroughs led to achievements in various generalizations of the Riemann hypothesis (Dijkgraaf 2020).

Quantum Mechanics

Richard Feynman once said, "Nobody understands quantum mechanics" (Kumar 2017). Kumar (2017) suggests that whenever "the weirdness of quantum mechanics haunts you, it is better to go back to its creators" and look at their original publications and ideas. The first half of this chapter, and parts of Chapter 2, were designed to do that very thing, to introduce the major scientists who introduced hugely significant contributions to the fields of quantum theory and then the transition to quantum mechanics. Describing quantum mechanics is connected to specific versions of the field (this is much like any other academic discipline, such as sociology). Kumar examines quantum mechanics from two different mathematical forms, one of which is known as "matrix mechanics" and the other as "wave mechanics." The basics of those two versions were explained in this chapter. Roland Omnes, in his book *Understanding Quantum Mechanics* (1999) states in his chapter on "Principles" (of quantum mechanics) that there are several approaches possible when examining quantum mechanics but narrows it down to: matrix mechanics, wave mechanics and Feynman path integrals. Omnes is similar to Kumar but he added importance to Feynman's work. The United States Department of Energy (2024) defines quantum mechanics as "the field of physics that explains how extremely small objects simultaneously have the characteristics of both particles (tiny pieces of matter) and waves (a disturbance or variation that transfer energy)." This relationship between particles and waves is what physicists call the "wave-particle duality" (United States Department of Energy 2024).

There are many things we know about quantum mechanics beginning with the simple fact that it is a subfield of physics that describes the behavior of particles; that is to say, atoms, electrons, photons and almost everything in the molecular and sub-molecular realm (Mann and Coolman 2022). Pratt (2021) describes how the word "quantum" is a Latin word correlated with "quantity," and *quanta* refers to the smallest amount of any physical entity. Blinder (2004) states, "Quantum mechanics is the theoretical framework which describes the behavior of matter on the atomic scale. It is the most successful quantitative theory in the history of science, having withstood thousands of experimental tests without a single verifiable exception…. A host of modern technological marvels, including transistors, lasers, computers and nuclear reactors are offspring of the quantum theory" (p. 17). Blinder may be overstating the value of quantum mechanics in these areas of discovery as scientific discoveries do not occur exclusive of other fields. Consider, for example, Pedrotti, Pedrotti and Pedrotti (2018) state the emergence of lasers, fiber optics, nonlinear devices, and a variety of semiconductor sources and detectors in the 1960s corresponded with the ever-expanding range of applications and developments from optics, physics, engineering and technology. Griffiths and Schroeter (2017) would also seem to disagree with Blinder's conclusion that quantum mechanics is a framework that has developed a quantitative theory that has withstood experimental tests without exception by stating that there is no general consensus as to what the fundamental principles of quantum mechanics are, how it should be taught, or what it really "means." Griffiths and Schroeter (2017) claim that any physicist can "do" quantum mechanics but the stories they tell themselves about what they are doing are as various as the tales of Scheherazade, and almost as implausible. (Note: The "tales of Scheherazade" is a reference to a collection of Middle Eastern folk tales compiled in Arabic during the Islamic Golden Age; it is often known in English as the "Arabian Nights.") Echoing Richard Feynman's sentiment about quantum mechanics cited earlier, Niels Bohr said, "If you are not confused by quantum physics then you haven't really understood it" (Griffiths and Schroeter 2017:xi). Recall that it was Bohr, in the Copenhagen interpretation, who underscored the ambiguity with quantum mechanics when he claimed that a quantum particle doesn't exist in one state or another, but in all of its possible states at once.

Quantum mechanics is an advanced science but it does have its shortcomings, or its oddities. It describes things so small that they are completely beyond the range of human senses. It stands to reason that we do not possess an innate intuition for the quantum world. However, as Susskind and Friedman (2014) explain, we can comprehend how to rewire our intuitions with abstract mathematics. Still, most people have a hard time with quantum mechanics not just because of the hard mathematics but because "our sensory organs are not built to perceive the motion of an electron. The best we can do is to try to understand electrons and their motion as mathematical abstractions" (Susskind and Friedman 2014:2). Classical mechanics is also filled with mathematical abstractions but quantum mechanics is different in two ways, according to Susskind and Friedman: (1) Different Abstractions, states are represented by different mathematical objects and have a different logical structure; and (2) States and Measurements, in classical mechanics, the relationship between the state of a system and the result of a measurement on that system is very straight-forward; in fact, it's trivial. In the quantum world, this is not true. States and measurements are two different things, and the relationship between them is subtle and nonintuitive.

Physics is generally revered for its establishment of universal "laws" and preciseness as a science but when quantum physics is involved vagueness creeps into its equations and theories (i.e., the "Matrix equation" and the "Uncertainty principle"). The introduction of such concepts and "The Many Worlds Interpretation," multiverses, parallel worlds, and quantum entanglement seem to make quantum physics less of science and more like nonfiction popular culture.

Quantum Entanglement

One such example of a seemingly counterintuitive phenomenon found in the domain of quantum mechanics is quantum entanglement. *Quantum entanglement* is the theory that two subatomic particles can be intimately linked to each other even if separated by billions of light-years of space. No matter how far apart particles are from one another in space, their states remain linked. "That means they share a common, unified quantum state. So observations of one of the particles can automatically provide information about the other entangled particles, regardless of the distance between them. And any action to one of these particles will invariably impact the others in the entangle system" (Sutter 2021). In this regard, despite their vast separation, any particle vibrating in one part of the universe, say because of the sound of your voice, can affect a molecule at the edge of the universe instantly. Quantum entanglement proponents would suggest that it is an illusion that particles scattered across the universe are separated from one another. Then again, as astrophysicist Paul Sutter (2021) explains, physicists developed the fundamental ideas behind entanglement as they worked out the mechanics of the quantum world in the early decades of the twentieth century. They decided that to properly describe subatomic systems, they had to use something called a *quantum state*. A quantum state reinforces the idea that in the quantum world, nothing is certain for example, you never know where an electron in an atom is located, only where it *might* be. Sutter (2021) states that the first physicist to use the word "entanglement" was Erwin Schrödinger and that he described entanglement as the most essential aspect of quantum mechanics, saying its existence is a complete departure from classical mechanics. Quantum entanglement, or some equivalent term, could never be used in the social sciences as it is too vague and unscientific. Imagine if a sociologist studying a group of people in Ireland concluded their findings were now applicable to all people around the world because they shared a "common, unified quantum state" while ignoring cultural differences, differences in socialization processes, and the uniqueness of individual personality traits. We would be laughed out of the academic community. Such is the oddity of the concept of quantum entanglement. (Note: This idea will be revisited in Chapter 9.)

Emspak and Hickok (2022) state that in 1964, physicist John Bell posited that changes can be induced and occur instantaneously even if the particles are very far apart, this proposal is known as Bell's Theorem. This theorem is well regarded in modern physics but it conflicts with other well-established principles such as Einstein's contention that information cannot travel faster than the speed of light. Einstein famously described this entanglement phenomenon as "spooky action at a distance" (Emspak and Hickok 2022; Sutter 2021). For more than 50 years, scientists around the world experimented with Bell's Theorem but were never able to fully test the theory; even so, in 2015, three different research groups were able to perform substantive tests that supported the theorem (Emspak and Hickok 2022). And yet, as Sutter (2021) points out, while entangled particles may influence one another, the issue of causality remains questionable as faraway particles could have been effected by many possible causes. In addition, "an observer at the faraway particle does not know if the local observer has disturbed the entangled system, and vice versa. They must exchange information with no faster than the speed of light to confirm" (Sutter 2021). In March 2022, NASA announced it would be sending a quantum entanglement experiment—called the Space Entanglement and Annealing Quantum Experiment, or SEAQUE—into space.

Physicists John Clauser, Alain Aspect and Anton Zeilinger won the 2022 Nobel Prize for Physics for their experiments with quantum entanglement. Their work highlighted previous findings that two or more particles can exist in an entangled state even if they are far apart. Clauser has conducted groundbreaking experiments using entangled light particles, photons. It is believed that this research confirms that quantum mechanics is correct and paves the way for quantum computers, quantum networks and quantum encrypted communication (The Nobel Prize 2022g). The scientists admit that it is "totally crazy" that the quantum entanglements theory actually appears to be legitimate. The idea that unseen particles, such as photons, can be linked, or "entangled," with each other is a notion that baffled Albert Einstein. As it turned out, Bohr's notion of quantum mechanics was correct and Einstein's was incorrect (Phys.Org 2022). Asked how quantum entanglement works,

Clauser told the Associated Press, "Why this happens I haven't the foggiest. I have no understanding of how it works but entanglement appears to be very real" (Phys. Org 2022). Clauser's fellow prize recipients also said that they could not explain the how and why behind the quantum entanglement effect. In this case, the inability to explain why a theory "works" is no entanglement to winning a Nobel Prize.

Time Reversal

In the quantum state, physicists ponder, "Is it possible to reverse time?" Time is supposed to move in only one direction—forward—and, "According to quantum mechanics, the final irreversibility of conceptual time reversal requires extremely intricate and implausible scenarios that are unlikely to spontaneously occur in nature" (Jeewandara 2020). However, scientists have demonstrated "time reversal" in a quantum computer, returning three qubits (the basic unit of quantum information) to their state a fraction of a second earlier (Osborne 2019). By designing an algorithm to artificially reverse a (thermodynamic) time arrow within a quantum computer, scientists have experimentally demonstrated time reversal by sending a qubit from a more complicated state to a simpler one (Osborne 2019). The arrow of time reference is relative to the second law of thermodynamics, which implies that entropy growth stems from energy dissipation of the system to the environment (Jeewandara 2020). Time arrows themselves would have to go in different directions (e.g., forward and backwards) in order for true time reversal (in Nature) to be possible. Quantum physicists at the University of Bristol, Vienna, the Balearic Islands and the Institute for Quantum Optics and Quantum Information are arguing that when small amounts of entropy are involved the second law of thermodynamics can be violated (University of Bristol 2021).

Experimental physicists working on time reversal state that in a two qubit quantum computer, experiments are successful around 85 percent of the time but when a third qubit was introduced, more errors occurred and the success rate fell to around 50 percent. "So developing a quantum computer that can reverse time on a large scale is not going to happen any time soon. Furthermore, it indicates time reversal in nature is unlikely because it is too complex" (Osborne 2019). What we can see from this version of "time reversal" is not at all like fictional portrayals of time travel where people can travel to the past, it is more like "the quantum version of pressing rewind on a video to 'reverse the flow of time'" (Jeewandara 2020). If you are expecting the introduction of "time machines" so that you can correct the mistakes of the past, don't hold your breath.

String Theory

String theory posits that the most fundamental particles we observe are not actually particles but tiny strings that only "look" like particles through our scientific instruments because they are so small. These string entities exist and vibrate in many dimensions and the vibrations produce effects that we interpret as atoms, electrons and quarks (Mann and Coolman 2022). It is a theory that attempts to merge quantum mechanics with Albert Einstein's general theory of relativity. "The name *string theory* comes from the modeling of subatomic particles as tiny one-dimensional 'string-like' entities rather than the more conventional approach in which they are modeled as zero-dimensional point particles. The theory envisions that a string undergoing a particular mode of vibration corresponds to a particle with definite properties such as mass and charge" (Greene 2022). In 1905, Einstein unified space and time with his special theory of relativity and in 1915 he further unified space, time and gravitation with his general theory of relativity. These were huge achievements but Einstein dreamed of even grander unification, a theoretical framework that would account for space-time, and all of nature's forces—something he called a unified theory (Greene 2022). For the last three decades of his life, Einstein worked at this goal to no avail (see Chapter 7). Physics evolved from classical to quantum mechanics and finally, in 1968, there appeared to be a monumental breakthrough in the unification goal. Gabriele Veneziano, a young theorist working at the European Organization for Nuclear Research (CERN), wrote a research paper describing how a 200-year-old formula, the Euler beta function, was capable of explaining much of the data on the strong force than what was being collected at various particle accelerators around the world (Chalmers 2018; Greene 2022). A few years later, three physicists, Leonard Susskind, Holger Nielsen and Yoichiro Nambu, significantly expanded upon Veneziano's insight by showing that the mathematics underlying his proposal described vibrational motion of minuscule filaments of energy that resemble tiny strands of sting, inspiring the name *string theory* (Greene 2022). As early as the 1970s there were questions about the ability of string theory to be tested empirically as the presumed strings were too small. The model being used was inconsistent for three spatial dimensions (our world) was embarrassing, but proponents kept hoping (Chalmers 2018). The shortcomings of string theory were emerging but despite this physicists in the 1980s had high hopes for string theory as they envisioned the theory's potentiality of uniting all four of nature's forces—gravity, electromagnetism, strong force and weak force—and all types of matter in a single quantum mechanical framework, suggesting it might be the long desired unified field theory (Greene 2022). For the past four decades, it has been Michio Kaku at the forefront in trying to keep string theory, especially a unified string field theory, alive and well.

In 2002, science writer John Horgan made a bet with physicist Michio Kaku that by 2020 no one will have won a Nobel Prize in Physics for work on superstring theory, membrane theory, or some other unified theory describing all the forces of nature (Horgan 2019). Horgan won the bet when it was announced that the 2019 Nobel Prize winners in Physics were Jim Peebles, Michel Mayor and Didier P. Queloz (Peebles for his theoretical discoveries in physical cosmology; Mayor and Queloz for the discovery of an exoplanet orbiting a solar-type star). The ambiguity of quantum mechanics pales in comparison to string theory. Horgan (2019) argues that physicists have yet to produce any empirical evidence for either string theory, loop-space theory or any other unified theory. They don't even have any good ideas for obtaining evidence.

Chances are, you have heard of Michio Kaku as he is not only considered one of the most brilliant physicists of the contemporary era, he is also active in promoting physics and science in the popular world appearing on countless news programs and podcasts. Kaku is a theoretical physicist at the City College of New York (CUNY) and has written several physics-related books. We will learn much more about Kaku in Chapter 9. Kaku, along with his colleague Keiji Kakkawa, are often credited as co-founders of *string field theory* and as a highly visible proponent of string theory he is often the target of critics, include Horgan and his specific challenge. Growing up, Kaku loved science fiction shows and books, especially those filled with time-traveling heroes, parallel universes, and intergalactic space travel. His nonfictional hero was Albert Einstein and it became Kaku's goal, or mission, to finish the work of Einstein in his quest to find a "theory of everything"—one that could tie together his theory of general relativity and quantum mechanics. However, with our current understanding of physics, these two theories are not compatible so Kaku came up with his version of string theory. The basic premise of *string theory* is to combine these two theories (general relativity and quantum mechanics) by assuming there are multiple universes and dimensions beyond the ones we know (American Physical Society 2022).

Let's return to the bet made between Horgan and Kaku. As explained by Horgan (2019), Kaku made the bet, twenty years earlier, for a number of reasons, beginning with the general reminder that much of physics is done indirectly. For example, we know that the sun is made of hydrogen gas, and yet no one has ever visited the sun. We know that black holes exist in space, yet they are invisible by definition. We know that the Big Bang took place approximately 13.8 billion years ago, and yet no one was there to witness it. Kaku then extends this form of logic to conclude that we do not need to build an atom smasher the size of the galaxy to prove string theory (Horgan 2019). Instead, Kaku, states, we need to look for echoes from the 10th and 11th dimensions as follows:

a. Within a few years, the Large Hadron Collider, the largest atom smasher on earth, will be turned on outside Geneva, Switzerland. It might be able to find "sparticles" or super particles, i.e., higher vibrations or octaves of the superstring.

b. Invisible dark matter, which makes up 90 percent of the matter in the universe, might be shown to consist of sparticles like photino. This might also verify string theory.

c. In this decade, gravity wave detectors should be able to record shock waves from colliding black holes, which might reveal the first quantum correction to Einstein's original theory of 1915. These quantum corrections can be compared to those predicted by string theory.

d. Within 20 years, NASA plans to send three gravity wave detectors into outer space. They should be sensitive enough to pick up the shock waves from the Big Bang itself created a fraction of a second after the instant creation (Horgan 2019).

Kaku concluded that this should be enough to prove, or disprove string theory. If not, then string theory will be shown to be a "theory of nothing." However, if the numbers agree, string theory will be heralded as the greatest achievement of the human mind and will have "read the mind of God" (Horgan 2019).

John Horgan's 2002 counter-argument (his defense for their $1,000 bet) begins with the "purely intellectual" hope that Kaku is correct in that string theory would represent the greatest of all scientific achievements. However, Horgan began to suspect as early as the 1990s that the quest for a unified theory is religious rather than scientific. "Physicists want to show that all things came from one thing: a force, or essence, or membrane wriggling in eleven dimensions, or something that manifests perfect mathematical symmetry. In their search for this primordial symmetry, however, physicists have gone off the deep end, postulating particles and energies and dimensions whose existence can never be experimentally verified" (Horgan 2019). Horgan's point about the oddity of creating alternate and multiple dimensions is amplified by his further criticisms of Kaku's defense of string theory in that the super colliders necessary to collect super particles would have to be enormous (54 miles in circumference); gaining access to infinitesimal microscales where superstrings supposedly wriggle would require an accelerator that could not be built; and the simple fact that Nobel prize judges have always been sticklers for experimental proof.

Relying on "echoes" from the 10th and 11th dimensions (as proposed by Kaku) is certainly a clue that string theory will be hard to prove, at least with our current level of knowledge and instrumentation. Another foundational idea of string theory that will be hard to prove is the belief that the Universe we live in is actually a hologram. The *holographic principle* states that what we experience in 3 dimensions could just be data bits of information that exist on the surface of some distant two-dimensional surface that is projected as a hologram to appear in three dimensions. Leonard Susskind insists that the holographic principle is not some speculation among most theoretical physicists and is instead, "a working, everyday tool to solve problems in physics" (Stromberg 2015). The thing is, there is no direct evidence that our universe is a two-dimensional hologram and there is no good way of testing the principle experimentally.

The ideas of a multiverse of inflationary cosmology, or "branches of the wave function" of quantum mechanics, and "parallel branes" of string theory are among other tenets that test our understanding of science and willingness to suspend what our senses tell us to be true. Sometimes, when discussing these terms, there seems to be an overlap but those doing work in these areas find the distinction. Cosmologists look at the multiverse as meaning different regions of spacetime, far away so that we can't observe them, but nevertheless still part of what one might reasonably want to call "the universe" (Carroll 2011). In inflationary cosmology, on the other had, these different regions can be relatively self-contained—"pocket universes." When these pocket universes are combined with string theory, the emergent laws of physics in the different pocket universes can be very different; they can have different particles, different forces, and even different numbers of dimensions. In this regard, they can be thought of as separate universes, even if they're all part of the same underlying spacetime. The quantum mechanics perspective describes reality in terms of wave functions, which assign numbers (amplitudes) to all the various possibilities of what we can see when we make an observation (Carroll 2011).

In his book *The Hidden Reality* (2011), Brian Greene begins by saying that there was a time when the word "universe" meant "all there is." Think of such an expression as "There is nothing in this universe that will stop me from solving this problem." The universe was an all-encompassing term and that is how most people view the idea of the universe. So, when most people hear of the idea of multiverses or parallel worlds it is a hard concept to accept. It is also a hard concept to prove and yet a number of physicists, especially string theory enthusiasts, continue to work on the theory. If there are multiverses and if they are to be understood, Greene reasons, it'll come from string theory. Greene also lumps a number of concepts together as synonymous—*parallel worlds* or *parallel universes* or *multiple universes* or *alternate universes* or the *metaverse*, or *megaverse*, or *multiverse*—as they're all among the words to embrace not just our universe but a spectrum of others that may be out there. Greene's theory of multiverses is something of the extreme, at least for those outside of the quantum world of science. He puts forth the string theory notion that our entire universe can be explained in terms of tiny strings that vibrate in 10 or 11 dimensions (as referenced earlier), implying the dimensions we cannot see. He states that within string theory, strings are not the only entities the theory allows for but also objects that look like large flying carpets or membranes and the idea that we may be living on one of those gigantic surfaces. Greene too is hoping that such an idea can be supported by empirical means via the Large Hadron Collider (LHC) at CERN. As of July 2022, the LHC had discovered three subatomic particles never seen before but it has not proven the existence of multiverses.

The "Many Worlds Interpretation" (MWI) of quantum mechanics holds that there are many worlds which exist in a parallel at the same space and time as our own. Proponents of MWI point to the existence of other worlds as a solution to quantum measurement problems. Critics counter that claiming that the calculations of a formula or a theory work in some other dimension is hardly a way of conducting science especially as such a theory cannot be proven empirically. After all, if the MWI approach was applicable to every aspect of life people could claim to be correct about any and every course of action by simply stating that in some other world their behavior was the correct course of option. Quantum physicists attempt to make the MWI theory plausible by claiming that "every time a quantum experiment with different possible outcomes is performed, all outcomes are obtained, each in a different newly created world, even if we are only aware of the world with the outcome we have seen" (*Stanford Encyclopedia of Philosophy* 2021). String theory added the idea of many worlds, or many dimensions, as part of its attempt to describe the whole universe under a single "theory of everything." A number of physicists are turned off by the idea that string theory can explain not only everything in our universe but other universes. Physicists that still believe in the value of string theory have begun to reevaluate the idea of an (near-)infinite number of possible universes, each with their own laws of physics (Moskowitz 2018). So, where does this leave string theory? Brian Greene (2022) believes that string theory is still a vibrant area of research but, "it remains a mathematical construct because it has yet to make contact with experimental observations."

Meanwhile, the world of fiction embraces tales of a multiverse. In the early

2020s, two of the more popular box office movies involved stories of a multiverse: *Spider-Man: No Way Home* (2021), which earned around $2 billion USD; and *Dr. Strange in the Multiverse of Madness* (2022), which earned over $1 billion USD. It is apparent that people are quite willing to entertain the thought of multiverses within the realm of popular culture; but, are they ready to learn about it within the context of physics?

Summary

In this chapter we learned about the development mechanics in physics. We began with a review of classical mechanics, often called Newtonian mechanics, the branch of physics and an area of mathematics that involves the study of motion of macroscopic objects under the action of forces or displacements and the subsequent effects of the physical bodies on their environment; and the examination of bodies that remain at rest. Newton's Laws of Motions are of particular relevance to classical mechanics.

The discussion of the development of quantum mechanics included a description of the significant contributors to the transformation from classical mechanics to quantum theory to quantum mechanics. Discussion began with Max Planck, the founder of quantum theory and his work on thermodynamics and wavelength distribution. The works of Niels Bohr; Ernest Rutherford; Erwin Schrödinger; Louis de Broglie; Werner Heisenberg, who represents a shift to quantum mechanics; Paul Dirac; Julian Schwinger; and Freeman Dyson followed.

The chapter concluded with an examination of both quantum mechanics and string theory. Both of these perspectives are highly respected in physics and yet perplexing, even among quantum physicists themselves. Richard Feynman famously said, "Nobody understands quantum mechanics." There are, of course, many known aspects of about quantum mechanics beginning with the simple fact that it is a subfield of physics that describes the behavior of particles and matter on the atomic scale. While classical physics is busy establishing concrete laws, quantum mechanics struggles with such variables as quantum entanglement and time reversal. String theory posits that the most fundamental particles we observe are not actually particles but tiny strings and that these string entities exist and vibrate in many dimensions and that the vibrations produce effects that we interpret as atoms, electrons and quarks. String theory is meant to be a unifying theory that can explain everything within the realm of physics. String theory, like quantum mechanics must contend with aspects that make the theory suspect, including the idea of multiverses, parallel universes and the Many Worlds Interpretation.

The importance of the material presented in this chapter is self-evident as this was a chapter on quantum mechanics and string theory but it's also important as it will serve as an vital foundation for the topics covered in Chapter 7 (Albert Einstein's Unified Field Theory); Chapter 8 (Stephen Hawking's Theory of Everything: The Origin and Fate of the Universe); and Chapter 9 (Michio Kaku: A Theory of Everything via Superstring Theory).

PART B

FROM EARLY SOCIAL THOUGHT TO SOCIAL PHYSICS TO SOCIOLOGY

As the natural sciences were developing (see Part A), there emerged an earnest attempt to explain human behavior via the scientific method. Chief among these academic disciplines is sociology. Part B consists of 3 chapters that highlight the transition from early social thought to social physics to sociology. In Chapter 4, we look at the early influences on sociology. These influences include philosophical speculation; the Age of Enlightenment; and Claude-Henri-Simon. Chapter 5 introduces us to the founder of sociology, Auguste Comte, and his ideas on positivism, social physics and sociology. We will learn about the many academic influences on his works including the effects of the Enlightenment; the Tradition of Order; the Tradition of Progress; the Tradition of Liberalism; and his mentor, Claude-Henri Saint-Simon. We will learn about social physics and why this term should've been kept instead of replacing it with the term "sociology." We will also learn about the foundation of sociology, much of which still remains intact today, nearly 200 years later. A brief look at how "social physics" is still used today will be included. Chapter 6 describes how sociology is a science. We will examine how science was a key to the origins and development of sociology; learn about the importance of social theory supported by research methods; and learn about the establishment of laws.

4

The Early Influences
on Sociology

Introduction

As the natural sciences, in particular physics, were emerging and developing over the past centuries so too was an attempt to develop social sciences that could explain human behavior. In fact, a number of the same early breakthroughs and discoveries in science discussed in Chapter 1 would overlap as early influences on sociology. Of particular relevance is the discussion on the major paradigms of thought and the influence of philosophy.

If you recall, the four major paradigms of thought are: tradition; faith; common sense; and enlightened, rational thought. Social thinkers in general, and sociologists in particular, have incorporated these paradigms of thought in their social theories since the classical period of social theory. Sociologists have long pointed out how social systems dominated by tradition and faith have led to numerous forms of social injustice and intolerance. Embracing enlightened, rational thought, on the other hand, has led to progressive changes in society that empowers all people, including those traditionally discriminated against by the power elites. Notions of common sense have always been a feature of any culture but often vary from society to society because of the socialization process, life experiences, cultural norms and values, and personal observations of events. As we shall learn in this chapter, the type of paradigm of thought that is embraced by societal leaders will have a tremendous impact on a society and its culture. Social thinkers who spoke out against societal ills on the basis of such things as tradition and faith (e.g., the "divine rights of kings") will have a great influence on the development of sociology.

Just as philosophical thought would influence the development of the natural sciences (e.g., Pythagoras' mathematical theorem) so too would it influence sociology. In fact, sociological theory began as philosophical thought but somewhere along the way a split between the two occurred that allows for a clear distinction between these academic disciplines that still exists today.

Philosophical Speculation

There has been philosophical speculation on the nature of society and social life at least as far back as the ancient Greeks. In fact, the term *philosophy* derives from the Greek words for "love of wisdom." In practice, philosophy involves the study of the fundamental nature of knowledge, reality, our very existence, and what constitutes ethical and moral behavior. Philosophy has always attempted to enhance an individual's problem-solving capacities and help us to analyze information and ideas through deep contemplation and reflection. To this day, philosophy remains mostly a discipline entrenched in the application of deep thought in its analysis of human life.

As with such other academic disciplines as physics, chemistry, and psychology, sociology would eventually emerge with its own parameters of specific interest and make its break from philosophy. To distinguish itself from its predecessor, sociology developed as a field that attempts to support its social theories with empirical research (systematic data collection). To this day, sociological theory overwhelmingly maintains a commitment to the scientific approach to the study of human behavior. Sociological theory also brings with it a *critical* aspect to its examination of social reality. That is to say, sociological theory examines societies, social institutions, and social systems as they exist in reality, rather than in the abstract. Such an approach is not about creating an ideal type of society and calling upon other societies to conform to that ideal (as was often the case with ancient philosophy).

So when did sociology make this break from philosophy? Scholars disagree on the precise answer to this question. As the term "sociology" was coined by Auguste Comte, a European (a Frenchman), and the field was initially developed by him (as we shall learn in detail in Chapter 5), most reviews of the antecedents of sociology understandably focus on European influences, as will be the case here. However, there is at least one non–European social thinker that should be acknowledged, Ibn Khaldun, also known as Abu Zayd 'Abd al–Rahman ibn Khaldun (Snell 2019). Khaldun (1332–1406) was born in Tunis, North Africa (present-day Tunisia), to an educated family and studied the Koran, mathematics and history. He achieved high political office serving as Prime Minister of Egypt; and he saw active military service (*New World Encyclopedia* 2023). Khaldun developed one of the earliest nonreligious philosophies of history; is generally considered the greatest Arab historian; is an early influencer of sociological thought; and has been called the father of the science of history (Snell 2019). Khaldun's most significant work is *The Muqaddimah* and in this introduction to history, he discussed historical methods and provided the necessary criteria for distinguishing historical truth from error (Snell 2019). His sociological publications centered on Arabic thought and culture; Islamic ideology; and an analysis of social institutions (Snell 2019). Prior to the European social thinkers we will learn about in the following pages, Ibn Khaldun argued that state rulers were not "divine rulers." He would spend two years in a Moroccan prison for saying such a thing. Ibn Khaldun was mostly unknown to the European thinkers in the generations that would follow and remains mostly unheard of today. However, having traveled through Morocco, including Fez and Marrakech, places of significance for Khaldun, I saw first-hand the tributes and acknowledgments that still exist to honor this scholar.

Niccolo Machiavelli

Sociologist Roberta Garner (2000) suggests that the story of sociology begins with Niccolo Machiavelli (1469–1527) and *The Prince*, a short book he wrote in 1513 (but was not published until 1532). This was an interesting era as during the period of 1450–1525, Europe was experiencing dramatic social change. For example, in 1453, the Turks captured Constantinople (now Istanbul) from the Greeks and demonstrated the proficient use of cannons and gunpowder. The eastern Mediterranean became part of the Islamic world, and European rulers, merchants, and adventurers felt pressure to expand westward and southward beyond the Straits of Gibraltar. In 1458, Johann Gutenberg printed the Bible on his movable-type printing press and spearheaded the movement of mass dissemination of the printed word. Prior to Gutenberg's invention, creating a book was arduous and time-consuming and generally written in Latin, meaning that the masses (who were mostly illiterate) had nearly no access to information that books provide. Because of the printing press, books and pamphlets such as *The Prince* became available to an audience eager to read about traditional institutions such as the military or the nobility suddenly being humanized. In 1492, Columbus "discovered" the "New" World, triggering the burst of expansion by European nations onto the rest of the world. In that same year, the sovereigns of Christian Spain completed their reconquest of the peninsula from Islamic rule and expelled the remaining Moors and Jews (Garner 2000). Italy was at the height of its Renaissance.

Machiavelli's lifetime was one of warfare. In 1512, the Medicis (an Italian bourgeois family that headed a powerful dynasty), also known as the House of Medici, had returned to Florence to reclaim power over it. (Florence was the home of Machiavelli and where he wrote *The Prince*.) Backed by the papal (Pope Leo X) and Spanish armies they ruthlessly earned victory. With royalty in their blood the Medicis also produced four popes: Leo X, Clement VII, Pius IV and Leo XI. The Medicis are a perfect example of a blend of "faith and tradition" (two of the four dominant paradigms of social thought) that Machiavelli (and other social thinkers we will learn about) would condemn. Following their conquest, the Medicis accused Machiavelli of conspiracy (because of his role with the previous government), and imprisoned and tortured him. He refused to admit to any wrongdoing and was released, after which he retired to his estate to contemplate politics and to rehabilitate his dislocated shoulders (Green 2022). The following year he completed *The Prince*, but over concerns for his own safety, it was not published until after his death in 1532.

The Prince, it can be argued, sparked sociological theory because in contrast with Plato and Aristotle, who would likely insist on an imaginary ideal society to serve as the model for princely behavior, it instead concerned itself with ruthless and tyrannical princes from the real world. Pigliucci (2022) agrees with this assessment by stating that in *The Prince*, Machiavelli, gives a "frank assessment of political realities rather than on pious fantasies" (p. 22). Machiavelli made it clear that royal rulers have no virtue and that any ruler who hopes to be the embodiment of virtue "will be gone before dinner time—to be replaced by someone more realistic about politics" (Green 2022:46). *The Prince* (*Il Principe*) was a controversial publication for its time, because it provided a realistic view of human actions and challenged the long-held belief that kings had a "divine right" to rule. (Books that speak the truth today are considered controversial, for that matter, too, especially if they are labeled "woke" by someone.) Until the Renaissance, most publications upheld general notions of normative behavior, were non-empirical, and did not observe, describe, or analyze actual human behavior. Having held a leading position in the Florentine government of Italy, and knowing some of the movers and shakers of the time, Machiavelli was privy to great insights regarding to the matters of how rulers maintained their power (Green 2022). Machiavelli (2006) included into his book all the violent, fierce, savage, coercive, and sometimes even compassionate acts that the ruler must implement in order to stay in power. *The Prince* was based on reality, observations of real people, and not just moral ideals. It is for this very reason that it shocked its readers and was widely censored and banned. This is the very type of publication that illustrates modern social science—to write about society as it really is, not only as the power elite says that it is, or should be; and to be critical of social institutions that do not operate in the best interest of the people. *The Prince* is essentially a guide on how to be an effective leader from the perspective of Machiavelli's experience as a leader in the Florence military. Though, some argue this treatise is a satirical look on how not to be an effective leader, others view Machiavelli as a realist because he was not concerned with how the world could be if it was perfect, but rather how it was based on his experiences. Machiavelli believed that a prince should be loved and feared, but if he can be only one of the two then he must choose fear. It was Machiavelli's experiences as a philosopher, diplomat, historian, politician, writer, poet and playwright that assisted him in his knowledge and workings of the socio-political world and allowed him the ability the articulate these experiences in so many published works. Other works of note written by Machiavelli include *Discourses on Livy*, *Art of War* and *Florentine Histories*. Interestingly, Mortimer N.S. Sellers (2015) states that *The Prince* and *Discourses on Livy* (*Discorsi Sopra la Prima Deca di Tito Livio*) allows some scholars to consider Machiavelli as the "father of modern constitutionalism" and *The Prince* as the starting point of "modern political science" (p. 216).

Martin Luther

Garner puts forth a relatively strong argument about the importance of *The Prince* as a focal point to mark the distinction between philosophical thought and a starting point for sociological theory. However, because of its initial limited readership, one might argue that a contemporary of Machiavelli, Martin Luther (1483–1546), would actually serve as a better representation. Luther, a German priest and professor of theology, was one of the first advocates of mass education. He also challenged the powerful social institution of the Catholic Church and its assertion that the only true interpretation of the Bible should come from religious leaders. Luther, in contrast, believed that it was the right, even the duty, of all Christians to interpret the Bible for themselves (Stayer 2000). For this to happen, the masses would have to learn to read, which required mass education. It was his time spent in the monastery at Wittenberg that allowed Luther the opportunity to learn about the Catholic Church from within. And while he appreciated the Church's general values and beliefs, he was displeased with its position on how to spread the word of the Bible to the people. Luther's proposals on how the Bible should be taught became so popular it encouraged others to share their doubts with the Church and protest its medieval ways (bear in mind, Luther lived during part of the medieval period). Among Luther's complaints of the ancient Catholic Church was the Communion of the Saints, Penance, Purgatory, infused justification, the Papacy, the priesthood, and sacramental marriage (Armstrong 2012).

One of the practices of the Church that Luther was most critical of involved the Church's papal practice of asking payment—called "indulgences"—for the forgiveness of sins, known then as indulging in sinful behavior. His campaign to stop the Church from selling indulgences to church members (to those who could afford to buy them) led to Luther nailing his 95 Theses to the door of the cathedral in Wittenberg, Germany, in 1517. This act also ignited the fires of the Reformation and Protestantism. These 95 Theses condemned the excesses and corruption of the Roman Catholic Church, especially "indulgences," as seen from Luther's perspective. Luther felt that one should be truly sorry for their sins and be granted absolution through penance rather than paying for absolution. The Castle Church in Wittenberg, Germany, was known as one of the most infamous churches for the collection of holy relics or religious artifacts as offerings for forgiveness. The Church would display the offerings and the viewer was granted forgiveness for "indulging" in sin (Brecht 1985). Such a practice was elitist and benefited only the wealthy of society. Sociologists would be against any social policy that would benefit only the rich.

Luther spent a year in hiding and later returned to Wittenberg in 1522 to promote his religion—Lutheranism—which focused on the education of the masses and teaching the study of God rather than the interpretation of scripture by an exclusive group of authority figures in the Catholic Church. Luther found continued support from several German royals that provided him with partial immunity, though he was still a fugitive in Germany (Soukup 2017). The Protestant Reformation had an ally with various royal families and people who felt the same way as Martin Luther. Protestant ideals were easily and efficiently being spread through parts of Europe through the use of technology as the printing press allowed for larger production of texts used to exert influence over the masses (Robinson 2017). Still, the Church did all it could to stop the masses from reading the Bible for themselves. Consider that in 1536, William Tyndale, an English theologian and scholar, who was the first to translate the Bible into Early Modern English, was convicted of heresy, executed by strangulation and his body then burned at the stake.

The sociological relevance of Luther's beliefs are plentiful and include: his willingness to criticize an existing social institution, and a powerful one at that; his willingness to criticize a social system that favored the rich over the poor (the sale of indulgences was an elitist practice); his promotion of the redistribution of wealth, an idea that had barely been developed by social thinkers at this point in time, Luther believed that once the poor and working-class members of society realized that they outnumbered the royal and wealthy members of society that they would resist their oppressors and demand the redistribution of wealth so that it was fair and equal for all; his fight for the abolishment of usury, the lending of money at high interest rates that can often not be paid off by the debtor thus keeping the poor, poor and the wealthy, wealthy (Singleton 2011); his willingness to go to court to fight for his convictions; his willingness to fight for equality in education for all people; and his fight for the right of individual freedoms, in that he questioned the legitimacy of power and authority by the few over the lives of people. There is (at least) one significant blemish to Luther's legacy and a view of him as an ideal, tolerant religious person. He was, at least according to the research presented by Thomas Kaufmann, an undeniable anti–Semite. Luther spoke very poorly of Jewish people throughout his life. He acknowledged that Jesus was born as a Jew but said that contemporary "Jewish blood" had now become "more watery and wild" and of "inferior quality" by comparison with Jesus's day (Kaufmann 2017:3). Kaufmann adds, "Luther took pre-modern anti–Semitism for granted, adopted it, and helped to spread it" (p. 4). Furthermore, Luther's place among theologians and the leader of the Protestant Reformation led to his followers accepting his views of Jews and tainted the Lutheran church over the following centuries (Kaufmann 2017). To this day, we recognize anyone who touts that a category of people as having "inferior genes" is a racist and promotes a racist ideology.

Although the sixteenth-century ideas of both Machiavelli and Luther provide us with good examples of what could be considered sociological thought, rather than philosophical thinking, we are still centuries away from the official birth of sociology.

Thomas Hobbes, John Locke and Jean-Jacques Rousseau

Thomas Hobbes (1588–1679), John Locke (1632–1704) and Jean-Jacques Rousseau (1712–1778) each provide us philosophical insights as to the nature of social order that would have an influence on early sociology.

Hobbes was born in Wiltshire, England, on April 5, 1588. His lifetime was part of an era where the medieval ways were being questioned but the replacement system was yet to be formed (Harrison 2003). Hobbes believed that the social order was made by human beings and not preordained by God or by the domain of traditional authority and therefore the people should be allowed to change it (Adams and Sydie 2001). Even under authoritarian rule, Hobbes believed that authority is given by the subjects themselves; that, only by their consent, the rulers maintain sovereign power. As a political and social theorist, Hobbes wondered what life and human relations would be like in the absence of government. In 1651, Hobbes published his greatest work, *Leviathan*. In this book he provides a disturbing account of society without government. From his viewpoint, society would be filled with fear, danger of violent death, and the life of a person would be solitary, poor, nasty, brutish, and short (Delaney 2024). In his brief introduction to *Leviathan*, Hobbes describes the state as an organism analogous to a large person. He shows how each part of the state parallels the function of the parts of the human body. The idea of society as an organism with each part serving a function will serve as a forerunner to the ideas of Auguste Comte, Herbert Spencer and the school of thought known as structural functionalism.

Among his other ideas that would influence early sociology was his realization that humans are shaped by religious and political beliefs, beliefs that can vary quite differently from person to person. Because individuals do not share the exact same beliefs as one another, they develop different self-interests. Self-interests are shaped by selective perception, and consequently, reality is a projection created by individuals based on their beliefs and their nature. Such notions will have an influence on the schools of thought of conflict theory and symbolic interactionism. Because people are guided by self-interests, Hobbes felt it important that society should instill a system of morals that would be the same for everyone; in this manner, conflict could be minimized. What Hobbes failed to realize is that tradition- and faith-based social systems were based on a system of shared morality dictated by those in power. Hobbes objected to this. And yet, he now proposed a social system based on morality as dictated by the government. This dilemma actually reflects a problem that many social thinkers (and social policymakers) have gone through since the days of Hobbes. How do we maintain social order without infringing on the individual rights of people? This is a question that many sociologists attempt to answer.

Hobbes also incorporated philosophy and natural science in his theories. For example, advancing on the individualism put forth by René Descartes ("I think, therefore I am"), Hobbes uses the individual as the building block from which all of his theories spring. He formulated his theories by way of empirical observation. Hobbes believed that everything in the universe was simply made of atoms in motion, and that geometry and mathematics could be used to explain human behavior. According to his theories, there were two types of motion in the universe: vital (involuntary motion, such as heart rate) and voluntary (things that we choose to do). Voluntary motion was further broken down into two subcategories that Hobbes believed were reducible to mathematical equations—desires and aversions. Desires were things one was moved to or that were valued by the individual, while aversions were fears or things to be avoided by the individual. Further, individuals' appetites constantly keep them in motion, and in order to remain in motion, everyone needs a certain degree of power. Thus, the pursuit of power is the natural state of humans. Humans are in a constant struggle for power, and above all else, they want to avoid a violent death (Delaney 2024).

Consequently, humans must find a way to maintain peace. Hobbes draws on the language of the natural law tradition of morality which emphasized the principles of reason. Hobbes reasoned that people would be willing to give up "individual rights" for the security offered by a peaceful cooperative society. He believed that a "social contract," an agreement among individuals, would accomplish this. But, because human nature would never allow this to happen (because of greed, jealousy, etc.), and with no way to enforce the contract, people would eventually break it in an attempt to control a greater share of power over others. Realizing this, Hobbes proposed that an authoritarian government would come to power in order to enforce the social contract by whatever means necessary. He gave this government the name *Leviathan* (from the Bible), meaning monster. Individuals would give up all of their rights to the leviathan except for the right to self-preservation. People might give up their rights to the leviathan, but by their very nature, they would not be able to abandon their passion and quest for power. This drive would need to be channeled into what Hobbes called "commodious living" (a condition in which human passions are no longer a source of destructive conflict), so that individuals could pursue more constructive goals such as trade, industry, and other business ventures. The government would insure that all individuals were free to maximize their self-interests while protecting them from each other (Delaney 2024).

In sum, there are a number of influences from Hobbes on sociology including: his idea that social order is made by humans and not preordained by God; the use of the organic analogy (an influence on structural functionalism); individuals have different self-interests and different political interests because of different life circumstances (an influence on conflict theory); perception is often selective (an influence on symbolic interactionism); advancing individualism as put forth by René Descartes; and a belief that natural laws (especially those found in geometry and mathematics) could be used to explain human behavior.

John Locke was born in a village in Somerset, England, on August 29, 1632. Locke grew up amid the civil disturbances which were plaguing seventeenth-century England. He was educated at home until the age of 14, when he went to Westminster School (Thomson 1993). In 1652, Locke attended Christ Church, Oxford, where he studied Aristotelianism and remained a student for many years. He would come to revolt against the medieval scholasticism of the Oxford curriculum and became more interested in the "new science" or "natural philosophy" introduced by Sir Robert Boyle, who ultimately founded the Royal Society (Thomson 1993). Among the ideas of Aristotle to influence Locke was *tabula rasa* ("scraped tablet" or "clean slate"), a concept that appears in Aristotle's *De anima* (fourth century BCE; *On the Soul*). The *tabula rasa* concept refers to the idea that every child is born innocent and thus, they are not born with "original sin" as some religions taught; instead, it is the child's surroundings that will affect how they will develop and turn out. For Locke, *tabula rasa* did not mean that children were literally born with a blank mind but rather were born without social predispositions. We can see the influence of Thomas Hobbes and his ideas on natural law and human rights in Locke's *Two Treatises of Government*. Rene Descartes also had an academic influence on Locke. Having already begun his studies in medicine and the physics of Descartes, Locke began to use such instruments as barometers, thermoscopes and hygrometers (Rickless 2014). Descartes also helped Locke form his own ideas about the universe and developing different classifications systems of species (Rickless 2014). Locke was close friends with Sir Isaac Newton; Newton had developed an interest in mathematics, planets, gravity and how the moon revolved naturally around the earth, thus leading to his ideas on "natural laws." This line of thinking inspired Locke to conjure up the idea that all citizens should enjoy natural rights as if they were laws.

Locke embraced many of the ideas presented by Hobbes in his theories on the state of nature and the rise of government and society. Hobbes, as we have learned, believed that the government should exist to insure that all individuals were free to seek their self-interests while protecting them from each other. Locke, too, realized that there are times when the government needs to enact *salus populi suprema lex esto* (a supreme law that allows the government to take extreme measures during times of drastic circumstances) (Cope 1999). Locke believed that such a policy should only be utilized when available laws are inadequate to handle emergency situations. As a proponent of a government with limited powers, Locke proposed that individuals engage in a "social contract" with other members of society as a means of maintaining some sort of civility in society. Locke and Hobbes shared a common view of the importance and autonomy of the individual in society. The extent to which they agreed varies, but one important belief was constant between the two social thinkers—people existed as individuals before societies and governments came into being. They each possessed certain rights and all had the freedom to do as they pleased, unrestricted according to Hobbes, and with some restrictions placed on them by God, according to Locke. This freedom of the individual was important for it represents the foundation for modern liberal democracy (Delaney 2024).

Besides a general right to self-preservation (relatively) free from government interference, Locke believed that all individuals had a natural right to appropriate private property. This natural right carried with it two preconditions of natural law. First, since the earth was given by God to all individuals, people must be sure to leave enough property for all to have, and second, nothing may be allowed to spoil. These conditions met, an individual was granted exclusive rights to any object that he mixed with his labor.

Locke agrees with Hobbes that, human nature being the way it was, people eventually would find a way around the natural law restrictions on property accumulation through the creation of money. People were granted the ability to accumulate unlimited money based upon their industriousness. This meant that some people acted more rationally than others and thus were more deserving of property. Locke so despised the use of money that he argued it led to the disproportionate and unequal possession of the Earth.

However, Locke recognized that money "turns the wheels of trade." He argues that riches consist of gold and silver and countries filled with mines have an interest in maintaining the gold standard. Such countries grow richer either through conquest or commerce. In his *Some Considerations of the Consequences of the Lowering of Interest and Raising the Value of Money* (1691), he states the importance of a uniform code and a steady measure of values. A few years later, in *Further Considerations* (1695), he argues against devaluing the standard that he had proposed earlier. He reestablishes his commitment to maintaining standards in money in his *An Essay for the Amendment of the Silver Coins* (1695).

Locke's *Two Treatises of Government* (1967/1689) has been viewed as the classic expression of liberal political ideas. It is read as a defense of individualism and of the natural right of individuals to appropriate private property. It served as an intellectual justification for the British Whig Revolution of 1689 and stated the fundamental principles of the Whigs (Ashcraft, 1987). It would also serve as a primary source for the American Declaration of Independence. The key elements in Locke's political theory are natural rights, social contract, government by consent, and the issue of private property. Labor becomes the source and justification of property. Contract or consent is the ground of government and repairs its boundaries. Locke also believed that society had the right to overthrow the government. Since a majority created it, they have the power to remove it. This introduces the idea that government should be accountable to the people. Clearly, Locke was in favor of a limited government. It is unfortunate however that the framers of the U.S. Constitution ignored Locke's *First Treatise of Government* (Chapter 1) wherein he condemned slavery as "vile and miserable."

The constitutional and cultural life of the United States was deeply influenced by Locke's *A Letter Concerning Toleration* (1991/1689), which argued for the rights of man and the necessity of separating Church and State. Locke wrote that the commonwealth seems to be a society of men constituted only for the procuring of, preserving, and advancing of their own civil interests. Locke referred to civil interests as liberty, health, and indolency of body; and the possession of outward things, such as money, lands, houses, furniture, and the like. It is the duty of the civil magistrate, by the impartial execution of equal laws, to secure unto all the people in general and to every one of his subjects in particular the just possession of these civil interests.

In *A Letter Concerning Toleration*, Locke detailed in great length the need for the separation of church and state. Locke states that whatsoever is lawful in the Commonwealth cannot be prohibited by the magistrate in the Church. Any law created for the public good overrides the church and any conflict with interpretations of God's will shall be judged by God alone, not by religious zealots. Further, the magistrate ought not to forbid the preaching or professing of any speculative opinions in any Church because they have no manner of relation to the civil rights of the subjects. He made two exceptions to the general defense of tolerance. Atheism and Roman Catholicism should not be tolerated. He stated that atheists do not believe in a God and therefore their word cannot be trusted since taking a solemn oath means nothing to them. Locke argued that the Roman Catholic Church was dangerous to public peace because it professed allegiance to a foreign prince. Locke generally goes out of his way in many of his theological writings not to take issue with the Christian faith and adherence to the Bible. He treated religion like any other subject; he uses an intellectual approach, something quite admirable and ahead of its time.

Together with Newton's *Principia*, Locke's *Essay Concerning Human Understanding* (1975/1690) effectively decided the issue in the battle between "gods" and "giants." Locke details in *Essay* the need for analysis and study in regard to issues of morality and religion. The *Essay* represents Locke's greatest philosophical contribution and centers on traditional philosophical topics: the nature of the self, the social world, God, and the ways in which we attain our knowledge of them. His initial purpose of thought was to halt the traditional analyses of the Cartesians (or the medievalists) and to derive a method of dealing with the important difficulties in normative conduct and theological discussion. In Book IV of the *Essay*, Locke reveals that he is at one with the rationalist theologians of his century in their antagonism toward those who would ignore reason. Locke (1975/1690) proclaims that reason must be our last judge and guide us in everything.

Whether or not Locke can be labelled a "rationalist" is debatable. Some social thinkers come to view a person as a rationalist if they ground their thoughts with reason as a means to interrupt the social world. Philosophers label Locke an empiricist. Thomson (1993), for one, argues that Locke was an empiricist, and describes empiricism as beginning "with sense experience and claims that all knowledge must be derived from it. … Empiricist principles reject the possibility of a priori knowledge of the world" (p. 210). Modern-day empiricists, including sociologists, would agree with the notion of rejecting *a priori knowledge*. However, grounding their thoughts with "reason" is not enough to be considered an empiricist. Systematic data collection and statistical interpretation are requirements of modern empiricism, and therefore in order to be labeled an empiricist, one must collect data and employ statistical analysis of such data. Thomson (1993) provides no evidence that Locke conducted empirical research; in fact, Locke's pursuit of a medical degree was hampered by this critical limitation. Philosophers may label Locke as an empiricist during his era, but as the criteria of empiricism have evolved, there are few modern social scientists that would label him an empiricist based on a contemporary perspective.

The debate over whether or not Locke is a true empiricist is relatively unimportant especially compared to his many other concepts and contributions that still have relevancy today. For Americans, perhaps the most important contribution from Locke is his liberal notions regarding the role of government. After all, he laid the foundation for much of the groundwork of the U.S. Constitution and the U.S. federal government. The passage of the Declaration that declares "unalienable rights" of life, liberty, and the pursuit of happiness are also from Locke's writings and especially evident by one's right to own private property. In addition, one of the most heated debates in contemporary society—the separation of church and state—was a concept articulated by Locke and embraced by the "founding fathers" of the United States.

Sociology would embrace many of these theories and thoughts of John Locke including: the idea that a child is not born with "original sin," or predisposition (sociologists say, no one is born a racist or a bigot, etc.); individuals are free to seek their self-interests but the government should protect us from one another and foreign entities; systematic data collection and statistical interpretation are requirements of modern empiricism; all humans have unalienable rights of life, liberty and the pursuit of happiness; individuals have the rights to own property; and that there should be a clear separation of church and state so that all people are free to worship, or not to worship, the religion of their choice. The early sociologists that embraced the idea that sociology should be modeled after the natural sciences also appreciated Locke's idea that all citizens should enjoy natural rights as if they were natural laws in the line of thinking of Newton.

Jean-Jacques Rousseau was born on June 28, 1712, in Geneva, Switzerland. He was baptized into the Calvinist faith. Rousseau studied music and devised a new system of musical notation; he would often earn a living throughout his lifetime by copying music. His earnings helped to secure his time to publish a number of significant works. In his second publication, *Discourse on the Origin of Inequality* (1755; known as *Second Discourse*), Rousseau described the process of how social institutions had developed extreme inequalities of aristocratic France, where the nobility and top officials of the church lived in luxury, while the poor peasants had to pay most of the taxes. The theme of his *Second Discourse* is that society alienates man from his natural self, thus creating a situation of inner dissension and of conflict with other men (Crocker 1968).

In 1762, Rousseau published his famous *The Social Contract*. According to Rousseau, society could only be accounted for, and justified as, a means for enabling men to advance to a higher level of achievement than could be arrived at in its absence. Rousseau believed that society was responsible for the development of the moral potentialities of man's original nature. He put forth the notion that all men are equal and that the State's conformity to natural law involved the maintenance of public order and the provision of opportunities for the happiness of individuals. Rousseau believed in a democratic society (perhaps naively a utopian society), but he also was aware of the potential of individuals acting in self-interest. Rousseau, like Hobbes and Locke, believed, therefore, that the State is to have a limited role in societal matters with its primary function to protect members from outside threat as well as internal self-concerning individuals.

To reach this desired end, Rousseau promoted the idea of "general will." "The central concept of Rousseau's political philosophy is the general will. Rousseau claims that a legitimate political order is one where the sovereign people are governed by their own general will: where the people are both rulers and subjects at the same time" (Bertram 2012:403). The idea of a "general will" is widely recognized as a theory that applies and intersects with current approaches to what we view as the "greater good."

It is interesting to point out that Rousseau had a different view on private property than most of his predecessors, especially John Locke. Rousseau believed that God created nature and that humans should not own nature, for if they did, it would lead to their corruption. This corruption would occur because of the jealousies among people in a given society that inevitably would arise because of the different amounts of property that individuals own. Rousseau believed that those without property ownership would eventually revolt against those who did own property (Gildin 1983). Property, then, according to Rousseau, should belong to all the people as a collectivity. In this manner, Rousseau was a forerunner to Karl Marx and his view of private property.

Rousseau's direct influence on sociology are many, starting with his insights on the social inequalities that existed in aristocratic France just decades prior to the French Revolution (which would begin in 1789, after his death) and his other observations in *Second Discourse* highlighted by the fact that people who feel alienated from society may lead to dissension and conflict with others; that society should be run by a "general will" of all the people; and, of special interest for Marxists in particular, that property should be owned by the collectivity and not by private individuals (and corporations).

The Age of Enlightenment (circa 1685–1815)

The "Age of Enlightenment" (also known as the "Age of Reason") is the collective term used to describe the trends and writings in Europe and the American colonies during the "long" eighteenth century: from the late seventeenth century to the ending of the Napoleonic Wars in 1815. The phrase—"Age of Enlightenment"—was frequently employed by writers of the period itself, convinced that they were emerging from centuries of darkness and ignorance into a new age enlightened by reason, science, and a respect for humanity. The Enlightenment was a period of dramatic intellectual development and change in philosophical thought. It was a time when humans began to use reason to discover the world and cast off the superstitions and traditions of the medieval world. This period of huge change in thought and reason was, in the words of historian Roy Porter, "decisive in the making of modernity" as centuries of custom and tradition were brushed aside in favor of exploration, individualism, tolerance and scientific endeavor, which, in conjunction with developments in industry and politics witnessed the emergence of the "modern world" (White 2018). The desire to discover natural laws that govern the universe led to scientific, political and social advances. While it would be inaccurate to suggest that the centuries prior to the Age of Enlightenment were completely devoid of invention, innovation and scientific thought, a number of long-standing ideas and beliefs were being challenged, abandoned and replaced during this era. Consider, for example, the previously mentioned John Locke, whose *Two Treatises of Government* (1689) advocated a separation of church and state, religious toleration, the right to property ownership and a contractual obligation on governments to recognize the innate "rights" of the people; and Thomas Hobbes, who similarly advocated new social contracts between the state and civil society as the key to unlocking personal happiness for all (White 2018).

The Enlightenment thinkers kept a watchful eye on the social arrangement of society. They emphasized the pursuit of happiness and fulfillment in the here and now rather than in the heavenly future. They stressed rational education and scientific understanding as the means to attain progress (Adams and Sydie 2001). Progress could be attained because humans hold the capacity for reason. Further, reason should not be constrained by tradition, religion or sovereign power.

The roots of sociology can be found in the work of the philosophers, social thinkers and scientists of the "Great Enlightenment," which had its origins in the scientific discoveries of the seventeenth century. That pivotal century began with Galileo's "heretical" proof that the Earth was not the center of the universe (see Chapter 1 for a further explanation), as both Aristotle and the Church had taught, and ended with the 1687 publication of Sir Isaac Newton's *Principia Mathematica* (Kornblum 1994). "Scientific experimentation (with instrumentation) was used to shed new light on nature and to challenge superstitious interpretations of the living world, much of which had been deduced from uncritical readings of historical texts" (White 2018). Science was now challenging the dogmatic rule of the Church and of monarchies, and a number of people became openly skeptical of religious teachings in general. The work of Enlightenment thinkers was not dispassionate inquiry for they were deeply disturbed by the power of the Church and its secular allies in the monarchy. The traditional powers did not tolerate freethinkers and persons of science were often tortured and executed (Garner 2000).

The Enlightenment is most readily characterized as "liberal individualism."

It was a movement that emphasized the individual's possession of critical reason, and it was opposed to traditional authority in society and the primacy of religion in questions of knowledge (Hadden 1997). According to Seidman (1983), liberalism arose as a reaction against static hierarchical and absolutist order, which suppressed individual freedom. The Enlightenment thinkers (including the philosophers and intellectuals of this period) put their faith in the power of human reason (thus, the reference to the "Age of Reason"). The insistence on the ability of people to think and act rationally was anathema to Church and State (Hadden 1997). Social thinkers were impressed by Newton's discovery of universal gravitation. If humanity could so unlock the laws of the Universe, God's own laws, why could it not also discover the laws underlying all of nature and society? Scientists came to assume that through a rigorous use of reason, an unending progress would be possible—progress in knowledge, in technical achievement, and even in moral values. The early sociologists, especially Auguste Comte, would certainly agree with this basic premise that just as laws are applicable to the natural world, so too are laws applicable to the social world. In order to reach this goal of establishing laws that could explain human behavior, education and the use of science would have to be taught to the people. Placing a premium on the discovery of truth through the observation of nature and experimentation rather than abiding by authoritarian sources such as the Bible and monarchs was something promoted by enlightened thinkers of this period, and of any period, for that matter.

The Enlightenment was more than a set of ideas; it implied an attitude, a method of thought—and as argued by this author, *the* major paradigm of thought. There was a clear desire to explore new ideas and allow for changing values. It is important to note that not all of the social writers that comprised the collectivity of enlightened reason were intellectuals. There were many popularizers engaged in a self-conscious effort to win converts. They were journalists and propagandists as much as true philosophers, and historians often refer to them by the French word *philosophes*. The philosophes valued both education and practical knowledge. They believed that educated persons would exercise their critical reason for their own happiness and, consequently, their acts and deeds would benefit society overall. The philosophes also placed a great deal of importance on practical knowledge—how to farm, how to construct bridges and dams, how to relate to follow citizens (Adams and Sydie 2001). Hard work and education were believed to be the foundation to human and social progress.

The American and French Revolutions

Near the end of the Enlightenment era there were two major socio-political revolutions that would have a significant social impact on the thinking of how societies should be structured and would influence the creation of sociology. These two revolutions are the American and French Revolutions, both of which sought to overthrow oppressive regimes and replace them with governments based on ideals of the rights of those governed. Both of these significant revolutions revealed that a number of individuals were going beyond the mere discussion of enlightened ideas and were actually putting them into practice. The American Revolution encouraged attacks and criticisms against existing European regimes. "Thomas Jefferson's preamble to the Declaration of Independence, a prime example of Enlightenment thinking, assumed that all 'rational' individuals would agree with the 'self-evident truths' that 'all men are created equal' and endowed with 'inalienable rights' of 'life, liberty, and the pursuit of happiness'" (Adams and Sydie 2001:12). By praising the value of democracy and citizens' rights, Jefferson was directly confronting tyrannical authority.

The British Empire directly felt the impact of the American Revolution, as it learned that the convictions and desires of the oppressed would not be tolerated by free-thinking citizens armed with the enlightened tools to fight back. Indirectly, it was the French who were perhaps influenced the most by the revolution in America. The citizens of France were no longer willing to be subjected to traditional forms of authority. The ideas of democracy had a great impact on the French people and provided a spark to ignite the French Revolution of 1789. The French revolutionary mob chanted, "Liberty.... We shall not yield" during its June 1789 riots (Rude 1988:57). The revolution symbolically began on July 14, 1789, with the well-known storming of the Bastille (the revolutionists believed ammunition was stored there), a medieval fortress and prison in Paris. The Bastille represented the royal authority center of the monarchy and came to represent the tyranny of the monarchs. As the monarchy fell, the feudal system in France collapsed along with it (Goodwin 1970; Hampson 1963). Years after the siege, King Louis XVI and his wife Marie Antoinette were found guilty of high treason and executed by guillotine.

Both the American and French revolutions brought about opportunities to build a new social order built on the principles of reason and justice. In France, these changes were indeed revolutionary as many nobles were killed and their dominant role in French society was ended forever (Cockerham 1995). A series of laws enacted between 1789 and 1795 produced a number of other fundamental social changes. Churches were now subordinated to the state and forbidden to interfere in politics and the conduct of civil government. Each social class was given equal rights under the law, and each son in a family was entitled to equal amounts of inherited property (as opposed to just the eldest son). The total impact of the French Revolution was far more intense than the American Revolution. The Americans were fighting for freedom from the imperial British government, while the French were fighting for the near-complete restructuring of society. Following years of wars and chaos, mostly under the reign of Napoleon until he met his political and military demise at Waterloo in 1815, France would find itself in a period of instability. A number of significant wars and revolutions would follow Napoleon's demise as well (see Chapter 5).

The long series of political revolutions ushered in by the French Revolution and continuing into the nineteenth century was a dramatic factor in the rise of sociological theorizing. The impact of these revolutions on many societies was enormous and resulted in many positive changes. It also attracted the attention of many early theorists who concentrated on the negative effects of such changes. These writers were particularly disturbed by the resulting chaos and disorder that revolution and war bring with them, especially in France. An interest in the issue of social order was one of the major concerns of classical sociological theorists, especially Auguste Comte and Emile Durkheim (Delaney 2024).

The Industrial Revolution

Another major development that began during the Age of Enlightenment that would influence early sociology was the Industrial Revolution. The Industrial Revolution began in the mid-eighteenth century (circa 1760) in England and quickly spread through many Western societies, including the United States and Canada. The Industrial Revolution was not a single event but, instead, a number of interrelated developments that culminated in the transformation of the Western world from a largely agricultural society to an overwhelming industrial system. The textile industry was especially huge at the inception of industrialization. Women and children were often employed in the textile industry during the early stages of industrialization because their smaller fingers were often better at threading the machinery. They worked long hours, often 16-hour shifts, for very little pay. The lack of child labor laws, unsafe working conditions, the lack of unions and collective bargaining rights, were among the many problems of early industrialization.

The Industrial Revolution involved the introduction of massive numbers of machines which resulted in a dramatic increase in productivity. This increase in productivity led to an increased demand for more machines, more raw materials, improved means of transportation, improved forms of communication, better-educated workers (the workers needed to be literate enough to operate the machinery and read instructions), and a more specialized division of labor. Large factories were built to house all of this production. The owners of the means of production needed more and more workers which spirited the great migration of people leaving their farms and rural ways of life in the hopes of finding gainful employment in the rapidly developing urban cities. Nearly all laborers worked long hours for little pay. Urban planning and development was either an afterthought or ignored completely. This resulted in large sections of sprawling cities with chaotic slums characterized by inadequate (or a lack of) sanitation and the emergence of urban crime resulting in a growing number of disenchanted, economically-poor people. The Industrial Revolution changed the face of Western society. No longer did the majority of people live in small, rural villages with an extended kinship system and produce for themselves most of what they needed in order to survive. The rise of trade had dissolved the subsistence economy of medieval society and created a system of political power based on financial wealth rather than ownership of land.

By the early nineteenth century, social thinkers and intellectuals were discussing the wide range of social problems that had never existed before industrialization. They were concerned about other related topics such as the influences of industrialization and modernity on societal change and social order. Social reformers were worried about the welfare of workers and abandoned children (among others) and wondered if, and how, society should intervene to help the less fortunate. Concerns over topics such as these have a direct influence on the development of sociology.

Claude-Henri Saint-Simon

Saint-Simon (1760–1825) was born into a noble French family and lived in comfort as a member of the aristocracy. He was a social reformer and of the one founders of socialism (Barnes and Fletcher 2023). He met Rousseau and was taught the leading ideas of the Enlightenment philosophers of France. In 1776, Saint-Simon joined the military. Three years later he became a captain, as the common practice of the aristocracy's enjoying rapid promotion. Under the orders of the absolute monarch, King Louis XVI, Saint-Simon served in the American Revolution as a volunteer on the side of the colonists. The monarch supported the colonists because of his disdain for the British. Saint-Simon fought under the command of George Washington at Yorktown. Fighting with the French in the colonial war in the West Indies, he was captured (1782) by the English and served a prison term of several months. In 1783, Saint-Simon went to Mexico and while there designed the concept of building a canal across Panama. The following year he returned to France.

Following the timeline already established previously in this chapter, we know that Saint-Simon's return to France occurs just prior to the French Revolution. He renounced his noble title and did not take part in the revolution. Saint-Simon did endorse the ideals of liberty, equality and fraternity. With his wealth, Saint-Simon also embraced the opportunity to make a fortune during the chaos of revolution- and post-revolution years by taking advantage of the sale at low prices of church and émigré property. He also purchased at a fraction of the price the land left behind by other aristocrats that fled France following the Revolution. (Over the years, his business partner would steal much of his fortune, however.)

At this point, one might wonder how an aristocratic military man and real estate mogul such as Saint-Simon would come to have a significant influence on the official introduction of sociology. Having already decided to leave government life, Saint-Simon claimed that Charlemagne (747–814; Saint-Simon was fond of claiming descent from Charlemagne), the first and greatest Holy Roman Emperor (800–814), had appeared to him in a dream and told him to become a "great philosopher." This vision persuaded him to pursue a career in "saving humanity." Sustained by the faith that he had a message for humanity, Saint-Simon lavished his wealth on a salon for scientists to come together and share ideas (like a "think tank"). He became actively involved in the newly established (1794) Ecole Polytechnique, a school established to provided students with a well-rounded scientific education with a strong emphasis in mathematics, physics, and chemistry, and to prepare them upon graduation to enter the national institutes of public works. Saint-Simon was especially involved in the study of physics. He often entertained distinguished scientists and formed friendships with a number of leading scientists and writers whom he helped to support.

There were a number of influences on Saint-Simon's academic works but especially such Enlightenment thinkers as Rousseau, Isaac Newton and Nicolas de Condorcet. Saint-Simon was tutored by Rousseau for a short period of time in his early life. Rousseau influenced Saint-Simon's ideas of scientific knowledge and how it applies to society and Claude-Henri gave credit to Rousseau for helping him to sharpen his mind into a tight metaphysical net. Saint-Simon maintained that Newton had uncovered the structure of the universe (structure is viewed here as recurrent patterns that could be observed and studied in astronomy) via his "Three Laws of Motion." He thought it was possible to study the structure of society and uncover its laws. In his work, Saint-Simon wrote about the necessity of creating a science of social organization. The term *organization* meant "organic structure" to him. He maintained that society, like an organism, was born and grew. The major challenge was to understand such growth (social change) and the forces behind social stability (social order). He believed that laws exist to explain these sociological issues of social organization, social stability and social change.

Saint-Simon was now ready to begin his academic publishing career. In his first publication, *Letters of an Inhabitant of Geneva to His Contemporaries* (1803), Saint-Simon proposed that scientists take the place of priests in the social order. He argued that the property owners who held political power could hope to maintain themselves against the propertyless only by subsidizing the advance of knowledge (The Editors of Encyclopædia Britannica 2023a). In his "Introduction to the Scientific Studies of the nineteenth Century" (1807), Saint-Simon stated that the observation of patterns over a long period of time was essential. Those observations must then be brought together in a general theory of history capable of explaining the fundamental causes of historical change, not only in the past and at the present time, but also in the future; for the causes of future events must already be in existence. The implication was that if one could forecast the future, then one might be able to shape the future as well. This line of thought was influenced by de Condorcet's belief that he could document the operation of progress in the past and project the course of history for the future. For de Condorcet, the idea of infinite perfectibility was a foregone conclusion (Coser 1977).

In his 1813 *Essays on the Science of Man*, Saint-Simon suggests that the methodology of a science should be:

1. Study the "course of civilization": and look for regularities, patterns and processes of change.
2. Observations will disclose patterns or "laws of social organization." The broad historical trends will outline the history of social evolution.
3. Once the laws are discovered, they can be used to reconstruct society on the basis of a plan.

As we can see, Saint-Simon believed that the study of society should be based on science, including the use of history and observation, as methodological approaches. In Chapter 5, we will see that Comte also stressed the historical method and the use of observation as a means of gaining knowledge.

Foreseeing the triumph of the industrial order, Saint-Simon called for the reorganization of society by scientists and industrialists on the basis of a scientific division of labor. His hierarchical view of society would be ushered in by positivism. *Positivism*, the reliance of scientific study, laws, regulations, and reason, was to be directed by the most "competent" members of society. Saint-Simon referred to the competent class as people like bankers, lawyers, industrialists and intellectuals.

Social action should be dictated by this class based on positivistic decision-making. Other categories of Saint-Simon's social strata included artists and poets (emotional persons) and those with strength and motor skills making up the social class of workers and organizers (Collins and Makowsky 2010).

In the *New Christianity* (1825), Saint-Simon called for a newer, more humanistic approach to Western religion (one that would incorporate the laws of positivism) so that it could serve as a guiding force to usher in the new social order of society. Saint-Simon believed that science and religious ideas would eventually combine to form a positivistic religion, or a *terrestrial morality* as he called it. (Once again, we will see this idea reemerge with Comte.) Saint-Simonian groups (followers of the ideas of Saint-Simon) sprung up all across Europe preaching the message of Saint-Simon's philosophy. They were bourgeoisie intellectuals and officeholders (both public and private) who were, not surprisingly, mainly bankers, industrialists, and intellectuals who considered themselves to be the "competent" class. The Saint-Simonians emphasized the need for order, disciple, efficiency, public control of the means of production, and the gradual emancipation of women.

The above represents a glimpse into the ideas and publications of Saint-Simon. In some instances it has been pointed out how Saint-Simon's ideas were similar to Comte's. In reality, this means that many of Comte's ideas were similar to that of Saint-Simon. It is this relationship between the two that makes for the most direct influence on the founding of sociology as Saint-Simon was the mentor of a young Auguste Comte. The two collaborated for 7 years until 1824 when there was a falling out between the two. Saint-Simon would die the following year. Auguste Comte would more successfully transform many of Saint-Simon's ideas and formulate them into a specific and challenging discipline called sociology.

Summary

In this chapter, we learned about the early influences on sociology. Just as philosophical thought influenced the development of the natural sciences so too would it influence sociology. Philosophy, like sociology, has always attempted to enhance an individual's problem-solving capacities and help us to analyze information and ideas through contemplation and reflection. To distinguish itself from its predecessor, sociology developed as a field that attempts to support its social theories with empirical research (systematic data collection and analysis). To this day, sociology maintains a commitment to the scientific approach for the study of human behavior. It also brings with it a critical aspect to its examination of social reality.

A number of early social thinkers had ideas that either indirectly or directly reflect those of sociological concern and include Ibn Khaldun, Niccolo Machiavelli, Martin Luther, Thomas Hobbes, John Locke and Jean-Jacques Rousseau. Among the ideas the overlapped with these philosophers and the early sociologists were: the notion that kings and monarchs do not have a "divine right" to rule and that the social order is to be designed by the people; the promotion of the right of free education for all people; the practice of "indulgences" was wrong; criticizing existing social institutions, when needed, was a morally ethical thing to do; individuals have civil rights (e.g., liberty, freedom and the pursuit of happiness); people can adhere to a chosen religion or be free from religion and that there must be a separation of church and state; individuals have different self-interests than one another; perception is often selective; a belief that natural laws could be used to explain human behavior; a child is not born with predispositions (e.g., no one is born a sexist or racist); the scientific method must be embraced when conducting social research; rationality and reason should serve as the guidelines when establishing a social structure and social order; and the promotion of equality among all people.

The Age of Enlightenment, also known as the "Age of Reason," also served as a precursor to sociology in a number of ways and especially its promotion of enlightened thinking via reason and science and demands for a respect for humanity. This was an age of dramatic intellectual development as centuries of custom and tradition were brushed aside in favor of exploration, individualism, tolerance and scientific endeavor. The desire to discover natural laws that govern the universe led to scientific, political and social advances in ways of thinking on how society should be run. Two major political revolutions—the American and French Revolutions—took place near the end of the Enlightenment era that would have a significant social impact on the thinking of how societies should be structured and would influence the creation of sociology. Another major development during this period was the Industrial Revolution. The Industrial Revolution was not a single event but, instead, a number of interrelated developments that culminated in the transformation of the Western world from a largely agricultural society to an overwhelming industrial system characterized by a large number of new social problems. The consequences of such a change became the domain of study for early sociologists and remains so today.

Claude-Henri Saint-Simon provides us with a direct link to Auguste Comte, the person who coined the term sociology (see Chapter 5). Influenced by the works of many great Enlightenment thinkers and once tutored by Rousseau as a youth, this former aristocrat and military man became an outstanding scholar admired by his contemporaries and amassed a following of disciples known as Saint-Simonians. At the end of his life, Saint-Simon served as the mentor to Comte. Comte would borrow and expand upon many of Saint-Simon's ideas and concepts.

5

Auguste Comte,
Social Physics and Sociology

Introduction

Auguste Comte is considered the official founder of sociology as he is the person who coined the term and set the early parameters of the discipline. In this chapter, we will learn about the life of this dynamic and often brilliant social thinker; the influences on his life; a sampling of his major concepts and contributions to the field; and how he settled upon the term "sociology" for his academic discipline of positive philosophy. We will discover that Comte initially preferred the term "social physics" over sociology. We will also learn about usages of the term "social physics" since Comte's era.

Auguste Comte (1798–1857)

Isidore Auguste Marie Francois Xavier Comte was born on January 19, 1798, in the southern French city of Montpellier during the era of chaos and instability that followed the French Revolution (see Chapter 4). Montpellier was under siege when Auguste was born. Growing up during a time of war left an important imprint on him to the point where he would value social order. To add to the instability in his own immediate setting, his parents were devout Catholics and ardent royalists, affiliations not conducive to one's personal safety at this time as the revolutionists were rebelling against the Church and the monarchy (Hadden 1998). Comte's parents had married in secret because the revolutionary government had closed the churches of Montpellier. His father, Louis-Auguste Comte, was a petty government official who was employed at a tax office, and a serious man who was opposed to the French Revolution (Standley 1981). Auguste Comte (he had shortened his name early on in life) and his father disagreed about most of their beliefs except for the idea that social order was of the utmost importance (Thompson 1975). Father and son had a big disagreement over Auguste's decision to become loyal to the French First Republic, which made him a republican and in opposition to the Catholic Church. Comte also announced that he ceased believing in God. As a result, Comte's relationship with his parents, and siblings (two sisters and one brother) were strained throughout the remainder of his life.

Despite limited family finances, Comte's parents were able to send him and his brother to the Lycee Joffre at Montpellier. Following his primary school education, Auguste attended the University of Montpellier and then École Polytechnique in Paris. He was a brilliant student of physics and mathematics and was also interested in economics, history and philosophy. He enjoyed meeting many of the eminent scientists of France. Comte came to view École as *his* school, and as a place that he wished to graduate with honors and hoped to teach after the end of his studies. His classmates recognized him as an outstanding student and as a leader. However, Comte was also often disorderly and unruly and in 1816 led a protest of students against the teaching methods of a geometry instructor. The school disciplined Comte and the other ringleaders of the revolt. École's new general, trying to keep in line with the new conservative government (that followed Napoleon's abdication), ordered the removal of Comte and his whole class. The government sent in troops to enforce the order. École Polytechnique was temporarily closed that year (1816) for restructuring and Comte was not allowed to return. Understandably, Comte's expulsion from École Polytechnique would have an adverse effect on his academic career.

Comte had gained a reputation as possessing an exceptional mind. His knowledge of mathematics would help him in his later years when he attempted to establish the validity of "laws" and their application to the study of society. He also had a terrific knowledge and understanding of physics, something that would become quite relevant. Comte was able to demonstrate unusual feats of memory such as reading pages of text and reciting it backwards by heart (Hadden 1997). By 1817, Comte was teaching journalism and mathematics in Paris. In the summer of that year, he was introduced to the French utopian socialist Claude-Henri Saint-Simon, then the director of the periodical *L'Industri*. Comte became Saint-Simon's secretary, or more accurately his protégé and the two were very close despite the vast differences in their ages. Saint-Simon was nearly sixty years old when the two met but he was impressed by Comte's brilliant mind and came to view him as his "adopted son." As Saint-Simon's apprentice, Comte was paid quite handsomely, but when Saint-Simon experienced financial troubles, Comte continued to work without pay. Comte and Saint-Simon each benefited from this collaboration and many of their ideas and concepts overlapped. In the year prior to Saint-Simon's death, the two social thinkers had a falling out and split over publishing rights for the *Plan des Travaux Scientifiques* (*Plan of Scientific Work*), which Saint-Simon published in 1824 but failed to acknowledge Comte. (Note: In 1822, Comte would publish a volume *Plan de Travaux Scientifiques Necessaires Pour Reorganiser la Societe*, in English, *Plan of Scientific Studies Required to Reorganize the Society*.) Comte would publish his first essays in various publications headed by Saint-Simon including *L'Industri*, *Le Politique* and *L'Organisateur*. We will learn more about the impact of Saint-Simon on Comte's academic development during the discussion of intellectual influences on Comte's life.

By the mid–1820s, Comte was busy making significant academic contributions. Beginning in April 1826, his lectures on his new science of positive philosophy attracted many outstanding French thinkers. From these lectures he developed his six volume *Course of Positive Philosophy*, which were published between 1830 and 1842. Because of his ideas on positivism and continued publications Comte had amassed a tremendous following.

Intellectual Influences on Auguste Comte

Every social thinker is a product of their time and Auguste Comte is no exception. In response to the political, industrial and scientific revolutions of his day, Comte was fundamentally concerned with an intellectual, moral and political reorganization of the social order. The key instrument necessary to reconstruct society, Comte believed, was the adoption of the scientific attitude. As an ardent positivist, he insisted that the goal of sociology involved the discovery of knowledge that would aid in the progressive improvement of society. Comte was influenced by the works of a number of individual theorists and schools of thought, including: English philosopher Francis Bacon, who emphasized inductive experimentation; English philosopher Thomas Hobbes; Italian astronomer, physicist and engineer Galileo Galilei; French philosopher Baron de Montesquieu; German philosopher Immanuel Kant, whom Comte considered the metaphysician closet to the positive philosophy; French philosopher Jacques-Benigne Bossuet, a bishop and influential spokesperson for the rights of the French church against papal authority; and, above all, Saint-Simon (Ashley and Orenstein 1985). During the early period of his life, Comte was also influenced by liberal political economists Adam Smith (referred to as the "father of modern capitalism") and Jean-Baptiste Say, a liberal French economist and businessman who developed the "Law of Markets" (production is the source of demand; if production is increased so too will demand increase; demand for one product creates a demand for other products). Comte was also impressed by historians William Robertson, David Hume, and G.W.F. Hegel.

There are five major influences on Auguste Comte and each will be briefly highlighted below.

The Effects of the Enlightenment

Comte believed that the purpose of science (especially sociology) was to study objective relationships of both structure and change in order to predict future events; after all, the goal of any science is the prediction of future behavior (discovery and explanation are the first two steps of science). It might be easy to think that Comte was a strong proponent of all the ideals of the Enlightenment proponents, especially with its focus on progress (Kobya 2018). However, Comte viewed many of the Enlightenment ideas as metaphysical in nature. Notions such as natural rights and individual freedom of thought and action were metaphysical because they were ungrounded in scientific analysis, according to Comte. As we shall see later in this chapter, Comte's general disregard for metaphysics (the philosophical study of concepts and reality outside of human sense perception) placed it in the second stage of his "Law of Three Stages"—a mere transitional phase from the theological to the positive stage in line with his historical, evolutionist way of thinking. While he understood the notions and principles of individual freedom, equality and sovereignty of the people, he viewed such terms as metaphysical as it was not possible to measure such things (e.g., are all people *truly* equal to one another?). He developed his scientific view of positivism to combat what he considered to be the negative and destructive philosophy of the Enlightenment (Ritzer 2000; Kobya 2018). Comte believed that, "sociology, a positive science, would show the way to progress to the western people without compromising order" (Kobya 2018:849). However, it must be pointed out that, Comte's Law of Three Stages, an evolutionary theory, also reveals the notion of historical progress, something he learned from various Enlightenment philosophers (Barnes and Fletcher 2023).

The Tradition of Order

The Enlightenment failed to establish a stable social order following the French Revolution of 1789 and that displeased Comte. The social instability and chaos that lasted throughout much of Comte's life upset him to the point where he often put a high premium on thinking about ways of maintaining social order. The traditionalists taught that a society not bound together by the ties of a moral community would collapse. (This line of reasoning is similar to the adage "United we stand, divided we fall.") Comte believed that society must have a legitimate authority with a hierarchal structure and full support of its citizens. From this standpoint, society is viewed as an organic functioning whole. The traditionalists believed that society is healthy only when the different parts (the different groups of people and different social institutions) are functioning in harmonious order. Comte embraced many of the ideas of the traditionalists: order, hierarchy, moral community, spiritual power, and the primacy of groups over individuals. In fact, Comte's concept of *social statics* can be directly traced to their influence (Delaney 2004).

Despite the value he placed on social order, Comte realized that in order for society to continue to evolve, it (and he) must promote progress.

The Tradition of Progress

As a person of science, Comte had to embrace the notion of progress. Recall our earlier mention of Comte having embraced the idea of the historical progress, something he learned from various Enlightenment philosophers. He would develop a theory that the human mind and societies evolved through a series of stages (see the later discussion on "The Law of Three Stages"). From the tradition of progress, Comte would be deeply influenced by Nicolas de Condorcet (Marie-Jean-Antoine-Nicolas de Caritat, Marquis of Condorcet), a French philosopher and mathematician. Condorcet's *Esquisse d'un Tableau Historique des Progres de l'esprit Humain* (*Sketch for a Historical Picture of the Human Mind*), written while he was hiding from Robespierre's police, continued (Anne Robert Jacques) Turgot's focus on the long, historical chain of progress culminating in modern rational man. Condorcet believed that he could document the operation of progress in the past and project trends that would continue. *Esquisse* was considered the most influential publication on the idea of progress ever written to that point in history. Condorcet saw science and technology as the means by which mankind would propel society into the future and reach a period near perfectibility wherein the human race would find a way to end suffering and deprivation. He knew society was nowhere near that point. He did, however, identify a number of epochs that humanity had evolved from through history to demonstrate his belief in progress: from savagery to pastoral community and thence to agricultural state (Condorcet 1795). His belief in progress convinced Condorcet that additional epochs, or stages would follow in the development of society.

Comte, as alluded to a number of times already, will develop his own concept, actually a "law" on how societies and the human mind progress through stages. This overall belief in progress was very important to Comte and led to the important concept of *social dynamics*, or "the fundamental laws of social dynamics" wherein he states the progress in a society is achieved through the right balance between opposing conservative and innovative forces (Population Council 2011).

The Tradition of Liberalism

Liberalism is a necessary component for progress to occur. Conservative thought results in stagnation and support of the status quo whereas liberal thinking allows for innovation and invention. As someone who promoted societal progress, Comte embraced social policies that would allow for such things as growth in commerce. In his *Course of Positive Philosophy*, Comte (1896) revealed his high regard for Adam Smith by calling him an "illustrious philosopher." Comte had mixed feelings about Smith's economic theories. On the one hand, Comte was critical of Smith and his successors for their belief in the self-regulating character of the market as he viewed *laissez faire* as a system conducive to anarchy. On the other hand, Comte's belief in the beneficial effects of the division of labor comes from Smith. Comte also agreed with Smith that the industrial form of the division of labor had awoken a potent form of social cooperation, which would allow mankind to drastically increase their production capacity. Comte would later recognize the potential for negative aspects of specialization (e.g., the worker could reach the point where they would not have to exert creative understanding of their work and, they may develop a lack of desire to exercise innovative thought).

Another area in which Comte is directly indebted to the liberal economists resides with the recognition that "industrialists," or the modern term "entrepreneurs," are critical to the liberal spirit of progress, innovation and evolution of the mind and society. Comte agreed with Smith's French disciple, Jean-Batiste Say, in making a distinction between the "capitalist" and the "entrepreneur." Comte believed that the entrepreneur would guide and direct activities in the new industrial system whereas the capitalist controls production and distribution. It can be pointed out today that the entrepreneur remains as a force in the post-industrial socio-economic systems as well.

Claude-Henri Saint-Simon

As we learned earlier, Comte met Saint-Simon in summer of 1817 in Paris and the two would collaborate on a number of works. In 1824, the two social thinkers broke from one another over a quarrel involving an intellectual disagreement. There is no doubt however, that Saint-Simon had a huge influence on Comte, both personally and especially professionally. Saint-Simon was an activist and promoted immediate social reform. He wanted, above all, to inspire the liberal industrialists and bankers, who were his backers, to take prompt steps for the reorganization of French society. Saint-Simon, if we recall from Chapter 4, lived quite a different life than Comte. He was a man of action, someone who traveled to many parts of the world, and someone who was eager to make an immediate and positive difference in society. Comte was not-so-worldly and was far more intellectually-inclined and as a result, he emphasized that theoretical work had to take precedence over reform activities. He believed that establishing the foundations of the scientific doctrine was more important in the short term than trying to affect any practical influence on matters of societal change. Despite this fundamental difference, Comte was most definitely influenced by Saint-Simon. In acknowledging his debt to Saint-Simon, Comte states, "I certainly owe a great deal intellectually to Saint-Simon … he contributed powerfully to launching me in the philosophic direction that I clearly created for myself today and which I will follow without hesitation all my life" (Durkheim 1928:144).

Ideologically, Saint-Simon envisioned planned societies linked together into a larger organized international community (something like a United Nations and an early forerunner of the concept of globalization). He was a firm believer in the validity of science and rationalism. He promoted positivism, the scientific approach to the study of society. Saint-Simon believed in the systematic collection of data, especially through observation, and then the establishment of laws based on these observations. Saint-Simon wanted to replace religious dogmatic thinking with science; however, because he realized that the average citizen was not educated well enough to comprehend the ideas of science, he believed science should be introduced to the masses via artists and artwork designed simple enough so that they could understand it. This is a straightforward idea utilized by many cultures (past and present) that rely on symbol drawings to illustrate instructions and information. Saint-Simon also pointed out this is why religion relies so heavily on art and imagery to illustrate ideals and concepts (it is hard to convey such abstract notions as Heaven, Hell, angels, etc., without artwork). Saint-Simon, as with nearly all sociological social thinkers, was a firm believer in technological growth and viewed advanced forms of technology as a sign of progress. His positivistic doctrine went hand-in-hand with his promotion of technology. Saint-Simon viewed industrialization and internationalism as clear examples of advancements in technology but once again believed that "average" people were incapable of comprehending the concept of a world-wide community. (This seems to be true even today as many people do not understand how global markets and the "supply chain" operate.) As a result, he believed that scientific and intellectual people should serve as the vanguards of society organization and growth. As we shall soon see, the ideas of Saint-Simon described here (along with other ideas) would be embraced, and more successfully formulated, by Auguste Comte.

One specific example of an influence of Saint-Simon on Comte to be shared here is the idea that changes in social organization take place (and are necessary) because of the development of human intelligence. Influenced by Newton's "Three Laws of Motion" (a foundation of classical mechanics, often called Newtonian mechanics; see Chapter 3), Saint-Simon thought it possible to study the structure of society and ultimately devised his own societal classification system based on three moral ideals. He believed that any scientific study of society has to look at the moral ideas of a period because at any particular time in history the form of organization of a society is a direct reflection of the prevailing social code. Saint-Simon claimed that there were three different moral ideas in Western Europe and each was separated from the others by a transition—during that period, one moral system declines and another replaces it. The process of replacement-transition results from accumulated scientific knowledge, which changes the philosophical outlook of the society. For Saint-Simon, there were "Three Moral Systems":

1. Supernatural-Polytheistic Morals: Greece and Rome
2. Christian Theism: Socratic science, feudalism, and Middle Ages
3. Positivism: Industrial society

As we shall see later in this chapter, Saint-Simon's three moral systems would have a direct influence on Comte's "Law of Three Stages," or the "Law of Human Progress." In particular, Comte's final stage of societal development would also be the Positive stage.

Positive Philosophy

Auguste Comte is the founder of positivism, a philosophical and socio-political movement which enjoyed a very wide diffusion in popularity in the second half of the nineteenth century (Bourdeau 2022). Comte came to embrace the concept of "positivism" while working with Saint-Simon. Saint-Simon promoted positivism as the scientific approach to the study of society through the systematic collection of data and the establishment of laws based on observation. Comte developed an entire philosophy around the idea of positivism in order to combat what he perceived as the short-comings of the Enlightenment.

When Comte was formulating and writing about positivism two hundred years ago most of the individual sciences, such as physics, chemistry, and biology, had been developing at a steady pace but none had yet to synthesize the basic principles of science into a coherent system of ideas (Hadden 1998). Comte envisioned a system that was led by an intellectual and moral basis and that allowed for science to intervene on behalf of the betterment of society.

Auguste Comte was among the early social thinkers who believed that the social world could be studied in the same manner as the natural sciences, through scientific observation and the establishment of natural laws. The study of society via the scientific method is generally referred to as *positive philosophy* or *positivism* as Comte would come to describe his new doctrine which described the natural order of both scientific knowledge and scientific methodology. Positivism is a system that promotes rationality, logic and mathematical proof (through observation and measurement) and rejects metaphysics and theism. Clearly influenced by Saint-Simon, it was important for Comte to design positivism to cope with both intellectual and moral challenges of the day (Ple 2000). Social positivists seek to discover social laws that will enable them to predict social behavior. Through observation of behavior, certain social relationships and arrangements should become identifiable; these observations could be explained as "facts" and in casual terms without interference of the researcher's value judgments. Therefore, positivism claims to be the most scientific, objective research tradition in sociology (Adams and Sydie 2001).

Comte's idea of positivism is based on the idea that everything in society is observable and subject to patterns or laws. These laws could explain human behavior (Simpson 1969). Comte did not mean that human behavior would always be subjected to these "laws"; rather, he saw positivism as a way of explaining phenomena apart from supernatural or speculative causes (Simpson 1969). Laws of human behavior could only be based on empirical data. Thus, positivism was based on research guided by theory, a premise that remains the cornerstone of sociology today. The very purpose of sociology as a discipline is to discover and define social patterns of development in society (Thompson 1975). Comte believed positivism would create sound theories based on sufficient factual evidence and historical comparisons to predict future events. The discovery of basic laws of human behavior will allow for the deliberate courses of action on the part of both individuals and society. Decision-making guided by science would, indeed, from this perspective, be positive. Positivism is the notion by which behavior can be predicted as a result of historical patterns and in order to solidify positivism as a useful mechanism for societal development, Comte found similarities in the deductions of physical science, as well as social science (Comte 1857). By utilizing the scientific approach to study behavior, scientists could now explain their discoveries and work toward the important goal of predicting future events. The ability to foretell behavior can help individuals, groups, organizations and societies plan accordingly. For example, we have discovered and explained how and why earthquakes occur, but ultimately, we need to be able to predict when they will occur in order to save lives. To that end, scientists have developed an early warning system via the MyShake app available (as of early 2023) to residents in California, Oregon, and Washington states. As we shall see in Chapter 6, the use of the scientific method in sociology is so common today it is treated as a given.

Positive philosophy enjoyed much success outside academic circles for many years as his social movement was active nearly everywhere in the world (Bourdeau 2022; Simon 1963). Perhaps the best example of spread of positive philosophy could be found in Brazil, which owes the motto on its flag "Ordem e Progresso" (Order and Progress) to Comte (Bourdeau 2022). Positive philosophy had also spread to Mexico; and positivists were active in England, the United States and India (Bourdeau 2022). Following the First World War, the positive philosophy was overmatched by other doctrines. (However, as we know, Comte's greatest contribution—yet to be discussed—still survives today.) Let's return to the influence of Comte on Brazil. Its current national flag—well known throughout the world—has a green field (which represents the Amazon rainforest) with a large yellow rhombus in the center (representing Brazil's abundant mineral wealth) bearing the blue disk/celestial globe, depicting a starry sky of twenty-seven small white-pointed stars (each star represents a specific state in Brazil) spanned by the white equatorial curved band with the National Motto: "Ordem E Progresso" (Portuguese for "Order and Progress") written in green (Bachman 2010). The motto of "Order and Progress" is adapted from Comte's motto of positivism, "Love as a principle and order as the basis; progress as the goal" (Bachman 2010). Following the military coup by positivist and republican troops that overthrew the Monarchy and which led Brazil to become a republic (1889), the Brazilian people widely supported Comte's ideas of positive philosophy (Bachman 2010). The Positivist Church of Brazil also emerged during this era. Positivism did spread to other South American nations, including Argentina. I presented a paper, "Positive Philosophy: A Social Force to Combat Dogmatism," at the First Ibero-American conference on Critical Thinking in Buenos Aires, Argentina in September 2005, and described the role of positivism in Argentina. The attendees from Argentina were not as pro-positivism as Brazilians.

Comte was not alive to see much of his positive philosophy take shape in socio-political form in Latin America. He did, however, see its development and growth as an academic discipline. He would be greatly alarmed to realize that many contemporary sociologists have abandoned the positivistic approach that was the centerpiece of his approach to the study of society. But, as we know, over time, things change.

Social Physics

As the description of positive philosophy above details, there are two distinct aspects of positivism. First is the academic aspect of positivism that highlights the need to study society and human behavior empirically through observation and other research methods in order to establish laws. The second aspect of positivism was how it was used as an inspiration by those who wished to move on to the next stage of development beyond theism and traditional rule of monarchs. Of primary concern here is the academic aspect of positive philosophy. With that in mind, we turn our attention to an early realization of Comte that he needed a name to describe his new social science.

Comte originally used the term "social physics" to describe his positivist science but later found out that Belgian astronomer, mathematician, social statistician and sociologist Adolphe Quetelet (1796–1874) had "stolen" the term from him (Coser 1977). Quetelet used the term "social physics" in his 1835 *On Man: Essay on Social Physics* which introduced the subject of physics of humans or human physics and attempted to reduce human existence down to physics via the application of a system of numbers to study human patterns and phenomenon. Quetelet incorporated his knowledge of astronomy and applied the principles of *mechanics* in his scheme of social physics (Aubin 2014). Comte could have still used the term *social physics* to describe his positive philosophy after all; he came up with the concept prior to Quetelet and he does receive credit for coining the term.

So, what is social physics? Social physics is a field of science which uses mathematical tools inspired by physics to understand human behavior. It is the study of social phenomena through the lens of physics and mathematics and dates back to the early seventeenth century when Thomas Hobbes, inspired by the works of Galileo, wrote in his 1655 treatise *De Corpore* (*On the Body*) that physical phenomena of society could be explained in terms of the universal law of motion. The idea substantively evolved in the early nineteenth century when Saint-Simon, in his 1803 book, *Lettres d'un Habitant de Geneve* (*Letters of an Inhabitant of Geneva to His Contemporaries*), conceptualized the application of the study of society of laws similar to those of physical and biological sciences. In the years to follow, Saint-Simon would go on to coin various terms and phrases, such as designating the study of society as the "physics of organized bodies," as contrasted with the "physics of brute bodies," the usages of which occurred in several of his 1815 articles (Online Encyclopedia of Human Thermodynamics 2011). In 1819, the term "social physics" appears in an essay written by Comte in *Le Producteur* (*The Producer*), a journal created by Saint-Simon (Online Encyclopedia of Human Thermodynamics 2011). Comte believed that a mechanistic science could help to explain society's complexities (Pentland 2015). Comte would refine the term *social physics* in a number of publications during the 1820s. For Comte, *social physics* is a science that concerns itself with social phenomena in the same manner as astronomical, physical, chemical and physiological phenomena; meaning that social behavior is subject to natural and invariable laws, the discovery of which is the goal of social researchers (Iggers 1958; Iggers 1959; Han and Wiita 2022).

In volume 6 ("Social Physics") of his *Course of Positive Philosophy* (1830–1842), Comte (1896) argued that social physics would complete the scientific description of the world that Galileo, Newton and others had begun. He stated that the human mind had learned to grasp celestial and terrestrial physics; mechanical, chemical, and organic physics; both vegetable and animal sciences; and therefore, just one science remained to be satisfied, social science. Comte promoted social physics as the means to guide social science and he did so because he felt the attempts to study society had fallen short. "The theories of social science are still, even in the minds of the best thinkers, completely implicated with the theologico-metaphysical philosophy and are supposed to be, by a fatal separation from all other science, condemned to remain so involved forever" (Comte 1856:399).

It was obvious to Comte two hundred years ago that we must embrace science to study humanity. He believed that social physics could unravel the complexities of social behavior and society's intricacies. He enjoyed the use of the term "social physics" because it resembled "physics," an academic field that relied on laws and precision (at least during his era). Comte believed that physics was the first field of knowledge to free itself from the grip of theology and metaphysics and for that reason Comte admired it. Social physics, then, *was* the perfect name for his positive philosophy as it made it clear that the study of human behavior and society must be done scientifically and with an ultimate goal to establish laws of human behavior. However, there was that pesky matter of Quetelet using the term *social physics* in a manner that displeased Comte so much that he decided he must find a new name for his positivistic science.

Sociology

As we all know, the term that Comte would use to replace social physics would be "sociology." In the fourth volume of the *Course of Positive Philosophy*, Comte proposed the word *sociology* for his positivist science. As Pickering (2000) states, it was specifically in 1839 that the term first appeared. It is important to point out that when Comte coined the term *sociology* he forever secured his place as the official founder of the discipline and guaranteed his importance to the field. (Note: While there may have been social thinkers who conducted social analysis that today might be called sociological, it was never labeled "sociological" until Comte created the term.) The word *sociology* is a hybrid term compounded of Latin and Greek parts; *socio* (Latin) for "society," and *ology* (Greek) for "the study of." Thus, sociology literally means, the study of society. The scientific principles articulated within his positive philosophy and social physics had already laid the foundation for the field of sociology. It was now up to Comte to try and establish parameters for the discipline as well as establish "laws."

The "Law of Three Stages" or the "Law of Human Progress"

Comte's first major publication was *A Prospectus of the Scientific Operations Required for the Reorganization of Society*, which he referred to as the "great discovery of the year 1822" (Hadden 1997). It is here that he describes the plan for an empirical science of society by introducing his evolutionary theory of the "Law of Three Stages," or the "Law of Human Progress." It involves the notion that the history of societies can be divided rather neatly into three distinct periods and that each kind of society is produced and supported by a different form of thought or philosophy (Hadden 1997). Because society of his day was experiencing a period of crisis and great disorganization, he set out to discover the causes or reasons for this phenomenon. He concluded that European societies were in the midst of a difficult transition from one stage to the next.

For Comte, evolution or progress was a matter of the growth of the human mind. The human mind evolved through a series of stages, and so too must society, he proposed. The transition is always difficult, filled with periods of great disorganization and reorganization based on the newly emerging form of thought. Comte argued that an empirical study of the historical processes, particularly of the progress of the various interrelated sciences, reveals a law of three stages that govern human development. He analyzed these stages in his major work, the *Course of Positive Philosophy*. The three different stages are:

1. **Theological (circa prior to 1300 CE):** During this stage of development, societies and the human mind are dominated by religious or supernatural explanations to explain what humans otherwise could not. Intellectual efforts were hampered by the assumption that all phenomena are produced by "supernatural beings." The highest point of this stage is the idea of a single God replacing the former belief of a proliferation of gods.

2. **Metaphysical (1300–1800 CE):** According to Comte, this stage is a mere modification of the first stage and centers on the belief that abstract forces control behavior. While Comte found this stage as an improvement over Stage 1, he viewed it as merely a transitional one because people could not handle a direct move from Stage 1 to Stage 3.

3. **Positive (after 1800 CE):** In this, Comte's final stage of societal development, there comes the realization that laws exist. Through the use of reason and observation to study the social world, human behavior can be explained rationally. This stage is highlighted by a reliance on science, rational thought, empirical laws and observation.

Before elaborating on each of these stages, let's recall that Saint-Simon also promoted the idea that societies evolved through 3 (moral systems) stages with the final stage as positivism. He also believed that a less-developed social system led by theism preceded the third stage.

According to Comte, the theological stage occurred prior to 1300 CE. This was a time when religion dominated society and unexplainable phenomena were attributed to supernatural beings or divinities. In this stage, the human mind is searching for the essential nature of things, especially one's origin and the purpose of life. Comte felt that this was a period of inferior and primitive knowledge. During the theological stage, priests and military men maintained social order, and the gods did man's thinking for him (Simpson 1969). The theological stage has three sub-stages: (a) animism—ordinary objects are turned into items of tremendous purpose and are worshipped because it is believed that all objects, places and creatures possess a distinct spiritual essence; (b) polytheism—belief and worship of many gods (i.e., God of water, God of rain, God of fire, and so on); this was a period of time where humans desired explanations and began speculating and attributing phenomena to various supernatural beings; during this time, humans were haunted by feelings of "awe" and "fear" (Schraff 1995); and (c) monotheism—the highest point of development in the theological stage wherein the idea of a single God replaces the former belief in a proliferation of gods; this stage came about because people became overwhelmed with the many gods, who appeared to always be at conflict with one another.

To illustrate this stage, ask yourself, "Why do heavy objects fall?" The theological response would be "because God, or some spirit, willed them to fall." Another example is the concept of a "miracle." Whenever something unexplainable happens that has a very positive outcome (e.g., a medical patient given no chance to survive suddenly recovers), theological-based responses are commonly something akin to, "It was a miracle," or, "It was God's will." A scientific response would be much more rational, as we know that such occurrences are merely things that are statistically rare, and just because an occurrence is statistically rare, that does not make it a miracle from God or some divine source—a causal effect has not been established. Science is not afraid to keep looking for the explanation for those events that are statistically rare; those hampered by theological thinking have already given up their thought process. Interestingly, when something very negative occurs that is statistically rare or highly unexpected, people do not call that a miracle. Religious persons reserve describing a statistically rare event only to that which is positive which is very insightful to the flaw of this line of thinking.

The metaphysical stage, which occurred between the 1300 and 1800, is only a slight progressive step beyond the thinking of the theological stage. This was a time of philosophical thought and there was a heavy reliance on nature and abstract forces. Comte deemed this stage as the least important of the three stages. It was merely a transitional stage necessitated by Comte's belief that an immediate jump from the theological to the positivist stage would be beyond the comprehension of the vast majority of people. Comte summarized the metaphysical stage as the sunset of theologism and the sunrise of positivism (Simpson 1969). To illustrate this stage, ask yourself the same question as in Stage 1—"Why do heavy objects fall?" The metaphysical response would be "it is the nature of heavy objects to fall."

The final stage is known as the positivist stage, which began circa 1800. This stage relies on science and knowledge based on empirical laws and observations. The insistent search for absolutes, origins and purpose is refocused into the study of laws. In this stage, the individual became the "object of science" as well as the "subject making science possible" (Simpson 1969:43). Industrialization and scientific moral guidelines of reasoning and facts dominate the scientific positivist stage. Once again, ask yourself—"Why do heavy objects fall?" The positivistic response would be: "The law of gravity dictates that heavy objects fall down, and certainly they do not ascend upward."

Beyond the evolution of the human mind, each of three stages, Comte believed, is correlated with certain political developments as well. The theological stage is reflected in such notions as the divine rights of kings. During this stage of development, people with some sort of allegiance to a god or deity were in charge of society. The metaphysical stage involves such concepts as the social contract, the equality of persons and popular sovereignty. The positivist stage entails a scientific or sociological approach to political organization. Quite critical of democratic procedure (primarily because it would allow the uneducated masses too much say in how future society would operate and would allow unqualified persons an opportunity to win elections), Comte envisioned a stable society governed by a scientific elite who would use the methods of science to solve human problems and improve social conditions. This is the very thing that the uneducated fear. Consider for example, during the height of the COVID-19 pandemic, it was primarily the uneducated that attacked scientists (especially Dr. Anthony Fauci, former Director of the National Institute of Allergy and Infectious Diseases and the Chief Medical Advisor to the President of the United States during the pandemic) that promoted the use of vaccines and social distancing. They believed that their own home remedies or the lack of any preventative actions were better courses of actions than listening to medical and scientific experts. That elected officials went against the advice of scientists is a nod to Comte's concern.

Although Comte recognized an inevitable succession through these three stages, he acknowledged that at any given point in time all three might exist simultaneously. It was Comte's hope, and belief, that in the future, humanity would be dominated by the ideals of positivism and that ideological and metaphysical thinking would no longer exist. Unfortunately, as we well know, his hopes and beliefs did not come true as there are still people who doubt the validity of science and turn to religion and metaphysics for answers to life's dilemmas and problems.

There are flaws to Comte's "Law of Three Stages" and in Chapter 10, "The Fate of Humanity," I will introduce my own updated version of this "Law of Human Progress." It will serve as a very important update to Comte's "Law" and connect with my theory of the fate of humanity. This approach also highlights the break from the positivistic approach.

Research Methods

In line with his doctrine of positivism, Comte insisted that sociology utilize the research methods of investigation of the natural science (observation, experimentation and comparison) along with the historic analysis of social events as a means of supporting theory and obtaining new knowledge.

When using observation, the scientist looks for specific facts in order to validate theories about specific phenomena of social behavior to create and establish laws. Comte claimed that no social fact can have any scientific meaning until it is connected with some other social fact (Simpson 1969). When using the observational method, the sociologist must make sure to record the all the key circumstances of the research procedure to assure that subsequent sociologists will be able to replicate the study. Comte believed that a person trained with the workings of the scientific method would be able to convert almost all impressions from the events of life into sociological data. A talented sociologist would be able to take this data and interrelate it with experience and knowledge of the subject area and work toward establishing patterns, and ultimately, laws. Thus, observation as a research method is much more than simply looking at things, it involves paying attention to details, relating the data to past observations, formulating theories about the observations, continuing the observations until patterns are discovered, and then, establishing laws of human behavior.

The second research method promoted by Comte is experimentation. Experimentation is generally better suited for natural scientists because it is easier for them to set up controlled environments. Conducting experiments in the active social world is far more difficult for social scientists because of the countless, and often unforeseen, number of variables to try and control. In addition, for moral and ethical reasons, sociologists do not have many opportunities to perform experiments. Still, sociologists can and do conduct experiments; and it is particularly common for ethnomethodologists to use breaching experiments. Field experiments are also possible and provide situations in which the researcher observers and studies subjects in their natural setting.

The third research method of investigation is comparison, which Comte divided into three subtypes. First, we can compare humans to lower forms of animals. Second, we can compare a variety of societies from different parts of the world. Third, we can compare societies to others in the same stage of development (Ritzer 2000). In the first type of comparison, Comte felt that there was great value in comparing whatever rudiments of social life are found among lower animals with that found among humans. Comte thought that the first germs of social relations could be discovered among the lower animals; according to Simpson (1969), this method has since proven of some advantage in such subsidiary fields of sociological study as the family, the division of labor and socialization. By Comte's comparing humans to lower animals, he undermined ruling classes that considered mankind a special species above all other species. The primary use of the comparison method, according to Comte, was the discovery of social structures, social classes, social functions and patterns of social behavior, which are universal. Such discoveries are made through the study of coexisting states of society in different parts of the world. Comparing coexisting societies is an important tool for positive sociology, but Comte believed that the comparison of consecutive stages through which society passes over time was also needed (Delaney 2024).

This is where the fourth, and chief scientific device of sociology, comes into play (Simpson 1969). The fourth method is the historical investigation of human evolutionary growth. Comte states, "Our existing state cannot be understood simply through study of as it is, but only by seeing it as part of the series of social states from which it has emerged and which have left their imprint upon our minds" (Simpson 1969:21). By attributing human reason to history, history provides more than "counsel" and "instruction"; it provides a "general direction" for humans to proceed.

Today, sociologists often rely on survey research, a research method not described by Comte. Surveys include e/mail questionnaires, phone surveys and face-to-face interviews. Other popular research methodologies include observational (or field) studies (which may involve participant or nonparticipant observation); unobtrusive research (measures of erosion and measures of accretion); content analysis; archival studies; and experiments, including breaching experiments.

Although Comte spent a considerably greater amount of time engaged in theorizing (in an attempt to establish laws of the social world) than he did in conducting research, his emphasis on utilizing the scientific method in support of theory established the foundation of sociology. That is, sociologists must conduct scientific research in order to claim any form of legitimacy with regard to theory formulation. The legitimacy of sociology, not only as a science, but as a discipline, is predicated on Comte's idea that theory and methods go hand in hand (Delaney 2024).

Social Statics and Social Dynamics

As Newton's theory of motion can be divided into statics, the study of equilibrium, and dynamics, the study of motion caused by natural forces, Comte pointed out that social forces exist in all societies, some of which are designed to maintain social stability and others that encourage change. Comte referred to these social forces as social statics and social dynamics. Through his notions of social statics and social dynamics, Comte established a direction for social research. He believed that just as biology found it useful to separate anatomy from physiology, it was just as desirable to make a distinction in sociology between statics and dynamics (Coser 1977). *Social statics* is a term used to described the social processes that hold society together (e.g., the criminal justice system, criminal laws, religion and schools) while *social dynamics* refers to mechanisms of change (e.g., inventions, innovations and entrepreneurship). Thus, Comte gave sociology not only its name, but also its initial orientation, its parameters, which distinguished it from other disciplines (Cockerham 1995).

In his description of social statics (sociologists today refer to this as *social structure*), Comte was anticipating many of the ideas of later structural functionalists (a significant school of thought found in sociology). As a product of the post–French Revolution in France and having been influenced by social thinkers from "The Tradition of Order," Comte possessed a lifetime fascination with the social processes designed to keep society intact. Bear in mind, throughout his life, France played witness to a number of significant revolutions and rule under a variety of leaders (1789, the French Revolution, which brought down the Monarchy, King Louis XVI and the ancient regime; 1799–1814, rule under Napoleon, who waged many wars; 1814–1830, the return of the Bourbon Monarchs—brothers of King Louis XVI—to the throne; 1830, the July Days, or the Revolution of 1830, and 1848, the Revolution of 1848) who had their own ideas on how society should be structured and maintained. It is understandable that a person who would want to promote a positive philosophy and a society based on scientific laws would prefer an orderly society where individuals and social institutions worked in harmony with one another in order to maintain societal stability. There are certain conditions and laws needed in order for harmony in society to occur. Comte developed a theory akin to his Law of Three Stages when describing the necessary elements for harmony in society: the individual, the family and society (Thompson 1975). At the most elementary level are individuals who often respond to stimuli emotionally and via primitive instincts rather than intellectually. Comte stated that individuals need to respond with reason and not with instincts in order for society to remain stable. Comte viewed the family as the transitionary stage from the individual to society. The family relationship was to provide a model for societal obedience. Society was the most important level of social stability as it provided for the needs of the people (e.g., employment and education opportunities). Comte believed it was especially important for the government to find ways to keep unemployment low because high rates of unemployment would cause distress and chaos. Subordination to government authority would be necessary but not to the degree where individualism was hindered. In fact, Comte promoted the idea of individualism because the creative and forward-thinking individuals of society stimulate further evolutionary thought. This evolutionary way of thinking is articulated by his concept of "social dynamics" (Delaney 2024).

As a proponent of social evolution, Comte devoted a great deal of attention to social dynamics (today's term would be *social change*). He found social dynamics to be more interesting and of greater importance than social statics. Social dynamics were important because social evolution would make society better overall. Social dynamics deals with the laws of social movement, or progress. With this line of thinking, we can recall Newton's laws of motion. Using the sociological perspective, I would state that a society in a progressive motion (Law of Societal Progressive Motion) will continue to gain momentum if acted upon by such forces as forward-thinking individuals who innovate, create inventions for the betterment of humanity and engage in entrepreneurship. Utilizing two of the research methods he promoted—the historic and comparative—Comte was able to explain social change in a variety of societies by examining their histories and comparing them to others. He could also examine a society in terms of its stage of development based on his criteria from the Law of Three Stages.

Social Physics After Comte

Let's recall that Comte originally preferred the term "social physics" to describe his positivist science. It was a great term and perhaps one he should have kept. Social physics made it clear that sociology is a field of science which uses statistical analysis to support its theories on matters of social behavior. Various connotations of the term dates back to the early seventeenth century and continued to Saint-Simon's "physics of organized bodies," and "physics of brute bodies." Auguste Comte coined the term "social physics" in 1819. He believed that social behavior is subject to natural and invariable laws, the discovery of which should be the goal of social researchers. When Comte found out Adolphe Quetelet was using the term differently than he envisioned it should be used, he abandoned the concept of *social physics* and replaced it with *sociology*. However, just because Comte stopped using the term *social physics* that does not mean it disappeared from academic discourse.

Scottish physicist James Clerk Maxwell references the experiences of social physicists in 1873 but describes how the field was transforming into "statistical physics" (Ball 2002). Ball (2002) states, "Statistics entering physics through the agency of social science soon came to dominate it. Erwin Schrödinger makes it clear in 1944 that he considers laboratory-scale physics to be statistical rather than deterministic" (p. 13). However, Ball (2002) adds, "Nonetheless, quantum probability would have had a rockier path if physicists had not already been prepared by the knowledge that a statistical approach does not preclude the existence of precise laws." Thus, laws can exist whether they are proven to be deterministic or simply statistically probable.

In the middle of the twentieth century, John Q. Stewart, an American astrophysicist and engineer worked on the development of social physics, or "social mechanics" (as he later came to call it), by developing physics-based equations and diagrams such as the construction of population potential maps (Barnes and Wilson 2014). This research would serve as a historical reference point as "social physics" of a more contemporary period often refers to this as "big data" analysis. Swedish geographer Reino Ajo used a variation of social physics in the same era as Stewart to show that the spatial distribution of social interactions could be described using gravity models (Ajo 1953).

By the end of the 1990s, American physicist Mark Buchanan took note of a large number of papers themed on social science viewed through the lens of physics while he served as an editor of *Nature*. This inspired him to write three "social physics" types of books: *Ubiquity* (2000); *Nexus* (2002); and *The Social Atom* (2007) (Online Encyclopedia of Human Thermodynamics 2011). In *Ubiquity*, Buchanan underscores what he describes as a newly discovered law of nature—with its footprints virtually everywhere—that the world is modeled on a simple template of a universal pattern of change, often placing us on the brink of instability. This discovery is what Buchanan calls the new science of "ubiquity." In *Nexus*, Buchanan (2002) highlights his research that reveals the hidden geometry behind the fundamental principles of the emerging field of "small-worlds" theory—the idea that a hidden pattern is the key to how networks interact and exchange information, whether that network is the information highway or the firing of neurons in the brain. Related to the subject area of *Nexus*, Albert-Laszlo Barabasi writes in *Linked* (2014), that there are deep links between all forms of human life. "Statistical mechanics," his variation of social physics, has led to what he calls the Barabasi-Albert model, something that he believes will allow him to demonstrate the link between all forms of behavior. In *The Second Atom* (2007), Buchanan puts for the notion that via observations, social physicists can predict whether neighborhoods will integrate, whether stock markets will crash and whether crime waves will continue or abate but examining patterns, not people.

More recently, there are those who are using the "social physics" label for their "big data" analysis that utilizes mathematical laws to understand the behavior of human crowds and human activity with consumer applications (e.g., credit card purchases, dining habits travel destinations and social media browsing) (George, Haas and Pentland 2014; Barnes and Wilson 2014) and human activity during pandemics (e.g., the COVID-19 pandemic) (Kastalskiy et al., 2021). Alex Pentland (2014) utilizes a social physics and "big data" scheme with the concept of "idea flow" when describing the way human social networks spread ideas and transform those ideas into behaviors. Thanks to the millions of digital breadcrumbs people leave behind via smartphones, GPS devices, and the internet, the amount of information we have about human activity is mind-boggling and all of this is available for sociologists and others that want to analyze human behavior (Pentland 2014). Pentland and his research teams have found that they can study *patterns* of information exchange in a social network without any knowledge of the actual *content* of the information and predict with great accuracy how productive and effective that network is, whether it's a business or an entire city. As we learned earlier in this chapter, Comte had already pointed out that his science of positivism was based on the idea that everything in society is observable and subject to patterns or laws; thus, these particular modern "social physicists" have not come up with something uniquely new when they suggest that they can study patterns of information as Comte had already promoted this. In fact, Comte said that everything in society is observable and subject to patterns and laws; he did not have access to "big data," however.

As demonstrated here by this sampling of the variations of the usages of "social physics" after Comte, and as shown throughout this chapter, Comte's once preferred term of "social physics" for his positive philosophy science has taken on many different perspectives. We will see the term "social physics" reappear in Chapters 10 and 12 of this book.

Summary

Auguste Comte is considered the official founder of sociology as he is the person who coined the term and set the early parameters of the discipline. We learned about his life and how it coincided with the chaos of the aftermath of the French Revolution of 1789. In fact, throughout most of his life, France was involved in various wars and regime changes. This fact would have a profound effect on him as he would come to value social stability and order (he would use the term *social statics*). There were five major influences on Comte discussed in this chapter: the effects of the Enlightenment (would influence his scientific view of *positivism*); the Tradition of Order (would lead to *social statics*); the Tradition of Progress (would lead to *social dynamics*); the Tradition of Liberalism (he came to see the value of entrepreneurs in the spirit of progress); and his mentor, Claude-Henri Saint-Simon. Many of Comte's ideas overlapped with that Saint-Simon's leading some to wonder which theorist should receive credit for key concepts; then again, it has been said that many publications with Saint-Simon's name on it were likely actually written by Comte.

Saint-Simon promoted the concept of "positivism" as the scientific approach to the study of society through the systematic collection of data and the establishment of laws based on observation. Comte expanded on these ideas and created an academic discipline called positive philosophy. For Comte, positivism is a system that promotes rationality, logic and mathematical proof (through observation and measurement) and rejects metaphysics and theism. Comte's idea of positivism is based on the idea that everything in society is observable and subject to patterns or laws. These laws could be used to explain human behavior.

Comte needed a term to describe his new science. He originally promoted "social physics" (a term he coined) but when he found out that Belgian astronomer Adolphe Quetelet used the term differently than he intended it to be used, he abandoned the term. For Comte, *social physics* is a science that concerns itself with social phenomena in the same manner as astronomical, physical, chemical and physiological phenomena; meaning that social behavior is subject to natural and invariable laws, the discovery of which is the goal of social researchers.

In the fourth volume of the *Course of Positive Philosophy*, Comte proposed the word *sociology* for his positivist science. The term has been used ever since. The word *sociology* is a hybrid term compounded of Latin and Greek parts; *socio* (Latin) for "society," and *ology* (Greek) for "the study of." Thus, sociology literally means, the study of society. The scientific principles articulated within his positive philosophy and social physics had already laid the foundation for the field of sociology. It was now time for Comte to try and establish parameters and laws for the discipline, some of which are discussed in this chapter.

The chapter concludes with a look at "social physics" since the time of Comte. As demonstrated, there are variations of the usage of "social physics."

6

Sociology as a Science

Introduction

Sociology is an academic discipline that entails a number of elements including: the sociological perspective; the use of a "sociological imagination"; and the scientific study of human behavior, groups, organizations and society. It is also a discipline guided by social theory that is supported by research methodology.

Among the basic tenets of the sociological perspective: individuals are, by their nature, social beings; individuals are, for the most part, socially determined; and individuals are capable of creating, sustaining and changing the social forms within which they conduct their lives (as in, humans are both "puppets of their society" but "they are also the puppeteers") (Eitzen and Sage 1989:5). The sociological perspective places great emphasis on the ways in which social forces, such as the social institutions of family, education, politics and economics influence human behavior.

The concept of the "sociological imagination" also highlights the importance of the social environment's influence on human behavior. The term "sociological imagination" was coined in 1959 by eminent sociologist C. Wright Mills (1916–1962). When examining human behavior, the sociological imagination approach incorporates the personal biography (life history) of an individual along with their current social environment. In this manner, the sociologist has a more complete understanding of the individual. Thus, Mills is encouraging sociologists to take life histories into account when analyzing behavior and not simply to employ a snapshot view of human behavior. This idea actually goes back to Comte, among others, who emphasized the importance of looking for patterns of behavior through such research methods as the historical process. Employing the sociological imagination also helps individuals to realize that many of their problems are not due to personal shortcomings but rather are the result of social forces outside of their control. To underscore this point, Mills (1959) made the distinction between "personal troubles" and "public issues." *Personal troubles* refer to actual shortcomings within the character or behavior of the individual that they are directly responsible for. For example, if someone is fired from a job because they consistently showed up late for work, left early, performed poorly, drank alcohol while working, and so forth, losing their job was their fault because of personal shortcomings. *Public issues* refer to things out of the control of the individual. For example, if someone loses their job because the owners of the company replaced human workers with artificial intelligence (e.g., robots) as a cost-savings mechanism, it is not the fault of the worker.

Science As a Key to the Origins and Development of Sociology

A third element of sociology involves the scientific study of human behavior, groups, organizations and society. Science has played a key role in sociology since its origin and historical development. In Chapter 5, we learned that Auguste Comte created the term "sociology" to describe his positive philosophy doctrine. *Sociology* is defined as the systematic study of groups, organizations, societies, cultures and the interactions between people. The term "systematic" refers to the scientific approach used by sociologists. By definition, sociology is a *science* as it focuses on attaining knowledge through the scientific method. The *scientific method*, in turn, is defined as the pursuit of knowledge involving the stating of a problem, the collection of facts through research methodology (e.g., observation and experiment), and the testing and analyzing of ideas/theories to determine whether or not they appear to be valid. Just as the natural scientists do, social scientists employ the scientific method as they maintain a strong commitment to testing their theories through statistical and systematic analysis. The scientific method possesses elements of logical reasoning and objectivity. *Logical reasoning* involves the discovery of causes for human behavior and social events following a rigorous pursuit of explanations; it is a system of forming conclusions based on a set of premises or factual information. When a direct connection between events is established we have a *causal explanation*. *Objectivity* refers to the researcher being self-conscious about their values, opinions and biases and making sure it does not interfere with the research process. Although it is impossible for anyone to be completely objective and value-free, the goal of sociological research is consistent with that of the natural sciences—to remain as detached as possible in order to best assure unbiased results.

Origins and Development of Sociology

The most significant aspects of the origins and development of sociology were discussed in Chapter 4, but a brief review and elaboration on the importance of science to sociology is provided here.

Sociology is one of the classic academic disciplines, having officially existed for nearly two centuries. It was inspired by the ideas and actions of social thinkers who challenged the dogmatism of faith and tradition that dominated European cultures in the centuries before the Enlightenment. The ideas of Ibn Khaldun, Niccolo Machiavelli, Martin Luther, Thomas Hobbes, John Locke and Jean-Jacques Rousseau were among those with philosophical origin stories connected to sociology. Although Comte found some of the notions of the Enlightenment to be too abstract, the core beliefs of embracing reason, science, respect for humanity, exploration, the natural rights of individuals, tolerance, a general belief in the progress of humanity and the desire to discover natural laws that govern the universe that led to scientific, political and social advances in ways of thinking on how society should be run remain as mainstays in sociology today. As we learned in Chapter 5, the traditions of "order," "progress," and "liberalism" were important influences on Comte and early sociology and still influence the discipline today.

From enlightened thinking and the "tradition of liberalism," contemporary sociologists have come to recognize that social constructs lead to the formation of diverse groups based on a variety of criteria including religion, gender, race and ethnicity, sexual orientation, age classifications (life cycle groupings), social class and so on. Sociology promotes the understanding and inclusion of others. The sociological perspective, while acknowledging that we are all unique individuals, holds that we are shaped by our social environment and our various group memberships. The sociological perspective also advances the notion that we can best understand ourselves, and our place in society, if we understand diverse groups. It is important to note, however, that if we only focus on the differences between people, we will fail to take note of the similarities between them. By acknowledging such similarities, it may become possible to achieve greater harmony among the diverse people of the world. It is by breaking away from the shackles of the conservative past that societies and humanity can progress today. If we do not embrace liberalism as an ideology, society risks returning to the evil ways of the past where rule was dominated by a select few (e.g., monarchies and dictators) and religious intolerance (e.g., churches that taught just one way of doing things in return for a false promise of a joyous afterlife).

The Industrial Revolution is often cited by sociologists as a key origin in the development of sociology and rightfully so, as this is when societies dramatically changed, mostly for the better (progress) but also at great cost (e.g., urban social problems and the beginning of serious man-made causes of harm to the environment). The Industrial Revolution dramatically altered the lives of people as the socio-economic systems of societies were modified radically. The population shift from primarily rural living to urban resulted in a number of social changes that drew the attention of social reformers, such as Saint-Simon and others that would become early sociologists. Today, many sociologists focus on the issues of urban life including high density living; heterogeneity (diversity); workers' dependency on a salary; many impersonal, casual and short-lived relationships; extreme social class distinctions; anonymity; formal social control (e.g., law enforcement agencies); higher cost of living; noise pollution; land, air and water pollution; less green spaces; and street crime. Conversely, industrialization brought many positives including: a vibrant city life; diversity of friendship groups; opportunities to climb the socio-economic ladder; a variety of occupational opportunities; plenty of entertainment options; agencies designed to help the less fortunate; personal freedom (anonymity has its advantages); opportunities to join voluntary organizations to help others; embracing the concept of urban community; and educational opportunities.

The industrial stage of development (what Comte called the "Positive" stage) was indeed a significant influence in the origin and development of sociology. As a reminder, in Chapter 10, an updated version of the "stages of development" of society and human thinking will be presented as we have gone beyond the positivist stage of development and thinking.

Science and Society

It was science, empirical science in particular, that would replace the paradigms of thought of tradition and faith. Science is among the prevailing themes of this book starting with Chapter 1 where many early breakthroughs and discoveries in science were reviewed; continuing with chapter reviews on physics and quantum mechanics and string theory and through our discussions on the early influences of sociology.

Embracing the fact that sociology *is* a science is what gives sociology credibility in the academic world. Science, as Plato said long ago, represents how knowledge differs from opinion and belief. Science is grounded by a commitment in the empirical testing of theoretical postulates and theories. Science, then, is a system of knowledge that is concerned with the phenomena found in the physical world including, of course, human behavior. Scientific knowledge, when done correctly, entails unbiased observations and discoveries and conducts data analysis in an attempt to uncover general truths and, ideally, fundamental laws. As defined by the Science Council (2023), "Science is the pursuit and application of knowledge and understanding of the natural and social world following a systematic methodology based on evidence." Scientific methodology includes the following procedures: Objective observation (measurement and data; possibly although not necessarily using mathematics as a tool); evidence; experiment and/or observation as benchmarks for testing hypotheses; induction (reasoning to establish general rules or conclusions drawn from facts or examples); repetition (can the results be replicated repeatedly); critical analysis; and verification and testing (critical exposure to scrutiny, peer review and assessment) (Science Council 2023).

The study of science and society early on led to what some refer to as the "sociology of science." When thinking of the roots of the sociology of science one often thinks of Karl Marx who is among "the earliest authors in whose work we find an overview of the general theses about the relationship between knowledge and social reality" (Scaristan 2014:67). Perelman (1978) writes that "science, in the works of Karl Marx, is a major force in shaping the economy as well as the theory used to describe it" (p. 859). For example, "Marx emphasized the importance of scientific progress in an address celebrating the revolution of 1848." "He passed over the role of the renowned revolutionaries of that uprising, choosing instead to analyze 'steam, electricity, and the self-acting mule … revolutionists of a rather more dangerous character'" (Perelman 1978:859). Scaristan (2014) points to Marx's 1857 *Outlines of the Critique of Political Economy*, the *Grundrisse* and his 1863, *Theories of Surplus Value* which offer a systematic conception of the relationship between science and economy organized around two large questions: the ideological connection between science (mainly social science) and reality; and the efficacy of science (mainly natural science) in the production, reproduction, and transformation of the foundation of society (Tucker 1978; Sacristan 2014). In *The Grundrisse*, Marx describes one of the ways in which the technological application of science has advanced productivity and hence given capitalism a scientific character. Technological advancements via science have replaced skillful workers, a sign of a paradigm shift in the economic productivity scheme of the capitalists (Tucker 1978).

An attempt to combine elements of social sciences and natural sciences is a hallmark theme of social physics. The intent of this book is far beyond that of other scholars including those who utilize the sociology of science approach since as Sacristan (2014) states, an approach that attempts to embrace the natural and social sciences seems far too ambitious from the point of view of the research programs most common today in the sociology of science. Nonetheless, many studies are conducted under the Marxist name today and there is a long-standing reputable journal called *Science and Society* that has appeared quarterly since 1936. This journal publishes academic articles that blend social and political theory, with first-order historical research in economics, philosophy and theoretical foundations in the natural sciences, literature, and the arts. It should also be noted that the study of science and technology has led some social theorists to a more interdisciplinary engagement with the findings of the natural sciences (Ritzer and Stepnisky 2018). Again, we can see how this reflects the social physics approach.

What Auguste Comte had created with his "Law of Three Stages" or "Law of Human Progress" was, of course, the idea that social thought and human society progresses through stages with significant stages identifiable as "paradigms of thought" (something that was discussed in Chapter 1). Thomas Kuhn (a physicist who turned to history of science, and then turned to philosophy of science) made a name for himself through his 1962 book *The Structure of Scientific Revolutions* wherein he gave an account of the development of science as being mostly stable until sparked by revisionary revolutions (Bird 2018). As popular as this publication once was we can see that Kuhn never identified or predicted a major paradigm shift or identified a fourth stage of human and societal development as significant and clearly articulated as demonstrated in this book (see Chapter 10).

As we shall see in the following pages sociology utilizes the scientific research methodologies of the natural sciences but also incorporates additional strategies due to the unique and more complicated subject area under study.

Social Theory Supported by Research Methods

The fourth element of sociology identified in the introduction to this chapter is the realization that sociology is guided by social theory that is supported by research methodology. It is social theory that directs sociologists in their quest to explain the social world. An important first step toward developing a social theory is the ability to think critically.

Critical Thinking

We learned from the previous discussion above that an important aspect of scientific methodology is critical analysis. However, before we can get to that point in the research process and social theory for that matter, we must develop critical thinking skills. One of the most important aspects of a liberal arts education is helping to develop students' critical thinking skills. As Idrasiene and associates (2021) state, "Critical thinking is recognized as one of the tools for the information and development of human and social capital" (p. 286). The authors add, "Critical thinking is treated as a developed and dynamic competence that encompasses both cognitive skills and dispositions … such as self-confidence and fairness" (p. 286). Possessing critical thinking skills allows the individual to speak intelligently on a number of diverse topics and ascertain the truth in what people, especially the power elite, have to say. It is especially important to think critically today as there are so many sources of misinformation that are being shared (via social media sites and biased cable news networks) by agenda-minded purveyors of falsehoods and consumed by a gullible public that does not take the time to fact-check or think critically. Critical thinking is not a skill that comes naturally for most people and therefore it becomes the responsibility of institutions of higher education to teach people how to analyze, evaluate and fact-check information in an effort to cultivate a higher level of thinking. Remember this the next time you hear someone say that a college education is not important in order to succeed in life. While it is true that it is not necessary for everyone to graduate from college in order to find a job and become a contributing member of society rarely, if ever, do any employers take time out from the work day to teach their employees critical thinking skills. The employer themselves likely lack critical thinking skills. In nearly all employment situations the employer is happy if their workers can perform their job duties. They are not concerned with their critical thinking skills such as an ability to analyze and synthesize information gathered from reliable sources instead of something they heard on a cable news channel. It is almost exclusively the domain of higher education to teach critical thinking skills.

So, what is critical thinking? *Critical thinking* is intellectually disciplined thinking that is clear, rational, open-minded, centered on reason and supported by evidence; it is a mental process of skillful conceptualization, analyzing, synthesizing and/or evaluating information gathered from, or generated by, observation, experience, reflection, questioning what biased others say is the truth, and an overall grounding in empiricism. Throughout the first five chapters of this book we have learned of the ideas of many brilliant thinkers and how they all possessed critical thinking skills. We will learn about additional social thinkers who are also quite brilliant and again it has much to do with the fact that they have the ability to think critically.

Social Theory

As individuals, we cannot help but contemplate the meanings of social events that directly impact on our lives; we immerse ourselves in our own limited social networks and concerns of immediate consequence to us. Some of us, however, ponder the big picture issues that affect society, the future of our planet and the world that subsequent generations are inheriting. We often wonder about the behavior of others and we are especially concerned with the behaviors of those who have a direct impact on our lives. And again, some of us, primarily social thinkers such as sociologists and philosophers, wonder about how the actions of some people, especially the power elites, affect the masses, society, the planet and the future of humanity. Social thinkers trained with critical thinking skills will look at the world through many lenses as they attempt to explain social events and human behavior.

As leading authorities on all matters of human behavior and social issues, sociologists attempt to explain nearly everything, from the mundane everyday life activities to the vast diversity of cultures worldwide. Sociologists are guided by theoretical constructs that help them in their attempt to explain human behavior. Because of this, social theory is one of the most important aspects of sociology. In fact, sociology majors and minors around the world are always required to take at least one social theory course in sociology in order to complete their degree requirements.

The term *theory* can be defined as a statement that proposes to explain or relate observed phenomena or a set of concepts. Theory involves a set of interrelated arguments that seek to describe and explain cause and effect relationships. A theory is a supposition or a system of ideas intended to explain something based on general principles that are independent of the thing to be explained. (This is akin to the principle that we were all taught in elementary school that you cannot use the word you are trying to define in the definition of that word.) A theoretical explanation of some event or behavior must involve principles that are not inclusive of that event or behavior. For example, when trying to explain why two siblings are always angry at each other and fighting one another the explanation cannot simply state, "The siblings are angry at each other, they get upset and that is why they fight one another." That theory has not provided us with any useful information or explanations independent of the behavior trying to be explained.

In everyday use, the layperson may be tempted to think that the word "theory" means something like an untested hunch, or a guess. But for scientists, a theory has nearly the opposite meaning. A theory is a well-substantiated explanation of an aspect of the world that can incorporate hypotheses, facts and laws. As explained by the American Museum of Natural History (2023a), "The theory of gravitation, for instance, explains why apples fall from trees and astronauts float in space. Similarly, the theory of evolution explains why so many plants and animals—some very similar and some very different—exist on Earth now and in the past, as revealed by the fossil record." Furthermore, "a theory not only explains known facts; it also allows scientists to make predictions of what they should observe is a theory is true." Scientific theories are testable. New evidence should be compatible with a theory. If it isn't, the theory is refined or rejected. The longer the central elements of a theory hold—the more observations it predicts, the more tests it passes, the more facts it explains—the stronger the theory (American Museum of Natural History 2023a).

The theory of evolution is the perfect example of how this works. The development of genetics after Darwin's death has greatly enhanced evolutionary thinking and yet even with these new advances, the theory of evolution still persists today, much as Darwin first described it, and is universally accepted by scientists

(American Museum of Natural History 2023a). Anyone with a basic level of intelligence accepts the theory of evolution as fact and this explains why educated and intelligent people looked upon Herschel Walker, a Republican candidate for Senate in the state of Georgia (in 2022), in complete wonderment (and amusement if not for the seriousness of the idea that someone could run for the U.S. Senate and not be able to comprehend how evolution works) when he asked, "Why do apes still exist if humans have evolved from them?" (Sonmez 2022). The sheer stupidity of such a question should have disqualified him from running for a political office but, unfortunately, politicians do not have to pass an intelligence test to hold political office. (Imagine if they did—we could easily clean house of many incompetent elected officials and political candidates.) Walker was speaking while making an appearance at Sugar Hill Church in Sugar Hill, Georgia (March 2022). Lead pastor of the Sugar Hill Church, Chuck Allen, replied to Walker by saying something equally disturbing, "You know, now you're getting too smart for us." One thing is for sure, Walker is not too smart for us, at least he's not too smart for educated people that understand how theory and science works. Walker did not win the election but it was much closer than it should have been in an era of science, rationality and enlightened thought. Clearly, a number of people that voted in that election lacked critical thinking skills.

With a focus on the social aspects of the world, sociologists utilize a specific type of theory, "social theory," a term generally synonymous with the term "sociological theory." Social theory is used in other disciplines of the social sciences and humanities, such as anthropology, political science, economics, history, cultural and media studies and gender studies (Harrington 2022). *Social theory* involves the use of abstract and often complex theoretical frameworks to describe, explain and analyze the social world; in particular, social events and the actions and behaviors of people; while also attempting to uncover patterns that may lead to the discovery of laws. Harrington (2022) defines social theory as the "ideas, arguments, hypotheses, thought-experiments, and explanatory speculations about how and why human societies—or elements or structures of societies—come to be formed, change, and develop over time or disappear." Social theory often challenges the status quo (e.g., disputing the legitimacy of the concept of the "divine rights of kings") as it examines society as it actually exists and attempts to support its notions of reality based on empirical research. Sociologists and social scientists will utilize a range of explanatory concepts, analytical tools and heuristic devices in their efforts to interpret statistical or qualitative data about particular empirical social phenomena (Harrington 2022).

Generally speaking, sociological theory is grounded in the scientific tradition of belief that social patterns exist; therefore, general laws can be created through empirical study. As Jonathan Turner (2003) states, "Scientific theories begin with the assumption that the universe, including the social universe created by acting human beings, reveals certain basic and fundamental properties and processes that explain the ebb and flow of events in specific contexts. Because of this concern with discovering fundamental properties and processes, scientific theories are always stated abstractly, reign above specific events and highlight the underlying forces that drive these events" (p. 1).

As described in Chapter 4, social theory branched off from philosophical thought with Machiavelli's publication of *The Prince*. This publication was deemed significant because it described society as it actually was and not some ideal described by the power elites. The true beginnings of sociological theory reside with Auguste Comte, the person who created the field of sociology. Comte's theories mark the beginning of the "classical" era of social theory; an era that would continue with such other social thinkers as Harriet Martineau, Herbert Spencer, Karl Marx, Emile Durkheim, Georg Simmel, Max Weber and George Herbert Mead among others. The contemporary era of social theory began around mid-twentieth century. This period of social theory is highlighted by the ideas of a collection of like-minded social thinkers whose combined efforts led to the formation of a "school of thought." In most cases, these schools of thoughts were influenced by social thinkers from the classical period, but odd concepts were modified or replaced and a vast array of new concepts introduced. There are, in fact, so many new sociological concepts and theories that it is literally impossible to chronicle them all (although I have written a number of social theory books that describe the major ones). This "schools of thought" approach to sociological social theory is easily understood when one realizes that in the social sciences, and sociology in particular, the disciplines have become very broad, while areas of specialty among individual theorists have become very narrow. Consequently, contemporary sociological theory has become dominated by "schools of thought" rather than by single theorists of the classical era.

We will take a fresh look at some of these classical and contemporary social theorists later in this chapter when we look at how past sociologists have viewed the idea of establishing laws.

Research Methods

In order for any academic discipline to declare itself a science, it must conduct research and maintain a commitment to the canons of the scientific method. Consequently, research methodologies serve as the backbone of sociology. Sociologists employ a variety of research methods, or ways of getting information, to collect data in their effort to support or disprove a theory. Sociologists may use any or all of six primary methods: survey research; observational (or field) studies; unobtrusive research; content analysis; archival studies; and experimentation. Note that some of these methods (e.g., observation and experimentation) are used in the natural sciences but other methods (e.g., survey) are more restricted to the social sciences. There is a simple reason for this, the subject area of social scientists is often quite different from that of natural scientists and the nature of the study far more complicated; thus, necessitating distinctive methodology strategies. The good news for social scientists who conduct social research is the advancements in technology have allowed for greater achievements in the field of research because of online databases; access to "big data" sets; access to multimedia resources; the Internet; and digital libraries, all of which are filled with vast amounts of data, information and knowledge waiting to be analyzed.

A brief examination of the six research methodologies utilized by sociologists is presented below. The first method is survey research.

Survey research is the most frequent, widely-used approach in sociology. Moreover, it is not only popular in sociology but widely used in a variety of social science disciplines. Chances are, you have taken at least one survey in your life and you have likely been asked many other times to respond to a social survey. There are three common types of social survey: E/Mail questionnaires; phone surveys; and, face-to-face interviews.

Conducting survey research is not a new phenomenon; in fact, it has been utilized for centuries. For example, many ancient civilizations (i.e., Athens and Rome) took a census of their populations. A census is a type of survey that involves questioning an entire population. The U.S. Constitution mandates (Article 1, Section 2) that a census is taken every 10 years in order to assure equal representation of all residents. This mandate once simply required a head count. However, today respondents are asked numerous questions including their phone number; ages of the occupants of that dwelling; and ethnicity and race. All of this data is stored by the government. In fact, every time we provide information to anyone, even when filling out warranty cards, grocery store discount card forms, credit and debit cards forms, and so on, we are generating data for databases, most of which finds its way to the "Big Data" realm of even larger and more complex data sets.

Survey research conducted by sociologists and most social scientists are certainly not massive undertakings like the Census Bureau's decennial census. Instead, *survey research* involves taking a sample (a subset) of a population and administering a questionnaire or interview. Survey sampling is conducted because it would be impossible to interview all elements of a larger population and therefore, survey researchers focus on a representative, random sample. This technique is very much considered part of the scientific method. As Martin Frankel (1983) explains, survey sampling "is a branch of statistics that concerns itself with the methods and techniques of selecting samples where results may be projected to a larger population" (p. 21). Thus, a researcher can gather significant data and information from a sample survey. Survey research also represents an effective method for measuring people's values, beliefs, attitudes, perceptions, motivations and feelings on topic areas not directly accessible via observation. Further, certain topics, such as those related to sexual activity, drug use, and other private matters are generally best addressed by survey research—just imagine if a researcher were to look through the windows of people's private homes to observe these behaviors in order to collect data (Delaney 2012).

The information and corresponding data gathered via the survey research method is very useful for sociologists, social scientists in general, market researchers, political campaigns, law enforcement agencies, health agencies and so on. Survey data is also responsible for a great deal of our current knowledge about our society and the global community. It is important to note, however, that survey research data is the result of *self-reporting*, that is, the researcher is relying on the validity of answers provided by respondents (Delaney 2012).

Although survey research is the most popular method in sociology, sociologists are quick to point out that the type of research strategy used in collecting data must be appropriate to the study under consideration. This may lead the researcher to go out to the field and observe behavior firsthand. *Observational research* involves focusing on a social situation and meticulously recording key characteristics and events found in a specific setting. Stangor (2004) explains, "Observational research involves making observations of behavior and recording those observations in an objective manner. The observational approach is the oldest method of conducting research and is used routinely in psychology, anthropology, sociology, and many other fields" (p. 126). Ethnography, a popular variation of observational research, involves the study of an entire social setting in which the researcher asks the subjects for their perspectives on social reality.

There are two primary categories of observational research: participant observation and nonparticipant observation. *Participant observation* involves the researcher joining the group under study in order to gain a greater understanding of what the people are doing and compare it with what they say. This approach gives the researcher a better understanding of the dynamics of the group, its cultural environment and provides greater credibility to the researcher's observations. Such a methodological approach is especially important when the researcher has little or no knowledge of the behaviors of the group (e.g., the structure and activities of a street gang). There are two basic subcategories of observational research: announced participant observation and unannounced participant observation. *Announced participant observation* involves the researcher interacting with the group under study, informing the group of their purpose, and witnessing firsthand, or participating in, group activities. The degree of participation commitment of researchers to these groups varies. For example, let's say a sociologist wants to study the activities of a street gang and that they have found entry into the gang (they were given permission by the gang to study them as a researcher), they could "travel" (hang out with, and go wherever the gang goes) with the gang for hours at a time on weekend nights or they might stay with the gang for weeks or months at a time. An announced participant observer researcher would not necessarily have to participate in group activities meaning that a gang researcher would not have to engage in gang activities.

Unannounced participant observation entails the researcher's interacting with a specific group under study without informing its members that they are being observed. With the example of gang research, the researcher would have to actually join the gang. The advantage of unannounced participation observation over the announced observer role is that it reduces the possibility of reactivity—the condition in which a participant being observed changes the way they behave. Group members are also unlikely to be guarded or to hold back information from the observer. There are a number of scenarios when people other than researchers might join a group in an unannounced participation observer role such as undercover law enforcement infiltrating a criminal enterprise. The advantage of the participant observation role is its flexibility method (compared to asking rigid questions off a questionnaire) and depth and intimacy of understanding of the subject matter that it brings to research. This is a big advantage for social scientists over natural scientists as in most scenarios the natural scientist cannot actually become a part of the world of study (e.g., the study of particles, molecules, viruses, the animal kingdom and so on). A disadvantage of this approach is the realization that sometimes researchers become too close to the group under study and they lose detachment or objectivity.

The second primary category of observational research is nonparticipation observation and like the two subcategories of participant observation, this is a direct form of observation. *Nonparticipant observation* involves the researcher observing the group under study from such a distance that the group is unaware of their presence. For example, the gang researcher may have never found an "entry" point into the group (did not receive an invitation to join the group as they lacked the proper contacts) or their type of study did not require a lengthy involvement with the gang. Under this scenario, the researcher may observe the behavior of gang members from an abandoned building by using binoculars and night vision goggles. While this may be a safer way of observing deviant or criminal behavior and eliminates the hassle of gaining permission to study a particular group (because the researcher does not have the contacts to gain entry), it has a major drawback in that the researcher is not afforded an opportunity to ask subject members questions in an attempt to elaborate on their observations. In this way, the social scientist is reduced to the role of a natural scientist conducting observational research.

The third research methodology available to sociologists is unobtrusive research. Whereas observational studies involve the direct observation of behavior and social events by the researcher, unobtrusive research entails indirect observation. *Unobtrusive research* is an indirect form of observation that examines physical traces left behind (by the subjects). This method is like doing detective work in that researchers examine physical traces of past behavior. Unobtrusive research allows the researcher to keep away from ongoing interactions. As True (1989) explains, "The word *unobtrusive* means that a person is not a part of the interaction and has no influence on it. When you're done collecting data, the interaction is over" (p. 119). From the evidence collected, the researcher attempts to piece together past behavior. Unobtrusive measures do not require the cooperation of those under study. There are two primary categories of unobtrusive measures: erosion and accretion. *Measures of erosion* reveal past behavior as a result of the wearing away of an item or area, such as worn-out carpet or pathways through backyards. Focusing on wear indicates, among other things, high traffic areas. *Measures of accretion* reveal evidence of past behavior based on deposited materials left behind (e.g., gang graffiti spray-painted on buildings, park benches, lamp posts and so on, indicate that a gang has claimed that area). The researcher need not have witnessed the spray-painting directly to realize that gang members committed the criminal activity of destroying property because they have left evidence of their criminal activity. An empty spray paint can would be another example of a measure of accretion.

The use of unobtrusive methods is important in forensic sociology. Forensic sociology is a subfield of sociology that, like all forms of forensics, involves the examination of evidence left at a crime scene. Forensic sociology focuses primarily on the intersection between professionals in the criminal justice and mental health service systems among other areas. Forensic sociologists are trained to help identify those most at risk to commit certain crimes; those most likely to be victimized by crime; and those who suffer from mental health problems that if left untreated might commit criminal activities.

The fourth research methodology strategy utilized by sociologists, and by nearly all those in science, is content analysis. *Content analysis* is an indirect form of observation of behavior that involves the examining of written or oral forms of communication (e.g., books, journal articles, newspapers, diaries, letters, and emails). With content analysis the researcher need not rely on conducting their own research in an attempt to support or disapprove a theory. Instead, they may choose to use existing sources of data (e.g., databases). Once this data has been collected, it exists as a form of written communication that can be analyzed by others for their own purposes—sociologists regularly use U.S. Census data for a variety of research projects. When conducting content analysis research, researchers examine the various forms of content and record instances relevant to the study at hand on tally sheets. An advantage of this methodology is that it is safe and economical. One of the significant disadvantages is that the researcher may not find what they are looking for and incorrectly conclude that absence of evidence is evidence of absence when this could very well be a false conclusion. Furthermore, relying on second-hand information, especially depending on the source (e.g., many Internet sources, personal diaries, and email correspondences), is subject to falsehoods, misinformation and lies. This is why scientists that conduct research and utilize content analysis rely on peer-reviewed sources (articles and books written by experts which are reviewed by several other experts in the field before the article is published in order to ensure the article's quality).

Archival research is the fifth research methodological approach available to social researchers. As with content analysis, archival research involves the use of existing data. An archive is a place where old documents are kept (or stored). The government, businesses, law firms, museums and libraries are all likely to have archives where they store old documents and oversized or oddly shaped files that do not neatly fit into other existing shelving. Much of this information simply never made it into any sort of digital files, digital libraries, institutional repositories or national library collections. For many private people, the attic or basement may serve as an archive where tax documents, baby photo albums, baby's first shoes, yearbooks and so on are stored. *Archival research* involves the analysis of documents and other materials found in the archives. Emile Durkheim (1951 [1897]) examined archival data (death certificates) from between 1841 and 1872 from seven European countries to conduct his famous research on suicide. Archival records contain a huge amount of information and must therefore be systematically coded by the researchers (Delaney 2012). As was the case with Durkheim, researchers that use archival records often do so for research purposes that had nothing to do with its original purpose.

The sixth primary research methodology option for social researchers is conducting experiments. Although experimentation may seem to belong solely in the domain of the natural sciences, researchers in the social sciences may also conduct experiments. *Experiments* are a research methodology that involves the researcher manipulating the independent variable and measuring the dependent variable to discover the relationship between the two. One advantage of the experimental method is that it generally allows the researcher to control the environment so that outside variables do not influence the study.

There exists a wide variety of experimental designs available to researchers, such as the "classic," or basic experimental design; a single-blind experiment (information is withheld from participants, such as one group receives the treatment vaccine but the other group receives a fake vaccine with neither group knowing whether they received the treatment or not—this is an effort to control for the placebo effect): and, a double-blind experiment wherein both the participant groups and the researchers do not know who has received the treatment, this is done to control for the placebo effect for both the participant and the researcher. In the "classic" experiment, the researcher starts off with two groups that are as identical as possible in all aspects relevant to the study. An initial measurement of the two groups is taken before the induction of a treatment, or independent variable. Researchers then introduce a variable, or treatment of some sort, to one group, identified now as the *experimental group* (or *treatment group*), while the second group, known as the *control group*, does not receive the treatment. The treatment introduced to the experimental group is the independent variable. Because experiments allow social researchers to test the effects of an independent variable on a dependent variable in an attempt to provide a causal inference, experimenters must be very specific in their description of the independent variable (the treatment) used in their experimental design. After a designated time, a second measurement is taken of both groups. If there is a change in the treatment group but not in the control group the experimenters may conclude that the treatment was effective. However, experimenters are careful not to draw conclusions after just one trial/experiment and will conduct numerous other trials to assure reliability (consistency of a measure) and validity (accuracy of a measure). Because social scientists that conduct experiments do so on humans, many precautions must be taken to assure ethical standards (e.g., obtaining consent forms from participants, protecting anonymity and confidentiality of participants; and avoiding deceptive practices).

One particular type of experiment utilized by ethnomethodologists (ethnomethodology is a "school of thought" in sociology) is the breaching experiment. Made famous by Harold Garfinkel, a *breaching experiment* involves deliberately interrupting the taken-for-granted world of actors as they interact with one another (Delaney 2024). Social realities are violated in order to shed light on the methods by which people construct social reality. (In breaching experiments, consent forms are not sought beforehand.) Breaching experiments are not formally conducted in laboratories like natural scientists conduct; rather, they are quasi-experimental field studies designed to modify the familiar. Examples would include setting up a bedroom inside an elevator in a college dorm; standing backwards inside an elevator; posting "wet paint" signs where there is no wet paint; and skits from hidden camera shows.

Social researchers are encouraged to use multiple research methods when they conduct their studies. Using multiple approaches is known as *triangulation*. Triangulation is used to overcome the shortcomings of one particular methodological approach while highlighting the value of using multiple approaches in the search or empirical verification.

Whether a researcher triangulates or not, the type(s) of research methodology utilized by the researcher represents either a quantitative or qualitative approach. Both approaches yield some sort of data. *Quantitative research* methods are the objective, logical tools of science that provide facts and figures describing patterns and events in social life. Social researchers who attempt to support their theories with statistical evidence use quantitative research. American sociology is especially quantitative primarily because of the use of computers used for statistical analysis on data sets, including "big data." Quantitative research is considered an objective research approach and it allows for measurement and prediction. Whereas quantitative research relies on the use of numbers and statistical analysis to objectively describe elements of a research study and attempts to explain "what" is going on; qualitative research relies on words and descriptions and attempts to answer "why" does a certain behavior occur? *Qualitative research* involves the use of methods (e.g., interviews) that provide a subjective analysis of human behavior and social events.

One final topic to discuss under the "research methods" umbrella is longitudinal research. *Longitudinal research* helps researchers to find patterns; these patterns may lead to the identification of laws. Longitudinal studies employ continuous or repeated measures to follow particular individuals, groups, organizations or societies over prolonged periods of time—often years or decades. Any serious scientist is attempting to establish laws of human behavior as mere snapshot views of human behavior and society fall short of the goal of sociology, certainly Comte's goal of sociology.

We finish this chapter by looking at a sampling of how past sociologists have viewed the ideas of establishing laws in the field.

Establishing Laws

The most brilliant social thinkers throughout the past couple millennium have attempted to establish laws; this is true both in the natural and social worlds. Arguably, establishing laws applicable to the social world should be the fifth key element of sociology to be added to the four others identified at the introduction of this chapter and described within it. In the following pages we will take a quick look at some of the social thinkers that influenced sociology, along with sociologists themselves that shared their thoughts on the idea of establishing laws pertinent to the social realm.

Social Laws

We begin with Thomas Hobbes who advanced the principle of individualism put forth by René Descartes ("I think, therefore I am"). Hobbes uses the individual as the building block from which all his theories develop. He formulated his theories by way of empirical observation. Hobbes believed that everything in the universe was simply made of atoms in motion and that if geometry and mathematics could be used to discover natural laws it could also be used to discover laws that could explain human behavior (as humans are also atoms in motion). According to his theories, there are two types of motion in the universe: vital (involuntary motion, such as heart rate) and voluntary (things that we choose to do). Voluntary motion was further broken down into subcategories that Hobbes believed were reducible to mathematical equations—desires and aversions. Desires stimulate human motion and social action toward that valued item, while aversions were items that individuals attempted to avoid either through action (removing oneself from an undesired environment) or inaction (never entering the undesired environment). Further, individuals' appetites constantly keep them in motion, and in order to remain in motion, everyone needs a certain degree of power. Hobbes also drew upon the language of natural law in his emphasis on the principles of reason (Delaney 2024). Hobbes was clearly in the early stages of developing a law that could explain human behavior based on mathematics and the application of a theory of motion based on the human actions of desires and aversions.

We can see the influence of Hobbes and his ideas on natural law and human rights in John Locke's *Two Treatises of Government*. Descartes also had an academic influence on Locke. Having already begun his studies in medicine and the physics of Descartes, Locke began to use such instruments as barometers, thermoscopes and hygrometers (Rickless 2014). Descartes also helped Locke form his own ideas about the universe and developing different classification systems of species (Rickless 2014). John Locke was close friends with Sir Isaac Newton and he developed an interest in mathematics, planets, gravity and how the moon revolved naturally around the earth, thus leading to Newton's ideas on "natural laws." This line of thinking inspired Locke to think of the idea that all citizens should enjoy natural rights as if they were laws. Newton's discovery of *universal gravitation* and his "Three Laws of Motions" led many social thinkers of this era to believe that if humanity could unlock the laws of the natural world that it would also be possible to discover and establish laws that explain the social world. Through a rigorous use of reason and the unending scientific progress that was occurring during the Enlightenment era it certainly seemed plausible that the discovery of social laws concerning humanity would be possible.

Rousseau was another one of these social thinkers that believed natural laws could be used to explain human behavior. Likewise, Immanuel Kant believed that Newton's science had provided adequate evidence that permanent "laws" existed in nature. It made him think that if humans could gain such insights of nature when nature does not provide any privileged access to its operation certainly it would be possible to attain such insights of the social realm. At the very least, Kant believed that social scientists were capable of sorting data into categories of knowledge: space, time and causality (Hadden 1997). Once this step was accomplished scientists would move on to the next steps of establishing laws of human behavior and human society. G.W.F. Hegel (1770–1831), on the other hand, did not believe that any amount of hard, positivist thinking or analysis could make any ultimate claims of "truths" about human behavior because the development of the human mind had not yet reached that point of growth in comprehension and understanding. We have come a long ways since the time of Hegel. Not only have a number of social scientists developed the mind capacity to think in such a manner as to discover and establish laws, we have large enough databases and the capabilities to analyze even "big data" sets thanks to computer analysis programming.

Saint-Simon, a firm believer in the validity of science and rationalism, promoted positivism as the means to establish laws. Systematic collection of data, especially through observation would achieve this goal. Like so many others of his era, Saint-Simon was influenced by Newton's "Three Laws of Motion" and came to understand that guidelines that lead to the establishment of natural laws could also be applied to establish social laws.

It has been established that Saint-Simon had a close professional relationship with Auguste Comte. As the founder of sociology, Comte made it very clear that the ultimate goal of this discipline was to look for patterns of behavior through various research methods, such as the historic process, and establish laws concerning human behavior, social structure and society. His positive philosophy is based on the idea that everything in society is observable and subject to patterns and laws. His "Law of Three Stages" represents an ambitious attempt to explain the evolutionary process of societal progress as well as the evolutionary growth of the mind.

Once a very influential sociologist, Herbert Spencer (1820–1903) also promoted the ideas of universal laws. He was among the early sociological giants and his life overlapped with Comte. Spencer is the theorist who coined the term "survival of the fittest" (Darwin coined the term "natural selection"), meaning those who are most successful at adapting to the changing environment are most likely to survive and to have children who will also be successful. The *survival of the fittest* concept was an important aspect of Spencer's theory on social evolution. In *First Principles* (1862) Spencer defined evolution as "a change from indefinite, incoherent homogeneity, to a definite, coherent heterogeneity; through continuous differentiations and integrations" (p. 216). Spencer (1862) elaborates, this brings about "in all cases a change from a more diffused or incoherent form, to a more consolidated or coherent form" (p. 211). Add to this, Spencer states, "Evolution is an integration of matter and concomitant dissipation of motion; during which the matter passes from an incoherent homogeneity to a definite coherent heterogeneity; and during which the retained motion undergoes a parallel transformation" (Nichols 1902: 136). Spencer argued that the law of evolution is universal. However, he does allow for the fact that forces can impede evolution and cause dissolution. Predicting whether a society will continue to evolve or whether it will dissolve can be assisted by using the laws of motion. Some *force* (e.g., economic capital, a new technology, new values and beliefs) sets into *motion* system growth. This motion, as it acts differently on various social units, sends them in different directions and "segregates" them such that their differences are "multiplied." Conversely, to the extent that integration is incomplete and/or the force that drives the system is spent and cannot be replaced, then dissolution of the system is likely. Thus, social systems grow, differentiate, integrate, and achieve some level of adaptation to the environment, but at some point the system may fall into a phase of dissolution. It is critical, for the very survival of a society, to continuously attempt to achieve, evolve, innovate and embrace progressive technological ideas or it will surely dissolve (Delaney 2024). The sociologist that conducts macro analysis of any given society should be able to notice patterns that will predict evolution or dissolution.

Not exactly a law, Vilfredo Pareto (1848–1923), a sociologist and economist, established the "Pareto Principle" (1906), also known as the "80/20 rule" that has two applications: (1) that roughly 80 percent of outcomes come from 20 percent of causes; and (2) that 80 percent of the wealth of a society is owned by 20 percent of the members of a given society. The original use of this principle was applied to Pareto's discovery that 80 percent of the land in Italy in 1906 was owned by just 20 percent of the population (Lavinsky 2014). According to the Brookings Institution, a nonprofit public policy organization based in Washington, D.C., in the United States, the top 20 percent wealthiest people owned 77 percent of the total wealth of the country (Sawhill and Pulliam 2019). Sociologists today routinely cite statistics on how the top 1, 5, 10 or 20 percent of the wealthiest members of society own a disproportionate amount of the wealth. This holds true throughout much of the world as well. Whether or not we can refer to this as a law or not is questionable, but it is factual information. The workers can only wish that the income gap between the top wage earners (CEOs) and a typical worker had a 4 to 1 ratio but, as we know, it is much worse. According to the Economic Policy Institute, CEOs were paid 399 times as much as a typical worker in 2021 (Bivens and Kandra 2022). As for the second aspect of the "Pareto Principle," there are many examples of the 80/20 rule, including: 20 percent of the input creates 80 percent of the result; 20 percent of the workers produce 80 percent of the result; 20 percent of customers create 80 percent of the revenue; 80 percent of the public uses 20 percent of their computers' features; 80 percent of crimes are committed by 20 percent of criminals; 80 percent of the population finds only 20 percent of it attractive; 80 percent of grief is caused by 20 percent of people in your life; and so on.

Emile Durkheim (1858–1917), a legendary early French sociologist who followed in the footsteps of Comte was a firm believer that sociology was a science and could establish laws. Studying with his teacher Emile Boutroux at the École Normale Supérieure, Durkheim came to view sociology as having a distinct method and field and that sociology was a legitimate science. Boutroux believed that science requires three assumptions to be met. The first is that science needs to have observable phenomena as its basis as without observable phenomena, there would be nothing to study. Second, science needs to be regulated by certain fixed natural laws. Third, science must look forward and assume that new phenomena are being produced (Gunn 1922). Influenced by Saint-Simon and Comte's ideas on positivism, Durkheim embraced and utilized the scientific method extensively when writing his dissertation and on his work on suicide. Commenting on the use of the scientific method when analyzing society, Durkheim states, "No further progress could be made until it was established that the laws of societies are no different from those governing the rest of nature and that the method by which they are discovered are identical with that of the other societies. This was Auguste Comte's contribution" (Lukes 1972:68).

German sociologist Georg Simmel (1858–1918) introduced the idea of "formal sociology" which emphasized finding patterns of social behavior that transcend specific situations (Cross 2019). Simmel's formal sociological method was a search for recurrent patterns or relationships that exist across a wide variety of social contexts; it "seeks to find patterns endemic to social organization" (Cross 2019:331). Simmel's approach to sociology also involved identifying a number of "social forms" and "social types" that consisted of predictable behavioral characteristics based on established patterns. He created a "social geometry" of social relations to identify complex social interactions and reduce them to simple patterns wherein constructs of an entire range of possible formations can be reduced to a relatively few postulates as a means of "rationalizing the then-young discipline of sociology into a discipline that could stand on an equal footing with the physical sciences" (Cross 2019:332). Simmel formulated theories on human interactions that would stimulate the creation of exchange theory wherein he attempted to identify universal characteristics of human behavior; among them, individuals are motivated to action to satisfy needs and pursue goals and that people expect some level of reciprocity. As Zerubavel (2007) noted, Simmel's conception of formal sociology "almost resembles physics in its quest for transhistorical as well as transcultural generality" (p. 132). As we can ascertain, Simmel was clearly interested in establishing laws based on patterns of behavior.

The anti-positivistic, neo–Kantian influence of thinkers like Heinrich Rickert influenced German sociologist Max Weber's (1864–1920) belief that reality is not reducible to a system of laws. He believed that no body of laws can exhaust a science of culture, nor can one ever expect to achieve complete predictability, since prediction is successful only within limited or closed systems. Society and culture are a result of an ongoing process, and consequently, history is never predetermined; it moves toward unknown ends. Weber felt that there could be no objective ordering of the historical process (Mommsen 1989). He regarded "historicism" as a "narrow-minded patriotism of the field" (Kaslar 1988:9). In response, Weber came to utilize the "ideal type" methodology to study society.

American sociologist Lester Ward (1841–1913) insisted that sociology identify social laws and he wrote of this throughout his publications. Ward encouraged the pursuit of knowledge of nature and of the universe and said that humanity must not be deterred by fear. Ward said that humanity must forge ahead in its pursuit of knowledge of the laws of the universe and of the social world. Ward thought that perhaps there is a law of human behavior to avoid situations that cause pain, arguing that the dread of pain alone teaches us to try and avoid situations that will result in harm. The very avoidance of pain and harm contributes to the law of "natural selection," Ward suggests (Delaney 2024). The problem with this suggested law is all the possible exceptions, especially those connected to emotions such as love and pain. Consider, for example, while we have learned to avoid the pain of fire, many of us have not learned to avoid the pain that lost love can create. Perhaps Ward was on to something but any law on pain would have to narrow its focus. Ward was fond of using the term "telesis" (planned progress) as it represented action toward a definite end and is intelligently planned and directed by the application of human effort.

Ward made it clear that sociology was concerned with the "law of the mind" rather than the "law of nature" (Commager 1967:234).

Thorstein Veblen (1857–1929), an American sociologist and economist said that there were economic laws that arose since industrialization that explain the productive capacity of industry: land, labor and capital (Veblen 1921). In his *Theory of the Leisure Class* (1899), Veblen described the consumption aspects of industry. He said that consumers engage in the "wasteful" behaviors of *conspicuous consumption* (purchasing items not necessary for basic survival) and *conspicuous leisure* (nonproductive use of time) because they had the time and the means to do so and because they gained some enhanced sense of self-esteem. The laws of conspicuous consumption and conspicuous leisure are still very applicable today but they are likely more akin to principles than anything else. Veblen also believed that people who engaged in conspicuous consumption and conspicuous leisure were wasting valuable time and valuable capital. Thus, Veblen stated that conspicuous consumption and leisure, prevailing aspects of the consumer society, led to what he called the "law of conspicuous waste."

Originating during the 1950s, primarily through the ideas of George Homans (1910–1989), social exchange theory is positivistic in that it assumes that human behavior can be explained by natural laws. Influenced in part by Simmel's idea of universal characteristics of human behavior, Homans created the "Five Propositions that Explain all Human Behaviors." Homans is the only theorist bold, brave, daring or unwise enough to dare claim that he could explain all human behaviors based on one of five propositions. He felt that human behavior was so predictable, so determined by patterns that they were subject to propositional laws.

Other theorists have since attempted unifying theories. Talcott Parsons (1902–1979) create structural functionalism in the 1950s as a macro-sociological theory designed to examine the characteristics of social patterns, structures and institutions. Parsons' structural functionalism, or more simply, functionalism, was an attempt to create a grand theory of society that would explain all social behavior, everywhere and throughout history. In the true sociological tradition of the idea that social theory should be supported by research methodology, Parsons made very clear in the preface to *The Structure of Social Action* (1949 [1937]) his commitment to empirical research as the guiding force behind his theory. In fact, many theorists, from Aristotle to Galileo to Comte to Einstein to Kaku have attempted unifying theories that can explain all aspects of their respect fields. Grand theories highlight the knowledge and expertise of proponents of a particular academic discipline and help to promote its quest toward gaining further and more advanced knowledge.

Modern Principles and Delaney's Laws

There have been a number of modern attempts to establish principles and laws that have a universal application. I will share a couple of examples you may have heard of and then share some of my own laws that were undoubtedly influenced by the ideas of others as each of us "stand on the shoulders of the giants" of the past, as the metaphor goes (and as attributed to Isaac Newton in a letter he wrote to Robert Hooke in 1675; but also attributed to Bernard of Chartres in 1159). It seems that whoever makes a mantra, principle or law famous generally receives credit for it.

The first theory to be described is the "finite pool of worry." When I teach students about the topic of social problems I explain that there are a variety of individual reactions and attitudes toward them including: indifference, few people worry about things that do not threaten them directly; fatalistic resignation, the passive acceptance of misfortune; cynicism, the idea that the misfortuned are to be blamed for their own troubles; religious retribution, the attitude that God is punishing humans for their sins; romanticizing, the unconsciously screening of observations to make them fit an ideal vision of the world; and social scientific, the attitude that through intellectual and empirical study, an objective solution can be found for any social problem. There is also a quite plausible principle to explain why some people do not rally behind a campaign designed to draw attention to, and stop, a particular social problem and that is referred to as the "finite pool of worry." The *finite pool of worry* states that humans have limited emotional resources for worry and therefore when they are already invested in something that really worries them because of a direct influence on their lives they cannot possibly take on additional worries. This principle makes logical sense when we consider that there are so many social problems of concern that if we fretted equally over every one of them it would be a burden that few, if any, of us could bear.

Most sociologists examine the role of power either at the macro level (e.g., how the power elites of a society wield power over the masses) or at the micro level (e.g., how a superordinate maintains power over subordinates or how within any group one person always has more power than the others). Sociologists also examine the role of power within personal relationships (e.g., love relationships or personal relationships). After examining countless relationships over a long period of time, the "Principle of Least Interest" developed. This principle suggests that the person who is least interested in maintaining a relationship can most easily walk away from the relationship. For example, in a romantic relationship one person will be more devastated than the other if there is a break-up. The person who is least interested in maintaining a relationship is the one with the power as they are more prepared to move on. This principle applies to nearly all social relationships including employment. If you are working for someone right now, or you have people working for you, who will be less concerned if that employment situation ends? The answer to that question tells you who has the power. Another thing we learn from this principle is that the person with minimum feelings invested in a relationship is the one with the power.

I have developed my own laws, including "The Law of Why Everything Happens." In short, everything happens because of what happened previously. Sociologists are trained to look for patterns of behavior. Saint-Simon stated that the observation of patterns over a long period of time was essential. His line of thinking was influenced by de Condorcet's belief that if we document past behaviors through current behaviors we could also project future behaviors. Contemporary sociologist Randall Collins (2004) introduced his "Interaction Ritual Chains" as "a theory of momentary encounters among human bodies charged up with emotions and consciousness because they have gone through chains of previous encounters" (p. 3). This theory supports my Law that everything happens because of what happened previously.

In Chapter 5, I introduced my "Law of Societal Progressive Motion," which states that a society in a progressive motion will continue to gain momentum if acted upon by such forces as forward-thinking individuals who innovate, create inventions for the betterment of humanity and engage in entrepreneurship. The concept of "motion" appears often in both the natural and social sciences and this Law is a modification of Newton's Laws of Motion.

Three other principles, or laws, that I am working on are: "The Law of Existence," the idea that any substance consisting of matter that actually exists but is lost, does in fact, still exist; it may be lost, but it exists somewhere in the Universe. This "Law" goes along with the "Law of Mass," which stipulates that everyone has to be somewhere. And then there is, "The Law of Opinions," the idea that people form opinions on a matter based on previous experiences and circumstances that now affect their way of thinking.

Summary

This chapter has three primary subject areas designed to highlight the idea that sociology is a science. First, science is the key to the origin and development of sociology and it is science that leads that leads to unbiased knowledge via observation, discovery and conducting data analysis in an attempt to support or disprove a theory.

Second, sociology is social theory supported by research methodology. It is social theory that directs sociologists in their quest to explain the social world. The ability to think critically is an important first step toward developing a social theory. Generally speaking, sociological theory is grounded in the scientific tradition of belief that social patterns exist; therefore, general laws can be created through empirical study. In order for any academic discipline to declare itself a science, it must conduct research and maintain a commitment to the canons of the scientific method.

Most brilliant social thinkers throughout the past couple of millennium have attempted to establish laws about the natural world and then the social world. Arguably, establishing laws applicable to the social world should be a key element of sociology. A review of a number of social thinkers who have established such laws or principles was presented.

By continuing to embrace its scientific roots in empirical research is what gives the field of sociology legitimacy. Sociology as science is what allows us to embrace the concept of "social physics." Sociology remains grounded in reality and attempts to explain human behavior, the social structure, culture and societies. We have not entered the realm of quantum mechanics and string theory with mathematical abstractions, the "many worlds interpretation," multiverses and parallel worlds (things which cannot be proven, at least as of now). Sociology would be best served to stick to the social aspects of physics and statistical analysis on tangible items. Then again, if one attempts to create a theory of everything, it will likely be necessary to think beyond the limitations of the known world.

PART C

PHYSICS:
THEORIES OF EVERYTHING

Not all physicists believe that it is possible to create a "theory of everything." They are not even sure that such a theory can theoretically exist, for that matter. However, the more brilliant among us, people like Albert Einstein, Stephen Hawking and Michio Kaku will see it as a challenge to try and establish such a grand theory.

In Chapter 7, we shall see how Einstein attempted to establish a theory of everything via a unified field theory. He had unified space and time with his special theory of relativity in 1905 and furthered unified space and time with gravitation in his general theory of relativity in 1915, so it seemed clear to Einstein that he could utilize his theory of relativity to unify the four fundamental forces of Nature (gravitational force; strong nuclear force; weak nuclear force; and electromagnetic force) in order to establish a theory of everything in his attempt to explain the physical universe. His research will also help create the field of *theoretical physics of cosmology*—the scientific study of the large scale properties of the Universe as a whole.

In Chapter 8, we will learn how Stephen Hawking attempted to create a theory of everything relying on quantum mechanics and Einstein's theory of relativity. Combining quantum theory and quantum mechanics along with Penrose's theory of space-time singularity, Feynman's sum-over-histories idea, and the "no-boundary proposal," Hawking explains the origin of the Universe via the Big Bang theory and argues that it is likely to be black holes that will cause its demise. The origin and fate of the Universe are critical aspects of Hawking's theory of everything.

In Chapter 9, we will learn of Michio Kaku's attempt of a "theory of everything" utilizing superstring theory. We will learn about the meaning of superstring theory; symmetry and supersymmetry; the idea that superstring theory can only work with multiple dimensions and parallel worlds; his work on the Big Bang theory; his work on robots and Artificial Intelligence (AI); the fate of humanity and the Universe; and whether Kaku still believes a theory of everything is possible.

7

Albert Einstein's
Unified Field Theory

Introduction

Albert Einstein is perhaps the most popularized and well-known genius recognized by name and image amongst the masses and certainly by those in the sciences. And while he was seemingly at ease with the world, he was intensely private (Feldman 2007). We know of him because of his various achievements that include: a theory of general relativity, which revolutionized our understanding of gravity, space and time; his work on the photoelectric effect; quantum theory of light; his theory that demonstrated the link between mass and energy ($E=mc^2$); his theories on Brownian motion (the existence of atoms and molecules); and the introduction of the cosmological constant. As stated by the National Academy of Sciences (2023), "Considered by many to be the greatest scientist of the twentieth century, Albert Einstein revolutionized scientific thought with new theories of space, time, motion and gravitation." In 1999, *Physics World* conducted a survey among the world's leading physicists (130 replied to the survey) and from this survey a ranking of the top physicists of all time was determined: Albert Einstein; Isaac Newton; James Clerk Maxwell; Niels Bohr; Werner Heisenberg; Galileo Galilei; Richard Feynman; Paul Dirac; Erwin Schrödinger; and Ernest Rutherford topped the list.

The admiration that the scientific community holds for Einstein is the result of a combination of genius, his academic achievements and his dream of accomplishing an even greater feat, creating a unifying field theory that would combine the four fundamental forces—gravitational force, strong (nucleus) nuclear force, weak (nucleus) nuclear force and electromagnetic force. As we shall see in this chapter, for the last three decades of his life, Einstein worked toward this unification goal in hopes of creating a theory that could explain everything (in the natural world).

Biography

Theoretical physicist Albert Einstein (1879–1955) was born in Ulm, Württemberg, Germany, on March 14, 1879, and just six weeks later his family moved to Munich (The Nobel Prize 2023a). Einstein's parents were secular, middle-class Jews.

His father, Hermann, after several false starts, opened an electrochemical factory in Munich with his brother Jakob. His mother, the former Pauline Koch, was the more cultured and widely read parent who also played the piano and had a genuine interest in German classical music, particularly Beethoven's piano sonatas (Whitrow 1967). While his mother was of stronger character than his father, the main intellectual stimulus in Einstein's early life came from his uncle Jakob, who was a trained engineer (Whitrow 1967). He had one younger sister, Maria, who went by the name of Maja (Feldman 2007; Kaku 2023). Michio Kaku (2023) explains that Einstein, at the age of 5, became fascinated by the idea that invisible forces could deflect the needle of a compass. This would lead to a lifelong fascination with invisible forces. Prior to his teenage years, Einstein had become quite religious and even composed songs in praise of God but this all changed after he read science books that contradicted his religious beliefs.

Einstein attended secondary school at Luitpold Gymnasium in Munich. He did not care for the Prussian-style educational system that he felt stifled originality and creativity. "One teacher even told him that he would never amount to anything" (Kaku 2023). Albert was impressed by a young medical student, Max Talmud (later Max Talmey), who often dined at the Einstein home. Talmud became an informal tutor and introduced Albert to mathematics and philosophy. Talmud also introduced him to a children's science series by Aaron Bernstein, *Naturwissenschaftliche Volksbucher* (1867–68; *Popular Books on Physical Science*), in which the author imagined riding alongside electricity that was traveling inside a telegraphy wire. This led Einstein to wonder all sorts of things, including "What would a light beam look like if you could run alongside it?" And "If light were a wave, then the light beam should appear stationary, like a frozen wave." Even as a child, Einstein realized that stationary light waves had never been seen, so there was a paradox (Kaku 2023). At age 16, Einstein wrote his first "scientific paper" titled "The Investigation of the State of Aether in Magnetic Fields" (1895). He wrote the paper and sent it with a letter to his uncle, Casar Koch. Much later it was published as part of a collection of articles (*The Collected Papers of Albert Einstein, Volume 1: The Early Years, 1879–1902*). The article was an explanation of magnetic induction effect, which predated pilot wave theory by thirty years. Einstein also mentions such topics as double refraction and the mysterious nature of electric current. The influence of Talmud was very evident. Einstein was interested in electromagnetic phenomena because his family had been involved in electrotechnology since 1882; his uncle Jakob, an engineer, patented a number of items manufactured by the family firm.

The Einstein brothers failed to secure a winning bid in a contract to electrify the city of Munich. They faced fierce competition from well-established companies outside of Bavaria (Feldman 2007). As a result, in early 1894, Einstein's family moved to Italy, first to Milan and a few months later to Pavia. Hermann had a relative in Italy that helped him find work. Albert was left at a boardinghouse in Munich and was expected to finish his education. By this time, Einstein already excelled at physics and mathematics and taught himself algebra, calculus and Euclidean geometry. He also studied music and philosophy and particularly enjoyed Immanuel Kant (having been introduced to his *Critique of Pure Reason* at age 13). Still, he grew increasingly upset by the Gymnasium's regimen and teaching style and by the end of the calendar year 1894 he joined his family in Pavia.

Einstein finished his secondary education at the Argovian cantonal school (a gymnasium) in Aarau, Switzerland, graduating in 1896. In 1896, with his father's approval, Einstein had also renounced his citizenship of the German Kingdom of Württemberg in order to avoid conscription into military service. While he lived in Aarau, Einstein lodged with the family of Jost Winteler and fell in love with Winteler's daughter, Marie. Interestingly, Albert's sister, Maja, later married Winteler's son Paul (Highfield and Carter 1994). Upon completion of his gymnasium education, Einstein enrolled in the four-year mathematics and physics teaching diploma program at the Swiss Federal Polytechnic School (following expansion in 1909 to full university status, it was renamed the Swiss Federal Institute of Technology). Marie Winteler, a year older than Albert, took a teaching position in Olsberg, Switzerland (Highland and Carter 1994). There were just 5 freshmen in Einstein's class including one woman, a twenty-year-old Serbian, Mileva Marić. Working side-by-side, the two budding physicists became very close to one another. Not much was known of the early relationship between Einstein and Mileva until after the deaths of both of them when love letters between them were discovered and published in 1987. Highfield and Carter (1994) base a great deal of their book, *The Private Lives of Albert Einstein*, on this content analysis of archival data between Einstein and Mileva. Based on these letters, it was revealed that the couple had a daughter, Lieserl, that Mileva delivered while she visited her parents in Novi Sad (Serbia) in early 1902. When Mileva returned to Switzerland, it was without child and the true fate of the infant is unknown but it is believed that she was either given up for adoption or that she died of scarlet fever (Highfield and Carter 1994). Einstein and Marić would marry in January 1903. Their first son, Hans Albert, was born May 1904 in Bern, Switzerland, and their second son, Eduard, was born in Zürich in July 1910.

Love letters written between Einstein and Marie Winteler prior to Eduard's birth acknowledged that Albert had preferred Marie all those past years and that he had been in love with her instead of his wife. He felt his time with Mileva was "misguided" and that he mourned the "missed life" that he had imagined he would have enjoyed if he had married Winteler instead (Wüthrich 2015). Rather than follow through with his desire to be with Marie, Albert entered into a relationship with Elsa Löwenthal in 1912, who was both his first cousin on his mother's side and his second cousin on his father's side (Calaprice and Lipscombe 2005). By the time Mileva learned of this infidelity, the Einstein family was living in Berlin (1914), and she took the boys and moved back to Zürich. Five years later (1919) the couple were granted a divorce on the grounds of having lived apart for five years. As part of the divorce settlement and a bit of cunning foresight on the part of Mileva, she made sure that part of the divorce settlement included the stipulation that should Albert win a Nobel Prize, he would give the prize money he received to her. Just two years later Einstein won the Nobel and he did sign over the prize money in its entirety to Mileva and she bought a house in Zürich (Pal 2021). Einstein would marry Löwenthal but his womanizing (he had many affairs) undermined this marriage (Highfield and Carter 1994). Nonetheless, Elsa stuck by his side. In 1936, Elsa died and

Albert was then looked after by his sister, Maja, his stepdaughter, Margot, and his secretary-housekeeper, Helen Dukas (Whitrow 1967).

Back to Einstein's academic and professional career, he graduated from the Swiss Federal Polytechnic School in 1900 with his bachelor's degree and was fully certified to teach mathematics and physics. However, as a student, he preferred to study on his own and skipped many classes, a behavior that did not go over well with his professors. In part, because of this, Einstein did not obtain solid letters of recommendation and he could not secure a teaching position. His father was also in dire economic straits. Albert felt as though he could not marry Marić and raise a family without a job. He took on menial tutoring jobs teaching children but was fired from even those jobs (Kaku 2023). He had certainly reached his low point in 1902. (Note: In 1901, Einstein became a Swiss citizen, a status he kept for the rest of his life.)

Through the help of the father of his lifelong friend Marcel Grossmann, Einstein was able to secure a position as a clerk in the Swiss patent office in Bern (Kaku 2023). Albert finally had a steady, albeit small, income (and that is why, on January 6, 1903, he married Marić). Einstein was able to complete his work tasks at the patent office rather easily and quickly and this afforded him much time to concentrate on his own academic and scientific interests. Two monumental events occurred in the year 1905 for Einstein. The first, he earned his doctorate in physics from the University of Zürich. The second, Einstein published four revolutionary physics papers, all of which were initially ignored. As Kaku (2023) explains, "This began to change after he received the attention of just one physicist, perhaps the most influential physicist of his generation, Max Planck, the founder of the quantum theory." (See Chapter 3 for a discussion on Planck.) Planck's continued admiring comments and his experiments that gradually confirmed Einstein's theories led to Einstein being invited to lecture at international meetings and conferences and his prestige grew every step along the way. "He was offered a series of positions at increasingly prestigious institutions, including the University of Zürich, the University of Prague, the Swiss Federal Institute of Technology, and finally the University of Berlin, where he served as director of the Kaiser Wilhelm Institute for Physics from 1913 to 1933 (although the opening of the institute was delayed until 1917)" (Kaku 2023). Einstein's work (which will be described later in chapter) was disrupted at the University of Berlin with the outbreak of World War I. As a lifelong pacifist, Einstein was only one of four intellectuals in Germany to sign a manifesto opposing Germany's entry into war. In November 1918, radical students seized control of the University of Berlin and held the rector of the college and several professors hostage. Together with Max Born (1954 Nobel Prize for Physics winner), Einstein brokered a compromise that resolved the situation (Kaku 2023).

In 1921, Einstein began the first of several world tours, it was during this tour that he learned he had won the Nobel Prize for Physics "for his services to Theoretical Physics, and especially for this discovery of the law of the photoelectric effect" (The Nobel Prize 2023b) rather than for his theory of relativity. (Note: The photoelectric effect as Einstein explained it appears later in this chapter.) Throwing shade at Einstein, the Nobel Committee decided that none of that year's nominations met the criteria as outlined in the will of Alfred Nobel. Based on the Nobel Foundation's statutes, the Nobel Prize can in such a case be reserved until the following year, and this statute was then applied, meaning that Einstein would receive his Nobel Prize for 1921 one year later, in 1922 (The Nobel Prize 2023b). However, Einstein was on a world tour during the Nobel December ceremony of 1922 and it was decided that he would not receive the award and give his speech in Stockholm in front of the Royal Swedish Academy, but instead, at the Nordic Assembly of Naturalists at Goteborg on July 11, 1923. The audience consisted of about 2,000 people, including the King of Sweden. This speech is considered his Nobel Prize speech even by the Nobel Prize Foundation. But, unlike usual Nobel lectures, this was not a presentation of the work that was cited in the award—for his work on the photoelectric effect—rather, Einstein gave a speech on the theory of relativity. There was not a single mention of his work on the photoelectric effect (Einstein 1923; Pal 2021).

The early 1930s played witness to the rise of the Nazi empire led by Adolf Hitler. The Nazis targeted Einstein because of his popularity, his nonsupport of the Nazi cause and because he was a Jew. In December 1932, Einstein decided to leave Germany forever (he would never return). Einstein moved to the United States and settled at the newly formed Institute for Advanced Study at Princeton, New Jersey, which soon became a mecca for physicists from around the world (Kaku 2023). He was one of the Institute's first professors, serving from 1933 until his death in 1955, and played a significant part in the Institute's early development (Institute for Advance Study 2023). Einstein was granted permanent residency in the United States in 1935 and he became an American citizen in 1940, although he also retained his Swiss citizenship. While Einstein's theories helped to develop the possibility of an atomic bomb, he was not invited to join the Manhattan Project in Los Alamos, New Mexico. Voluminous declassified Federal Bureau of Investigation (FBI) files years later revealed that the U.S. government worried that Einstein's history with peace and socialist organizations did not make him a good candidate to work on such a project. Einstein did help the U.S. war effort in other ways, however, including evaluating designs for future weapons systems and by auctioning off priceless personal manuscripts including his handwritten copy of his 1905 paper on special relativity which sold for $6.5 million—it is now located in the Library of Congress (Kaku 2023). Nonetheless, Einstein, who promoted peace over war, supported Oppenheimer in his opposition to the development of the hydrogen bomb and instead, called for international controls on the spread of nuclear technology.

Einstein and Oppenheimer were colleagues and friends. They first met in 1932 during Einstein's visit to the California Institute of Technology (Caltech; as part of his world lecture tour), where Oppenheimer served as a theoretical physics professor and taught such courses as quantum theory, the quantum theory of radiation and statistical mechanics. Oppenheimer spent the majority of his time developing a strong physics department at the University of California Berkeley but commuted back and forth between the two campuses and usually spent one term each year on the Caltech campus (California Institute of Technology 2023). Einstein and Oppenheimer had many conversations on such topics as life, politics and science. As Oppenheimer was facing scrutiny with the U.S. government following the Manhattan Project for his past associations with peace advocates and communists, Einstein advised him to not give legitimacy to such a "kangaroo court." Oppenheimer, however, dismissed Einstein's advice. Publicly, Einstein always stood by Oppenheimer and said to the press, "I admire him not only as a scientist but as a great human being" (*The Indian Express* 2023). The two physicist friends became official colleagues in 1947 at the Institute for Advanced Study in Princeton when Oppenheimer took over as the director of the Institute (from 1947 to 1966). Oppenheimer, then, became Einstein's boss, but the true relationship was that of colleagues and friends.

Einstein enjoyed more intimate conversations with his fellow physicists while at Princeton. During the winter of 1943–44, Einstein; Bertrand Russell, the British logician, philosopher, and gadfly; Wolfgang Pauli, the "boy wonder of quantum physics," who formulated the "exclusion principle" in 1925 and postulated the existence of the neutrino in 1930; and Kurt Gödel, whose "incompleteness" theory of 1931 shattered the link between logic and mathematics that Russell's monumental work *Principia Mathematica* had attempted to forge, all met at Einstein's home at 112 Mercer Street in Princeton on a weekly basis (Feldman 2007). The four men spent their days thinking, writing, and periodically, lecturing, either within the Institute or elsewhere at professional meetings. While the meetings did not make history, one can imagine the conversations these brilliant thinkers engaged in.

During the last years of his life Einstein became increasingly drawn to antiwar activities and to advancing civil rights of African Americans. He was offered the position of president of Israel in 1952 by David Ben-Gurion, but he turned it down (Kaku 2023). Einstein died on April 18, 1955, at Princeton, New Jersey.

Let's now take a look at some of Einstein's key contributions to physics and then we'll conclude with an examination of his attempt to create a unified field theory.

The 1905 Papers: Einstein's Annus Mirabilis

As stated by the Library of Congress (2023), Albert Einstein published four papers in 1905 that would change the world of physics. So significant were these papers that 1905 is referred to as Einstein's *annus mirabilis*, or miracle year. (The term *annus mirabilis* refers to a year in which an unusual number of remarkable things occurred.)

The first of these 1905 papers (received by the editor of the German journal *Annalen der Physik* on March 18, 1905), "On a Heuristic Point of View Concerning the Production and Transformation of Light," "explained the already-observed photoelectric effect—by which beams of light cause metals to release electrons which can be converted into electric current—by suggesting that light be thought of as discrete packets, or quanta, of energy particles" and earned Einstein a Nobel Prize in Physics in 1921 (National Academy of Science 2023). Einstein's examination on the photoelectric effect, where electrons are released when light hits a material led him to put forth the notion that light consists of "discrete packets" as opposed to the widely accepted wave theory of light. This discovery later advanced the theory of wave-particle duality in quantum mechanics (Library of Congress 2023). As Kaku (2023) explains, Einstein applied the quantum theory to light in order to explain the photoelectric effect. If light occurs in tiny packets (later called photons), then it should knock out electrons in a metal in a precise way. "Einstein's light quanta and energy conservation equation successfully explained the photoelectric effect and other effects that the wave theory of light and Maxwell's theory failed to. You might imagine that such a breakthrough would have been welcomed with open arms from the physics community. Not so, unfortunately" (Bembenek 2017). Einstein's photon concept met with great resistance until, as stated earlier in this chapter, it was promoted by Max Planck. The resistance in the physics community can be explained primarily because Einstein had dared to call out the wave theory of light which had seen much success with explaining physical phenomena, especially under the guidance of Maxwell's theory. Tampering with something that had given so much in the way of explanation offended most physicists (Bembenek 2017).

The second paper (received by the editor of *Annalen der Physik* on May 11, 1905), "On the Movement of Small Particles Suspended in Stationary Liquids Required by the Molecular-Kinetic Theory of Heat," focuses on Brownian motion, the erratic random movement of microscopic particles in a fluid as they collide. "This paper helped to move the theory of atoms into reality by offering a way for scientists to count and observe their behavior during experiments" (Library of Congress 2023). As Kaku (2023) explains, in this paper, "Einstein offered the first experimental proof of the existence of atoms. By analyzing the motion of tiny particles suspended in still water, called Brownian motion, he could calculate the size of the jostling atoms and Avogadro's number." Avogadro's number refers to the number of units in mole (or mol, in chemistry, a standard unit for measuring large quantities of very small entities such as atoms, electrons, ions, molecules or other specified particles) of any substance (defined as its molecular weight in grams), equal to $6.02214076 \times 10^{23}$. While Kaku and others focus on Einstein's analysis of the existence and proof of atoms, upon reading his paper we also see the importance of the molecular-kinetic theory of heat. Einstein (1990) begins by stating, "It will be shown in this paper that, according to the molecular-kinetic theory of heat, bodies of microscopically visible size suspended in liquids must, as a result of thermal molecular motions, perform motions of such magnitude that these motions can easily be detected by a microscope. It is possible that the motions to be discussed here are identical with the so-called 'Brownian molecular motion'; however, the data available to me on the latter are so imprecise that I could not form a definite opinion on this matter" (p. 123). Einstein (1990) adds, "If it is really possible to observe the motion to be discussed here, along with the laws it is expected to obey, then classical thermodynamics can no longer be viewed as strictly valid even for microscopically distinguishable spaces, and an exact determination of the real size of atoms becomes possible. Conversely, if the prediction of this motion were to be proved wrong, this fact would provide a weighty argument against molecular-kinetic conception of heat" (p. 123). In this 1905 paper, Einstein then applies his calculations much to the much-later fascination of the physics community; that is, appreciation came after Planck gave the theory kudos years later.

In his third paper (received by the editor of *Annalen der Physik* on June 30, 1905), "On the Electrodynamics of Moving Bodies," Einstein argues that the speed of light is fixed and not relative to the observer and this is true whether the source is moving or stationary (Library of Congress 2023). As Feldman (2007) states, this paper "demolishes Newton's absolute time and space" [theory] (p. 31). This is also where Einstein laid out the mathematical theory of *special relativity*. "The Special Theory of Relativity tells us that a moving object measures shorter in its direction of motion as its velocity increases until, at the speed of light, it disappears. It also tells us that moving clocks run more slowly as their velocity increases until, at the speed of light, they stop running altogether" (The Physics of the Universe 2023). Special relativity theory is limited to objects that are moving with respect to inertial frames of reference (e.g., in a state of uniform motion with respect to one another such that one cannot, by purely mechanical experiments, distinguish one from the other [The Editors of Encyclopædia Britannica] 2023b). These two ideas—the speed of light is fixed and special relativity—are organized by Einstein based on the principle of relativity and the principle of the constancy of the velocity of light which are defined as follows:

1. The laws governing the changes of the state of any physical system do not depend on which one of the two coordinate systems in uniform translational motion relative to each other these changes of the state are referred to.
2. Each ray of light moves in the coordinate system "at rest" with the definite velocity V independent of whether this ray of light is emitted by a body at rest or a body in motion. Here, where "time interval" should be understood in the sense of the definition in § 1 (Einstein 1990:143–144).

It is in Einstein's fourth paper of 1905 (received by the editor of the German journal *Annalen der Physik* on September 17, 1905) "Does the Inertia of a Body Depend Upon its Energy Content?," that he introduces arguably the most famous equation in history: $E=mc^2$ (Library of Congress 2023). In this equation "E" equals energy, "m" equals mass and "c" equals light; thus, Energy equals mass times the speed of light squared. Kaku (2023) states that this paper was submitted almost as an afterthought and that the equation came about as the result of his relativity theory. "This equation showed that the energy of a body at rest equals its mass times the speed of light squared. The speed of light, or c, is 299,792,458 meters/second. That is a huge amount of energy that could be released, which would later be confirmed through the advent of nuclear bombs and reactors" (Library of Congress 2023). Put another way, the speed of light is about 186,283 miles per second—a universal constant known in equations as "c," or light speed (Stein 2023). This equation is the foundation for Einstein's special relativity theory and serves as the basis for much of modern physics. The speed of light is considered so immutable that it has helped to establish international standard measurements such as the meter, and by extension, the mile, the foot and the inch; and through other equations, the kilogram and the temperature unit Kelvin (Stein 2023). The speed of light calculation and its associated laws are so well-established that physicists and science fiction writers alike cannot help themselves but contemplate faster-than-light travel (Stein 2023). So far no one's been able to demonstrate a real warp drive (such as that associated with the 1960s *Star Trek* TV series), but that does not stop the pursuit of such an actual breakthrough. (Note: On *Star Trek* they created the concept of a "warp bubble" around the spaceship, inside of which space is literally warped.)

It must be noted, if you actually read this fourth paper (as I have read all of them) you will *not* find the actual E=mc² equation and that is because Einstein did not in fact use it in this paper. This is because Einstein used "V" to mean the velocity of light in a vacuum and "L" to mean the energy lost by a body in the form of radiation (Einstein 1990; Byrd 2021). In this paper the E=mc² equation was not written out as a formula but as a sentence in German that said (translated into English), "If a body gives off the energy L in the form of radiation, its mass decreases by L/V²" (Einstein 1990:174).

As an additional note, John S. Rigden, in his 2005 book, *Einstein 1905: The Standard of Greatness*, argues that Einstein wrote 5 papers in 1905. The article in question (the one missing from the above descriptions), "A New Determination of Molecular Dimensions" was his doctoral dissertation that was submitted to *Annalen der Physik* on April 30, 1905, but not published until 1906. Rigden (2005) also points out that while these five papers were all submitted over a six-month period, "it would be misleading to suggest that in the spring of 1905, a flood of profound ideas suddenly popped into his mind. Indeed, Einstein had been ruminating about these ideas for some years, until the spring of 1905, when he began furiously writing papers" (p. 4).

Theory of Relativity

Einstein explains that mathematics deals exclusively with the relations of concepts to each other without consideration of their relation to experience. He adds that physics too deals with mathematical concepts; however, these concepts attain physical content only by their clear determination of their relation to the objects of experience. This is especially the case for the concepts of motion, space and time (Einstein 2016).

The theory of relativity is that physical theory which is based on a consistent physical interpretation of these three concepts. The name "theory of relativity" is connected with the fact that motion from the point of view of possible experience always appears as the *relative* motion of one object with respect to another (e.g., of a car with respect to the ground, or the earth with respect to the sun and the fixed stars). Motion is never observable as "motion with respect to space" or, as it has been expressed, as "absolute motion." The principle of relativity in its widest sense is contained in the statement: The totality of physical phenomena is of such a character that it gives no basis for the introduction of the concept of "absolute motion," or shorter but less precise: There is no absolute motion (Einstein 2016).

Einstein acknowledges that it may seem that such an insight would gain little from such a negative statement but adds that in reality, it is a strong restriction for the (conceivable) laws of nature. "In this sense there exists an analogy between the theory of relativity and thermodynamics. The latter too is based on a negative statement: There exists no perpetuum mobile" (Einstein 2016).

The development of the "theory of relativity" proceeded in two steps: first came the "special theory of relativity" and second the "general theory of relativity." The latter presumes the validity of the former as a limiting case and is its consistent continuation (Einstein 2016). The special theory of relativity retained the basis of classical mechanics in the fundamental sense that laws of nature are valid only with respect to inertial systems. As we shall soon see, the general theory of relativity would expand on the initial shortcomings of the special theory of relativity.

Einstein's third paper of 1905, "On the Electrodynamics of Moving Bodies," introduced us to his special theory of relativity. However, from 1905 to 1915, Einstein was consumed with a crucial flaw in his theory: it made no mention of gravitation or acceleration (Kaku 2023). "His friend Paul Ehrenfest had noticed a curious fact. If a disk is spinning, its rim travels faster than its centre, and hence (by special relativity) meter sticks placed on its circumference should shrink. This meant that Euclidian plane geometry must fail for the disk" (Kaku 2023). To correct his theory, Einstein formulated a theory of gravity in terms of the curvature of space-time. "To Einstein, Newton's gravitational force was actually a by-product of a deeper reality: the bending of the fabric of space and time" (Kaku 2023).

To address the above concerns, Einstein turned to the "Principle of Equivalence" (a fundamental law in modern physics, which describes that inertial and gravitational forces are similar in nature and usually indistinguishable). From this principle, Einstein realized that a body has an inertial mass (resistance to acceleration) and a heavy mass (which determines the weight of the body in a given gravitational field, e.g., that at the surface of the earth).

These two quantities, so different according to their definition, are according to experience measured by one and the same number. There must be a deeper reason for this. The fact can also be described thus: In a gravitational field different masses receive the same acceleration. Finally, it can also be expressed thus: Bodies in a gravitational field behave as in the absence of a gravitational field if, in the latter case, the system of reference used is a uniformly accelerated coordinate system (instead of an inertial system) (Einstein 2016).

In November 1915, Einstein finally completed the general theory of relativity. This completed general theory of relativity not only generalized his special theory of relativity but also provided a new theory of gravitation. Among other things, it predicted the gravitational bending of light rays (Dukas and Hoffmann 1979). The completion of the general theory of relativity allowed for the continuation of his ultimate achievement, his theory of relativity. A bit of controversy surrounds the story of Einstein's completion of his theory of relativity. As Kaku (2023) explains, Einstein had given six two-hour lectures at the University of Gottingen wherein he thoroughly explained an incomplete version of general relativity that lacked a few necessary mathematical details. The mathematician David Hilbert, who had organized the lectures at his university and had been corresponding with Einstein, completed these details and submitted a paper on general relativity just five days before Einstein as if the theory were his own. Among physicists today, the equations are viewed as derived from Einstein and Hilbert but the theory itself solely to Einstein.

The lecture that Einstein delivered to the Nordic Assembly of Naturalists at Gothenburg on July 11, 1923, in lieu of an actual Nobel Prize speech in Stockholm in front of the Royal Swedish Academy provides us with a great review of the key aspects of his completed theory of relativity. Einstein states, "The special theory of relativity is an adaptation of physical principles to Maxwell-Lorentz electrodynamics. From earlier physics it takes the assumption that Euclidian geometry is valid for the laws governing the position of rigid bodies, the inertial frame and the law of inertia.... From Maxwell-Lorentz electrodynamics it takes the postulate of invariance of the velocity of light in vacuum (light principle)" (Einstein 1923:484).

Einstein explains that according to the special relativity principle, the laws of Nature must be covariant relative to Lorentz transformations; therefore, the theory provides a criterion for general laws of Nature. The theory also led to a modification of the Newtonian point motion law in which the velocity of light in a vacuum is considered the limiting velocity, and it also leads to the realization that energy and inertial mass are of like nature (Einstein 1923). Furthermore, "the special relativity theory resulted in appreciable advances. It reconciled mechanics and electrodynamics" (Einstein 1923: 485).

Addressing the two issues of gravity and acceleration, Einstein looked at Viennese philosopher and physicist Ernst Mach's modification of the law of inertia. Mach had criticized the concepts of space and time that were a part of Newtonian physics and became an inspiration to the young Einstein (Infeld 1950). Mach argued that the inertia should be interpreted as an acceleration resistance of the bodies against *one another* and not against "space." "This interpretation governs the expectation that accelerated bodies have concordant accelerating action in the same sense of other bodies (acceleration induction)" (Einstein 1923:488). (Note: The description of speed in terms of Mach 1, Mach 2, etc., is attributed to Ernst Mach.) Einstein found Mach's interpretation as even more plausible according to general relativity which eliminates the distinction between inertial and gravitational effects.

It amounts to stipulating that, apart from the arbitrariness governed by the free choice of coordinates, the $g\mu v$-field shall be completely determined by the matter. Mach's stipulation is favored in general relativity by the circumstance that acceleration induction in accordance with the gravitational field equations really exists, although of such slight intensity that direct detection by mechanical experiments is out of the question (Einstein 1923: 488).

Einstein (1923) concluded his lecture on the theory of relativity by describing "the most important concept of Riemannian geometry, 'space curvature,' on which the gravitational equations are also based, is based exclusively on the 'affine correlation'" (p. 490). Riemann had explained "curvature as a departure from flatness of a space, or space-time, which is approximately, flat or Euclidean" (Schilpp 1970). Einstein adds, "By seeking the simplest differential equations which can be obeyed by an affine correlation there is reason to hope that a generalization of the gravitation equations will be found which includes the laws of the electromagnetic field" (p. 490).

It was his theory of relativity that Einstein felt should have earned him a Nobel Prize. Many physicists agree, with some arguing, that a second Nobel should have been awarded to him years after his 1921 Prize.

Quantum Theory

As described in Chapter 3 (see Planck), early twentieth-century physics was highlighted by two major transformations: Einstein's theories of relativity and Planck's groundbreaking work on quantum theory. Quantum theory proposed that energy exists as discrete packets—each called a "quantum." A *quantum* refers to a quantity, or an amount of something; specifically, the smallest discrete unit of a phenomenon (e.g., a quantum of light is a photon; a quantum of electricity is an electron); it is the most basic building block and cannot be broken into smaller parts. "This new branch of physics enabled scientists to describe the interaction between energy and matter down through the subatomic realm" (American Museum of Natural History 2023b). Infeld (1950) states, "Quantum theory deals with the laws that describe how matter is built out of these elementary particles and what the forces are between them as revealed in spectral lines, in radioactive phenomena, or in the process of fission" (p. 85).

Planck introduced the quantum of energy in his experimental investigations of black body radiation in 1900. He was followed by the young Einstein who proposed the "light quantum hypothesis" in 1905 (Singh 2006). "Einstein was the first person to have a clear realization that Planck's introduction of energy quanta was a revolutionary step and thus one which would have larger significance for physics than just for the problem of black body radiation" (Singh 2006:173). Einstein played a major role in the development of quantum theory with his first paper of 1905 wherein, among other things, he applied the quantum theory to light in order to explain the photoelectric effect. "Einstein actually helped create quantum theory with his description of the photoelectric effect, in which particles of light can drive electric currents" (Frank 2023). Both Planck in 1900 and Einstein in 1905 used quantum theory to understand problems of radiation. "Einstein in 1907 was the first to apply it to the problems of matter. This was the problem of specific heat of solids" (Singh 2006:176). Einstein clearly found value with quantum theory, at least early on and in the manner utilized by Planck. As Lalli (2013) explains, the totality of Einstein's 1905–1925 breakthroughs in the original quantum theory amounts to an impressive list of contributions. By the late 1920s, however, he had grown disillusioned with the way the theory was developing via physicists like Niels Bohr and Werner Heisenberg (Frank 2023).

Ever happy with his pioneering breakthroughs in the theory of general relativity—such as wormholes, higher dimensions, the possibility of time travel, the existence of black holes, and the creation of the universe—Einstein was becoming increasingly isolated from the rest of the physics community because of quantum theory (Kaku 2023). Quantum theory was already unraveling the secrets of atoms and molecules and as a result, the majority of physicists were working on the quantum theory, not relativity (Kaku 2023). Einstein certainly had his doubts concerning quantum theory (and perhaps he viewed it as an unwanted rival to his relativity theories).

Einstein saw quantum theory as a means to describe Nature on an atomic level, but he doubted that it upheld "a useful basis for the whole of physics." He thought that describing reality required firm predictions followed by direct observations. But individual quantum interactions cannot be observed directly, leaving quantum physicists no choice but to predict the probability that events will occur. Challenging Einstein, physicist Niels Bohr championed quantum theory. He argued that the mere act of indirectly observing the atomic realm changes the outcome of quantum interactions. According to Bohr, quantum predictions based on probability accurately describe reality (American Museum of Natural History 2023b).

As we can see, Einstein is trying to hold onto the old idea that physics is a hard science, based on observation and experimentation and not on conjecture, probabilities and indirect observations. As described in Chapter 3, this is the problem with much of physics today; it has entered the realm of make-believe, especially string theory with such abstract and improvable (to date, anyway) notions as different dimensions, multiverses, parallel worlds and alternate universes. But even Einstein, as a theoretical physicist, did not personally turn to mathematical calculations to support his theories. Feldman (2007) explains, "Einstein had not turned into a mathematician.... Mathematics for him was never the point, only a tool for doing physics" (p. 152).

Things got heated between Einstein and Bohr (see Chapters 2 and 3 for a discussion on Bohr) and the two Nobel winners engaged in a series of sophisticated "thought experiments" wherein Einstein "tried to find logical inconsistencies in the quantum theory, particularly its lack of a deterministic mechanism" (Kaku 2023). He simply could not accept an interpretation in which the principal object of the representation—the wavefunction—is not "real." Einstein's famous quote sums up his feelings about quantum theory's introduction of fundamental randomness into the discipline saying, "God does not play dice with the universe." The implication of this statement is that the existence of the universe is not a matter of randomness. It should also be made clear that Einstein was not suggesting that a religious God created the universe; instead, he was referring to the laws of Nature. What Einstein means by the word "God" is the mathematical laws of Nature. At best, the idea of God could be someone, or something, that formulated the laws and then left the universe alone to evolve according to these laws. "Thus, his use of the word God is to be interpreted as the existence of natural laws of great mathematical beauty, whatever form they might take" (Natarajan 2008:656). As for Einstein's religious views, he believed in a God of philosophy, not religion (Baggott 2018). Kaku (2023) states, Einstein "believed there was an 'old one' who was the ultimate lawgiver.... [Einstein] did not believe in a personal God that intervened in human affairs but instead in the God of the 17th century philosopher Benedict de Spinoza—the God of harmony and beauty." Spinoza's God reveals himself in the lawful harmony of all that exists (Baggott 2018). Benedict de Spinoza (in Hebrew, Baruch; in Latin, Benedictus; 1632–1677) was born in Amsterdam. Spinoza described what he meant by God in great detail but suffice it to say, for him, God was an "absolute" with infinite attributes each of which expresses eternal and infinite essence—it was Nature (Nadler 2020).

Einstein was convinced that his God was infinitely superior and subject to strict adherence to the physical principles of cause and effect and thus, there is no room for free will as everything is determined by the laws of Nature (Baggott 2018). However, returning to Einstein's quote that "God does not play dice with the universe" and taking into consideration his interpretation of God as Nature and Nature as fixed by set laws, Natarajan (2008) reminds us of a key feature of quantum mechanics, namely Heisenberg's famous "Uncertainty Principle" which is based on the idea that Nature *is* inherently random. As we can see then, Einstein was fighting an uphill battle against the developing quantum theory and emerging quantum physics that so many physicists were now embracing even as his own attempt of a clever quote was falling off the intended mark of making a profound impact.

Einstein and Bohr (and a number of Bohr's young followers, including Pauli and Werner Heisenberg) publicly debated the merits of quantum physics at the prestigious 1927 Solvay Conference on Physics held from October 24 to 29 in Brussels, Belgium and attended by the top physicists of the day. Einstein believed that quantum physics was just a fad but of course, he would be proven wrong. Years later, Einstein was still on the attack. He co-authored a paper, "Can Quantum-Mechanical Description of Physical Reality Be Considered Complete?," written by Einstein, Podolsky and Rosen (nicknamed EPR) in the *Physical Review* (May 15, 1935) refuting quantum theory. EPR put forth the notion that "in a complete theory there is an element corresponding to each element in reality" and yet with quantum theory the knowledge of elements is not complete (Einstein et. al. 1935). The press shared Einstein's skepticism of the "new physics" but once again, the physics community supported Bohr. Nonetheless the EPR paper introduced topics that form the foundation for much of today's physics research (American Museum of Natural History 2023b). In addition, experiments conducted since this time have confirmed that the quantum theory, rather than Einstein, was correct. Still, "what Einstein had actually shown was that quantum mechanics is nonlocal—i.e., random information can travel faster than light. This does not violate relativity, because the information is random and therefore useless" (Kaku 2023).

It should be clear that Einstein was a founder in the development of quantum theory and if for no other reason, he felt this gave him the right to judge the further growth of the theory. He realized, however, that it was time to move onto the next challenge, the biggest challenge for any social thinker, to create a theory of everything, or in the case of physics, a unified field theory.

Unified Field Theory

By the late 1920s, and as previously stated, Einstein became increasingly isolated from the mainstream of modern physics not only because he unsuccessfully challenged the developing version of quantum theory but because he spent the last thirty years of his life attempting to devise a unified field theory. For someone who had unified space and time with his special theory of relativity in 1905 and furthered unified space and time with gravitation in his general theory of relativity in 1915, it seemed natural to him to want to continue to develop a unified field theory utilizing his theory of relativity that would "geometrize all the forces of Nature and not just gravity" (Natarajan 2008:658). In particle physics, a *unified field theory* is "an attempt to describe all fundamental forces and the relationships between elementary particles in terms of a single theoretical framework. In physics, forces can be described by fields that mediate interactions between separate objects" (Sutton 2023). Sutton (2023) states that James Clerk Maxwell formulated the first field theory in his theory of electromagnetism and that Einstein developed a field theory of gravitation. Einstein attempted to create a unified field theory that combined electromagnetism and gravity. The unification goal was to find a common source of both gravitation and electromagnetism. Einstein worked with the brilliant mathematician Walter Mayer in an attempt to create a series of equations that could accomplish such a goal (Forse 1963). In early 1929, Einstein turned over to the Prussian Academy of Science a six-page report that expressed mathematically the unification of certain laws governing gravity and electromagnetism. However, Einstein knew it was only a partially successful attempt to develop a single mathematical formula from which the laws of gravity and electromagnetism could be derived (Forse 1963). Einstein had hoped his theory of relativity could help him accomplish this attempt at unification. Spoiler alert, Einstein, and every physicist since him, have failed to accomplish this feat.

The biggest obstacle in this attempt of unification has to do with the conversion of bosons (subatomic particles) to fermions (any member of a group of subatomic particles having off half-integral angular momentum) and vice versa. The matchup of leptons and quarks doesn't work as well as it did in previous steps of unification and would call for a new class of particles. Thoughts about these new set of particles often come under the title of "supersymmetry." In this regard, it seems that there would have to be supersymmetric boson particles for all the fermions and supersymmetric fermion particles for all the bosons.

In the quantum theory realm, there were inroads to developing unified field theories such as, in the 1940s, quantum electrodynamics (QED, the quantum field theory of electromagnetism), was fully developed (Sutton 2023). During the 1960s and 1970s, particle physicists discovered that matter is composed of two types of basic building block—the fundamental particles known as quarks and leptons (mentioned above). *Quarks* are elementary particles, and a fundamental constituent of matter, that combine together to form particles called hadrons, the most stable of which are protons and neutrons; quarks are bound by strong force. Quarks are so small they cannot be broken down into smaller components, making them the smallest things we know of. *Leptons* are also subatomic particles that cannot be broken down into smaller parts; they respond only to the electromagnetic force, weak force, and gravitational force and are not affected by the strong force; they include the electron (Sutton 2023). As described in Chapter 3 of this book, in 1968, there appeared to be a monumental breakthrough in the unification goal when Gabriele Veneziano working at CERN wrote a research paper describing how a 200-year-old formula was capable of explaining much of the data on the strong force than what was being collected at various particle accelerators around the world. In the 1970s, there was a development in quantum field theory for the strong force called quantum chromodynamics.

While the above examples of unified field theories represent significant achievements, none of them accomplished what Einstein hoped to accomplish. Einstein attempted to unify the four fundamental forces into one single equation. The four forces are: gravitational force; strong nuclear force, weak nuclear force and electromagnetic force. Even the far-fetched superstring theory in ten dimensions has failed to accomplish this (Dudas 2006). Proponents of "superstring" theory reserve hope that their theory will ultimately produce a "theory of everything" (Feldman 2007). Not yet, however. Among other problems, no variation of string theory can be verified experimentally. Michio Kaku, speaking like a true string theory advocate, dismisses the need for experiments, "The real problem is purely theoretical: if we are smart enough to completely solve the theory, we should find all of its solutions…. So far, no one on Earth is smart enough" (Feldman 2007:148). Physicists attempting to create a theory of everything are in real trouble if they have abandoned experimentation (science) and admit that they cannot even come up with a theory in the first place. In chapter 9, we will examine Kaku's attempt to create a theory of everything.

A "theory of everything" must take into account the study of the physical Universe. Einstein first started to incorporate this fundamental fact into his unified field theory in a paper he published two years after first proposing his general theory of relativity (Narlikar 2007). "A key concept of General Relativity is that gravity is no longer described by a gravitational 'field' but rather it is supposed to be a distribution of space and time itself" (NASA 2011a). Initially, Einstein's theory was able "to account for peculiarities in the orbit of Mercury and the bending of light by the Sun, both unexplained in Isaac Newton's theory of gravity. In recent years, the theory has passed a series of rigorous tests" (NASA 2011a). Among the things Einstein accomplished via these insights was the fact that he helped to launch the new branch of *theoretical physics of cosmology*. NASA (2011b) defines *cosmology* as "the scientific study of the large scale properties of the universe as a whole. It endeavors to use the scientific method to understand the origin, evolution and ultimate fate of the entire universe." As with any field of study, cosmology involves the formation of theories or hypotheses about the universe which make specific predictions for phenomenon that can be tested with observations (NASA 2011b).

Einstein's theory led him to predict that the Universe is dynamic—expanding or contracting. However, this contradicted the prevailing view that the universe was static, so he reluctantly introduced a "cosmological constant" (dark energy in today's parlance) term to his equation (Kaku 2023; Hawking 2007; Narlikar 2007; Wadia 2007). In 1929, astronomer Edwin Hubble (of whom the famed Hubble telescope is named after) found that the universe was indeed expanding, thereby confirming Einstein's earlier work. Hubble discovered a fuzzy nebulous object in the sky and determined that it lay outside of the Milky Way, proving that our galaxy was just one small drop in the enormous universe (Tillman and Harvey 2022). "Using General Relativity to lay the framework, Hubble measured other galaxies and determined that they were rushing away from us, leading him to conclude that the universe was not static but expanding" (Tillman and Harvey 2022). When Einstein met Hubble during a visit to the Mount Wilson Observatory near Los Angeles in 1930, he declared the cosmological constant to be his "greatest blunder" (Kaku 2023;

Hawking 2007). Recent satellite data, however, have shown that the cosmological constant is probably not zero but actually dominates the matter-energy content of the entire universe and is now a very important part of modern cosmology as it's the best explanation we have for the effects of dark energy on our expanding universe; thus, indicating that Einstein's "blunder" was not such a mistake after all and apparently determines the fate of the universe (Kaku 2023; Siegel 2023; Hawking 2007).

As an additional note to Hubble's legacy, Tillman and Harvey (2022) explain, while NASA's Hubble Space Telescope is probably best known for its astounding images, its primary mission was cosmological. "By more accurately measuring the distances to Cepheid variables, stars with a well-defined ratio between their brightness and their pulsations, Hubble helped to refine measurements regarding how the universe is expanding. Since its launch, astronomers have continued to use Hubble to make cosmological measurements and refine existing ones" (Tillman and Harvey 2022). Clearly, Einstein's contributions to cosmology were quite significant, even if mostly accomplished indirectly.

Einstein's split with mainstream physics came at the very height of his career when he was just in his late 40s. He discounted quantum mechanics and clashed with Danish physicist Niels Bohr, launching a feud that would last until his death in 1955 (Folger 2004). Einstein found quantum mechanics to be too quirky even though he had introduced a fourth dimension into his equations of general relativity to describe gravity. In cases where gravity was extremely strong, his theories broke down. His gravitation theory actually led to the discovery of what we now call "black holes," a phenomenon wherein objects of such enormous density have gravity so strong that it traps even light. And yet, Einstein hoped to rework his general relativity equations to eliminate the concept of black holes entirely (Folger 2004). Einstein felt that there must have been a mathematical error in his formulas that allowed for the discovery of a phenomenon. Nonetheless, in 1939 Oppenheimer "used general relativity to show in detail how black holes could form from collapsing stars. Yet Einstein was undeterred. Throughout the 1940s, he continued his fruitless search for a revolutionary new theory, even as quantum mechanics advanced at a blinding pace" (Folger 1940s). As described in Chapter 3, Oppenheimer and Sweet proved (in their 1939 paper, "On Continued Gravitational Contraction") that black holes were not merely mathematical errors in Einstein's general relativity theory and that large stars could collapse to form black holes. Much to his dismay, Einstein was proven wrong again. Still, he pursued the goal of a unified field theory at a time when other physicists scoffed at such a notion.

In recent years, however, this goal of finding a unified field theory has become a central goal of a number of physicists, but with string theory as the favored candidate for a unified understanding of the basic laws of the physical universal (Institute for Advanced Study 2023). Today, most proponents of string theory pay homage to Einstein as a man "ahead of his time." "Still, his disdain for quantum mechanics might well have distanced him from today's unifiers. He tried to circumvent quantum physics by geometrizing electromagnetism in gravitation's image. String theorists have taken the inverse route by quantizing gravitation" (Feldman 2007:158).

It should be noted too, that while Einstein enjoyed his position at Princeton's

Institute for Advanced Study, one that afforded him the luxury of pursuing his theoretical aspirations without the burdensome commitments of teaching (and all the tasks associated with it, such as time constraints, grading tests and so on) and having to deal with administrative nonsense; without graduate students to bounce ideas off of, he did not have a platform to grow. He also did not have an opportunity to create a legacy of followers who could most directly carry on his ideas and works. Despite this, Einstein seems to have done quite well for himself as his name is synonymous with brilliance and genius and he did advance physics in many ways.

Summary

Albert Einstein is undoubtedly one of the most famous scientists of all time, even people outside of the sciences have likely heard of him. Having name recognition is one thing but having knowledge of this brilliant physicist is quite another. In this chapter, we learned a great deal about Einstein.

Einstein was born in Ulm, Württemberg, Germany on March 14, 1879, and died in Princeton, New Jersey, on April 18, 1955. The year 1905 was a hugely monumental one for Einstein—so much so it is referred to as his *annus mirabilis*—as he published 4 papers so significant it would transform physics and the way we view the universe. A lifelong pacifist, Einstein was able to escape Germany during the rise of Hitler's Nazi empire. In December 1932, he moved to the United States and settled at the newly formed Institute for Advanced Study at Princeton, New Jersey, which soon became a mecca for physicists from around the world.

Einstein's 1905 papers during his "miracle year" did not pay immediate dividends but they sure did revolutionize physics. His first paper "On a Heuristic Point of View Concerning the Production and Transformation of Light," "explained the already-observed photoelectric effect—by which beams of light cause metals to release electrons which can be converted into electric current—by suggesting that light be thought of as discrete packets, or quanta, of energy particles and earned Einstein a Nobel Prize in Physics in 1921" (National Academy of Science 2023). The second paper, "On the Movement of Small Particles Suspended in Stationary Liquids Required by the Molecular-Kinetic Theory of Heat," focuses on Brownian motion, the erratic random movement of microscopic particles in a fluid as they collide. It is in his third paper, "On the Electrodynamics of Moving Bodies," that Einstein introduces his special relativity theory. In his fourth paper of 1905, "Does the Inertia of a Body Upon its Energy Content?," Einstein introduces arguably the most famous equation in history: $E=mc^2$ (although, as explained in this chapter, this actual equation does not appear in this form but rather in sentence form with different characters to signify energy, mass and light).

Einstein considered his "Theory of Relativity" as his crowning achievement. There were two preceding steps, first was the "special theory of relativity" (introduced in 1905) and second was the "general theory of relativity" (developed between 1905 and 1915). This theory was able to unify principles of mechanics, electrodynamics, gravity and acceleration. Einstein was also a founder of quantum theory, a new branch of physics which enabled scientists to describe the interaction between energy and matter down through the subatomic realm. By the mid–1920s, a number of physicists had taken the ideas of quantum theory to create quantum mechanics and this greatly displeased Einstein. He insisted that his theory of relativity was still superior to that of quantum mechanics.

By the late 1920s, Einstein had become increasingly isolated from the mainstream of modern physics not only because he unsuccessfully challenged the developing version of quantum theory but because he spent the last thirty years of his life attempting to devise a unified field theory. He had unified space and time with his special theory of relativity in 1905 and furthered unified space and time with gravitation in his general theory of relativity in 1915, so it seemed natural to him to want to continue to develop a unified field theory utilizing his theory of relativity that would "geometrize all the forces of Nature and not just gravity." Einstein correctly realized that a "theory of everything" must take into account the study of the physical universe. His research would help create the field of *theoretical physics of cosmology*—the scientific study of the large scale properties of the Universe as a whole. He found that the universe was dynamic and not static as previously believed. However, he introduced a "cosmological constant" to his formula as a type of appeasement to others to show that the universe was static (not expanding or detracting). Edwin Hubble proved that Einstein's original idea was correct and although the cosmological constant now seemed like a "great blunder" it actually turned out to help future physicists explain such things as dark energy and the expanding universe.

When Einstein pursued the idea of a unified theory at the exclusion of other scientific quests, his contemporaries, lacking in true scientific vision, scoffed at such an endeavor. If there is one thing to fault Einstein for, it was that he turned his back on quantum mechanics and ignored the important developments in fundamental physics for nearly 30 years as he worked on his unified field theory. As Einstein himself admitted in 1954, "I must seem like an ostrich who buries its head in the relativistic sand in order not to face the evil quanta" (Gross 2007:8). But, even quantum mechanics evolved and was ultimately abandoned by some for string theory. Today, a number of physicists, especially superstring physicists, are attempting to establish a unified theory just as Einstein did that incorporates the four fundamental forces: Gravitational Force; strong nuclear force, weak nuclear force and electromagnetic force.

For all his contributions and foresight, Einstein remains as an inspiration for physicists, especially those in speculative areas.

8

Stephen Hawking and the Origin and Fate of the Universe

Introduction

Often, individuals seem to be remembered for certain distinguishable characteristics in addition to their outstanding achievements. When people hear Albert Einstein's name, especially those outside of science, they likely conjure up an image in their mind of the famous photo of him sticking out his tongue as an older man. It's an iconic image because he was such a serious scientist who made formidable discoveries about the Universe and sticking out one's tongue is a silly thing to do, and in many contexts, a rude thing to do. That particular photo of Einstein was taken on March 14, 1951—his birthday—as he was leaving his 72nd birthday party at Princeton University, which had been swarming with photographers and understandably, he was tired of smiling all night (Hamer 2019).

For the world famous theoretical physicist and cosmologist Stephen Hawking, the unfortunate first thing the non-scientific person thinks of in order to remember him is the fact that he was wheelchair bound and communicated first with his finger to control a computer and voice synthesizer. Once he lost use of his hands, he depended on twitching a cheek muscle to communicate. He relied on this for nearly all of his adult life. At the age of 21, Hawking was diagnosed with amyotrophic lateral sclerosis (ALS), a type of motor neuron disease and initially given just two years to live. The degenerative condition progressed slower than expected and he continued working for decades (Science Alert 2023). As we will learn in this chapter, among his accomplishments was his work on the "big bang theory," the prevailing scientific explanation as to how the Universe started. Demonstrating both his sense of humor and willingness to embrace popular culture, Hawking appeared on the TV Show *The Big Bang Theory* seven times, the most famous episode being "The Hawking Excitation" (first aired date, April 5, 2012). In addition to Hawking talking with the character Sheldon Cooper, a theoretical physicist, about physics, he spoke with another character, Howard. It was revealed in this episode that Hawking had previously worked (fictitiously) with Howard and he made a point of saying that Hawking had a great sense humor and to honor him, Howard made a remote control toy of

Hawking in a wheelchair (like a remote control car). All of Howard's friends thought it was in poor taste so he never showed it to Hawking. At the end of the episode, Hawking mentions that he always thought there should be a toy of him in a wheelchair. In addition to appearing on *The Big Bang Theory*, Hawking made hundreds of appearances on other television shows (i.e., *The Simpsons*, *Futurama*, *Star Trek: The Next Generation*, *Stargate*), late night TV programs (i.e., *Late Night with Conan O'Brien*), news programs such as *60 Minutes* and also appeared in many movies.

As we shall learn in this chapter, Stephen Hawking was a brilliant physicist who, among other things, attempted a theory of everything relying on quantum mechanics and Einstein's general theory of relativity.

Biography

Theoretical physicist Stephen William Hawking (1942–2018), known as Stephen Hawking, was born January 8, 1942, in Oxford, Oxfordshire, England, exactly 300 years after the death of Galileo, as Hawking himself liked to point out (Hawking 1993). Hawking estimated that about two hundred thousand other babies were also born that day but didn't know whether or not any of them were later interested in astronomy. Hawking was born in Oxford even though his parents were living in London. However, in 1942 it was better to be born in Oxford because of World War II and the Germans' agreement that they would not bomb Oxford and Cambridge in return for the British not bombing Heidelberg and Göttingen (Hawking 1993). Hawking remarked that it was a pity that such a civilized sort of arrangement couldn't have been extended to more cities. Then again, if humanity was truly civilized, war wouldn't exist at all.

Stephen's father, Frank, came from Yorkshire and his grandfather, Stephen's great-grandfather, had been a wealthy farmer. However, he had purchased too many farms and had gone bankrupt in the agricultural depression at the beginning of the twentieth century. This left Frank Hawking's family badly off financially but they did manage to send him to Oxford where he studied medicine. Frank would go on to secure a career in medicine and became a specialist in tropical diseases. While conducting research in East Africa, the hostilities of impending war broke out, leading Frank Hawking to set off in 1939 to return to England with the intention of volunteering for military service. However, upon his arrival back in London he was informed that his skills would be far more usefully employed in medical research (White and Gribbin 1992).

Stephen's mother, Isobel, was born in Glasgow, Scotland, the second child of seven of a family doctor. The family moved south to Devon when she was 12 years old and like the Hawking family, was not well off. Nonetheless, her family managed to send her to Oxford where she studied philosophy, politics and economics. Although both Frank and Isobel had attended Oxford their paths never crossed. After Oxford, Isobel had various jobs, eventually becoming a secretary for a medical research institute during the early stages of the war and that is how she met Frank Hawking (Hawking 1993). The two met at work, fell in love, married, and had their first child, Stephen, in 1942. When Stephen was just two weeks old, the family moved to Highgate, north London. Stephen's sister, Mary, was born eighteen months later; she went on to become a doctor. Philippa, Stephen's youngest sister was born when he was nearly five and adopted brother Edward joined the family as a baby when he was fourteen.

During and just after the war, Highgate was an area in which a number of scientific and academic people lived and as Hawking (1993) states, "In another country they would have been called intellectuals, but the English have never admitted to having any intellectuals" (p. 3). The children of this area and era were sent to Byron House School, which was very progressive for the times. Hawking, however, complained that the laid-back style of teaching (opposed to drilling things into students) stunted his intellectual growth stating that he did not learn to read until the late age of eight, while in comparison his sister Philippa was taught to read by more conventional methods and could read by age four. The Hawkings lived in a tall, narrow Victorian house which Frank and Isobel purchased at a cheap price during the war (when everyone thought London was going to be bombed flat). Hawking (1993) stated, "In fact, a V-2 rocket landed a few houses away from ours. I was away with my mother and sister at the time, but my father was in the house" (pp. 3–4). Fortunately, Frank was not hurt and the house was not badly damaged. But, playing in a nearby bomb site down the road was the norm for Stephen and his friend Howard as they grew up following the war. Howard's parents were not intellectuals like the other parents of the neighborhood and he attended the council school, not Byron House. As a result, Howard learned of football and boxing, sports that the Hawking parents never considered following.

When Stephen was eight, the family moved twenty miles north to the city of St. Albans in Hertfordshire. Upon arrival, Stephen attended the St. Albans High School for Girls, which despite its name took boys up to age ten. After just one term, Frank Hawking left on one of his yearly visits of Africa, this time for about four months. Isobel did not like being alone that length of time, so she took Stephen and his two sisters to visit her school friend Beryl, who was married to the poet Robert Graves. They lived in a village called Deya, on the Spanish island of Majorca. This was just five years after the war, and Spain's dictator, Francisco Franco, who had been an ally of Hitler and Mussolini, was still in power (he would, in fact, remain in power for another two decades). When the Hawking family returned to England from Majorca, Stephen attended another school in St. Albans.

Placed in the top academic stream, at age ten, Stephen began his studies at the local private school, St. Albans School, a well-known and academically excellent abbey school, situated in the heart of the city and possessing close ties with the ancient city cathedral. Hawking both showed signs of intellectual capability but also of social awkwardness and an inability to speak clearly—his friends dubbed his speech "Hawkingese" (White and Gribbin 1992:9). All of this had nothing to do with any early signs of illness; he was just an "eccentric and awkward, skinny and puny" kid (White and Gribbin 1992: 9). In a story often retold in Hawking biographies, when Hawking was twelve years old, two of his schoolmates made a bet about his future, John McClenahan bet that Stephen "would never come to anything"; Basil King, said that he would "turn out to be unusually capable" (Ferguson 2012:20).

Although he was in the top tier of the academic hierarchy in the English educational system for his age category, his teachers only came to regard him as a little above average in the top class (White and Gribbin 1992). Three hours of homework daily, including the weekend, was the norm for the top students of the St. Albans School. But, such is the price for future success. Stephen and his friends managed to find time to have fun, mostly creating and playing board games. The Hawking household had all the appearances of eccentricity. The home was clean but cluttered with books, paintings, old furniture and strange objects from various parts of the world. Neither Isobel nor Frank Hawking seemed to care too much about the state of the home. Stephen's bedroom was also cluttered and described as a "messy magician's lair, the mad professor's laboratory and the messy teenager's study all rolled into one" (White and Gribbin 1992:12).

Frank Hawking was significant in Stephen's childhood life in two ways: first, by his regular and prolonged absences every summer; and second, by allowing Stephen to spend time in his laboratory in Mill Hill where he enjoyed looking through microscopes and going through the insect house where he kept mosquitoes infected with tropical diseases. This worried Stephen as there always seemed to be a few mosquitoes flying around loose. Stephen had taken to heart that his father always seemed to work with a chip on his shoulder as Frank felt other people were not as good as him but because they had the right background and connections had gotten ahead of him. Frank warned Stephen of this. Frank influenced Stephen to go into physics instead of medicine because, "It doesn't matter what school you went to or to whom you are related. It matters what you do" (Hawking 1993:11).

Isobel Hawking influenced Stephen's political ideas. She, like many English intellectuals of the period, had been a member of the Communist Party in the thirties, gradually moving towards the Labour Party by the fifties. Isobel was an enthusiastic supporter of the Campaign for Nuclear Disarmament and actively encouraged Stephen to join her on demonstrations and political rallies. Stephen never became a communist, but his interest in politics and left-wing sympathies never left him (White and Gribbin 1992).

Toward the end of his academic years at St. Albans School, Stephen Hawking and his friends drew a great deal of attention and admiration from the entire town for their successful foray in building a computer called LUCE (Logical Uniselector Computing Engine). Put together out of recycled pieces of clocks and other mechanical and electrical items, including an old telephone switchboard, LUCE could perform simple mathematical functions (Ferguson 2012). When a new head of computing at St. Albans School, Nigel Wood-Smith, took over the post many years later, he found LUCE and threw it away with along with other unused pieces of equipment. It was only years later did it dawn on Wood-Smith of the potential historical significance of LUCE (White and Gribbin 1992).

It was now 1959. The Hawking family sans Stephen had left for India for a year. Stephen had to stay behind to study for, and take, university entrance exams. At age 17, Hawking's headmaster thought he was too young to apply for Oxford. However, his father insisted that he attempt to gain entrance to Oxford. In March 1959 he took his scholarship exams and a few days later found out that he had indeed earned a scholarship to Oxford University. His focus was physics. Hawking found his studies to be quite easy. Unnervingly, there was a prevailing attitude at Oxford at this time that was "very antiwork" (Hawking 1993:14). Students were supposed to be brilliant without effort, or to accept their limitations and settle for a lesser degree, "To work hard to get a better class of degree was regarded as the mark of a gray man—the worst epithet in the Oxford vocabulary" (Hawking 1993:14). This seems unnerving because we, especially professors, always encourage students to work hard in order to achieve intellectual heights not previously thought to be imaginable. Hawking (1993) does admit that he was not proud of this lack of work attitude but admitted that at the time he went along with the thought process of his classmates. Hawking passed his final exams and earned his Bachelor of Arts degree in physics from Oxford in 1962.

The Cambridge Years

Having achieved high marks at Oxford, Hawking had his choice of what university to attend in his pursuit of a doctorate degree. Hawking's primary interest was in theoretical physics and there were two possible areas of interest. One was cosmology, the study of the very large. (Note: As defined by NASA in Chapter 7, *cosmology* is the scientific study of the large scale properties of the universe as a whole.) The other was the study of elementary particles, an area that Hawking found less attractive because there were no significant inroads in this area at the time. Oxford did not have anyone working in cosmology but at Cambridge there was Fred Hoyle, the most distinguished British astronomer of the time. Eager to study under Hoyle, Hawking began his studies at Cambridge in 1962 but much to his dismay, Hoyle—who is famous for coining the term "Big Bang" theory by mocking it on a March 28, 1949, BBC Radio broadcast—decided not to take on any more students as he began to travel abroad a great deal. Hawking's supervisor would instead be Denis Sciama, whom Hawking had never heard of before. However, Hawking (1993) later wrote that he was likely better off with Sciama because he was always available and served as a good mentor whereas Hoyle was seldom around. By the time he finished his Ph.D. studies at Cambridge in 1966, Hawking would become the champion of the "Big Bang" theory in contrast to Hoyle who had shunned it. (Note: We will revisit Hoyle and his views on the "Big Bang" theory later in this chapter.)

Hawking's first year at Cambridge was a struggle. Ferguson (2012) explains, "Hawking's failure to get Hoyle as his supervisor and his mathematical deficiencies were setbacks, but no more than typical for a first-year graduate student. While he struggled to catch up on general relativity and find a way through the mathematical maze needed to understand it, a far more unusual and merciless problem was overtaking him the autumn of 1962, threatening to make all this effort meaningless" (p. 34). Hawking (1993) describes how he had not done much mathematics at school or at Oxford and as a result he found general relativity very difficult at first and did not make much progress. Hawking had also noticed during his last year at

Oxford that he was "getting rather clumsy in my movements" (Hawking 1993:15). Following his first term at Cambridge, Hawking went home to St. Albans for Christmas and his physical problems were too obvious to conceal from his parents. Frank Hawking took his son to the family doctor who, in turn, referred him to a specialist. Shortly after his twenty-first birthday, Hawking found himself in St. Bartholomew's Hospital in London for tests. He was diagnosed with amyotrophic lateral sclerosis (ALS), often referred to in the United States as "Lou Gehrig's disease" (named after the famous New York Yankees baseball player who was diagnosed with the disease in 1939 and died less than two years later).

According to the ALS Association (2023), "ALS, or amyotrophic lateral sclerosis, is a progressive neurodegenerative disease that affects nerve cells in the brain and spinal cord." "Amyotrophic" comes from the Greek language. "A" means no. "Myo" refers to muscle. "Trophic" means nourishment. So, amyotrophic means "no muscle nourishment," and when a muscle has no nourishment, it "atrophies" or wastes away (ALS Association 2023). "Lateral" identifies the areas in a person's spinal cord where portions of the nerve cells that signal and control the muscles are located. As this area degenerates, it leads to scarring or hardening ("sclerosis") in the region. The progressive degeneration of the motor neurons in ALS eventually leads to their demise. As scary as the disease itself is, consider the fact that for about 90 percent of all cases, there's no known family history of the disease or presence of a genetic mutation linked to ALS (ALS Association 2023). Even today, ALS is fatal. The average life expectancy after diagnosis in two to five years, but some patients may live longer, even for decades (Hospital for Special Surgery 2023).

When Hawking was diagnosed with ALS it would come as no surprise that medical professionals gave him just two years to live. Hawking (1993) recounts how, at first, the disease seemed to progress fairly rapidly and he questioned why he should keep working at his research because he did not expect to live long enough to finish his Ph.D. However, as time went by, the progression seemed to slow down. For two years he was able to walk with a cane and his depression was replaced with hope. His mentor, Sciama, now encouraged Hawking to finish his thesis (Ferguson [2012]). Added to this bit of encouragement, Hawking recognized that he now understood general relativity and was making progress in his research. But what really made a difference in his attitude on life was getting engaged to a woman, Jane Wilde, whom he had met at about the time he was diagnosed with ALS. "This gave me something to live for," said Hawking (1993:16).

Hawking's office in the Department of Applied Mathematics and Theoretical Physics at Cambridge was next door to Jayant Narlikar, one of Hoyle's research graduate students with whom Hawking had become friends. Narlikar was working with Hoyle on possible modifications to general relativity that might reconcile the "Steady State" model (a view that the universe is always expanding but maintaining a constant average density) with recent observations that called it into question. This challenge piqued Hawking's interest (Ferguson 2012). Hawking, with no malicious intent toward Hoyle or Narlikar, worked for months on the equations and calculations and, perhaps, found the material more fascinating than his own work (White and Gribbin 1992). In June 1964, Hoyle decided to make a public announcement of his findings at a meeting of The Royal Society in London. This would precede the publication of the work he had conducted with Narlikar's help. Hawking traveled to London to attend the conference. Hoyle spoke to around one hundred people; at the end there was warm applause. When the floor was opened to questions, Hawking rose (with the help of his cane) and challenged one of Hoyle's results, stating, "The quantity you're talking about diverges" (White and Gribbin 1992:68). Visibly upset, Hoyle replied, "Of course it doesn't diverge." Defiantly, Hawking replied, "It does." The audience was dead silent in amazement at the exchange between a brash young physicist and a proven scientist. Hoyle asked, "How do you know?" Hawking said slowly, "Because I worked it out." The audience laughed (White and Gribbin 1992; Ferguson 2012). Furthermore, everyone thought Hawking had "worked out" the math then and there but, of course, he had spent months working on this without Hoyle's knowledge and with Narlikar's awareness. Hoyle considered Hawking's method of conveying what he had "worked out" to be unethical but Hawking and others in the physics community pointed out that Hoyle had been unethical in announcing results which had not been verified. It turned out that Hawking was correct. Hawking would write a paper ("On the Hoyle-Narlikar Theory of Gravitation," published in 1965) summarizing the mathematical findings which led him to realize this. While still trying to sort out his own Ph.D. work with Sciama, Hawking had managed to make inroads within the rarefied atmosphere of cosmological research.

Hawking was able to maintain his friendship with Narlikar and Hoyle would continue to work with Narlikar. Narlikar went on to become an astrophysicist who is a proponent of steady-state cosmology. Along with Hoyle, they developed the conformed gravity theory, commonly known as the Hoyle-Narlikar theory. This theory reduces Einstein's general relativity in the limit of a smooth fluid model of particle distribution constant in time and space.

Hawking was introduced to the work of a young applied mathematician, Roger Penrose, who was then based at Birkbeck College in London. The son of an eminent geneticist, Penrose had studied at University College in London and had gone on to Cambridge in the early fifties. Penrose studied the fate of a star when it has no nuclear fuel left to burn and collapses under the force of its own gravity. Building on the work of such physicists as Subrahmanyan Chandrasekhar and John Archibald Wheeler, Penrose had found that even if the collapse isn't perfectly smooth and symmetrical, the star will inevitably be crushed to a tiny point of infinite density and infinite curvature of space-time, a singularity at the heart of a black hole (Ferguson 2012). Inspired by the Penrose theory of space-time singularity, Hawking would write his dissertation thesis on the topic. His theory reversed the direction of time, and considered what would happen if a point of infinite density and infinite curvature of spacetime—a singularity—exploded outwards and expanded. And, suppose the universe began like that? Suppose space-time, curled up tight in a tiny, dimensionless point, exploded in what we call the "Big Bang" and expanded until it looks the way it does today. Is this how the universe possibly began, he wondered? Guided by intellectual questions such as these, Hawking's thesis was completed and his lifelong pursuit of finding the origin of the universe, the fate of the universe and creating a theory of everything had begun.

Hawking obtained his Ph.D. degree in applied mathematics and theoretical physics, specializing in general relativity and cosmology, in March 1966. His essay, "Singularities and the Geometry of Space-Time" shared top honors with one by Penrose to win that year's Adams Prize, one of the most prestigious awarded by the University of Cambridge.

On July 14, 1965, Stephen Hawking and Jane Wilde married. The couple would later have three children together, Robert, Lucy and Timothy. In the winter of 1965, Hawking applied for a research fellowship at Gonville and Caius College in Cambridge. He was awarded the fellowship following his graduation at Cambridge. The couple lived in an apartment close to Stephen's office on campus. In 1968, Hawking became a member of the Institute of Astronomy at Cambridge. In 1969, his health was starting to diminish more quickly. He needed the help of crutches to walk about and eventually he was forced to rely on a wheelchair. On a trip to Geneva in 1985, Hawking contracted pneumonia and ended up losing his voice. A computer programmer developed a speech synthesizing program that would later serve as Hawking's communication board. Stephen and Jane Hawking were officially divorced in 1990. Hawking then married Elaine Mason, a nurse who Stephen had fallen in love with. Stephen and Elaine divorced in 2006. From that point on, Stephen spent more time getting closer with his children. In July 2009, President Barack Obama bestowed upon Hawking the Presidential Medal of Freedom, the highest honor a civilian can receive in the United States.

On March 14, 2018, Hawking died. He lived for more than 50 years after he was diagnosed with ALS. At the end, he could not speak or move his limbs. In his last years, he communicated by squeezing his cheek muscles and "blinking" an infra-red switch that was activated and he was able to scan and select characters on the screen in order to compose speeches, surf the internet, send emails and "speak" through a voice synthesizer (University of Washington 2021). His body was cheated out of physical movement but his intellect was not impaired.

As we shall see in the following pages, Hawking found a way to make many hugely significant contributions to cosmology, physics and science in general. His embracement of popular culture helped to solidify his status as a cultural icon. His book *A Brief History of Time* (1988), a landmark volume in science writing and in world-wide acclaim and popularity spent 147 weeks on the *New York Times* bestseller list and a record-breaking 237 weeks on the *Times of London* bestseller list and has sold more than 10 million copies. Some sources state that more than 25 million copies have been sold (Durrani 2018).

Promoting a Theory of Everything

The primary relevancy of Stephen Hawking to this book is his promotion and attempt to establish a "theory of everything." In Chapter 7 we learned of Einstein's attempt to establish a theory of everything via a unified field theory. Einstein updated Newton's theories of gravity and time and space via his mathematical theory of "special relativity" (introduced in 1905), the first step toward his "theory of relativity" (the second step was the "general theory of relativity," developed between 1905 and 1915). He had unified space and time with his special theory of relativity in 1905 and furthered unified space and time with gravitation in his general theory of relativity in 1915, so it seemed clear to Einstein that he could utilize his theory of relativity to unify all the forces of Nature in order to establish a theory of everything in his attempt to explain the physical universe. Einstein concluded that the universe is dynamic, that is to say, expanding or contracting. Einstein's research helped to create the field of *theoretical physics cosmology*. (Cosmology, in terms of trying to comprehend the meaning of the universe, has been around for tens of thousands of years.) As White and Gribbin (1992) explain, "Cosmology is the study of the Universe at large, its beginning, its evolution, and its ultimate fate. In terms of ideas, it is the biggest of big science.... More than any other branch of science [however], cosmology can be studied by using the mind alone. This is just as true today as it was seventy-five years ago, when Albert Einstein developed the general theory of relativity, and thereby invented the science of theoretical cosmology" (p. 21). Smeenk (2017) explains that cosmology, which began as a branch of theoretical physics through Einstein's work, is a science that, due to both theoretical and observational developments, has made enormous strides in the past 100 years.

As established previously in this chapter, Hawking was a cosmologist—having obtained his physics doctorate from Cambridge University with a specialty in general relativity and cosmology—and since the field of cosmology involves the scientific study of the large scale properties of the Universe as a whole it is easily understandable that he would endeavor to establish a theory that could explain everything—the origin of the universe, its evolution and its ultimate fate. In the Preface to his *Black Holes and Baby Universes and Other Essays* (1993), Hawking states, "I do not agree with the view that the universe is a mystery, something that one can have intuition about but never fully analyze or comprehend. I feel that this view does not do justice to the scientific revolution that was started almost four hundred years ago by Galileo and carried on by Newton" (p. viii). Hawking continues by pointing out that these early scientists showed that at least some areas of the universe do not behave in an arbitrary manner but are governed by precise mathematical laws. We have since established mathematical laws that govern everything we normally experience. Hawking (1993) acknowledged more than thirty years ago that there is still a great deal that we don't know or understand about the universe; but, the remarkable progress we have made, particularly in the last hundred years, should encourage us to believe that a complete understanding may not be beyond our powers. It is no wonder, then, that Hawking believed he could create a "theory of everything."

Hawking's "theory of everything" is one wherein all of physics is explained by combining quantum mechanics and Einstein's theory of relativity into a unified approach which explains the laws of the Universe (Powers 2018). The importance of incorporating quantum mechanics in his theory of everything is that it is a field of physics that describes the forces of nature that are very small; it explains how extremely small objects simultaneously have the characteristics of both particles (tiny pieces of matter) and waves (a disturbance or variation that transfers energy) that physicists refer to as "wave-particle duality" (Department of Energy 2023; Ferguson 2012). Hawking's theory of everything was a big picture view of the Universe while incorporating the role of even the smallest particles within it.

Not all physicists believe that it is possible to create a "theory of everything." They are not even sure such a theory can theoretically exist, for that matter. However, the more brilliant among us, people like Einstein, Hawking and Kaku will see it as a challenge to try and establish such a theory.

Quantum Theory and Quantum Mechanics

In his quest to establish a theory of everything Hawking, like most theorists in the mid- and late-twentieth century attempted to combine quantum theory and relativity theory into one complete, unified theory—Einstein himself spent the last three decades of his working life on this problem but failed to come up with a solution. A full theory of quantum gravity still eludes mathematicians. Focusing on how relativity and quantum mechanics interacted at the beginning of time, Hawking was able to make progress to such an extent that by the early 1980s he was posing the question of whether there ever had been a beginning to time at all (White and Gribbin 1992). To understand how he came to this startling hypothesis we have to look at quantum theory as developed by the outstanding American physicist Richard Feynman, an approach known as the "sum-over-histories" or "path integral" approach (White and Gribbin 1992:176). In simplest terms, Feynman was saying that particles do not have one history but rather have every possible history. This means that scientists cannot say exactly how a particle traveled from point A to point B, but by calculating all the possible routes from A to B, they can find the most likely path. Such a vague approach in physics underscores a fundamental difference between classical physics and quantum theory and quantum mechanics as, in the quantum world, certain predictions can only be made in terms of probabilities. Classical physics would provide a precise answer to the question as how long it takes a particle to travel from A to B based on the particle's initial velocity and the forces acting on it. In quantum theory, it is possible to merely give a probability that the particle in question can be detected at any given location at any time (Pössel 2006). In string theory, "the probability of given string interactions can be calculated as a path integral—in addition to all possibilities a string can travel through space, the sum is over all possibilities the string can deform and wiggle on the way" (Pössel 2006).

It was pointed out earlier in this text that quantum theory and quantum mechanics (and string theory, for that matter) is often incomprehensible. "Niels Bohr, one of the physicists who pioneered the quantum revolution used to say that 'anyone who is not shocked by quantum theory has not understood it,' while Feynman, probably, the greatest theoretical physicist since the Second World War, went even further, and was fond of saying that nobody understands quantum mechanics" (White and Gribbin 1992:177). White and Gribbin (1992) put forth the notion that it is not important to fully understand how *wave-particle duality* can occur, but to find a set of equations that describe what is going on and make it possible for physicists to predict how electrons, light waves, and the rest will behave. "The sum-over-histories approach was Feynman's contribution to this more pragmatic form of 'understanding' at the quantum level, and in the late 1970s Hawking applied it to the study of the Big Bang" (White and Gribbin 1992:177). Starting with black hole singularities, Hawking applied the quantum approach to calculating the history of the entire Universe.

Origin of the Universe

In a lecture given at the "Three Hundred Years of Gravity" conference held in Cambridge in June 1987, on the three hundredth anniversary of the publication of Newton's *Principia*, Stephen Hawking (1993) described the problem of explaining the origin of the Universe as a bit like the old question: Which came first, the chicken or the egg? "In other words, what agency created the Universe, and what created that agency? Or perhaps the Universe, or the agency that created it, existed forever and didn't need to be created" (Hawking 1993:85). One of the biggest challenges in establishing a theory of everything, Hawking reasons, is scientists tend to shy away from such questions, feeling that they belong to metaphysics or religion rather than to science (Hawkings 1993). However, Hawking points out that science has made huge strides in establishing laws that can explain the mysteries of time and space.

Hawking states that early on there were basically two schools of thought about whether and how the Universe began. The first school of thought reflects many early traditions, such as the Jewish, Christian and Islamic religions, which held that the universe was created in the fairly recent past (6–7,000 years ago). The second school of thought dates back to people such as Aristotle who, because he did not like the idea of an implied divine intervention involved with the creation of the Universe, preferred to promote the idea that the universe has always existed and would exist forever. This perspective also generally incorporates the idea that human progress is achieved following natural disasters that set the human race right back to the beginning (Hawking 1993). Both of these schools of thought resulted in the same ultimate conclusion that the universe was essentially unchanging with time. Either it was created in its present form, or it has endured forever as it has today (through a series of quasi-reboots). Whether one chooses to believe that the universe was a recent creation or has existed forever was a matter of religion or metaphysics, respectively.

This Side A or Side B option gets more complicated with time. In 1781, philosopher Immanuel Kant wrote his famous *The Critique of Pure Reason* and stated that there were equally valid arguments both for believing that the universe had a beginning and for believing that it did not. His analysis was based on reason, not on empirical observations of the Universe. Reason, according to Kant dictated that if the universe was unchanging, what is there to observe (Hawking 1993)?

By the nineteenth century, empirical science had entered the arena of the beginning, evolution and fate of the universe. Geologists realized that based on rock formations and fossils the earth would have had to have existed for hundreds or thousands of millions of years. This type of scientific factual information was not accepted by creationists, in fact, there are still some people today who cannot accept scientific truths. Other scientific discoveries of note by such scientists as Newton and Einstein have already been discussed in this text so let's jump ahead to the importance that Hawking places on Edwin Hubble's 1929 discovery of the expansion of the Universe. With the knowledge that we have today, NASA (2023) explains that Hubble had proven that not only was our Universe home to millions of other galaxies, but the Universe itself was expanding as well. Hubble studied the light emitted from various galaxies and discovered that the light appeared displaced toward the red end of the spectrum. "It became apparent that our universe was ceaselessly expanding outward, and all galaxies housed within it were moving away from one another. This phenomenon, known as redshift, reveals that the farther a galaxy is away from us, the redder its light will appear…. The idea of an expanding universe is a key underpinning of the Big Bang Theory. Hubble's observations provided the earliest insight into the origins of our universe" (NASA 2023). Hawking had zeroed in on the Hubble's ideas as to the origin of the universe as the notion of galaxies being on top of each other between ten and twenty thousand million years ago. "At this time, a singularity called the big bang, the density of the universe and the curvature of space-time would have been infinite. Under such conditions, all of the known laws of science would break down" (Hawking 1993:89).

As described earlier in this chapter, Hawking wrote his dissertation thesis on the ideas of Penrose's theory of space-time singularity. His work with Penrose led to the development of a new set of mathematical techniques for dealing with the origin of universe using singularity. Their work showed that there was an implied beginning to space and time—the Big Bang—and an end, through black holes, but it could not predict how the universe *should* begin (anyone seeking the answer to that question should seek religious guidance) (Hawking 1993).

The influence of Feynman's sum-over-histories idea (that every particle has every possible path, or history, in space-time) has been discussed. Hawking was also influenced by Jim Hartle (a frequent collaborator) and the two collaborated on an article entitled "Wave Function of the Universe" (1983). Hawking (1993) describes how they proposed that the state of the universe should be given by a sum over a certain class of histories. This class consisted of curved spaces without singularities, which were of finite size but which did not have boundaries or edges. The "no-boundary proposal" envisions the cosmos having the shape of a shuttlecock. "Just as a shuttlecock has a diameter of zero at its bottommost point and gradually widens on the way up, the universe, according to the no-boundary proposal, smoothly expanded from a point of zero size" (Wolchover 2019). Hartle and Hawking derived a formula describing the whole shuttlecock—the "wave function of the universe" that encompasses the entire past, present and future at once—making moot any need for speculation of the origin of creation, a creator, or any transition from a time before (Wolchover 2019). The no-boundary proposal makes it clear that it is pointless to ask what came before the Big Bang as there is no notion of time available to refer to, Hawking said at a lecture at the Pontifical Academy in 2016. "It would be like asking what lies south of the South Pole" (Wolchover 2019).

Hawking (1993) points out that while science may solve the problems of how the Universe began, it cannot answer the question: Why does the Universe bother to exist?

A Brief History of Time

Hawking's career was centered on establishing a "Theory of Everything" that could explain such big picture questions as "What is the Origin of the Universe?" and "What is the Fate of the Universe?" His significant publications were works toward answering these and other such grand questions. Some of his works have been mentioned already but a few more and one in particular, stand out and deserve special recognition here as they provided us with great insights on such concepts as the "Big Bang" theory, black holes and singularities.

Hawking's first published book (co-authored with G.F.R. Ellis and others) was *The Large Scale Structure of Space-Time* (1973). In this extremely technical book, Einstein's general theory of relativity is applied in the authors' research on black holes in space and singularities are explored. As described in the Preface, the authors conclude that Einstein's general theory of relativity leads to two remarkable predictions about the universe: first, that the final fate of massive stars is to collapse behind an event horizon to form a "black hole" which will contain a singularity; and secondly, that there is a singularity in our past which constitutes, in some sense, a beginning to the universe.

In 1981, Hawking (and Martin Rocek) published *Superspace and Supergravity: Proceedings of the Nuffield Workshop* which involved a collection of highly technical pedagogical lectures given at a workshop on how to devise a new theory of gravity. *Superspace* and *supergravity* are concepts that could help Hawking and others try to explain the make-up and origin of the universe. *Superspace* was first used by John Wheeler (see his co-authored book, *Gravitation*) to describe the configuration space of Einstein's general relativity theory. Hawking and others were applying the concept of *superspace* to research in curved space-time. In their Introduction of *Superspace and Supergravity*, Hawking and Rocek (1981) put forth the notion that supergravity theories could better explain the many divergences that plague quantum field theory than could other gravitational theories (i.e., Newtonian).

The most famous and significant publication by Hawking was *A Brief History of Time* (1988), a book that has sold over 10 million copies. As Hawking (2001) wrote in the Foreword of *The Universe in a Nutshell*, he never expected the book to be so popular and yet there it was, on the *London Sunday Times* bestseller list for over four years, which was longer than any other book had been and was certainly remarkable for a book on science that was not easy going. *A Brief History of Time* was organized in a linear fashion, with most chapters following and logically depending on the preceding chapters. This appealed to some readers but Hawking (2001) believed that others "got stuck in the early chapters and never reached the more exciting material later on" (p. vii).

In 1996, the illustrated, updated and expanded version of *A Brief History of Time* was published as *The Illustrated A Brief History of Time* and that is the edition we will look at here. In this edition of *A Brief History*, Hawking acknowledges again that he was surprised by the popularity of the original text, especially because much of the material was very technical and science-driven. And yet, Hawking surmised that the success of the book could be attributed to the public's interest in such profound questions as "Where did we come from?" "And why is the universe the way it is?" In this illustrated and updated version of *A Brief History*, Hawking attempted to make the material more accessible to the everyday reader. However, the key concepts and areas of science that drove Hawking in his quest to explain the mysteries of the origin and fate of the universe abound.

In Chapter 1, "Our Picture of the Universe," Hawking describes the evolution of scientific theories over the centuries beginning with Aristotle and going on to such other theorists as Copernicus, Galileo, Johannes Kepler, Newton, Kant, Hubble, and Charles Darwin. Hawking describes how scientists are still trying to finish Einstein's dream of a unified field theory that could describe everything in the Universe. In Chapter 2, "Space and Time," Hawking describes in great detail and illustration the development of scientific thought on the nature of space-time, curvature and geodesics (the shortest possible line between two points on a sphere or other curved surface). This chapter concluded with Hawking pointing out that he and Penrose showed that Einstein's general theory of relativity implied that the universe must have a beginning and possibly, an end. Much of the material found in Chapter 3, "The Expanding Universe," has been described previously and can be summarized as a chapter that explains how, in less than half a century, humanity's view of the universe, formed over millennia, has been transformed. "Hubble's discovery that the universe was expanding, and the realization of the insignificance of our own planet in the vastness of the universe, were just the starting point. As experimental and theoretical evidence mounted, it became more and more clear that the universe must have had a beginning in time, until in 1970 this was finally proved by Penrose and myself, on the basis of Einstein's general theory of relativity" (Hawking 1996:67). However, Hawking pointed out that beginning in the 1970s it became necessary to turn our understanding of the universe from the extraordinarily vast to the extraordinarily time. To do this, quantum mechanics (discussed in Chapter 4) would be applied to the study of the Universe. Combining theories of the vast with those of the tiny into a single quantum theory of gravity was Hawking's goal. Hawking also discussed the "uncertainty principle" formulated by German scientist Werner Heisenberg, according to which the speed and position of a particle cannot be precisely known due to Planck's quantum hypothesis.

In Chapter 5, "Elementary Particles and Forces of Nature," Hawking traces the history of the investigation of the nature of matter, Aristotle's four elements; Democritus's notion of indivisible atoms; John Dalton's ideas about atoms always combining in certain groupings to form molecules; J.J. Thomson's discovery of the existence of a particle of matter called electrons that resided inside atoms; Ernest Rutherford's discovery of atomic nucleus and protons; James Chadwick's discovery of neutrons; Murray Gell-Mann's research on smaller quarks; the discovery of a variety of quarks (referred to as six "flavors"); and antiquarks (as the universe expanded and cooled, the antiquarks would annihilate with the quarks but there would be more quarks than antiquarks).

Black holes will be discussed later in this chapter but that was the topic of Chapters 6 and 7. Hawking gives credit to American scientist John Wheeler for coining the term "black hole" but states that the idea itself goes back at least 200 years to a time when there were two theories about light: one, which Newton favored, was that it was composed of particles; the other was that it was made of waves. "We now know that really both theories are correct. By the wave/particle duality of quantum mechanics, light can be regarded as both a wave and a particle" (Hawking 1996:104). Hawking explains in this chapter that to understand how a black hole might be formed, we first need an understanding of the life cycle of a star; he explains this cycle. Hawking describes black holes as regions of space-time where extremely strong gravity prevents everything, including light from escaping from within them and explains that they form during the collapse of massive stars. Hawking also describes *wormholes* (a hypothetical connection between widely separated regions of space-time) and the possibility of astronauts falling through one and coming out in another region of the universe. In Chapter 7 ("Black Holes Ain't So Black"), Hawking describes how black holes are not actually black after all, they glow like a hot body, and the smaller they are, the more they glow. Thus, and paradoxically, smaller black holes might actually be easier to detect than large ones. Hawking believes that black holes consist of radiation and because of this, they will "evaporate" over time, rather than continue to exist forever as scientists had previously believed.

"The Origin and Fate of the Universe" is the title of Chapter 8 of *A Brief History* and in this chapter, Hawking describes how the universe began with the "Big Bang" and how the Universe would have likely appeared differently if it grew in size slower or faster than it actually did—in brief, the Universe would likely have collapsed if it grew slower or had been almost empty if it grew faster. In Chapter 9, "The Arrow of Time," Hawking describes "arrows of time" as bits of understanding of the world (there are three arrows: the thermodynamic arrow of time; the psychological arrow of time; and the cosmological arrow of time). His "no boundary proposal" implies that the universe will expand for some time before contracting back again. His ultimate goal in trying to understand the arrows of time is its incorporation into a complete unified theory that would explain everything in the universe. Chapter 10 ("Wormholes and Time Travel") is a topic that piques the interest of scientists and nonscientists alike as the idea of time travel, despite the impracticality of the notion, is one that intrigues many people, and the existence, or creation of, wormholes that violate space-time dimensions is itself captivating. Utilizing his *chronology protection conjecture* leads Hawking to conclude that it is certainly impossible to travel to the past and doubts it'll ever be possible to travel to the future. In the final chapter, "The Unification of Physics," Hawking ponders whether there will ever be a unifying theory in physics. Hawking states that it would be very difficult to construct a complete unified theory of everything in the universe all at once so instead he has made progress toward this goal in a step-by-step format. He did not accomplish this goal before his death. Hawking did state, however, "If we do discover a complete theory, it should in time be understandable in broad principle by everyone, not just a few scientists. Then we shall all, philosophers, scientists, and just ordinary people, be able to take part in the discussion of the question of why it is that we and the universe exist" (Hawking 1996:233).

It should be noted that a film *A Brief History of Time* was released in 1991 based on the life and work of the cosmologist, Stephen Hawking. Unlike the book, this film was really a biography of Stephen Hawking and includes clips of his lectures, interviews with friends and family, along with some physics. The film also depicts Hawkings struggles to overcome his paralysis and how he managed to excel in spite of his physical challenges.

In 2001, *The Universe in a Nutshell* was published and in it Hawking returns with an illustrated sequel and variation of *A Brief History of Time* describing the breakthroughs that had occurred in the years since the release of his acclaimed work. Hawking discusses advancements from supergravity to supersymmetry, from quantum theory to M-theory, and from holography to duality. He describes the new frontiers of science where superstring theory and p-branes may hold the final clue to the puzzle and advances his latest attempt to combine Einstein's general theory of relativity and Feynman's idea of multiple histories into one complete unified theory that will describe everything that happens in the universe. In 2002, *The Universe in a Nutshell* was awarded the Aventis science book prize and praised for making such a complex subject matter more accessible for all readers (Yates 2002).

The "Big Bang"

To this point, it has been established that Fred Hoyle, a British astronomer, coined the term "Big Bang" theory. Hoyle was always convinced that the Universe is indeed expanding, but the density of the matter is invariable, because of the homogeneous development of new matter at all times—known as the "Steady State" theory established by Hoyle and his former colleagues Herman Bondi and Thomas Gold (Sack 2018). Any notion of an event akin to a "big bang" was mostly just a mathematical game played by a few experts, as much as anything for their own amusement, even at the beginning of the 1960s (White and Gribbin 1992). Hawking took note during his days at Oxford and obviously while at Cambridge that the cosmologists were beginning to believe in the notion of the "Big Bang" theory as a plausible explanation for starting point of the Universe. This inspired more theoretical calculations, leading to new predictions, and more observations, including those by Hawking himself. Inspired by the Penrose theory of space-time singularity, Hawking would write his dissertation thesis (1965) on the topic and his theory reversed the direction of time, and considered what would happen if a point of infinite density and infinite curvature of space-time—a singularity—exploded outwards and expanded. "I was interested in the question of whether there had been a big bang singularity, because that was crucial to an understanding of the origin of the universe. Together with Roger Penrose, I developed a new set of mathematical techniques for dealing with this and similar problems" (Hawking 1993:91). This Big Bang explosion, Hawking reasoned, would be the explanation as to how the universe began. By the time Hawking promoted the no-boundary proposal it was clear that the "Big Bang" theory was *the* explanation for the beginning of the universe. Hawking said of the "Big Bang's" mainstream popularity of the 1970s: "By 1976, the Big Bang theory was so well established that American physicist Steven Weinberg was able to write a best-selling popular book, *The First Three Minutes*, describing the early stages of the Big Bang, how the Universe had emerged from the superdome state of the cosmic egg" (White and Gribbin 1992: 81–82).

Hawking explains the "Big Bang" theory and how it is responsible for the origin of the Universe: One-tenth of a second after the "the beginning" (or after the "bounce," as many cosmologists of the 1960s would have argued), some 15 billion years ago, the density of the Universe was 30 million times greater than the density of water. The temperature was 30 billion degrees (in kelvin, denoted by the letter K), and the Universe consisted of a mixture of very high energy radiation (photons) and material particles including neutrons, protons and electrons, but also more exotic, unstable particles created ephemerally out of pure radiation. (Think Einstein's $E=mc^2$.) One second later, the Universe had cooled dramatically—all the way down to ten billion K. At that time, the density was just 380,000 times the density of water. The first nuclei of deuterium formed just 14 seconds from the beginning. Hydrogen, the simplest atom, formed first. Just 3 minutes and 2 seconds after the Big Bang, the temperature had cooled to below one billion K. At this point, almost all the deuterium nuclei were able to combine in pairs to form nuclei of helium. Thirty-four minutes after the Big Bang, the temperature was down to 300 million K and the density of the Universe was only 10 per cent of the density of water but it took a further 700,000 years for the Universe to cool enough to allow electrons to become attached to the nuclei and form stable atoms. At this point, the temperature of the Universe had fallen to about 4,000 K (roughly the temperature at the surface of the Sun today), and nuclei and electrons were at last able to hold together to form stable atoms (White and Gribbin 1992).

Hawking explains, for most of the past 15 billion years, protons, neutrons and electrons have been bound up in stars and galaxies formed out of this primeval stuff as gravity pulled clouds of gas together in space (White and Gribbin 1992). The "Big Bang" had done its job, it created the Universe. What could end the Universe? Black holes.

Black Holes

"More than anything else, Hawking's name is associated with black holes—another kind of singularity, formed when a star undergoes complete collapse under its own gravity" (May 2021). In *The Illustrated A Brief History of Time* (1996), Hawking describes black holes as regions of space-time where extremely strong gravity prevents everything, including light from escaping from within them and explains that they form during the collapse of massive stars. Hawking suggested that the formation of the earliest black holes occurred in the chaotic environment of the earliest moments of the "Big Bang" and that numerous objects containing as much as one billion tons of mass but occupying only the space of a proton developed. These objects were called *mini black holes* and were unique in that their immense mass and gravity require that they be ruled by the laws of relativity, while their minute size requires that the laws of quantum mechanics apply to them also (Tikkanen 2023).

Hawking worked primarily in the field of general relativity and particularly on the physics of black holes. In 1971, Hawking proposed the "Black-Hole Area Theorem," also known as the "Second Law of Black Hole Mechanics," which states that the total horizon area of a classical black hole cannot decrease over time. In 2021, a team of U.S. physicists confirmed it for the first time using observations of the gravitational wave event GW150914 (Isi, Farr, Giesler, Scheel and Teukolsky 2021). Hawking's theorem was a parallel of the second law of thermodynamics, which states that the entropy, or degree of disorder within an object, should never decrease.

In 1974, however, Hawking argued that black holes could have entropy and emit radiation over very long timescales if their quantum effects were taken into account. This phenomenon was dubbed "Hawking radiation" and remains one of the most fundamental revelations about black holes. MIT physicist Maximilian Isi states that it all started with Hawking's realization that the total horizon area in black holes can never go down. The gravitation wave signal research conducted by Isi and associates indicates that black holes can generate a new black hole, along with a huge amount of energy that rippled across space-time as gravitational waves. The horizon area of the new black hole, however, would not be smaller than the total horizon area of its parent black holes. This phenomenon is something Hawking calculated in 1974, in accordance with the predictions of quantum theory, that black holes emit subatomic particles until they exhaust their energy and finally explode. Another aspect of the Hawking radiation, as mentioned earlier in this chapter, is that black holes are not completely black. A black hole can glow, like an ember, or if it is hot enough, you can have a *white* black hole. A white black hole would have the size of a bacterium but the mass of a continent; such black holes, while theoretically possible, are not known to be naturally produced anywhere in the universe (Maldacena 2011). (For a fuller understanding of black holes see Hawking's explanation in *The Illustrated A Brief History of Time*.)

Hawking's contributions to the study of black holes in the 1970s were considered revolutionary and earned him many exceptional honors and accolades, for example, in 1974 the Royal Society (the oldest national scientific society in Britain) elected him one of its youngest fellows.

Fate of the Universe

When looking at the future, or the fate, of the Universe, Hawking (1993) states that scientists believe that the Universe is governed by well-defined laws that in principle allow one to predict the future. "But the motion given by the laws is often chaotic. This means that a tiny change in the initial situation can lead to change in the subsequent behavior that rapidly grows large. Thus, in practice, one can often predict accurately only a fairly short time into the future. However, the behavior of the universe on a very large scale seems to be simple, and not chaotic" (Hawking 1993: 154–155). Hawking adds, "One can therefore predict whether the universe will expand forever or whether it will recollapse eventually. This depends on the present density of the universe. In fact, the present density seems to be very close to the critical density that separates recollapse from indefinite expansion. If the theory of inflation is correct, the universe is actually on the knife edge" (Hawking 1993:155). Hawking seems to be on the verge of predicting doom for the Universe but instead he cops out by saying, "So I am in the well-established tradition of oracles and prophets of hedging my bets by predicting both ways" (Hawking 1993:155).

In *The Illustrated A Brief History of Time* (1996), Hawking describes the possible role of God, or a god, in the Universe (he discussed God a number of times when writing about the "Big Bang") in relation to the closed surface theory. "The idea that space and time may form a closed surface without boundary also has profound implications for the role of God in the affairs of the universe. With the success of scientific theories in describing events, most people have come to believe that God allows the universe to evolve according to a set of laws and does not intervene in the universe to break those laws. However, the laws do not tell us what the universe should have looked like when it started—it would still be up to God to wind up the clockwork and choose how to start it off" (Hawking 1996:181). This is when Hawking (1996) gets profound by adding, "But, if the universe is really completely self-contained, having no boundary or edge, it would have neither beginning nor end: it would simply be. What place then, for a creator?" (p. 181).

In *The Universe in a Nutshell* (2001), Hawking is a little more precise with his predictions of the future as he ponders whether society will be a safe and comforting vision like that portrayed in *Star Trek* (Hawking admits to be being a fan of the franchise and he appeared in an episode of *Star Trek: The Next Generation*). Hawking concludes that the future of science won't be like the comforting picture painted in *Star Trek*: a universe populated by many humanoid races, with an advanced but essentially static science and technology. "Not much of this will happen in the next hundred years, which is all we can reliably predict. But by the end of the next millennium, if we get there, the difference from *Star Trek* will be fundamental" (Hawking 2001:171).

Hawking made a very bold prediction about the fate of Earth just prior to his death. Making a video appearance at the Tencent WE Summit in Beijing in November 2017, Hawking warned that the human race will perish on Earth after we turn it into a sizzling fireball in less than 600 years. He declared that humans must "boldly go where no one has gone before" if we hope to continue our species (Murphy 2017). In other words, humans needed to colonize other planets in order to survive as a species. (Notice how in the early twenty-first century, there has been increased attention given to travel to outer space.) He cited sociological concerns of overcrowding and increased energy consumption as the major causes of turning the planet into a ball of fire (Murphy 2017).

So, there you go. For anyone who wanted something more specific from Hawking in terms of what he thought was going to happen in the future, he does not predict the fate of the Universe but he does say that Earth will be a fireball by 2600 because of human behavior. At least he factored humans into his "theory of everything" a little bit.

A Theory of Everything Revisited

Hawking chased a dream of creating a "Theory of Everything." Every year, every scientific discovery made by him and other scientists seemed to shine a brighter light of hope onto that dream. In 2001, Hawking wrote, "In 1988 when *A Brief History of Time* was first published, the ultimate Theory of Everything seemed to be just over the horizon" (p. viii). In 1993, the first edition of Hawking's *New York Times* bestseller book *Black Holes and Baby Universes* was published. This book consists of 13 essays that, among other things, helped to transform the way people thought about physics; explained how black holes can give birth to baby universes; and provided an understanding of our universe and reality itself. It also reflected Hawking's belief that a "Theory of Everything" was certainly possible and in reach. Such a theory, Hawking believed, would help to explain everything in the Universe.

First published in 2002, Hawking provides us with an even clearer view of his vision of the Universe and his hope for a unified theory in *The Theory of Everything: The Origin and Fate of the Universe*. Based on a series of seven lectures that he gave at Cambridge University, Hawking explains his views on the history of the Universe; the most important scientific theories about space, time and the cosmos; the role of General Relativity; the "Big Bang"; and the life cycle of a star. In this book, Hawking is still mostly optimistic that science will discover the ultimate laws of nature. There are hints that he no longer believes he will be the one to establish the "Theory of Everything" as he believes that a unified theory will occur one day if our level of intelligence increases. Even then, a theory of everything would really be an infinite sequence of theories with each describing the Universe with more accuracy than the previous theory. (In 2014 a film titled *The Theory of Everything*, a biographical romantic drama film set at the University of Cambridge details the life of the theoretical physicist Stephen Hawking adapted from Jane Hawking's *Traveling to Infinity: My Life with Stephen* was released.)

In yet another *New York Times* bestseller, *The Grand Design* (2012), co-authored with Leonard Mlodinow, Hawking again writes about the origin of the Universe but also discusses how quantum theory predicts the "multiverse"—the idea that our universe is just one of many universes that appeared spontaneously out of nothing, each with different laws of nature. Such a notion alters his earlier conception of a "Theory of Everything." *Brief Answers to the Big Questions* (2018), yet another *New York Times* bestseller for Hawking, is a publication by Hawking that addresses the possible fate of the Universe by asking such questions as "Will humanity survive?," "Should humans colonize space?," and "Does God exist?"

Hawking's "Theory of Everything" relies on several assumptions. Toward the end of his life he began to doubt if he could ever complete such a theory especially in light of Kurt Gödel's "Incompleteness Theorems" (there were two of them and they were concerned with the limits of provability in formal axiomatic theories) that implies that pure mathematics is exhaustible; meaning that, no matter how many problems one solves, other problems (e.g., pertaining to the laws of physics) will remain. Thus, one could never allow for *everything* and therefore a theory of everything would be impossible.

As with Einstein before him, Hawking failed to establish a "Theory of Everything."

Summary

Stephen Hawking was born on January 8, 1942, in Oxford, Oxfordshire, England and is perhaps the most unique of all geniuses discussed in this text as he was able to communicate his intellectual brilliance despite the challenges of having the ALS (amyotrophic lateral sclerosis) disease nearly his entire adult life.

Hawking was distinctive too in the manner that he presented his academic findings in that some of his publications were considered too technical for the average person to comprehend while other publications contained scientific breakthroughs in book form filled with illustrations. Hawking also enjoyed being a part of the world of popular culture endearing himself to those who might not otherwise know how to relate to him.

Classically educated at Oxford and Cambridge, Hawking sought out early to try and explain the origin and fate of the Universe. He planned on transforming this information into a unified "Theory of Everything." Hawking obtained his Ph.D. in applied mathematics and theoretical physics, specializing in general relativity and cosmology. His 1966 essay, "Singularities and the Geometry of Space-Time" won him the prestigious Adams Prize and was a sign of things to come. Hawking's "Theory of Everything" is one wherein all of physics is explained by combining the quantum mechanics and general relativity theory into a unified approach which explains the laws of the universe. His hugely best-selling *A Brief History of Time* helped to explain such profound questions about the origin and fate of the universe.

It is his work on the "Big Bang" theory and black holes that makes Hawking so famous. Working with mathematician Roger Penrose and incorporating aspects of Einstein's general theory of relativity, Hawking developed a new set of mathematical techniques for establishing the beginning of time—this beginning was the result of a big bang explosion. Aspects of the Big Bang are explained in this chapter. The end of time would come about because of black holes. Hawking revolutionized the study of black holes.

The chapter concluded with a final look at Hawking's view of the fate of the universe and his thoughts about whether or not a theory of everything in physics was possible.

At age 76, Hawking died at his home in Cambridge, England.

It is worth noting that Hawking never won a Nobel Prize in Physics and this seems harder to believe than Oppenheimer having never won a Nobel (see Chapter 3). There are a number of speculative reasons given as to why he never won a Nobel but there was some vindication and round-about recognition of his work when in 2020 Roger Penrose shared (not with Hawking but with Reinhard Genzel and Andrea Ghez) the Prize for his research on black holes proving that they could exist according to the theory of general relativity—something he worked on with Hawking—and that they are connected to the creation and fate of the Universe.

9

Michio Kaku:
A Theory of Everything
via Superstring Theory

Introduction

Trying to establish an all-encompassing hypothetical framework that would explain the physics of the entire Universe in a single "Theory of Everything," as we found out in the preceding two chapters, eluded the combined genius of Albert Einstein and Stephen Hawking. Who would next dare try to establish a "Theory of Everything?" Would someone step up to the plate and attempt such feat? The answer is yes and his name is Michio Kaku.

Kaku's interest in developing a theory of everything came about when he was in fourth grade and read about the death of Albert Einstein who was described as a wonderful scientist. He learned that Einstein discovered many great things in his lifetime that made him world famous but that he died before he could finish his greatest work—establishing a unified field theory (a theory that would unify the four fundamental forces of the universe: the strong nuclear force, the weak nuclear force, gravity and electromagnetism). Curious about Einstein and his unified field theory, Kaku searched the Palo Alto libraries to try and find more information about unified field theory but he couldn't locate any books or articles on the subject. He did come across a few college texts on quantum mechanics but at age eight, Michio found them largely incomprehensible. Additionally, they didn't make even a passing reference to the unified field theory (Kaku and Thompson 1995).

Michio would turn to his teachers, who had no answers for him. As he got older and met physicists, they too were of no help when he asked about Einstein's unified field theory. Most physicists, Kaku found, felt that Einstein was either too far ahead of his time or that it was downright presumptuous to believe that anyone could unite the four forces in the Universe (Kaku and Thompson 1995). Kaku decided early on to make it his mission to complete Einstein's quest of a unified field theory and he felt that string theory would be the tool that would help him accomplish that goal. By the 1980s, Kaku had begun to lose hope on this idea and then he found the theoretical breakthrough he was looking for, "superstrings." Physicists

John Schwartz and Joel Scherk had predicted in the 1970s that "strings" could be the theoretical answer in advancing physics.

As we shall learn in this chapter, Kaku, arguably among the most brilliant physicists alive today, not only attempted to unite the four forces of Nature as Einstein had attempted, he did so as a proponent of superstring theory. We will also learn about symmetry and supersymmetry; the idea of the existence of multiple dimensions and parallel worlds; the Big Bang; robots and Artificial Intelligence (AI); humanity's future; the end of the universe; and whether or not a theory of everything is possible.

Biography

Theoretical physicist Michio Kaku was born on January 24, 1947, in San Jose, California. His Japanese parents are of Tibetan ancestry. His grandfather immigrated to the United States to help with the 1906 cleanup operation for the San Francisco earthquake (Famous Scientists 2024a). Kaku's parents were *kibei*—a term often used in the 1940s to describe Japanese Americans born in the United States who returned to America after receiving their education in Japan. Their *kibei* status was part of the reason the U.S. government confined them in a concentration camp during World War II (Encyclopedia.com 2019a). Following the war, Kaku's father, Toshio, went to work as a gardener and his mother, Hideok (maiden name, Maruyama) as a maid. When Michio was born, his parents worked hard to provide their son with the very best possible opportunities for higher education.

Growing up as a child, Michio loved science fiction shows and books that were filled with time-traveling heroes, parallel universes and intergalactic space travel. Kaku found magic, fantasy and science fiction stimuli for his active imagination and led to his lifelong love and pursuit to study the impossible. As he grew older, he put science fiction aside and turned to physics in order to pursue the study of the impossible (American Physical Society 2024). Kaku states, "Without a solid background in advanced physics, I would be forever speculating about futuristic technologies without understanding whether or not they were possible. I realized [to know,] I needed to immerse myself in advanced mathematics and learn theoretical physics. So that is what I did" (American Physical Society 2024).

A key and specific influence on the young Kaku was Albert Einstein. On the day Einstein died (April 18, 1955), Michio's teachers told his class that the physicist had died before he could complete his biggest discovery—a "theory of everything." Michio was fascinated by this story and focused on the part of how Einstein had never finished his theory. As a young grade school student Kaku began his quest to learn more about Einstein and his work. "Although his family was poor, they whole-heartedly supported Michio's curiosity, letting him build experiments in the house and taking him to local university libraries. Michio was determined to understand what this incomplete theory was all about" (American Physical Society 2024).

By the time Kaku got to high school, he had fully developed his passion for physics and his parents were supporting him any way they could. For example, they helped him construct a huge electron volt accelerator for a science fair. "Michio constructed a 2.3eV atom smasher in his garage. This particle accelerator was made of 400 pounds of scrap metal, 22 miles of copper wire, and generated a magnetic field 20,000 times greater than the Earth's" (American Physical Society 2024). Michio explained to *Asian Week* reporter Jon Matsumoto, "We were on the football field at Palo Alto, winding twenty-two miles of copper wire! The magnetic field it finally created was so powerful that if you put DC into it and you had fillings in your teeth, it would literally rip the metal out of your mouth" (Encycopedia.com 2019a). This ambitious project earned him a spot at the National Science Fair. There, it caught nuclear physicist Edward Teller's (the father of the hydrogen bomb) attention, and earned Kaku a full-ride to Harvard University (American Physical Society 2024; Encyclopedia.com 2019a; Famous Scientists 2024a).

Teller took on Kaku as a protégé, awarding him the Hertz Engineering Scholarship. Kaku graduated summa cum laude from Harvard in 1968 and was first in his physics class. Kaku next attended the University of California at Berkeley and worked at the Berkeley Radiation Laboratory as a research assistant. He earned his Ph.D. in 1972 (Kaku 2024a). In 1972, he held a lectureship at Princeton University.

Kaku's graduate studies occurred during the Vietnam War. Before inevitably being drafted, Kaku decided to join the military in 1968. He completed his U.S. Army basic training at Fort Benning, Georgia, and his advanced individual training at Fort Lewis, Washington. However, he was not deployed. A doctor had found that he had too much sugar in his blood making him borderline diabetic. As an infantryman, the Army decided not to send him to Vietnam. After his two year military stint, his service to this country was completed. Interestingly, Kaku (1994) recalls his training at Fort Benning (the largest infantry training center in the world) that involved throwing live grenades under the grueling Georgia sun and seeing the deadly shrapnel scatter in all directions and how his thoughts began to wander. He wondered about how many promising scientists were "snuffed out by a bullet in the prime of their youth?" (Kaku 1994:164). He came to realize that infantry training was rigorous and designed to toughen the spirit and dull the intellect. And yet, during night infantry training, while going through the obstacle course, which meant dodging live machine-gun bullets, froglegging under barbed wire, and crawling through thick brown mud, he paid attention to the "beautiful crimson streaks made by thousands of machine-gun bullets sailing a few feet over my head" and began to visualize in his head how strings could be twisted into loops and turned inside out (Kaku 1994:165). Because he rarely had any paper or pencils while practicing with machine guns, he forced himself to mentally conceive of the world as bits of strings—a clear foreshadowing of things to come in his professional career. When he had the chance, he would write down his ideas and when his military stint was over he kept working on these thoughts during his doctoral studies and after graduation.

As physicists picked up where Einstein left off, one solution that has excited the field is string theory. String theory combines the theory of general relativity and quantum mechanics by assuming there are multiple universes and dimensions beyond the ones we know (American Physical Society 2024). After earning his Ph.D. from UC Berkeley, Kaku joined in on this pursuit. He co-founded string field theory, a subset of string theory. String field theory uses the mathematics of fields to explain string theory (American Physical Society 2024).

Kaku became a visiting professor at the Institute for Advanced Study in Princeton, and at New York University. He then moved on to the City College of The City University of New York (CUNY) to conduct research on quantum mechanics. He currently holds the Henry Semat Chair and Professorship in theoretical physics at CUNY where he has taught for over 30 years. He has taught at Harvard and Princeton as well.

In his quest to find a "theory of everything," Kaku has conducted a great deal of research and published significant works. "He is the author of several scholarly, Ph.D. level textbooks and has had more than 70 articles published in physics journals, covering topics such as superstring theory, supergravity, supersymmetry, and hadronic physics" (Kaku 2024b). Kaku also has a knack for writing physics books in such a manner as to popularize science. Among his publications are *New York Times* best sellers: *Physics of the Impossible* (2008), probes the very limits of human ingenuity and scientific possibility including teleportation, time machines, force fields and interstellar space ships; *Physics of the Future* (2011), a time-traveling tour of the future and a look at inventions that will transform human lives; *The Future of the Mind* (2014), the scientific quest to understand, enhance, and empower the mind and a look at the latest advancements in neuroscience; and *The God Equation: The Quest for a Theory of Everything* (2021), as the title implies, the quest for a theory that explains everything. Other books include, *Hyperspace* (1994), a scientific odyssey through parallel universes, time warps, and the 10th dimension; *Beyond Einstein* (1995), the cosmic quest for the theory of the universe; *Visions* (1997), how science will revolutionize the twenty-first century; *Parallel Worlds* (2005), a journey through creation, higher dimensions, and the future of the cosmos; and *Physics of the Future* (2011), how science will shape human destiny and our daily lives by the year 2100. A closer examination of many of these books will be provided later in this chapter.

Anyone familiar with popular culture, news and entertainment programming, physics or science in general should know who Michio Kaku is as he is a media darling. He is indeed a popularizer of science. On his own homepage it states, "Kaku has starred in a myriad of science programming for television including Discovery, Science Channel, BBC, ABC, and History Channel. Beyond his numerous best-selling books, he has been a featured columnist for top popular science publications such as *Popular Mechanics, Discover, COSMOS, WIRED, New Scientist, Newsweek,* and many others" (Kaku 2024b). He is also a contributor to "CBS: Mornings" and is a regular on news programs around the world. He has made guest appearances on all major talk shows from morning, day-time and late night shows.

Kaku's ambition remains the quest for uniting the four fundamental forces of Nature along with quantum mechanics into a single grand unified theory of everything and he believes his string field theory is the answer (Kaku 2024b).

Beyond Einstein

As already established, Kaku sought to create a theory of everything and this quest was inspired at an early age upon learning about the life (and death) of theoretical physicist, Albert Einstein. Einstein, as we have learned, was trying to create a unified field theory that would unite the four forces of Nature. Kaku and Thompson (1995) elaborate on the meaning of the four forces by first clarifying that a *force* is anything that can move an object. "Gravity is an attractive force that binds together the solar system, keeps the earth and planets in their orbits, and prevents the stars from exploding" (Kaku and Thompson 1995:6). Kaku and Thompson (1995) add, "In our universe, gravity is the dominant force that extends trillions upon trillions of miles, out to the farthest stars; this force, which causes an apple to fall to the ground and keeps our feet on the floor, is the same force that guides the galaxies in their motions throughout the universe" (p. 6). The electromagnetic force holds atoms together; it makes the electrons (with negative charge) orbit around positively charged nucleus of the atom. Electromagnetic force determines the structure of the orbits of the electrons and it also governs the laws of chemistry (Kaku and Thompson 1995). On our planet, the electromagnetic force is often strong enough to overpower gravity (e.g., electromagnetic forces/charges by rubbing a comb, for example, makes it possible to pick up scraps of paper from a table) (Kaku and Thompson 1995).

Within the nucleus of an atom, the electromagnetic force is overpowered by weak and strong (nuclear) forces. The strong force is responsible for binding together the protons and neutrons in the nucleus. In any given nucleus, all the protons are positively charged. When the strong nuclear force is unleashed, the effect can be catastrophic (e.g., when the uranium nucleus in an atomic bomb is split deliberately, the enormous energies locked within the nucleus are released explosively in the form of a nuclear detonation). When certain nuclei (e.g., uranium, with ninety-two protons) break apart they leave fragments and debris, which we call radioactivity. "Therefore, yet another, weaker force must be at work, one that governs radioactivity and is responsible for the disintegration of very heaving nuclei. This is the weak force" (Kaku and Thompson 1995:8).

Without these four forces of Nature, life would be unimaginable. "The atoms of our bodies would disintegrate, the sun would burst, and the atomic fires lighting the stars and galaxy would be snuffed out" (Kaku and Thompson 1995:8). Physicists such as Einstein, Hawking, Kaku and others have attempted to united, these four forces into one grand theory so that they can discover a unifying theory of everything. Through the use of quantum mechanics, physicists have had less of problem finding a way to unite the three electromagnetic forces but the final force—gravity—has long eluded physicists. Gravity is so unlike the other forces that even combining a quantum mechanics approach has failed to lead to a unified field theory.

During the 1980s, physics was reaching an impasse as gravity alone stubbornly stood apart and aloof from the other three forces. Kaku found this ironic as the classical theory of gravity was the first to be understood through the work of Newton. The introduction of the quantum theory of gravity was supposed to help establish a theory of everything that could incorporate the four forces of Nature.

Kaku (1994) states, "All the giants of physics have had their crack at this problem, and all have failed" (p. 136). Einstein, Werner Heisenberg and Wolfgang Pauli (the Heisenberg-Pauli unified field theory) all faced a dead end even after spending decades tediously filling up tables of figures for the spectral lines of various gases, or calculating the solutions to Maxwell's equations for increasingly complicated metal surfaces (Kaku 1994). Kaku wrote in 1994 that "the greatest scientific problem of all time" was uniting the quantum theory with gravity, thereby creating a Theory of Everything (p. 136). "This is the problem that has frustrated the finest minds of the twentieth century. Without question, the person who solves this problem will win the Nobel Prize" (Kaku 1994:136).

Superstring Theory

Kaku and Thompson (1995) wrote in their co-authored book *Beyond Einstein*, that it would take a fresh approach, a new theory, if there was ever to be a solution to the quest for a unified field theory—a Theory of Everything. "Although there are still some unresolved questions concerning this theory, the excitement among physicists is palpable; throughout the world, leading physicists are proclaiming that we are witnessing the genesis of a new physics. This theory is called 'superstrings,' and a series of astonishing breakthroughs in physics within the last decades have culminated in its development, indicating that we are finally closing in on the unified field theory: a comprehensive, mathematical framework that would unite all known forces of the universe" (Kaku and Thompson 1995:3). Proponents of superstrings claim that the theory could be the ultimate "theory of the universe" (Kaku and Thompson 1995:3).

Kaku and Thompson (1995) describe how physicists, generally cautious in their approach to new ideas, were quite excited about the future of the physics because of superstring theory. "Princeton physicist Edward Witten has claimed that the superstring theory will dominate the world of physics for the next fifty years. 'Superstring theory is a miracle, through and through' he said recently" (Kaku and Thompson 1995:3). Kaku and Thompson provide other examples of exaggerated praise of the grandeur of superstring theory. The excitement ultimately centered on the idea that perhaps finally a theory had been created that could explain the four forces of Nature in one comprehensive format. Witten, an American mathematical and theoretical physicist, worked at the Institute for Advanced Study (IAS) in Princeton, New Jersey, in the 1990s (as of 2024 he was a professor emeritus at IAS) and Kaku (1994) stated that he dominated the world of theoretical physics at this time. Kaku describes Witten as a person who sits and stares out the window manipulating and rearranging vast arrays of equations in his head preferring to do calculations in his mind. It should not come as a surprise that Witten is also working on a Theory of Everything. He believes that superstring theory may need 26 dimensions and not just 10 dimensions if it hopes to explain the nature of both matter and space-time (Kaku 1994). In a 2017 interview with *Quanta Magazine* (a leading publication covering developments in physics, mathematics, biology and computer science), Witten admits that superstring theory is such a rigorous [or vague] theory the way that physicists define it that it is hard for mathematicians to create formulas and mathematical structures to study [prove] it (Wolchover 2017).

In Chapter 3 of this text a definition of string theory was provided as follows: a theoretical framework in physics that posits that the most fundamental particles we observe are not actually particles but tiny strings that only look like particles through our scientific instruments because they are so small. Kaku and Thompson (1995), along with some of their contemporaries prefer superstring theory over string theory. Both theories are a part of the same field with string theory as the generic term for the whole field while a primary distinction of superstring theory is that it includes properties of supersymmetry (to be discussed later in this chapter). Kaku and Thompson state that *superstring theory* assumes that the ultimate building blocks of nature consist of tiny vibrating strings. If correct, this means that the protons and neutrons in all matter, everything from our bodies to the farthest star, are ultimately made up of strings.

One of the problems with superstring theory is the realization that nobody has seen these strings because they are much too small to be observed. Kaku and Thompson (!995) describe them as "about 100 billion billion times smaller than a proton" (p. 5). While skeptics of superstring theory laugh at the notion of such tiny strings making up all matter of nature, proponents of the theory state that our world only appears to be made of point particles because our measuring devices are too crude to see these tiny strings (Kaku and Thompson 1995). Superstring theory replaces point particles with strings in order to explain the diversity of particles and forces in nature. Kaku and Thompson (1995) describe superstring theory as similar to a violin string in that it can be used to "unite" all the musical tones and rules of harmony. Historically, the laws of music were formulated only after thousands of years of trial-and-error investigation of different musical sounds leading to a musical scale. Similarly, in superstring theory, the fundamental forces and various particles found in nature are nothing more than different modes of vibrating strings. The gravitational interaction, for example, is caused by the lowest vibrating mode of a circular string (loop) (Kaku and Thompson 1995). These vibrating strings, smaller than the smallest subatomic particles, twist, fold and vibrate, they create matter, energy and according to this theoretical perspective, create matter, energy and the forces of Nature (e.g., electromagnetism and gravity). There are many oddities associated with superstring theory. One of them involves the by-product of anomalies when marrying quantum mechanics with relativity. "Anomalies are tiny but potentially deadly mathematical defects in a quantum field theory that must be canceled or eliminated. A theory just doesn't make sense in the presence of these anomalies" (Kaku and Thompson 1995:96). Anomalies mean that errors will occur when using superstring theory to make predictions. Rather than correcting the mathematical errors, superstring theorists devised an alternative solution—the use of the concept of multiple dimensions; specifically, the superstring model is in ten dimensions. (We will look at the concept of multiple dimensions later in this chapter.)

It is interesting to point out that Kaku and Thompson (1995) describe the concept of "cosmic strings." As we know, superstrings are said to be incredibly tiny vibrating objects but some physicists believe that following the Big Bang there may have been gigantic cosmic strings floating in space that were even larger than the galaxies themselves. "According to this theory, the vibrations left in the wake of these ancient wriggling cosmic strings are the galactic clusters we see in the heavens, including our own" (Kaku and Thompson 1995:154). Superstring theorists go as far as to suggest that cosmic strings likely explain the "clumpiness" of the universe (the idea that a number of stars of a given galaxy are "clumped" together).

Symmetry and Supersymmetry

Most of us appreciate *symmetry*—balanced and proportionate similarity that is found in two halves of an object. That means that one-half is the mirror image of the other half. Examples include feathers of a peacock and the wings of butterflies and dragonflies which have identical left and right sides. When these animals have been injured and no longer have symmetry, they do not look as Nature intended and generally do not look as appealing. Symmetry can come in the form of equality based on left and right; top and bottom, or diagonal. This book is divided into four parts, each with 3 chapters. I would not feel comfortable if one part had 2 chapters, another had 3 or 4 chapters and so on. I prefer symmetry in the Table of Contents! I have a colleague who prefers Pringles potato chips because they are symmetrical whereas all other brands of potato chips the individual chips are asymmetrical. There are numerous studies that show symmetrical faces are found to be more attractive than asymmetrical ones, and this seems to be true across cultures and times (Simmons, Rhodes, Peters and Koehler 2004; Lents 2019). (Note: In Chapter 3 the concept of "quantum entanglement" was discussed and how such a notion could not be applicable to the social sciences. The idea that symmetrical faces are found to be more attractive than asymmetrical ones across cultures and times makes one ponder if such a concept as "cultural entanglement" is indeed possible. This is a topic worth pursuing at another time and publication.)

In physics, the most obvious example of symmetry is a crystal or gem. As Kaku and Thompson (1995) explain, "crystals and gems are beautiful because they have symmetry—they retain the same shape if we rotate them at certain angles" (p. 99). In physics, *symmetry* is "the concept that the properties of particles such as atoms and molecules remain unchanged after being subjected to a variety of symmetry transformations or 'operations'" (Augustyn 2021). Kaku and Thompson (1995) state, "When we apply symmetry to physics, we demand that the equations remain the same when we make certain 'rotations.' In this case, rotations (actually, shufflings) occur when we change space into time, or electrons into quarks. We say our relations retain a beautiful symmetry if, after making these rotations, the equations remain the same" (p. 99). Symmetry in physics, then, allows for creation of certain physical laws that would be valid at all places and times in the universe. We know, however, that the Universe is not symmetrical. So, can symmetry help physicists trying to establish a theory of everything?

Kaku and Thompson (1995) describe how symmetry explains why all the potentially harmful divergences and anomalies, sufficient to kill other theories, cancel each other perfectly in the superstring theory. In fact, superstring theory includes many symmetries and physicists appreciate the fact that symmetries are essential to eliminate potentially fatal problems that face any relativistic quantum theory.

Supersymmetry is the idea that the fundamental particles of nature are connected through a deep relationship (Sutter 2021). Supersymmetry is a complex mathematical framework that was developed to enhance the shortcomings of the symmetry framework. Supersymmetry helps to fill in the gaps, it predicts a partner particle for each particle in the Standard Model of particle physics (this Model explains how the basic building blocks of matter interact and are governed by the four fundamental forces). Supersymmetry would unite the interactions of three forces—electromagnetism and the strong and weak nuclear forces. It would also link the two different classes of particles known as fermions and bosons (CERN 2024a). Fermions (named in honor of Enrico Fermi) and bosons (named for Satyendra Nath Bose) are the two fundamental kinds of particles that make up the subatomic universe. Fermions are the building blocks of the natural world: the quarks, the electrons and the neutrinos. Bosons are the carriers of the fundamental forces of nature. Sutter states that we still do not have an understanding as to why the universe is split into these two major camps. Supersymmetry is supposed to be able to provide us with an explanation of the connection between fermions and bosons. However, Sutter, among others has doubts about the capabilities of supersymmetry as a theory and its ability to help unite a field theory of Nature. He states that the only way to access the realm of supersymmetry is to recreate the conditions of the early Universe, such as in a giant particle collider.

The Large Hadron Collider (LHC) is, as the name suggests, a giant particle collider. It's capable of accelerating particles to nearly the speed of light and then smashing them together, achieving the highest energies possible—conditions not found in the universe since the first moments of the Big Bang. The LHC was explicitly designed to hunt for signs of supersymmetry by finding evidence for supersymmetric particle partners in the collision debris. The results however showed no such evidence. After years of searching and loads of accumulated data from countless collisions, there is no sign of any supersymmetric particle. "In fact, many supersymmetry models are now completely ruled out, and very few theoretical ideas remain valid" (Sutter 2021). Sutter concludes his review of supersymmetry by saying that while every possible model of this theory has not been ruled out, the future of supersymmetry is in serious doubt.

Multiple Dimensions

When we discuss the dimensions of reality that surround us on a daily basis we generally think of three: length, width and depth of all objects in our universe (the x, y and z axes respectively). When we watch television, look at our computer screens and view most movies at the theater, we see things in two dimensions—depth is missing. Some scientists believe that there are many more dimensions than three. In fact, the theoretical framework of superstring theory posits that the universe exists in ten different dimensions (Williams 2014).

The concept of a fourth dimension had reached the realm of the intellectual world by the late–1800s. So common was this concept in some circles that playwrights mocked it. In 1891, Oscar Wilde wrote a spoof on the idea of a fourth dimensions in "The Canterville Ghost." H.G. Wells incorporated in his 1894 novel, *The Time Machine,* several mathematical, philosophical, and political themes and popularized the new idea in science that the fourth dimension might also be viewed as time, not necessarily space (Kaku 1994). If scientists were thinking about four dimensions, might they think about more than four?

Einstein had pondered the idea of the existence of five dimensions when he received a letter (in 1919) from an unknown mathematician, Theodor Franz Kaluza, from the University of Königsberg (in what is now the city of Kaliningrad, Russia). In this letter, Kaluza proposed a novel way of writing a unified field theory that combined Einstein's new theory of gravity with the older theory of light written by Maxwell. The idea of five dimensions seemed outlandish to Einstein but it intrigued him, nonetheless. In 1926, Swedish mathematician Oskar Klein suggested that the fifth dimension was likely shaped like a circle and was so small that it could not be observed directly. For decades Einstein would return to the Kaluza-Klein theory (as it came to be known upon revision) as he worked on his unified field theory (Kaku and Thompson 1995).

By the 2010s, superstring proponents were working with the premise that there were ten dimensions. The first four were identified above (length, height, depth and time) but an elaboration on the fourth dimension is necessary—this is the dimension that governs the properties of all known matter at any given point. If we could see on through to the fifth dimension, we could see a world slightly different from our own that would give us a means of measuring the similarity and differences between our world and other possible ones. In the sixth dimension, according to superstring theorists, we would see a plane of possible worlds, where we could compare and position all the possible universes that start with the same initial conditions as this one (e.g., the Big Bang). In theory, if you could master the fifth and sixth dimensions, you could travel back in time or go to different futures (Williams 2014). Whereas in the fifth and sixth dimensions the initial conditions that determined the start of the universe are the same as in the seventh dimension, you have access to the possible worlds that start with different initial conditions. The eighth dimension also gives us a plan of such possible universe histories, each of which begin with different initial conditions and branches out infinitely (which explains why they are called "infinities") (Williams 2014). "In the ninth dimension, we can compare all the possible universe histories, starting with all the different laws of physics and initial conditions. In the tenth and final dimension, we arrive at the point in which everything possible and imaginable is covered. Beyond this, nothing can be imagined by us lowly mortals, which makes it the natural limitation of what we can conceive in terms of dimensions" (Williams 2014). One has to wonder, with the active imaginations that physicists utilized to create these dimensions (especially beyond the fourth), what is to stop others from making up other dimensions beyond ten?

After all, who's to say that additional dimensions aren't so tightly curled up that we don't notice them; or as Williams states, we mere mortals cannot imagine what other dimensions might exist? Others would counter, let's stick with known reality, the reality that we can prove (with known mathematical equations, if necessary).

Before Creation and the Big Bang

In *Hyperspace* (1994), Kaku discusses the question often asked by children who are told that God made the heavens and the earth, "Did God have a mother?" This deceptively simple and innocent question is difficult for elders of a church to answer and parallels a scientific question, "Was there anything before the Big Bang?" If religious leaders answer, "Yes, God had a mother" then there will be follow-up lineage questions such as "Did God's mother have a mother, and so on." If God did not have a mother then the question is "Where did God come from?" Has God been in existence since eternity, or is God beyond time itself? And, if yes, how is that possible?

As we have learned from physics, the idea of the Universe's creation by God has been replaced by the concept of the "Big Bang." Kaku spent time wondering what, if anything happened prior to the Big Bang. Not surprisingly, he applied superstring theory to this thought. Kaku believes that the Big Bang perhaps originated in the breakdown of the original ten-dimensional universe into a four- and a six-dimensional universe. Thus, we can view the history of the Big Bang as the history of the breakup of ten-dimensional space and hence the breakup of previously unified symmetries (Kaku 1994; Kaku and Thompson 1995). While scientists have found ample evidence (e.g., the fact that the stars are receding from us at fantastic velocities; the distribution of the chemical elements in our galaxy are in almost exact agreement with the prediction of heavy-element production in the Big Bang and in the stars; the earliest objects in the universe date back to 10 to 15 billion years, in agreement with the rough estimate for the Big Bang; and the Big Bang produced a cosmic "echo" reverberating throughout the universe that should be measurable by our instruments) to support the Big Bang theory as the origin of the Universe there is no evidence of what Kaku proposes (that there was originally a ten-dimensional universe).

Ten years after the above defense of the creation of the Universe, Kaku (2005) once again defended the Big Bang theory as the most viable explanation for the creation of the Universe. *In Parallel Worlds* (2005) Kaku reiterates that the Big Bang theory is not based on speculation but on hundreds of data points taken from several difference sources, each of which converge to support the theory.

Robots and Artificial Intelligence (AI)

In his book *The Future of the Mind* (2014), Kaku states that the two greatest mysteries in all of nature are the mind and the Universe. Our advanced technology has allowed us to photograph galaxies billions of light-years away, manipulate the genes that control life, and probe the inner sanctum of the atoms, but the mind and the universe still elude and tantalize us. In this book, Kaku discussed a number of fascinating topics, including unlocking the mind; telepathy; telekinesis; memories and thoughts; dreams; mind control; altered states of consciousness; reverse engineering the brain; and the mind as pure energy. However, the topic to be discussed here (primarily because of its relevancy to Chapter 10), is the artificial mind.

In Chapter 10 of *The Future of the Mind*, "The Future Mind and Silicon Consciousness," Kaku describes AI mostly in terms of robots and silicon consciousness. Kaku describes how an IBM computer called Watson did what many critics thought was impossible: it beat two contestants on the TV show *Jeopardy!* Millions of viewers watched Watson methodically destroy its opponents on national TV, answering questions that stumped the rival contestants, and thereby claimed the $1 million prize money. IBM had built a machine with a truly monumental amount of computational firepower with the ability to process data at the astonishing rate of five hundred gigabytes per second (or the equivalent of a million books per second) with sixteen trillion bytes of RAM memory (Kaku 2014). There were many people already sounding the alarm of the potential danger of having AI-powered machinery and technology. Ken Jennings (still a darling for *Jeopardy!*, the highest-earning American game show contestant and current host of the show) said with his on-air final comment following his loss to Watson, "I for one welcome our new computer overlords" (McNamara 2011).

While Kaku praised the artificial intelligence capabilities of Watson he countered that thought with the realization that one could not go up to Watson and congratulate it for winning; or slap it on its back or share a champagne toast with it as signs of a "job well done." Watson would not know what any of that meant; in fact, it was unaware that it had won at all. "All the hype aside, the truth is that Watson is a highly sophisticated adding machine, able to add (or search data files) billions of times faster than the human brain, but is totally lacking in self-awareness or common sense" (Kaku 2014:215). Kaku described the progress of AI in the early 2010s as astounding in terms of its ability to perform calculations faster than any human. On the other hand, Kaku countered, progress has been painstaking slow in building machines that can think for themselves (meaning, that they still relied on a human master to control and operate them). Robots, Kaku said, are totally unaware that they are even robots. However, Kaku also noted that the computer power had been doubling every two years for the past years under Moore's law, and some say it is only a matter of time before machines eventually acquire self-awareness that rivals human intelligence. (Note: Moore's Law will be briefly discussed again in Chapter 10.) This is exactly what scares many people who follow AI closely—the idea of robot consciousness as this new reality could decide the future of the human race (Kaku 2014). (Note: This topic will be discussed in Chapter 10.)

Before robots take over they must conquer a number of problems. One such problem confronting robots is the lack of pattern recognition. As Kaku explains, the best robots can barely recognize simple objects like a cup or a ball. "When a robot walks into a room, it has to perform trillions of calculations, breaking down the objects it sees into pixels, lines, circles, squares, and triangles, and then trying to make a match with the thousands of images stored in its memory…. Our brains are subconsciously performing trillions of calculations, but the process seems effortless to us" (Kaku 2014:218). Robots also lack common sense; they do not understand simple facts about the physical and biological world. There isn't an equation that can be programmed to teach robots or AI devices aspects of the commonsense world. Furthermore, as Delaney (2019) articulated in his book *Common Sense as a Paradigm of Thought*, ideas of what constitutes common sense are not common among all people and common sense behaviors are actually learned behaviors, not innate behaviors. As of now, robots and AI lack consciousness. Kaku compares their level of consciousness to that of a worm or slow insect (Level I consciousness on Kaku's scale). "Robots will have to be able to create a model of the world in relation to others if they are to enter Level II consciousness…. Current robots view humans as simply a collection of pixels moving on their TV sensors, but some AI researchers are beginning to create robots that can recognize emotions in our facial expressions and tone of voice" (Kaku 2014:222). When robots reach Level II consciousness they will realize that humans are more than just random pixels, and that they have emotional states. This is what many of us fear, what if robots interpret certain humans' actions or emotional states as dangerous, will they act upon that (especially if they are weaponized)?

Kaku introduces another topic of concern regarding robots as their level of intelligence and degree of consciousness increases—will they learn to lie? While we tend to think of robots as being coldly analytical and rational, always telling the truth, what is to stop them from lying once they become integrated into society? As their degree of consciousness increases, they may find the need to lie or at least tactfully restrain their comments (Kaku 2014). This is not a far-fetched idea as humans who may own robots will want them to be tactful, especially in a public sphere, and will therefore teach/program them to lie or conceal the truth so that they do not offend people, tip-off competitors, or any of the other many reasons that humans do not always tell the truth for "good" reasons.

It is when robots become self-aware that we have the most to worry about and this is especially true based on what and how they were programmed. Anyone who has watched Sci-fi movies such as *The Terminator* franchise will have an idea of what "bad" robots can do to humanity.

Humanity's Future

In *Visions* (1997), Kaku describes various ways that science will revolutionize the twenty-first century and chief among these was fusion. Kaku (1997) predicted that within the next thirty years, fossil fuels will become increasingly scarce and prohibitively expensive. He also warned of the effects of global warming. As a result, there was the need for alternative sources of inexhaustible power and Kaku promoted: fusion power, breeder reactors and solar energy. Kaku states that the United States has enough coal reserves to last perhaps five hundred years but if it relies on this fossil fuel, the environmental damage caused by acid rain, the greenhouse effect, and air pollution will seemingly rule out any significant role for coal in the future. Physicists, and scientists in general, are working on ways to assure that fusion is a vital energy source, Kaku assures. A breeder reactor refers to a nuclear reactor that produces more fissionable material than it consumes to generate energy. Breeder reactors produce fissionable plutonium from waste uranium but they also come with a risk of accidents, as well as the risk of sabotage or theft. Kaku admits that so far, breeder reactors have been a great disappointment in producing energy at a significant level. Furthermore, nuclear reactors cannot be used in cars and trucks and therefore can make only a small dent in the overall energy needs. The most promising solution to the energy crisis of the future is solar energy. Solar cells (commonly called photovoltaic cells) use yet another principle from quantum physics. In principle, solar energy is unlimited as the sun will always be there—and when it's not, we will all be dead anyway and have no need for energy. Kaku (1997) also believes that electric cars will continue to improve and as they do, they will help to lessen our overall dependency on oil. Advancements in the technology of lasers will assist laser printing, laser surgery and create a laser industry (e.g., fiber optics, X-ray lasers, 3-D TVs, holograms).

The advancements mentioned above should all occur between 2020 and 2100, according to Kaku. Beyond that date, new technologies will likely come into play. The most intriguing of these is the antimatter engine (such as the source of energy for the starship *Enterprise* on the *Star Trek* series). The science is not there yet to create antimatter engines but Kaku believes it will be by 2100. Making any other predictions about the future, especially those based on technologies not yet developed, are speculative. Kaku ponders something else from sci-fi, portable ray guns. Science has developed laser beams which can blast through steel, and in fact, there is almost no limit as to how powerful the laser beams can be. However, the idea of a portable power pack that can be held in your hand and used as ray gun (or as they use on *Star Trek*, phasers) seems unlikely. The idea of "force fields"—transparent, impenetrable walls made of pure energy—another common feature of science fiction also seem unlikely based on the limitations of the four forces of Nature. A "fifth force" would have to be discovered, Kaku believes, in order for force fields to come to fruition. Transporters and replicators also seem highly unlikely. *Star Trek* fans are used to the idea of humans and other objects being transported from place to place (as in, "Beam me up, Scotty"). Warp-drive engines used in space travel also seem impossible to Kaku. In these previous mentioned examples it's the idea of taking something apart, atom for atom, shooting it across space, and then reassembling it, is beyond comprehension and certainly beyond any physics known to science. And finally, Kaku states that the idea of invisibility is also impossible. In the 1897 novel, *The Invisible Man*, H.G. Wells' hero becomes invisible during an accident. His body floats in the fourth dimension, just slightly off the three dimensions of our Universe, and hence appears invisible to us, although he can see everything that happens in our three-dimensional world. Kaku (1997) says this is impossible because there is no known way of making someone invisible. Others would say it's impossible for that reason and because there is no proof of a fourth dimension.

In *Physics of the Future* (2011), Kaku states that physicists rank everything, even human civilizations, by the energy it consumes. Following the end of the Ice Age (10,000 years ago), civilizations began to utilize agriculture, and horses and oxen were soon domesticated, which increased our energy to 1 horsepower. The agricultural revolution spawned ingenious ways to create, maintain and expand wealth. At the end of the eighteenth century, the next revolution occurred, the Industrial Revolution. As described in great detail by sociologists, the rise of industrialization would dramatically change society. The creation of the internal combustion engine gave humans command over hundreds of horsepower. Kaku (2011) argues that the third wave of civilization since the Ice Age is the Information Age. The energy used in the Information Age is quite excessive as information, measured by electrons' circulation around the world on fiber-optic cables and satellites, is constantly flowing in the financial world, commerce, entertainment and communications at the speed of light. Kaku summarizes by saying that humanity's exponential rise in energy consumption will eventually catch up to us with very negative consequences (primarily environmental).

Kaku puts forth the notion that the key to the future for humanity is wisdom. Society must embrace education and science. Dictators and those who hate democracy will attack education and science and those are the people we must worry about as they will contribute to the end of humanity. Kaku (2011) states, "The key to a democracy is an educated, informed electorate that can rationally and dispassionately discuss the issues of the day" (p. 406). Our current civilization is drifting away from this ideal more and more every year.

The End of the Universe

In Chapter 10, "The End of Everything" of *Parallel Worlds* (2005), Kaku begins by describing the Norse legend of Ragnarok—the final day of reckoning. This day of reckoning is accompanied by cataclysmic upheavals including blinding blizzards, ruinous earthquakes, famine and men and women that perish helplessly in great numbers. Out of the ashes, however, will arise a new earth that gives birth to a new race of humans (somewhat similar to what happened following the Ice Age). Mythologies around the world have similar themes of doom and gloom scenarios of the end of times (Kaku 2005).

Kaku (2005) describes how physics is predicting a doom and gloom scenario for the universe but not because angry gods are fighting one another as in Norse legends and mythologies but because the laws of physics and hard data indicates that the final days of the universe will occur and most likely without a rebirth. Kaku is basing this conclusion on data from the Wilkinson Microwave Anisotropy Probe (WMAP) satellite which indicates that a mysterious antigravity force is accelerating the expansion of the Universe. "If it continues for billions or trillions of years, the universe will inevitably reach a big freeze similar to the blizzard foretelling the twilight of the gods, ending all life as we know it" (Kaku 2005:288). Kaku (2005) adds, "This antigravity force pushing the universe apart is proportional to the volume of the universe. Thus, the larger the universe becomes, the more antigravity there is to push the galaxies apart, which in turn increases the volume of the universe. This vicious cycle repeats itself endlessly, until the universe enters a runaway mode and grows exponentially fast" (p. 288). Eventually, Kaku reasons, all thirty-six galaxies in the local group of galaxies that make up the entire visible Universe are in danger; albeit not for the far, far, far distant future.

Kaku also applies the second law of thermodynamics to the fate of the Universe. This second law states that the total amount of entropy (chaos or disorder) in the universe always increases. Thus, everything must eventually age and run down. Taking into consideration the fact that life is driven by the natural laws of evolution, and that total entropy still increases, because additional energy fueling life is constantly being added by the Sun, the second law of thermodynamics, when applied to the entire universe, means that the universe will eventually run down. "The stars will exhaust their nuclear fuel, galaxies will cease to illuminate the heavens, and the universe will be left as a lifeless collection of dead dwarf stars, neutron stars, and black holes. The universe will be plunged in eternal darkness" (Kaku 2005:290).

Kaku ponders in this same chapter of *Parallel Worlds* whether or not intelligent beings can survive. The first step, according to Kaku, is that humans must reach a state of intelligence wherein they can abandon their frail bodies of flesh and blood and assume robotic bodies as mechanical bodies can withstand the cold much better than flesh. But, even machines must obey the laws of information theory and thermodynamics, making life extremely difficult, even for robots. Kaku (2005) adds, "Even if intelligent creatures abandon their robotic bodies and transform themselves into pure consciousness, there is still the problem of information processing. As the temperature continues to fall, the only way to survive will be to 'think' slower … spread over [a period] of billions of years" (p. 300). Thinking slower over a period of billions of years may allow intelligent creatures a chance to witness cosmic quantum transitions taking place in the universe. One might wonder, "Will any of these changes help intelligent beings?" And, are these intelligent beings even "human" anymore?

Regardless of form—robotic or our current frail bodies—Kaku states that any intelligent species in the Universe will inevitably be forced to confront the ultimate death of the Universe and the death of any life forms that may exist within it. Kaku (2005) then proposes a possible solution—far-fetched for most of us, but not for superstring theory proponents—the survival of an intelligent species may likely be dependent upon an escape into a parallel universe.

We certainly do not have the technology to develop travel to parallel worlds— if they even exist—but considering Kaku says the Universe will not end for at least billions of years, there is time to work on this. Then again, will humanity last even a fraction of that time? It helps if you are a superstring theorist, or superstring enthusiast, to believe in this possible solution for the future of humanity via travel to a parallel world or another dimension.

Is a Theory of Everything Possible?

In 2021, Kaku published *The God Equation*, a book that, more or less, summarizes his major past works and ideas (e.g., wormholes, time travel, the creation of the universe, Big Bang, inflation, gravitation, supersymmetry, holographic universe, and parallel universes) as he attempts to formulate a theory of everything by using superstring theory. Aspects of superstring theory and the theory itself have already been explained in this chapter and yet there is more to add as Kaku is always trying to make this theory accessible to general public. While on his press tour promoting *The God Equation* I heard Kaku repeat some simple sound bites such as this one he posted on X (formerly Twitter) on March 21, 2021: "In string theory, the notes on a vibrating string are subatomic particles. Physics is the harmonies on a string. Chemistry is the melodies on these strings. The universe is a symphony of strings. The 'mind of God' is the cosmic music resonating through 11th dimension hyperspace" (Kaku 2021a). Earlier in this chapter it was revealed that Kaku and Thompson (1995) used the example of a violin string to describe how superstring theory can be used to "unite" all the musical tones and rules of harmony.

Kaku wished to create a theory of everything because he wanted to finish Einstein's dream and because Hawking's use of quantum mechanics and quantum theory alongside general relativity were not adequate enough to finish the job. Breakthroughs in theoretical physics led to string theory and then superstring theory and Kaku believed that superstring theory would help him establish a unifying theory that could unite quantum mechanics and the four forces of Nature.

In *The God Equation*, Kaku (2021b) discussed the 2019 discovery by astronomers of a black hole. Billions of people saw the stark image, a red ball of hot fiery gas with a black, round silhouette in the middle, splashed across newspapers and websites around the world. The black hole that was photographed by the Event Horizon Telescope lies inside the galaxy M87, 53 million light years from Earth. A number of remarkable astronomical discoveries like this one have rejuvenated interest in Einstein's theory of gravity. Most physicists had stopped conducting research in Einstein's general relativity for the past 50 years in favor of quantum theory (Kaku 2021b). Einstein, as discussed in Chapter 7 of this book, had given up on quantum theory. But now, it seemed more relevant than ever to combine relativity theory with quantum theory, especially if one hoped to establish a theory of everything.

Stein and Wood (2023) summarize string theory as "the idea in theoretical physics that reality is made up of infinitesimal vibrating strings, smaller than atoms, electrons or quarks. According to this theory, as the strings vibrate, twist and fold, they produce effects in many, tiny dimensions that humans interpret as everything from particle physics to large-scale phenomena like gravity." As we know, Kaku and a few others have held that string theory could possibly help establish a "theory of everything," "a single framework that could unite general relativity and quantum mechanics, two theories that underlie almost all of modern physics" (Stein and Wood 2023). So far, quantum mechanics continues to do a very good job of explaining the behavior of very small things and general relativity works well explaining how very large things happen in the Universe but trying to merge these two theories into one has not worked out so well (Stein and Wood 2023). It was hoped that string theory, or superstring theory, could resolve the conundrums between the two but that has not been the case (so far) (Stein and Wood 2023).

Recall a couple of points made in Chapter 3 of this book. First, in 2002, science writer John Horgan made a bet with physicist Michio Kaku that by 2020 no one will have won a Nobel Prize in Physics for work on superstring theory, membrane theory, or some other unified theory describing all the forces of nature (Horgan 2019). Horgan won the bet when it was announced that the 2019 Nobel Prize winners in Physics were Jim Peebles, Michel Mayor and Didier P. Queloz. Second, the ambiguity of quantum mechanics pales in comparison to string theory as "physicists have yet to produce any empirical evidence for either string theory, which was invented more than 40 years ago, loop-space theory or any other unified theory. They don't even have good ideas for obtaining evidence" (Horgan 2019). No experiment has definitively proven the significant aspects of string theory and if this is the case, how can it be a leading contender for a theory of everything? Perhaps it is a flawed framework and just providing a false framework for theoretical physics.

Kaku (2021b) remains convinced that string theory is not only a viable path toward a theory of everything, it ultimately "could be our only salvation" (p. 196).

Summary

Theoretical physicist Michio Kaku was born on January 24, 1947, in San Jose, California. His Japanese parents are of Tibetan ancestry. Kaku followed in the footsteps of Albert Einstein and Stephen Hawking in trying to establish a "Theory of Everything." Kaku's interest in developing a theory of everything came about when he was in fourth grade and read about the death of Albert Einstein who was described as a great scientist. He learned that Einstein discovered many great things in his lifetime that made him world famous but that he died before he could finish his greatest work—establishing a unified field theory.

Kaku was a major figure in the development of string theory and then superstring theory, the next stages of development from quantum physics. String theory combines the theory of general relativity and quantum mechanics by assuming there are multiple universes and dimensions beyond the ones we know. A primary feature of superstring theory is that it includes properties of supersymmetry. Kaku believed that superstring theory would be the solution to creating a "Theory of Everything."

In his quest to find a "Theory of Everything," Kaku has conducted a great deal of research and published significant works. He is the author of several scholarly textbooks and journal articles covering such topics as string theory and superstring theory; symmetry and supersymmetry; multiple dimensions; parallel worlds; the Big Bang; robots and Artificial Intelligence (AI); and the fate of humanity and the universe. All of these topics are discussed in this chapter.

Kaku is also a popularizer of science as he is a regular in the realms of popular culture, news and entertainment programs. He has appeared on a wide variety of television networks, social media sites and has served as a featured columnist for top popular science publications such as *Popular Mechanics*, *Discover*, *COSMOS*, *WIRED*, *New Scientist*, *Newsweek*, and many others.

String theory, in any form, has been criticized because no experiment has definitively proven its significant aspects. The realization that multiple dimensions and parallel worlds must exist in order for this theory to hold up makes it highly questionable. Nonetheless, Kaku is convinced that superstring theory is the solution to finding a "Theory of Everything."

PART D

A THEORY OF EVERYTHING FROM THE SOCIAL PHYSICS PERSPECTIVE

For some time now, a limited number of social theorists have attempted to create a "theory of everything." We just learned in Part C of this book that some physicists have attempted to create a theory of everything that explains the origin and fate of the Universe, a seemingly appropriate component of such a grand theory. Physicists that attempt to create a theory of everything also find themselves trying to find a way to create a theory that explains the operations of the four forces of Nature in one unified coherent fashion so that they can add that to their theory of everything. It is easy to wonder why a unified field theory of Nature's forces is that critical. After all, it would seem that the ability to explain the aspects of the four forces of Nature independently (a great achievement) should be enough to incorporate with a theory of everything. In that regard, desperate theoretical physicists would not have to create the concepts of multiple dimensions and parallel worlds just to make their theories work. Can you imagine sociologists or psychologists using such concepts as "multiverses" and "parallel worlds" as explanations for the social and personal problems that confront humans on this planet? It is laughable to even imagine. Imagine politicians claiming that they have solved social problems (e.g., homelessness, poverty, crime, violence, etc.) and reduced taxes in every realm of the multiverse except for the one we reside in. Would that make people in this realm happy? Would that make people want to vote for them? Classic physics, the field that was respected as a "true science," insisted on following the rules of science and mathematics where their theories were supported by evidence and empirical data. We often marveled at the pure science of physics and mathematics.

Attempting a "theory of everything" from the social physics perspective provides us with the advantage of utilizing the knowledge already gained from the field of physics on certain matters, such as the properties of the forces of Nature, without the unnecessary worry of trying to create a unified field theory, and from the field of sociology to incorporate the role of human behavior. This combined knowledge can be merged in order to create a "theory of everything" from the social physics perspective which is concerned with: The Law of Human Progress and the role of Artificial Intelligence; the fate of humanity; questions surrounding a possible afterlife; the fate of Earth; and the fate of the Universe.

With this in mind, Chapter 10 describes social physics and its connection to a "theory of everything"; expands upon the stages of human progress by adding a fourth stage, Artificial Intelligence (AI); describes the positives and negatives of this AI stage of human progress; and warns of AI singularity. Chapter 11 describes the fate of humanity; specifically, is there a future for humans? Chapter 11 also describes whether or not there is an afterlife and if yes, what are the possible scenarios? And, in Chapter 12, the fate of Earth and the Universe are explained.

The answers provided in these three chapters reveal the social physics theory of everything.

10

Social Physics, Human Progress and Artificial Intelligence (AI)

Introduction

In the previous three chapters we learned of three specific attempts to create a "Theory of Everything" from leading physicists: Albert Einstein, Stephen Hawking and Michio Kaku. As established by their own parameters, they all failed. All physicists have failed, in fact. Einstein failed because he could not create a unified field theory, something that was his stated goal. Other physicists since him, including Hawking and especially Kaku attempted to finish the job Einstein started. We already learned what happened with those endeavors. Hawking and Kaku also attempted to explain the origin and fate of the Universe and thus, truly attempted to reach the realm of *everything* in their respective "theories of everything" from a physics point-of-view. Often, when theories do not work utilizing quantum mechanics, and especially string theory, theoretical physicists will claim that their theories do in fact work in other dimensions. Claiming that a theory works in a fifth, sixth and so on dimension does not help sociologists when they analyze and try to help solve social problems in this world. Certainly social policymakers and economic analysts cannot create theories and strategies on how to combat social problems (e.g., homelessness, poverty, economic inequality) only to watch them fail miserably and claim in the post-evaluation process or when explaining to their constituents that the policies would have worked in a different dimension. Such an explanation would be met with great negative responses, ridicule, possible termination of employment and most certainly, a lack of further funding.

The primary distinction between social physics (and the social sciences in general) and quantum physics is the fact that the former must deal with the known world of existence while the latter can speculate on made-up worlds and accept the realization that such speculative theorizing is similar to that found in metaphysics.

Social Physics and a Theory of Everything

Every academic discipline and practitioner engaged within it has the advantage of utilizing and benefiting from the trials and tribulations and knowledge attained by those who came before them. The academic fields found within the realm of early science have been making significant breakthroughs for thousands of years, dating back to the late Neolithic period at the very least. Astronomy developed in many parts of the world many thousands of years ago and this breakthrough is still helping scientists today make major discoveries. Mathematics and measuring devices such as rulers, protractors and weighing scales have been around for millennia and this academic discipline is critical for conducing calculations that assist scientists in expressing ideas, formulating theories and developing models that explain phenomena so that they can be measured, quantified and explained. Mathematics helps science to progress.

Mathematics and astronomy are among the sciences to assist the development of physics. Ibn Sahl (940–1000 CE), a Persian mathematician and physicist of the Islamic Golden Age, studied Ptolemy's *Optics* and came up with the optical properties of curved mirrors and lenses that are critical aspects of Snell's law (also known as Snell-Descartes law) of refraction—an equation that determines the angle at which a ray or beam of light is refracted when a visible light enters a transparent material such as glass at an angle (Kurtus 2022). The invention of the first optical telescope was invaluable to Galileo Galilei. The ideas of English physicist and mathematician Isaac Newton on motion (Newton's Laws of Motion, first published in 1687, remain, with few exceptions, to be a mostly accurate account of nature) and gravity are fundamental to physics and other fields; and Newton along with Gottfried Wilhelm Leibniz for developing calculus in the seventh century. Calculus is an advanced branch of mathematics and is critical for the sciences of physics and astronomy.

Continued developments in physics helped to raise this science to the top of the hierarchy of respect. During his lifetime, Auguste Comte (1798–1857), came to view physics as the pinnacle of sciences. He admired its dedication to conducting scientific inquiry and utilizing precise mathematical measurements. Unfortunately for Comte, he missed the countless developments in physics that followed his death. He would have admired classical mechanics which developed powerful mathematical tools for obtaining answers to theoretical questions, establishing laws and mathematically describing the motions of bodies and aggregates of body. Undoubtedly, he would have been less than impressed with string theory and perhaps even quantum mechanics.

As we learned in Chapter 5, Comte, the founder of sociology, was among the early social thinkers who believed that the social world could be studied in the same manner as the natural sciences, through scientific observation and the establishment of natural laws. Comte referred to the study of society via the scientific method as "positive philosophy" or "positivism." Comte was so impressed with physics that he originally wanted to use the term "social physics" to describe his positivist science but later found out that Belgian astronomer, mathematician, social statistician and sociologist Adolphe Quetelet (1796–1874) had "stolen" the term from him (Coser 1977). Quetelet (as we learned in Chapter 5) used the term quite differently than what Comte had in mind. So, Comte could have still used the term *social physics* to describe his positive philosophy considering, after all, he came up with the concept prior to Quetelet. With the current state of sociology—having seemingly lost its primary mission of the scientific study of society and human behavior as it actually is and the many younger sociologists who see the discipline as a place to wage a crusade with their own socio-political agendas—the field would have certainly benefited if it were still called "social physics." The term social physics makes it very clear that the discipline is meant to be a science, not an "art." Professors of social physics would have to keep a focus on matters of the scientific study of human society. Social physicist students would know that they were a part of a true scientific discipline.

It has been established, then, that social physics is a field of science that uses mathematical tools (research methodology and statistical analysis) inspired by classical physics to understand human behavior. It is the study of social phenomena through the lens of physics and mathematics. The term "social physics" was coined by Auguste Comte in 1819 in an essay which appeared in *Le Producteur* (*The Producer*), a journal created by Saint-Simon. As described in Chapter 5, Comte believed that a mechanistic science could help to explain society's complexities (Pentland 2015). Comte would refine the term *social physics* in a number of publications during the 1820s. For Comte, *social physics* is a science that concerns itself with social phenomena in the same manner as astronomical, physical, chemical and physiological phenomena; meaning that social behavior is subject to natural and invariable laws, the discovery of which is the goal of social researchers (Iggers 1958; Iggers 1959; Han and Wiita 2022). Goldberg (2014) states that Comte and others in the nineteenth century "aspired to explain social reality by developing a set of universal laws—the sociological equivalent of physicists' quest to create a theory of everything."

The topic of social physics in the contemporary era was discussed in Chapter 5. Among persons using the "social physics" label are those who incorporate "big data" analysis utilizing mathematical laws in an attempt to understand the behavior of human crowds and human behavior is Alex Pentland, an MIT professor who is considered among the leading data scientists in the world. Amir Goldberg (2014) goes as far as to describe Pentland's *Social Physics: How Good Ideas Spread—The Lessons from a New Science* as an example of a "theory of everything." Goldberg is over hyping the book by saying that, because important details such as the afterlife, the fate of the earth and the fate of the universe are not described.

The usage of the term "social physics" is important for anyone contemplating a "theory of everything" as it makes one realize that the worlds of both physics and sociology are critical. The approach used here is to incorporate physics (and the related natural sciences), sociology (and the related social sciences and humanities) and the rejection of metaphysics and theism. It is important to incorporate both physics and sociology because humans are a part of Nature and thus, utilizing a social physics approach to create a theory of everything is essential.

Among the early American sociologists to recognize the fact that humans are a part of Nature is Lester Frank Ward (1841–1913). Ward is generally acknowledged as the "father of American sociology" and he is the American sociologist who was instrumental in establishing sociology as an academic discipline in the United States (Editors of Encyclopædia Britannica 2023c; Delaney 2024). Ward has even been described as the American Aristotle (Commager 1967; Chugerman 1965). Ward was very optimistic about the role of the social sciences, and especially sociology, in their ability to help humanity achieve basic happiness and equality. Ward shared Comte's idea that sociology had a fundamental purpose of helping to teach the means necessary to improve society. In his two volume *Dynamic Sociology,* (considered Ward's most important publication as its breadth of coverage of the genesis of sociology details a great number of topics critical to the establishment of the legitimacy of early American sociology) Ward describes the "reciprocal relations of man and the universe." In Chapter 8 of Volume 2 of *Dynamic Sociology,* Ward addresses two special problems: (1) What is the attitude which nature assumes toward man? and (2) What is the attitude which man should assume toward nature? Ward believed that these two fundamental questions must be answered if society hopes to successfully self-direct itself toward progress. As a proponent of sociologists leading the way in guidance toward societal progress, we can see why such an issue is of utmost importance to Ward. Ward's answers to these two questions are lengthy and drawn out throughout the text. However, he does make significant main points for us to consider. First, he states that "nature stands to man in the relation of the whole to a part" (Ward 1883:3). Ward adds, "Man is an integral part of the universe, and, in order to be correctly conceived and properly studied, he must be conceived and studied as an objective phenomenon presented by nature" (p. 3). Nature is also the creator of Man such as it created every other object (e.g., animals, trees, rocks, metal or gas) in the universe. Humans are simply one of the many products of nature. "Nature, therefore, occupies the relation to man of cause to effect, of antecedent to consequent" (Ward 1883:4).

With regard to the answer to his second question—What is the attitude which man should assume toward nature?—Ward (1883) states, "Man finds himself an integral part of this great unconscious creative whole called nature, only a minute fraction of which can by any possible means be brought within the range of his experience" (p. 11). However, in our pursuit of knowledge of nature and of the universe, Ward said humanity must not be deterred by fear; we must find a way to evade the action of natural laws without apprehension as nature has no consciousness nor intelligence. "Man's right to probe and penetrate the deepest secrets of the universe is absolute and unchallenged" (Ward 1883:12). Thus, Ward is stating that humanity must not be held by the chains of doubt and that we must forge ahead in our pursuit of knowledge of the laws of the universe. Ward would surely be pleased by humanity's space exploration programs (Delaney 2024).

Ward, like Comte, would also be pleased, presumably, by the pursuit of a "theory of everything" that incorporates the laws of nature, humanity and our place in the Universe. Consequently, we can see, once again, the value of social physics within the framework of a "theory of everything."

Human Progress

For Comte, positivism was a doctrine based on the idea that everything in society is observable and subject to patterns or laws. This idea is parallel to that of the natural sciences in that everything should be explainable by laws, or a unified explanatory theory. Comte believed that laws could be established to explain human behavior (Simpson 1969). By this, Comte did not mean that human behavior would always be subjected to these "laws"; rather, he saw positivism as a way of explaining phenomena apart from supernatural or speculative causes (Simpson 1969).

In order to establish laws, practitioners must first theorize about social phenomena and then devise mechanisms of study in order to collect and analyze data in an attempt to either support or disprove a theory. Comte established this very fundamental scientific approach as the foundation of positivism, later to be called sociology. To this day, the most basic principle of sociology is the realization that this discipline is: theory, methods and everything else (the subject areas under study). Most sociologists, like most practitioners of any academic discipline (including physicists), think small and focus on specific behaviors. Others dare to think big, and even hope to create a "theory of everything."

The very purpose of sociology as a discipline is to discover and define social patterns of societal development. Comte believed positivism would create sound theories based on sufficient factual evidence and historical comparisons to predict future events, important elements when attempting to create a "theory of everything." The discovery of basic laws of human behavior would allow for deliberate courses of action on the part of both individuals and society. Decision-making could be made on rational, positivistic grounds. Utilizing the positivistic approach would allow social scientists to create sound theories—based on factual evidence and historical comparisons—to predict future events. The ability to predict future events could clearly benefit individuals and societies.

The Law of Three Stages

Throughout this text we have learned of numerous theorists from many academic disciplines that have created "laws," often utilizing stages, or steps. One of the most famous early theories involving laws with stages is Isaac Newton's (1642–1726) "Three Laws of Motion." Newton's work has influenced nearly every physicist, even hundreds of years following his death. Newton influenced Claude-Henri Saint-Simon's idea that societies progressed through three stages. Saint-Simon believed that it was possible to study the structure of society by examining its historical moral development and idealism. Saint-Simon felt that any scientific study of society has to look at the moral ideas of a period because at any particular time in history the form of organization of society is a direct reflection of the prevailing social code. He studied the moral systems of development in Western Europe and found that as societies progressed, one moral system replaced the previous one. This process of replacement-transition results from accumulated scientific knowledge, which be believed changes the philosophical outlook of the society. You may recall that for Saint-Simon the "Three Moral Systems" are: (1) Supernatural-Polytheistic Morals; (2) Christian Theism; and (3) Positivism.

Saint-Simon's three moral systems ideals of human progress would have a direct influence on Auguste Comte's "Law of Three Stages," or the "Law of Human Progress." Comte believed that human progress could be measured based on where people stood in the evolutionary chain of development. (Note: Just as Comte cautioned that every society is subject to periods of crisis and great disorganization that may interfere with its progress, I too would point out that there are many periods of time in any stage of human development where humanity may not actually be "evolving" but simply moving onward and transitioning to the next stage of development.)

Comte's first stage of human progress was the "Theological" (circa prior to 1300 CE), a stage of development wherein the human mind and societies as a whole are dominated by religious or supernatural explanations to elucidate what humans otherwise could not. In this first stage, natural phenomena are explained as being the result of supernatural or divine powers and it matters not whether the religion is polytheistic or monotheistic as either one presumes miraculous powers or wills are believed to produce the observed events (The Editors of Encyclopædia Britannica 2020). The second stage, "Metaphysical" (1300–1800 CE), was a mere modification of the first stage and centers on the idea that abstract forces control behavior. While Comte found this stage as an improvement over Stage 1, he viewed it as merely a transitional one because people could not handle a direct jump from Stage 1 to Stage 3. With metaphysics, no genuine explanations result: questions concerning ultimate reality, first causes, or absolute beginnings are unanswerable. "The metaphysical quest can lead only to the conclusion expressed by the German biologist and physiologist Emil du Bois-Reymond: *'Ignoramus et ignorabimus'* (Latin: 'We are and shall be ignorant')" (The Editors of Encyclopædia Britannica 2020). Comte's third stage of human progress is the "Positive" stage (after 1800 CE). In this stage of societal development and development of human mind, there comes the realization that natural laws exist and that they are separate of any notion of a God or gods. Through the use of reason and observation to study the social world, human behavior can be explained rationally. This stage is highlighted by a reliance on science, rational thought, empirical laws and observation (Delaney 2024). Abandoning theological and metaphysical explanations afforded humankind the chance to reach "full maturity of thought" (The Editors of Encyclopædia Britannica 2020) once such primitive forms of explanations were replaced with scientific ones.

The Fourth Stage of Human Progress

As Comte was an early- and mid-nineteenth-century social theorist who promoted positivism and attempted to established a new academic discipline of sociology modeled after social physics and Enlightenment principles, he had no need to worry about creating a fourth stage of human progress. Science was the crowning achievement of intellectual development in Comte's era. He certainly had no need to conjure a fourth stage of human progress. In fact, the positivistic (scientific) stage has dominated human thought and spearheaded significant and instrumental changes in everyday life and our level of knowledge about our planet, surrounding galaxies and our Universe since its inception.

It would take something monumentally epic to state that we have reached a point of human progression that goes beyond the positivistic stage but we have indeed reached that point. This fourth stage of human progress is *artificial intelligence* (AI). The concept of "artificial intelligence" has been around since 1956 when John McCarthy coined the term at the Dartmouth Summer Research Project on Artificial Intelligence (DSRPAI) hosted by McCarthy and Marvin Minsky. The field grew modestly but today it is omnipresent. We will learn more about AI in the following pages but to make sure everyone has a working idea of its meaning, artificial intelligence (AI) refers to the ability of a digital computer or computer-controlled robot to perform tasks commonly associated with intelligent beings (Copeland 2024).

Social Physics and Human Progress (Delaney's Law of Human Progress)

The major paradigms of thought were discussed in Chapter 1 of this book. A paradigm of thought was defined as a model of thinking and a way of viewing reality for a community of like-minded people and their associated behavioral patterns—especially in connection with social interaction. The four major paradigms of thought were identified as tradition; faith; common sense; and enlightened, rational thought. We can see a direct connection of two of these paradigms of thought (faith and enlightened rational thought) to Comte's first and third stages of human progress. It was enlightened rational thinking that gave rise to scientific discovery and explanation and inspired Comte's ideas on positivism and social physics.

Here, the major paradigms of thought are modified and applied into an evolutionary theory of human progress with the addition of the fourth stage of development of artificial intelligence (AI). The four stages are listed below:

1. Tradition—Whereas Comte's first stage of the "Law of Human Progress" began with the theological, there was a way of thinking and doing things prior to the introduction of faith and religion, namely, tradition. Tradition refers to a way of thinking, behaving, or doing something that has been utilized by people of a particular grouping over a long period of time. It is an inherited, established, or customary pattern of thought, action or behavior passed on from generation to generation dating back to the earliest humans and lasting for thousands of years. Before humans learned to read and write, such traditions were passed down via oral communication. In this stage of human development, a strong authoritarian leader (e.g., a clan leader in primitive societies or a dictator in later times) or a central government prevails over citizens' daily lives. Over a period of centuries the intrusive concept of "royalty," with birth rights valued over merit, would be a prime characteristic of this stage of human development. Traditional forms of thinking are not conducive for innovative types of thought and human progress. Traditions remain important for many people and in many societies but as time moved on, new forms of thought would emerge.
2. Faith—As Saint-Simon (Christian Theism) and Comte (theological) acknowledged religious or supernatural explanations became popular prior

to, or during, the Middle Ages. The concept of "faith" is preferred here as it is a more all-encompassing term that recognizes the same basic ideas—that adherents to a certain faith are taught to choose courses of action that abide by specific belief systems that have been enacted by elders (representatives of God or holy entities). While people may have "faith" in any number of things, such as an auto mechanic's ability to repair a problem with their car; a doctor to perform a medical procedure properly; or, that a friend will be there for you in a time of crisis; faith generally refers to, as it does here, either a strong belief in God or the doctrines of some religion or spiritual way of life. Faith almost always implies a firm belief in something even when there is no evidence or proof (e.g., the existence of God and an afterlife that involves Heaven or Hell). As with the tradition-based form of human progress, faith is generally quite conservative in the socio-political realm and is generally used in the maintenance of social order. Also like the tradition-based realm, faith remains important for many people despite its obvious flaws as a method to assist human progress and assist in the evolution of humanity.

3. Enlightened, Rational Thought—This is the stage of development that both Saint-Simon and Comte referred to as "Positivism." The positivistic stage of human progress followed the Enlightenment, a time of great scientific discovery. The Positive stage also began during industrialization, a time of great societal change. This was an era when social thinkers realized that "laws" could be applied to the social world just as they were being applied to the natural world. Through the use of reason and observation to study the social world, human behavior could be explained rationally. Science, then, would help humanity progress to greater heights never before attained. Enlightened, rational thought allowed for countless discoveries and innovations that have assisted humanity in progressive and evolutionary thought. Science has allowed for the development of new technologies that assist us in everyday life. The examples of how science has helped humans progress are nearly endless but include: advancements in medicine, communications, construction, clothing, cooking, basic hygiene, travel, ways of understanding the world, inventions and innovations, education, improvements in agriculture, more sports and leisure opportunities, exploration of Earth, the oceans, and space; science helps us to become better informed citizens; it helps to stimulate creativity; and it increases our fundamental levels of knowledge. There is absolutely no doubt that science has made the world better even when we recognize that the power of science in the wrong hands can cause problems for others (e.g., those who would weaponize scientific breakthroughs to harm others, the environment or the planet).

4. Artificial Intelligence (AI)—We have clearly reached a point in human society wherein we are being dominated by artificial intelligence. Just as each of the previous stages of human development did not eliminate the previous ones, AI has not eliminated the others either. However, AI *is* omnipresent, its presence is felt in nearly all spheres of life and while it has been around, in one form or another, for decades, artificial intelligence is becoming increasing powerful

now. Just like those who prefer tradition or faith over science, and those who prefer enlightened, rational thought over AI, we cannot wish it away as it has been become commonplace and is widespread in nearly all facets of life. AI is everywhere. In the following pages, we will learn more about the positive and negative impacts of AI and its impact on human progress.

(Note: The paradigm of thought of "common sense" is not a part of a specific stage of human progress because, as explained in Chapter 1, it is an aspect of all eras, but dominant in none.)

Artificial Intelligence (AI)

Before we discuss the meaning of artificial intelligence let's first understand that human *intelligence* refers to the ability to acquire and apply knowledge and skills which is characterized by the capability to learn or understand and develop complex cognitive feats. Colom and associates (2010) define "intelligence" as a general mental ability for reasoning, problem solving, and learning. "Because of its general nature, intelligence integrates cognitive functions such as perception, attention, memory, language, or planning" (Colom et al 2010). Reasoning, problem solving, and learning are crucial facets of human intelligence. People should be able to reason about virtually any issue and theoretically solve problems. However, there are widespread individual differences in the ability to reason, solve problems, and learn which lead to human differences in the general ability to cope with challenging situations (Colom et al 2010). Psychologists have developed hundreds of tests for the standardized measurement of intelligence with varying degrees of reliability and validity.

When we say that something is "artificial" it means that it is intentionally made by human skill (manufactured) opposed to being natural (e.g., artificial flavoring or artificial flowers). Artificial intelligence (AI) as described earlier in this chapter refers to the ability of a digital computer or computer-controlled robot to perform tasks commonly associated with intelligent beings (Copeland 2024). The United States Department of State, per the National Artificial Intelligence Act of 2020, states, "The term 'artificial intelligence' means a machine-based system that can, for a given set of human defined objectives, make predictions, recommendations or decisions influences real or virtual environments." Darrell M. West (2018), a senior fellow at the Center for Technology Innovation at the Brookings Institution, states that AI is generally thought to refer to "machines that respond to stimulation consistent with traditional responses from humans, given the human capacity for contemplation, judgment, and intention." Advancements in AI since its humble beginnings have allowed it to "incorporate intentionality, intelligence, and adaptability in their algorithms. Rather than being mechanistic or deterministic in how the machines operate, AI software learns as it goes along and incorporates real-world experience in its decision-making" (West 2018). An *algorithm* refers to a process or set of rules with precise steps to take to be followed in calculations or other problem-solving operations written in a computer program. AI systems contain algorithms for operating and processing. As AI systems advance, their algorithms begin to notice patterns not in their programming. The concern is, what will these AI systems do if/when they become self-aware and create algorithms for their own benefit and perhaps the determinant of humanity? Is that even possible? A sort of "rise of the machines," similar to that of the *Terminator* movie franchise?

The History and Development of AI

The genesis of AI can be traced to British logician and computer pioneer Alan Mathison Turing who, in 1935, described an abstract computing machine consisting of a limitless memory and a scanner that moves back and forth through the memory, symbol by symbol, reading what it finds and writing further symbols. The actions of the scanner are dictated by a program of instructions (similar to an algorithm) that are also stored in the memory in the form of symbols (Copeland 2024). "This is Turing's stored-program concept, and implicit in it is the possibility of the machine operating on, and so modifying or improving, its own program. Turing's conception is now known simply as the universal Turing machine. All modern computers are in essence universal Turing machines" (Copeland 2024). The first true AI programs would have to await the arrival of stored-program electronic digital computers. "In other words, computers could be told what to do but couldn't remember what they did" (Anyoha 2017). Not only were computers quite primitive in the early 1950s, the cost of leasing a computer was extremely expensive, up to $200,000 a month and only the most prestigious universities and big technology companies could afford such a luxury (Anyoha 2017).

Turing was already promoting the idea of "thinking" machines, beginning with those that could learn how to play chess at the level of human beings. In 1950, Turing had the idea of the "Turing Test" which specified that computers needed to complete reasoning puzzles as well as humans in order to be truly "thinking" in an autonomous manner (West 2018). The earliest successful AI program was written in 1951 by Christopher Strachey, later director of the Programming Research Group at the University of Oxford. Strachey created a program that allowed a thinking machine to play a complete game of checkers at a reasonable speed (Copeland 2024). The first AI program run in the United States was also a checkers program, written in 1952 by Arthur Samuel for the prototype of the IBM 701. Samuel's program greatly improved upon Strachey's checkers program (Copeland 2024). His improvements eventually led to the program winning one game against a former Connecticut checkers champion in 1962. It would take more than three decades later (1997) before an IBM computer (Deep Blue) would beat a chess world champion (Garry Kasparov) for the first time. "Deep Blue derived its prowess through brute force computing power. It used 32 processors to perform a set of coordinated, high-speed computations in parallel. Deep Blue was able to evaluate 200 million chess positions per second, achieving a processing speed of 11.38 billion floating-point operations per second, or *flops*. By comparison, IBM's first supercomputer, Stretch, introduced in 1961, had a process speed of less than 500 flops" (IBM Heritage 2024).

The idea of a "thinking machine" was transformed to an intelligent machine by

Stanford Professor John McCarthy who coined the term "Artificial Intelligence" and defined it as "the science and engineering of making intelligent machines" (Manning 2020). McCarthy, who received a BS in mathematics from Caltech (1948) and a Ph.D. in mathematics from Princeton (1951), is considered a pioneer in the fields of artificial intelligence, computer science and interactive computing systems. He coined the term "AI" in connection with the Dartmouth College Artificial Intelligence Conference held at Dartmouth College in 1956 where he was a professor at the time and which many of the world's leading thinkers in computing attended (Moor 2006). "As part of refining his ideas about AI, he also invented the programming language LISP in 1958" (Computer History Museum 2023). McCarthy created LISP (List Processor) by combining elements of IPL (Information Processing Language), a computer language tailored for AI programming (established by Newell, Simon and Shaw) with lambda calculus (a formal mathematical-logical system) (Copeland 2024). Allen Newell, a researcher at the RAND Corporation (Santa Monica, California) and Herbert Simon, a psychologist and computer scientist at Carnegie Mellon University (Pittsburgh, Pennsylvania; Cliff Shaw was the system programmer), created a physical symbol system hypothesis that states that process structures of symbols are sufficient, in principle, to produce artificial intelligence in a digital computer and that, moreover, human intelligence is the result of the same type of symbolic manipulations (Copeland 2024). IPL had a library of 150 basic operations, working with lists and symbols were among its basic achievements.

Throughout the 1960s, there were modest improvements in AI. In 1970, Marvin Minsky, an original co-host along with John McCarthy of the DSRPAI conference, was quoted in *Life* magazine: "from three to eight years we will have a machine with the general intelligence of an average human being" (Anyoha 2017). There was progress but not to the degree of the early proponents of AI. Among other problems to emerge was the realization that there was not enough memory or processing speed through the early 1990s to accomplish anything truly useful. Thus, while human minds had conjured ideas on how computers could create an AI revolution, the technology did not exist yet to allow that to happen. Add to that, the previously mentioned prohibitive factor of costs, added to the lack of AI funding from universities and private agencies as they wanted to see immediate results. Deep Blue's 1997 chess victory over a reigning world chess champion was significant as it demonstrated that a computer could outsmart a human that was an expert at a specialized task. While the funding for AI was still lagging, public interest in AI following Deep Blue's victory sparked a huge interest in artificial intelligence.

In the early 2000s, a number of computing robots were gaining victories against humans: In 2005, a Stanford robot won the DARPA Grand Challenge by driving autonomously for 131 miles along an unrehearsed desert trail; two days later, a team from CMU won the DARPA Urban Challenge by autonomously navigating 55 miles in an urban environment while adhering to traffic hazards and all traffic laws; and then, the big event that drew much media attention, the February 2011 victory of IBM's question answering system, Watson, that defeated two of the greatest *Jeopardy!* champions, Brad Rutter and Ken Jennings, and by a significant margin. The twenty-first century also played witness to the validation of a variation of Moore's law (a prediction made by American engineer Gordon Moore in 1965 that the number of transistors per silicon chip doubles every year) that computing power doubles roughly every 18 months, which continued to hold true. Computers now possessed processing power far beyond that of previous generations and, it could input and process much larger datasets ("big data"). Our current era has outpaced human intelligence. We can now collect "big data" so quickly with such large sums of information that no one person could ever process. Humans have to turn to AI to process all this information. Even if Moore's law begins to slow down, humans will never be able to catch up with the technology and computers with AI will likely always surpass us. AI systems have shown the ability for "deep learning"—in which neural networks have four or more layers, including the initial input and final output. "Moreover, such networks are able to learn unsupervised—that is, to discover features in data without initial prompting" (Copeland 2024). A *neural network*, then, is a method utilized in AI that teaches computers to process data in a way that is inspired by the human brain; it is a type of machine learning process, called deep learning that uses interconnected nodes or neurons in a layered structure that resembles the human brain.

Another rather unique example of an AI robot gaining a victory over a human occurred at D'Youville University in Buffalo, New York, May 11, 2024, when AI Robot Sophia, created by Hanson Robotics, served as commencement speaker instead of a human. University President Lorrie Clemo (a personal friend of this author) "justified" the decision by saying, "A major role of higher education is to be an instructor for innovation, and to prepare students for both the opportunities and challenges of the future. This event will represent an intersection of technology and education" (D'Youville University News 2024). The decision was a controversial one on campus with some in favor and others with reservations. As for the speech itself, it was quite non-traditional. "Sophia, dressed in a D'Youville sweatshirt, answered questions from a student on stage. She talked about the future of technology in hospitals and joked about the best place in Buffalo to get chicken wings" (Minkewicz 2024). Many students preferred a more personable speech; some faculty were upset over the amount of money spent on the commencement address especially in light that they have worked without a contract for almost three years; but, others were open to the idea of an AI robot giving the commencement speech as they recognize that AI is already an undeniable part of their lives (Minkewicz 2024). Meanwhile, at Northeastern University, President Joseph E. Aoun's commencement address included his informing graduates, "No machine can match your creativity, innovation" (Lloyd 2024). Aoun added, "AI simply cannot think across different contexts." As we shall see later in this chapter, others have come to, or worry about, a different conclusion.

In the early 2020s, it was ChatGPT that was all the rage. ChatGPT is an AI chatbot that uses natural language processing to create humanlike conversational dialogue (Hetler 2024). A *chatbot* is a computer program designed to simulate conversation with human users, especially over the internet; they are conversational tools that perform routine tasks efficiently. People like using chatbots because they help them to get out of doing tasks on their own (e.g., work assignments and school assignments); they are especially helpful when the human does not have the intelligence or willingness to do the work. GPT stands for "Generative Pre-trained Transformer," which refers to how ChatGPT processes requests and formulates responses. ChatGPT is a form of generative AI—a tool that lets users enter prompts to receive humanlike images, text or videos that are created by AI (Hetler 2024). ChatGPT is a specific chatbot developed by OpenAI (a private research laboratory founded by a group of entrepreneurs and researchers including Elon Musk and Sam Altman in 2015) and launched on November 30, 2022. OpenAI is backed by several investors, with Microsoft being the most notable (Hetler 2024). OpenAI also created Dall-E, an AI text-to-art generator (it enables users to create new images with text to graphics). Investors couldn't wait to pour money into OpenAI's ChatGPT, Microsoft alone made a $10 billion investment (Hiltzik 2023).

ChatGPT utilizes specialized algorithms to find patterns within data sequences. The transformer pulls from a significant amount of data ("big data") to formulate a response. Human trainers can program a chatbox with voice data to replicate the voice of anyone and then create a speech (such as a politician running for office) or a back-and-forth conversation. In most cases, it is virtually impossible to distinguish between the AI version of the person and the real human. Throughout 2023, OpenAI programmers pumped in all sorts of data from, of course, existing sources, including allegedly, millions of articles from the *New York Times* in order to train automated chatbots on how to compete with the news outlet as a source of reliable information (Merchant 2024). The *New York Times* filed a lawsuit against OpenAI and joined a class-action lawsuit filed by illustrators, the photo service Getty Images, the Author's Guild, anonymous social media users and many others, all alleging that companies like Open AI stand to profit from their work but being passed off AI creations. The Hollywood screenwriters' (Writers Guild of America) and actors' (The Screen Actors Guild-American Federation of Television and Radio Actors) strike of 2023 was centered on better pay and working conditions but also provisions on artificial intelligence as their intellectual property was being stolen, or could be stolen for AI purposes (e.g., the actors wanted guardrails on how the technology could be used to recreate their performances and screenwriters wanted to make sure that studios would refuse to produce AI-generated scripts).

In 2024, Google introduced a free (plus "convenience fees") AI app for smartphones called Gemini. The embedded technology enables people to quickly connect to a digital brain that can write for them, interpret what they're reading and seeing and help manage (or, perhaps manipulate) their lives. With the advent of the Gemini app, Google will cast aside the Bard chatbot that it introduced the previous year in an effort to catch up to ChatGPT created by Microsoft (*The Citizen* 2024). The Gemini chatbot, like all other chatbots, is designed to get people used to relying on technology instead of their own brains to write, interpret what they're reading and perform a number of other tasks in their lives (CBS News 2024). The implications of all this is quite frightful.

In many occupational fields people fear AI chatbots. This is especially true in education. "The notion that generative AI systems are at root 'plagiarism machines' has become increasingly widespread among their critics, and social media is teeming with opprobrium against AI" (Merchant 2024). Brett Becker, an assistant professor in the School of Computer Science at University College Dublin believes there are positive aspects of AI education (AIEd). He believes that AIEd will assist in social mobility; address achievement gaps; enhance teacher expertise; and address teacher retention and teacher shortages (Becker 2017).

The U.S. Federal Trade Commission (FTC) has open investigations on OpenAI because of its conversational AI bots. OpenAI's technology hit the market of business and social worlds so quickly and with such an immense impact that the FTC never had a chance to look into and develop regulatory guidelines. Now it will be playing catch-up. Among the concerns of the FTC is that OpenAI chatbots may produce "false, misleading, disparaging or harmful statements about people" (Edgerton and Nylen 2023:C3). In February 2024, in an effort to "catch-up," the Federal Communications Commission (FCC) outlawed robocalls that contain voices generated by AI, a decision that sends a clear message that exploiting the technology to scam people and mislead voters won't be tolerated. The regulation empowers the FCC to fine companies that use AI voices in their calls or block the service providers that carry them (Associated Press 2024).

Positive Aspects of AI

With AI's ability to collect and process vast amounts of data, make predictions based on informed decisions and automate tasks, it lends itself as a valuable tool for improving productivity, enhancing creativity, as well as taking on complex problems in a variety of fields all the while saving time and eliminating biases (so long as the algorithm has not been programmed to discriminate against certain persons, groups or categories of people). A number of people and entities promote the advantages of artificial intelligence as they see positive aspects of AI. Nikita Duggal (2023), for example, describes 10 benefits of artificial intelligence:

1. Reduction in Human Error—AI can significantly reduce errors and increase accuracy and precision. Decisions taken by AI in every step is decided by information previously gathered and guided by a set of algorithms. When the algorithms are programmed properly, these errors can be reduced to null.
2. Zero Risks—The use of AI robots can eliminate risks to humans in a number of tasks, including defusing a bomb, going to space, exploring the deepest parts of the oceans, and machines with metal bodies are resistant in nature and can survive unfriendly atmospheres.
3. 24 × 7 Availability—Humans cannot work all day long; we tire over time and need rest, and most of us do not want to work 7 days a week, let alone 24 hours a day, even if we had the stamina to do so. (The popular adage for most humans today is that they seek a "life/work" balance.) AI can work endlessly without breaks and think much faster than humans even while performing multiple tasks at a time with accurate results. (They have no personal life and therefore they do not need a "life/work" balance.) Further, while humans find tedious, repetitive jobs boring, AI devices have no sense of boredom.
4. Digital Assistance—Most technologically-advanced companies utilize digital

assistants which eliminate the need for human personnel; they can deliver user-requested content; they can interact with humans as chatbots; and they do not have to be paid a salary with benefits.

5. New Inventions—AI is at the forefront of creating numerous innovations and technologies (e.g., detecting breast cancer in women at an earlier stage); although, because AI is dependent on human-made algorithms, this advantage is somewhat limited right now.

6. Unbiased Decisions—So long as the algorithms are not programmed with built-in biases, AI will make decisions that are unbiased, devoid of emotions and that are highly practical and rational.

7. Perform Repetitive Jobs—A big advantage of AI is that it will perform repetitive tasks, without complaining, and as a result, necessary, mundane tasks are completed in a timely and efficient manner.

8. Daily Applications—Here, we are talking about the "apps" that people are utilizing on a regular basis found on their mobile devices and the Internet. Clearly, humans love these AI shortcuts that provide us valuable information (e.g., for weather, maps and communication).

9. AI in Risky Situations—It is much better for humans to utilize an AI robot to perform perilous tasks on our behalf in dangerous situations including law enforcement and military scenarios.

10. Medical Applications—AI applications are being used and expanded upon in many areas ranging from diagnosis and treatment to drug discovery and clinical trials. AI-powered tools can help medical personnel with potential risky health procedures.

AI is helping the development of science in many ways including analyzing "big data," identifying meaningful trends in these large datasets and simulating complex scenarios. For example, generative AI can be used to fight and prevent fraud by analyzing patterns in data and identifying potential risk factors so companies can spot indicators of potentially fraudulent behavior. In violent crowd situations, AI security systems can be used to identify and round up violators via facial recognition programming, a technique utilized in soccer stadiums in Europe and Latin America to prevent hooliganism (Olson 2024). Frey, Patton, Gaskell and McGregor conducted a study wherein they mined social media data from marginalized communities to look for street gang activity in Chicago. The researchers felt that the algorithms lacked the ability to accurately interpret the off-line context of the communications so they hired former gang members as domain experts for contextualizing social media data in order to create inclusive, community-informed algorithms. The ultimate goal was to help prevent gang activity via communication analysis (Frey et al 2018).

In sports, athletic trainers and coaches are utilizing AI Statcast-tracking technology to keep track of athletes' performances as a pre- and post-test means of measuring injury recovery. Data is also collected on athletes from sensors who utilize "wearables" and cameras and AI processes player performance in real time. This promotes data-driven decision-making by coaches and athletes to enhance practice and game plans. Through AI data analysis of high-level box-score statistics, teams can also get a better understanding of their own team and of their opponents' strengths, weaknesses and patterns by using AI algorithms to evaluate data collected on opponents. This gives teams that use AI a competitive edge (Liu, Mahapatra and Mayuri 2021).

Facial recognition is being used to unlock many cellular phone devices. Smart cars/self-driving cars, known as autonomous vehicles, while in their infancy in the early 2020s, are being developed at an increasing rate and this is something that can benefit everyone but especially those who cannot drive traditional automobiles (e.g., people with physical limitations). AI is utilized in many other areas in positive ways as well. In education, artificial intelligence can provide detailed feedback to students on their performance, allowing them to better understand their strengths and weaknesses. Similarly, AI can analyze data on waste production, collection and disposal in an environmental effort to help save the planet; it can help optimize supply chains to reduce waste; monitor and promote sustainable manufacturing processes; and assist scientists to develop alternative energy sources (other than fossil fuels). AI can help musicians create and produce music, for example, a new Beatles song ("Now and Then") and music video was released in 2023, even though two members of the band were long deceased (the song was originally recorded in the 1970s as a demo by John Lennon but was cleaned up with audio-enhancing technology).

As we can see from this brief overview sampling, AI has its hands in all sorts of fields. In fact, there have even been chatbots created to deal with grief. For example, HereAfter AI, a U.S.-based company allows people to upload memories, creating a "life story avatar" with which family and friends can interact. Loved ones hear meaningful stories about you after you have died and can interact with your avatar after your death. There is a holographic avatar and conversational AI bot version as well (Steinbauer 2023). You can decide for yourself if this is a great idea or just a bit creepy.

Negative Aspects of AI

There are a number of very serious concerns regarding artificial intelligence and consequently, it is easy to identify a number of specific negative aspects of AI. Duggal (2023) identifies seven disadvantages of AI:

1. High Costs—It takes a great deal of ability, plenty of time and financial resources to create a machine that can stimulate human intelligence. AI also needs to operate on the latest hardware and software to stay updated, thus making it quite costly.
2. No Creativity—A big disadvantage of AI is that it cannot learn to think outside the box. AI is capable of learning over time with pre-fed data and past experiences, but cannot be creative in its approach. This lack of creativity is connected to a loss of human influence. An overreliance on AI technology can result in reduced human empathy and reasoning (Thomas 2023).
3. Unemployment—One variation (application) of AI is a robot, which

is displacing occupations and human workers and thus increasing unemployment. At the start of 2024, the numbers of those unemployed because of AI robots was relatively small but the application of robots had just begun. Some estimates have it that by 2030, tasks that account for up to 30 percent of hours currently being worked in the U.S. economy could be automated—with Black and Hispanic employees left especially vulnerable (Thomas 2023).

4. Contributing to Human Laziness—AI applications automate the majority of tedious and repetitive tasks. Since humans no longer have to memorize things (like basic mathematical formulas such as the "multiplication tables") or solve puzzles to get the job done, we tend to use our brains less and less. This addiction to AI can cause problems to future generations. Human laziness is something quite noticeable, especially among younger people who prefer to look everything up on their AI devices rather than figure things out in their heads (e.g., doing simple math in their heads) or simply put things to memory (e.g., remembering facts and figures of historic events). As a college professor, I have increasingly noticed over the years that students will ask me questions that I have already provided the answers to in course information tabs or in a course syllabus but they are just too lazy to read the instructions. They are increasingly relying on AI to do their homework and write their term papers; again, instead of doing the research themselves and actually learning the material. Clearly it is not just college students taking the easy way out, people in many spheres of life and in their personal lives are doing the same thing—taking the easy way out. AI is most definitely contributing to the laziness of humans.

5. No Ethics—Ethics and morality are important human features that can be difficult to incorporate into an AI. In a 2019 Vatican meeting titled, "The Common Good in the Digital Age," Pope Francis warned against AI's ability to "circulate tendentious opinions and false data" and stressed the far-reaching consequences of letting this technology develop without proper oversight or restraint (Thomas 2023).

6. Emotionless—Humans have emotions. Having emotions can be positive as it allows us to function as a team, something especially important for management, but emotions also cloud judgments, can lead to biases, cause mental breakdowns and shortcomings, and lead to a loss of productivity, among a slew of other problems. Computers and AI machines have no feelings. They are designed to function with maximum efficiency and pesky emotions are never a part of the decision-making process.

7. No Improvement—As of now, AI cannot improve itself; once it is programmed, based on current technology and pre-loaded facts and past experiences, it cannot advance itself, it is dependent upon humans for adjustments and improvements.

There are a number of other very significant disadvantages of a world inundated with artificial intelligence. Consider, we have no idea who created the vast majority of algorithms that go into AI technology, we do not know the true motives beyond any AI algorithm including whether or not they are safe or biased. In other words, there is a lack of transparency (Thomas 2023). AI security systems used to help control criminal activity (described earlier as a positive aspect of AI) could be used as a form of social surveillance by repressive governments and corporations. AI can be used to track a person's movement, as they are in many countries already (Thomas 2023). Many people naively embrace a cashless society and do not carry cash with them for purchases and instead, choose to pay everything with non-cash forms of legal tender. This is a very dangerous situation as it creates a lack of data privacy and allows for companies and governments to track a consumer's every purchase. "While there are laws present to protect personal information in some cases in the United States, there is no explicit federal law that protects citizens from data privacy harm experienced by AI" (Thomas 2023). Built-in biases in AI algorithms may be used to compromise diversity, equity and inclusion (DEI) initiatives.

History has documented many instances of scientific and innovative creations that were designed to help humanity that were transformed by nefarious persons (e.g., military powers and paramilitary groups and autocratic governments) for the purpose of warfare and control over a populace. As a result, we must be very concerned about AI-fueled autonomous weapons. If any major military power pushes ahead with AI weapons development (e.g., robotic armies), a global arms race is virtually inevitable and the endpoint of this technological trajectory is catastrophic (Thomas 2023). According to the World Economic Forum, among the developments of AI weaponry is the Lethal Autonomous Weapon Systems (LAWS): machines engineered to identify, engage and destroy targets without human control (Effoduh 2024). Drones are already used by militaries and paramilitary groups and although they rely on human commands through a set of communication channels and algorithms, they can be infiltrated by adversaries. Fighter jets are being piloted by AI systems without humans inside the plane and without humans commanding them. Not only do we have to worry that AI weapons can be hacked we have to worry about the realization that they can simply make mistakes (e.g., mistake "friendlies" for "hostiles").

The idea that AI weapons and defense systems can be hacked leads us to another obvious concern; namely, that *any* AI system can potentially be hacked. That includes systems that control power grids and financial institutions. Speaking of the financial industry, AI technology has become involved in everyday finance and trading processes. "As a result, algorithmic trading could be responsible for our next major financial crisis in the markets. While AI algorithms aren't clouded by human judgment or emotions, they also don't take into account contexts, the interconnectedness of markets and factors like human trust and fear" (Thomas 2023). Because AI algorithms can make thousands of trades at a blistering pace and may do so even to make small profits, "selling off thousands of trades could scare investors into doing the same thing, leading to sudden crashes and extreme market volatility" (Thomas 2023).

With developments in AI, the spread of misinformation has reached new heights and levels of concerns. AI is being used by all sorts of persons to create fake news for a variety of reasons (e.g., to cause panic, for political purposes, and to discredit reputable persons). Within the political realm, governments and political actors around the world use AI to generate texts, images and video in an attempt to manipulate public opinion in their favor and to censor content that is critical of their position. Political misinformation flows in the opposite direction as well; that is to say, AI generated misinformation can be directed toward political leaders to make them think their constituents feel/believe a certain way about a socio-political issue. It is nearly impossible for elected officials to know the difference between real correspondences and fake ones. Consider, researchers conducting a recent study for Brookings sent 32,398 emails to legislative offices, some written by citizens, others generated by AI, which can deliver thousands of letters that appear genuine in seconds. The study found legislative offices could not discern which were fake (Kull and Thomas 2023). It's situations like this where AI is guilty of bias because the algorithm is designed to deceive.

There are those sounding the alarm that things are only going to get worse. "We are just seeing the beginning of what will become a flood of false inputs drowning genuine input and further undermining public confidence" (Kull and Thomas 2023:A16). Misinformation leads to another problem caused by AI, the creation of "deepfakes." *Deepfakes* are the AI manipulation of facial appearance through deep generative methods. While images of people is nothing new, deepfakes are far more realistic than "cheapfakes" and harder to detect. Homeland Security (2023) describes deepfakes as a serious problem and defines them as "an emergent type of threat falling under the greater and more pervasive umbrella of synthetic media, utilize a form of artificial intelligence/machine learning (AI/ML) to create believable, realistic videos, pictures, audio, and text of events which never happen." Deepfakes are used to spread false information or to manipulate the public opinion by creating fake videos of people saying or doing things that they never actually said or did. Deepfakes have been used to create fake or false social media profiles for non-existent people called *sockpuppets*. These fake accounts are used for propaganda purposes and perpetuate fake news or false narratives and have been involved in catfishing schemes.

Another significant negative aspect of AI and operating systems such as ChatGPT is the large amount of energy it takes to fuel such operations. While AI systems vary widely in energy consumption depending on their complexity and usage, they generally require significant amounts of electricity to process and analyze data efficiently according to the World Economic Forum (2024). ChatGPT responses require around ten times the electricity of a Google search and with 100 million users of ChatGPT every week that extra energy demand adds up; that's just users on one platform (World Economic Forum 2024). AI requires significant computing power, and generative AI systems might already use around 33 times more energy to complete a task than task-specific software would (World Economic Forum 2024). Right now, AI's energy use represents a fraction of the technology sector's power consumption, which is estimated to be around 2–3 percent of total global emissions (World Economic Forum 2024) but we are at the early stages of AI development.

AI Singularity

In Chapter 9, Michio Kaku described the progress of AI in the early 2010s as astounding in terms of its ability to perform calculations faster than any human. He also warned about the dangers of robots if they reach Level II consciousness and begin to interpret certain humans' actions or emotional states as dangerous as he worries that they may act upon those concerns if they deem humans as threats. If robots are weaponized, their threat to humanity becomes greatly heightened. As of now, robots have not reached Level II consciousness and they seemingly lack the ability to think outside of their algorithm programming but all that could change and then we have to wonder if humanity is safe from AI. We should be very concerned if AI progresses in intelligence so quickly that it becomes sentient and acts beyond humans' control and in a malicious manner.

AI chatbots are already passing themselves off as human beings in text conversations (Lewis 2023) and this concerns many people who are closely following the developments of artificial intelligence. These concerns are shared by Geoffrey Hinton, a pioneering researcher and the "Godfather of AI" who quit his role at Google in 2023 so that he could more freely speak about the dangers of the technology that he helped create (Grantham-Philips and O'Brien 2023). According to Hinton, one of his main concerns is how easy access to AI text- and image-generation tools could lead to more fake or fraudulent content being created, and how the average person would "not be able to know what is true anymore" (Prakash 2023). Homeland Security (2023) reinforces this sentiment through a variation of the old adage that most people abide by—I believe what I see with my own eyes—by saying that the natural inclination of people is to believe what they see and that is what makes technology like AI so dangerous. Hinton warns of "bad actors" using AI in ways that could have detrimental impacts on society—such as manipulating elections or instigating violence (Grantham-Philips and O'Brien 2023).

Hinton echoes another sentiment shared in this overall discussion of AI; namely, that AI chatbots will one day (soon) become more intelligent than humans. Add to this, the realization that AI lacks a sense of (human) ethics and the uncontrollable growth of artificial intelligence will eventually wipe out humanity (Duggal 2023). This moment is referred to as the "AI singularity." *AI singularity* refers to the point in time when artificial intelligence becomes more intelligent than humans with the fear that it becomes self-aware and uncontrollable. This point in time also represents a new level of intelligence wherein AI has a reached a level that humans cannot achieve. It would also be the polar extreme in the fourth stage of human progress. The best estimate for when complete AI singularity will occur is between 2050 and 2060, although there is not a consensus on this date (some suggest the AI singularity process has already begun) (Talagala 2021). Ray Kurzweil, a computer scientist, futurist, top Google engineer, and a prophet of AI, believes AI will pass the Turing test (the point where computers effectively achieve humanlike intelligence) and will reach singularity by 2045 and acquire superhuman intelligence and will be capable of growing and expanding on its own (Luskin 2023). "This is akin to 'runaway' AI, where we lose control and AI begins to train itself and act as a truly sentient, independent entity" (Luskin 2023). In an article that appeared in *Time* magazine, Kurzweil describes AI Singularity as "the moment when technological change becomes so rapid and profound, it represents a rupture in the fabric of human history" (Grossman 2011:43). Kurzweil first made this bold prediction of AI Singularity by 2045 in his 2005 book, *The Singularity is Near.*

Technological singularity is something that Comte never envisioned. If humanity survives AI singularity, it will be time to add a 5th stage to the "law of human progress."

Summary

In this chapter, we learned about the roles of social physics, the "Law of Human Progress" and Artificial Intelligence (AI) in the theory of everything. We were reminded why Auguste Comte came to view physics as the pinnacle of sciences and why he wanted to model his new academic discipline of positivism after it. Eventually, his positive philosophy would be named "sociology" but he never wavered from his original insistence that society should be studied scientifically and that the discovery of "laws" should be among its primary goals. Furthermore, his preferred usage of the term "social physics" made it clear that he was rejecting metaphysics and theism as the guiding forces of society.

As Comte observed, it was proposed here that the human mind and society have continued to evolve (even while experiencing periods of great crisis and fragile organization) to the point where we have been in the fourth stage of human progress. This fourth stage is the Artificial Intelligence (AI) stage and it reinforces the validity of social physics concept all the more as we have evolved to the point where a new paradigm shift in thought has become prevalent. This results in an updated version of the "Law of Human Progress"—one that incorporates and blends the four paradigms of thought with Comte's three stages of human development. This new "Law of Human Progress" has the following stages: Tradition; Faith; Enlightened, Rational Thought; and Artificial Intelligence (AI). We have clearly reached a point in human society wherein we are being dominated by forces of AI as its influence is omnipresent.

The history and development of AI was presented and we learned that it can be traced back to British logician and computer pioneer Alan Mathison Turing in 1935 who promoted the idea of "thinking machines." The idea of a "thinking machine" was transformed to an intelligent machine by John McCarthy who coined the term "Artificial Intelligence." A number of developments in the field eventually led to the development of chatbots.

Many positives of AI were discussed. Certainly AI can help social physicists and sociologists conduct mathematical calculations on "Big Data" at lightning speeds compared to that of the early physicists and that is a major bonus for such practitioners not trained in calculus and other advanced forms of mathematics. AI also detects patterns (both in the natural and social worlds) to assist the social scientist. More than a dozen positive outcomes of AI were discussed.

There are also many deep concerns (negative aspects) related with AI and a world inundated with artificial intelligence. The ultimate worry centers on the concern with AI reaching the point someday wherein they begin to think outside of the programmed algorithms and perceive humans as threat. The concept of "AI singularity"—the point in time when artificial intelligence becomes more intelligent than humans with the fear that it becomes self-aware and uncontrollable—was introduced. If this happens, we will have reached the polar extreme in the fourth stage of human progress. It may also represent the ultimate threat to humanity. Assuming humanity survives AI singularity, it will be time to add a 5th stage of human progress.

11

The Fate of Humanity
and the Afterlife

Introduction

Sociologist Niklas Luhmann (1927–1998), born in Luneburg, Germany, was one of the most prominent German, and arguably, European social theorists of the twentieth century. Having witnessed firsthand his country's defeat in a World War and German occupation by foreign troops, Luhmann was led to conclude that modern society was not a better place (than compared to the past) to live. Thus, like any social thinker, Luhmann was a product of the climate of his times. His research centered on how society functions and the role of social systems in society. Luhmann's published works were an attempt to formulate a universal or grand theory of social systems and through it all, he maintained a commitment to producing abstract and often elaborate frameworks for analyzing social reality. His resulting theories were far more complicated than the publications of Max Weber (Delaney 2024). Luhmann found no reason to make theory uncomplicated, because, as he explained, life itself is complex. In an attempt to understand social life, Luhmann studied all sorts of specific aspects of society. As Mathias Albert, a political science professor at the University of Bielefeld, Germany (where Luhmann taught) states, Luhmann wrote about all sorts of specific aspects of society, from minuscule studies of specific historical semantics to studies of love and passion, notions of differentiations and operative closure (self-referentiality, autopsies) of function systems, and political theory (Albert 2019). Luhmann (1983) described theory as not "something you invent or produce yourself; it is something already available which only needs interpretation and refinement" (p. 987). He remained steadfast in the idea that grand theory can, and should, be the primary goal of sociological theory.

Like Luhmann (and certainly other social thinkers), I have researched and published on a wide variety of topics on human behavior and of societal interest and importance and this has been invaluable as a precursor to writing a "theory about everything" as anyone who attempts to do so should have knowledge of the mundane and of the major events of the world as well as the diverse forms of human behavior.

My research includes such universal forms of behavior and social interest as friendship and happiness; popular culture and lessons learned from popular culture;

shameful behaviors; extensive coverage on one of the most enduring, lasting and powerful social institutions found in all societies, sports and leisure; and a close examination of one of the oldest social institutions of human society, religion. I have also conducted research and examined many negative aspects of society including violence, both interpersonal and institutional; murder and mayhem; doomsday cults; organized crime; street crime, with a specialty in street gangs; prison life; collective violence and riots; war; terrorism; genocide; and I have warned that the planet's environment is so compromised it is likely already too late to save it for future generations of humans. I have published on such other macro topics as the four paradigms of thought (tradition; faith; enlightened rational thought; and common sense) while describing the limitations of common sense in everyday social interactions and promoting the need to embrace enlightened, rational thought and science. I have also warned about the deterioration of democracy, human rights and rational thought in the twenty-first century in the United States and across the globe. The "diversity of darkness" and the prevalence of shameful behaviors by so many people in so many forms have led to what I have referred to as "Darkened Enlightenment"—the idea that the growing darkness that surrounds us threatens enlightened thinking and the very existence of humanity. The rise of populism and nationalism around the world; the deterioration of freedom and human rights globally; the growing economic disparity between the rich and the poor; attempts to devalue education; a growing disbelief in the legitimacy of science; attacks on the environment; pseudoscience as a by-product of unreasoned and irrational thinking; the ever-deepening political swamp; the power elites and the deep state; and the variations of Big Business that impact our daily lives, are all contributing to the concept of "Darkened Enlightenment" and most assuredly will lead to the premature mass extinction of humanity, as we know it, here on Earth.

My publications on social theory and learning about countless numbers of social thinkers, including sociologists and philosophers, have contributed to my thoughts on a theory of everything. Having immersed myself into the field of physics for the past few years has opened my mind to other important social thinkers whose ideas were shared in earlier chapters. All of this, my past publications, continued exploration of new ideas and subject areas, and my varied life experiences that have included traveling all of the United States as well as much of the globe and meeting many diverse people with wide-ranging ideas of life and the future, have helped to shape my views that make up the primary subjects of these two final chapters: the fate of humanity; the afterlife; the fate of the Earth; and the fate of the Universe. In this chapter, we will explore the fate of humanity and the afterlife.

The Fate of Humanity

While humans are capable of periodic acts of generosity toward others, including strangers, the harms we cause ourselves, one another and the environment are surely dooming humanity to a premature mass extinction. To put this in perspective, we should realize that the Universe does not care about humans or the planet

Earth as we are but an insignificant speck in the vastness of an ever-expanding Universe (see Chapter 8) filled with a seemingly infinite number of celestial bodies. In an interesting illustration of the insignificance of a human life on the planet Earth, let alone the Universe, the TV show *Resident Alien*, in an appropriately titled episode, "141 Seconds" (first aired date February 28, 2024), pointed out that a human life on Earth lasts 141 seconds in comparison to the length of time the planet has existed. It takes some advanced mathematics to try and figure out if this calculation is true. In 2020, Sandra Maria, writing for *Medium*, provides us with such calculations:

> Your age when you die = 85 years (2,680,560,000 seconds)
> Earth's Age = 4.5 billion years (1.433×1017 seconds)
> 85/4,500,000,000 = 0.000,001,890% (1.890 e-8)

Roughly, your life span will be two-millionths of one percent of the age of the earth. Compared to a human life span of 85 years, it would be like a life-form that lasts 141 seconds (Maria 2020). I asked a colleague of mine in the mathematics department to "do the math" and see if he could replicate this 141 seconds concept. When he did the calculations, he informed me that an average human actually only lives for 50.6 seconds in comparison to the lifespan of the planet. This figure indicates that the human life span in comparison to the life span of the planet Earth is even more insignificant that the 141 second concept. It's interesting too, to use the age of 85 as the benchmark for human life, as the life expectancy for an American living in the United States (in 2021) was only 76.1 years (it is higher for women than men) (Centers for Disease Control and Prevention, National Center for Health Statistics 2022). Life expectancy varies based on one's racial/ethnic background (non–Hispanic Asian Americans live the longest) and by the nation one lives (e.g., people live longer in the United Kingdom and shorter in Mexico). Suffice it to say, the planet Earth has been around a long time—estimates place it at 4.5 billion years and each of us humans, if we live a full life, can expect to live around 75 or 80 years, plus or minus a few years.

As individuals, we know that our "shelf life" is very limited. One of the primary questions being asked in this chapter, however, is, "What is the fate of humanity?"

The Realistic Fate of Humanity: Premature Mass Extinction

The fate of humanity is a premature mass extinction. This extinction will happen relatively soon, at least in the grand scheme of the timeline of planet. We know humanity is doomed for a number of reasons but let's begin with the double threat of the impending reality that we face the imminent sixth mass extinction and that our environment is under constant attack by forces from Nature and humans.

Mass Extinctions (ME) and Attacks on Our Environment

Barnosky and associates (2001) state that a *mass extinction* (ME) occurs when the planet loses more than three-quarters of its species in a geologically short interval of time, usually during a few hundred thousand to a couple of million years.

However, a critical event such as a meteorite impact may trigger a mass extinction in a relative instant moment. Our planet has already endured five ME in the past 540 million years (Wake and Verdenburg 2008; Andryszewski 2009; Delaney and Madigan 2021). On average, mass extinctions occur about every 65–70 million years (with the extinction time period lasting millions of years). The past five ME are the result of forces of nature (worldly or celestial). (Note: Mass extinctions are named after the geological time period which they occurred.) The last ME occurred about 65 million years ago. So, we are due for another ME soon. Many environmentalists including Delaney and Madigan (2021) provide documentation that we are already in the 6th ME period. The inevitability of a ME results in the predictable end of the life expectancy of nearly all species (some species such as cockroaches, crocodiles, lizards, turtles and small animals can, and will likely, survive).

The earth's environment is under constant "attack" by forces of nature and humanity. Long before humans rose to the top of the food chain, nature had begun, and continues, to attack the environment in a variety of fashions including: glaciation; volcanic eruptions; global warming and cooling (currently, caused in great part by human-assisted climate change); lightning strikes; natural wildfires; storms (often assisted by human-caused climate change), including superstorms, hurricanes, droughts/water shortages, floods/tsunamis, snowstorms, and tornadoes; the influx of invasive species from one ecosystem to another (often assisted by humans); and vapors emitted into the air from sulfur springs and the decay of dead vegetation and animal species. The planet has even been attacked by outer-worldly forces such as asteroids, meteorites and comets. A *meteorite* is any object that survives entering the earth's atmosphere and lands on the surface; an *asteroid* is a rocky object that orbits the sun and has an average size between a meteoroid and a minor planet; and *comets* are large objects made of dust and ice that orbit the Sun, best known for their long, streaming tails that are leftovers from the formation of the solar system some 4.5 billion years ago. If these outer-worldly forces are big and powerful enough, an impact on earth could wipe out vast areas of the planet and the entire human race itself could face extinction. The asteroid bombardment that killed the dinosaurs some 65 million years ago would've wiped out humanity as well. The first 5 ME were all caused by forces of nature (see Table 11.1) and the sixth ME could also be caused by a force/s of nature.

Table 11.1: The First 5 Mass Extinctions (ME) and Their Causes

ME#	Name/When it Began	Cause(s)
1	End-Ordovian (440 million years ago)	Glaciation
2	End-Devonian (365 million years ago)	Glaciation and Global Cooling
3	End-Permian (250 million years ago)	Asteroid and Volcanism
4	End-Triassic (200 million years ago)	Asteroid, Volcanism and Climate Change
5	End-Cretaceous (65 million years)	Asteroid and Volcanism

As we can see from Table 11.1 the first five ME were caused by forces of Nature, inner-worldly, outer-worldly or both. Humans were neither affected or the cause of these ME as they had not yet populated the planet.

Tens of millions of years after the fifth ME, the humanoid species began to evolve. For multiple millennia now, humans have, arguably, been the most evolved creatures on the planet. There are many of us who now worry that humans are slowly, or rapidly, depending upon one's perspective, destroying the Earth's environment. Humans are certainly capable of destroying much of it quickly with nuclear and chemical warfare; but, it is the sustained and persistent slow death that we have been inflicting upon our environment that is contributing to the demise of humanity.

Depending on one's definition of what constitutes a "human," archeologists estimate that our species has existed for about 150–200,000 years. Humans are a member of the bipedal primate species in the Hominidae (the great apes) family, having diverged from apes 6 million to 8 million years ago and a dozen humanlike species removed (Pickrell 2006; Delaney and Madigan 2021; Smithsonian Institution 2024a). Current day humans are Homo Sapiens, a Latin term for "thinking humans." Unlike other animal species, humans have developed a high-level brain, a bipedal gait (the way of walking or running on two legs, with the body's weight supported by the hind limbs), and opposable thumbs. As intellectually developed as humans have become, we have done a poor job as stewards of the environment. Our overall blatant disregard for the planet's environment and diverse ecosystems has not only led to the direct extinction of many species (animal, plant and marine) but is contributing to the sixth ME and human demise. We have treated the earth as a dumping ground for our human-made toxins and trash.

Of all the Earth's organisms, humans place the highest demands on the environment and therefore represent the greatest threat. Humans exploit both other species and the environment. "Scientists who set out to quantify humanity's impact on our 46,755 fellow species have found that we are the most prolific exploiters of animals—by far. Compared with wild predators that have roughly the same body size as us and have similar appetites, we capture or kill nearly 100 times as many vertebrate species, on average" (Errico 2023:A5). Orcas, for instance, have a range that's similar to humans, along with comparable social behaviors. And yet, of the 121 types of vertebrates eaten by the so-called killer whales, humans also consume 83 of them—along with 10,337 others in the ocean alone. On land, jaguars, among the most fearsome cats of the Americas, eat nine different types of prey. Humans use all nine of these same species, plus 2,698 others that live in the territory where jaguars and people overlap (Errico 2023). Humans have developed a wide array of skills that allow us to survive in a variety of environments and as a result, we have access to a wider range of animal species than is typical for large vertebrates. "Another reason for our outsized degree of mayhem is that we don't just consume other species for food. We also use them to make clothing, produce traditional medicines, create souvenir trinkets and keep us company, among other things" (Errico 2023:A5). Boris Worm and his colleagues analyzed data from the International Union for Conservation of Nature, which keeps track of wildlife species across the globe to see how well their populations are faring to come to the above conclusions reported by Gina Errico. Worm concluded that humans exploit about one-third of the wild vertebrate species (Perkins 2023). About 55 percent of exploited species are kept as pets, and an additional 8 percent or so—primarily birds, reptiles and amphibians—are used to make products. While our preindustrial ancestors may have engaged in sustainable harvesting behavior, modern humans exploit nearly one-third of all living vertebrate species often for nonfood purposes—an indisputable sign that we are out of balance with the natural world (Errico 2023).

Humans exploit the environment in another way, arguable far more harmful manner, by exceeding the earth's "carrying capacity." The earth has a limited "carrying capacity" to support life. *Carrying capacity* refers to the maximum feasible load the planet can sustain just short of the level that would end the environment's ability to support life (Catton 1980; Delaney and Madigan 2021). In other words, carry capacity is tied to the number of organisms that can be supported in a given area (ecosystem) based on the natural resources available without compromising present and future generations. Once the environment is sullied, the carrying capacity shrinks, thus negatively altering its ability to sustain life. Scientists seem to agree that the actual carrying capacity in terms of humans that the earth can handle is between 9 and 10 billion people (Wilson 2002; Delaney and Malakhova 2020). As of March 2024, the world's population was nearly 8.1 billion. In brief, over the generations, but especially recently, humans have contributed to the deterioration of the earth's carrying capacity. Not only have countless plant and animals species died off at an alarming rate because of the compromised environment, our growing population has placed great strain on our land's topsoil that is used to grow crops and raise cattle, sheep, chickens and other animals used for food consumption. The Earth's carrying capacity has especially been stretched to its limit because of human dependency on the conversion of fossil fuels to meet our energy needs (e.g., for gasoline, heating oil and diesel). This dependency on the burning of fossil fuels has led to a number of serious problems that are felt around the world, including climate change, the greenhouse effect and a compromised ozone.

Measuring human dependency on fossil fuels varies somewhat depending upon the source cited. For example, the World Bank (2019) estimates that nearly 80 percent of the world's total energy consumption comes from fossil fuels; this is down from the record high 95 percent in 1970 (Delaney and Malakhova 2020). The relative abundance of fossil fuels and the large profits made by corporations that control its production, distribution and sale all but guarantees our continued dependence. Among the obvious problems associated with a reliance on fossil fuels for energy are burning fossil fuels compromises air quality and causes physical harm to anything alive; ocean acidification; dramatic changes in weather patterns; the transportation of oil can result in ocean spills and cause ecological damage to plants and animals; global warming; a rise in CO_2 levels; extraction processes can cause long-lasting damage to local ecosystems; and fossil fuels are a nonrenewable resource. The rise in CO_2 levels is of particular concern as it has been well-established by the scientific community that the atmospheric CO_2 count must not exceed 350 ppm (parts per million; the ratio of carbon dioxide molecules to all other molecules in the atmosphere). As of February 2024, the CO_2 count reached an all-time high of 424.55 ppm, a figure far beyond the safe zone (National Oceanic & Atmospheric Administration 2024). The consequences of such a high level of carbon dioxide in our atmosphere is deadly and will contribute to the extinction of humanity.

Human reliance on fossil fuels is just one of the contributing problems to the deterioration of the environment. The description of the "carrying capacity" pointed to the problem of human overpopulation. *Overpopulation* is generally defined as an excessive number of people in an area to the point of overcrowding, depletion of natural resources, an impaired quality of life, or environmental deterioration. Overpopulation would also lead to food insecurity (the limited or unreliable access to foods that are safe and nutritionally adequate), malnutrition (a condition resulting from insufficient intake of biologically necessary nutrients) and world hunger (hunger aggregated to the global level) (Delaney and Madigan 2021). In many parts of the world the effects of overpopulation are in clear evidence. The 2023 edition of the United Nation's "State of Food Security and Nutrition in the World" report reveals that in 2022, between 691 and 783 million people faced hunger; 2.4 billion people experienced moderate or severe food insecurity; and 900 million faced food insecurity. Over 3.1 billion people could not afford a healthy diet and many children under the age of five suffer from malnutrition (United Nations 2023). Although food insecurity affects more people in rural areas, consumption of highly processed foods is increasing in peri-urban (zones of transition from rural to urban land uses) and rural areas. As Herbert Spencer warned, widespread hunger and the lack of access to safe, nutritious and sufficient food places a society at risk of *dissolution*—a condition that occurs when society ceases to evolve and remains stagnant or is incapable of providing necessary resources to its people. Another critical resource necessary for the survival of humans (and all living lifeforms) is water. We will learn about the harm humans are causing to fresh water supplies shortly.

The United Nation's report also emphasized the impact of urbanization on agrifood systems and projects that almost seven in ten people will live in cities by 2050. The UN (2023) warns that governments and policymakers must consider urbanization trends and their effects on food security, hunger and malnutrition. Sociologists have longed studied the effects of industrialization and how it has changed the course of human history in a vast array of ways and that includes urbanization and our role in shaping the environment. Generally speaking, human impact on the environment has been quite negative and has increasingly led to simplified-growth ecosystems because of our producing virtual monocultures (areas where primarily one type of crop grows). "Whether we are talking about massive cutting of trees to build homes and businesses, the plowing of prairies for crops and the allocation of huge tracts of land for ranching and farming, cultivating natural grass growth to conform to well-manicured lawns, and especially, the mass migration to cities, humans have greatly reduced the biological diversity of living things that exist in the 'wild' ecosystems" (Delaney and Madigan 2021:72).

Twenty years ago, I first used the term "enviromare" in print. An *enviromare* is an environmentally produced nightmare which causes great harm to humanity and the physical environment (Delaney 2005). Enviromares are all connected to various forms of pollution that are linked to nature (ecosystems, the biospheres, etc.) but caused by a number of social forces. A very brief review of these enviromares is presented below:

1. Air pollution—The most important need for all living species is oxygen. Breathing polluted air can lead to a number of health-related problems and if our environment's atmosphere becomes polluted, entire ecosystems may become compromised. A reliance on fossil fuels is the most obvious culprit that contributes to air pollution. Indoor air can also be compromised when the air outside is of poor quality.

2. Water pollution—Arguably, water is the second most important need of humans (and other living species) that must be met. Despite the obvious importance of clean, safe, drinking water for all people, data provided from WHO and UNICEF on access to clean water, adequate sanitation and hygiene paints a not so pretty picture: 2 billion people lack access to safely managed drinking water at home, 8 out of 10 of these people live in rural areas; nearly half of the world's population (3.6 billion people) do not have access to safely managed sanitation in their homes, and nearly one-half billion people practice open defecation; and 2.3 billion people lack basic hygiene services, including soap and water at home, this includes 670 million people with no handwashing facilities at all (Centers for Disease Control and Prevention 2022). The United Nations released a report in 2023 stating that 26 percent of the world's population doesn't have access to safe drinking water and 46 percent lacks access to basic sanitation (Associated Press 2023). A report released by UNESCO in 2023 states that 10 percent of the global population lives in countries with high or critical water stress and up to 3.5 billion people live under conditions of water stress at least one month a year (Associated Press 2023). The longer one goes without water, or clean water, the greater the potential negative effects on health. Nonetheless, a great deal of our water is not clean, and humans are responsible for a great deal of water pollution. "The National Institute of Environmental Health Sciences (2023) defines water pollution as any contamination of water with chemicals or other hazardous substances that are detrimental to human, animal or plant health." Any body of water can become polluted, regardless of its size and location, and this is due in part to atmospheric transport of pollutants; global warming; deforestation; rubbish and fecal matter being dumped in water; fuel spillages; corroded water piles that release harmful chemicals, such as lead; agricultural by-product runoffs; industrial harmful pesticides; oil spills; and hazardous wastes and human neglect.

3. Land pollution—Assuming there is breathable air and clean water, the next need humans must secure is food and shelter. Humans are land creatures, and we are designed to find shelter on land. We build our homes, domesticate animals, establish businesses and so on, all on land. And while a certain amount of the food we eat comes from marine ecosystems, we grow, hunt or gather most of our food on land (Delaney and Madigan 2021). *Land* is defined as the thin layer of topsoil on the earth's surface. *Land pollution* refers to the deposition of solid or liquid waste materials on land or underground in a manner that can contaminate the soil and groundwater, threaten public health and cause unsightly conditions and nuisances (Nathanson 2023). The

waste materials that cause land pollution are broadly classified as municipal solid waste (MSW, also called municipal refuse). There are many sources of land pollution including: manufacturing; mineral extraction; abandonment of mines; national defense activities; accidental spills; illegal dumping; leaking underground storage tanks; pesticide use; fertilizer application; construction and demolition (C&D) waste debris and hazardous waste; nonhazardous garbage, rubbish, and trash from homes, institutions (e.g., schools, commercial establishments and industrial facilities); plastics and microplastics; and natural sources such as hurricanes and floods (Nathanson 2023; Environmental Protection Agency 2023). Contaminated lands can pose a variety of health and environmental hazards including soils filled with toxic chemicals that may seep into nearby ground and surface waters, where they may be consumed by humans, animals and plants; they may be distributed to other areas as wind-borne dust; and the effects may cause acute or chronic health problems (EPA 2023a).

4. Solid Waste Pollution—Almost any item can eventually become an example of solid waste, as solid waste is often a polite way to describe garbage. Solid waste that is not disposed of properly becomes land pollution and blight on communities. As the world's pollution continues to expand, we have more and more people producing trash. This necessitates the need for more landfills and treatment plants. Large urban municipalities already have a hard enough time disposing of their trash and often ship it hundreds or thousands of miles away (making it someone else's problem). The solid waste enviromare is only going to get worse and most assuredly compromise the quality of life of humans and continue to harm the environment causing a ripple effect of other problems such as the release of toxic chemicals (pollutants or contaminants) in our soil and air; contaminate water supplies; disease; air pollution; marine plastic pollution; and overall negative impacts on wellbeing.

5. Noise pollution—Of all the enviromares, noise pollution is the least likely to significantly contribute to human extinction. Noise pollution is primarily an urban pollutant, but large industry and the sounds emanating from farmers' machinery often intrudes on the lives of people in rural areas. Generally, it is one's quality of life that is compromised more than the environment (Delaney 2005; Delaney and Madigan 2021). *Noise pollution* refers to any intrusive, unwanted or disturbing sounds that that a person finds to be annoying. The EPA (2023b) states, "The fact that you can't see, taste or smell it [noise pollution] may help explain why it has not received as much attention as other types of pollution." Still, noise pollution adversely affects the lives of millions of people and studies have shown that there are direct links between noise and a slew of health problems include: stress related illnesses, high blood pressure, speech interference, hearing loss, sleep disruption, and lost productivity (EPA 2023b).

6. Celestial Pollution—This enviromare refers to space junk; or, what NASA calls "orbital debris." Orbital debris is any human-made object in orbit about the Earth that no longer serves any useful purpose (NASA 2024a). "More than

25,000 objects larger than 10 cm are known to exist. The estimated population of particles between 1 and 10 cm in diameter is approximately 500,000. The number of particles larger than 1 mm exceeds 100 million. As of January 2022, the amount of material orbiting the Earth exceeded 9,000 metric tons" (NASA 2024a). Space junk can cause a great deal of harm to our satellite systems or the International Space Station. Falling orbital debris that does not burn up while hurtling toward earth could cause significant damage to human and other living lifeforms along with local ecosystems.

7. Chemical and Nuclear Pollution—In the original presentation of the seven enviromares, chemical and nuclear pollution is listed fourth. However, for the purpose of this specific topic, it was saved until last so as to make the greatest impact. Air, water and land pollutions are already causing havoc on the environment in a significant manner and are the cause of death for humans, animals and plant lives. Some lifeforms are dying on a daily basis because of those enviromares, the rest of us are being impacted over time, and humanity is playing a delusional game of craps thinking it will win in the long run; it won't. The danger of chemical and nuclear pollution, especially via warfare, is the possibility of immediate human extinction. And, that is why the sudden and instant demise of humanity is always possible. Before we consider a chemical or nuclear war, let's first look at chemicals. The World Health Organization (WHO) (2024) states that there are more than 160 million chemicals known to humans. About 40,000 to 60,000 of them can be found in commerce; 6,000 of these account for more than 99 percent of the total volume of chemicals in commerce. Chemicals, whether of natural origin or produced by humans (e.g., industrial and agricultural products such as pesticides, petroleum products and process metals), are a part of our environment. Some chemicals serve specific purposes while others are unwanted by-products, including wastes, or products of combustion such as toxic gases and particles from industrial emissions and burning fuel (WHO 2024). In 2019, a small number of chemicals for which data are available were estimated to cause 2 million deaths from a variety of health outcomes including poisonings, heart diseases, chronic respiratory diseases and cancers. "Chemical pollution also negatively impacts a range of facets of the ecosystem, which can harm human health" (WHO 2024). The story goes on and on. Nuclear energy offers a cleaner alterative to burning fossil fuels so why hasn't it become a number one source for energy? It's because of all the problems, or potential problems associated with nuclear energy including: the threat of core reactor meltdown; human operating errors; concerns over how to safely transport and store nuclear radioactive waste; toxic exposure; and the threat of the development and use of nuclear weapons. Nuclear accidents can destroy human life and the immediate ecosystems. (Note: We will take a look at nuclear war later in this chapter.)

The brief description of these enviromares, mass extinctions, the stress humans are placing on the planet's carrying capacity; human dependency on fossil fuels, urbanization and poor agricultural techniques give us a glimpse as to why it is easy to say the havoc humans are causing to the environment is a contributing factor to the fate of humanity. Still not convinced that humans are harming the environment to a dangerous extent? There's still a matter of ocean acidification; harm caused by plastics and microplastics; deforestation; and marine debris.

Ocean acidification comes about as a result of the increased output of CO_2 and climate change. Ocean acidification, in fact, should not be an afterthought compared to global warming; instead, it should be recognized as a twin concern. The Smithsonian Institution (2018) states, "Ocean acidification is sometime called 'climate change's equally evil twin,' and for good reason: it's a significant and harmful consequence of excess carbon dioxide in the atmosphere that we don't see or feel because its effects are happening under water." At least one-quarter of the carbon dioxide released by burning fossil fuels doesn't stay in the air, but instead dissolves into the ocean. "Since the beginning of the industrial era, the ocean has absorbed some 525 billion tons of CO_2 from the atmosphere, presently around 22 million tons per day" (Smithsonian Institution 2018). Ocean acidification is a global threat to the world's oceans, estuaries, and waterways. Think of the oceans as like sponges that are absorbing increasing amounts of carbon dioxide from the atmosphere. Acidification harms the planet's environment in general and the marine ecosystem, including reef-building corals and marine lifeforms specifically (NOAA Fisheries 2024). Added to this, is the reality that humans eat food from marine sources and the threat to humanity is a double-edged sword.

Initially, the introduction of *plastics* (a material consisting of a wide range of synthetic or semi-synthetic materials that use polymers as a main ingredient) seemed like a crowning achievement of human convenience as this unnatural product was versatile, sanitary, durable, lightweight, could be molded into different shapes and sizes, helped with storage and was easy to manufacture. Since plastics were first mass-produced following the Second World War, they became the preferred product for consumer and manufacturing goods. It took decades before people took a serious look at the harm they were creating; this harm was caused by the simple fact that plastics were not biodegradable. This meant that, every plastic product ever produced still existed and soon became a leading cause of pollution; especially land and water pollution. Our landscapes and landfills are filled with plastic products. But, it is our oceans and waterways that plastics are, arguably, causing the greatest harm. The United Nations Environment Programme (2024) reports that, every day, the equivalent of 2,000 garbage trucks full of plastic are dumped into the world's oceans, rivers and lakes. "Plastic pollution is a global problem. Every year 19–23 million tonnes of plastic waste leaks into aquatic ecosystems, polluting lakes, rivers and seas" (United Nations Environment Programme 2024). Furthermore, "Plastic pollution can alter habitats and natural processes, reducing ecosystems' ability to adapt to climate change, directly affecting millions of people's livelihoods, food production capabilities and social well-being" (United Nations Environment Programme 2024). There is so much plastic garbage in the oceans that islands of plastic garbage have formed (to be discussed later in the chapter). As big of a concern as plastics pollution is for the environment, humanity and other living species, is microplastics. *Microplastics* are tiny plastic particles that result from both commercial product development and the breakdown of larger plastics (National Geographic 2024). Microplastics are dangerous because, essentially, we cannot get rid of them and humans and animals alike end up ingesting them. Research indicates that humans, on average, consume a credit card's size worth of microplastics each week (Xia 2019). Lee and associates (2023) have found that microplastics can cause a wide variety of harm to humans including, but not limited to, abnormalities in internal organs; sharp microplastic particles can cause toxicity; endocrine disruptions including various cancers; reproductive-system disorders; respiratory and cardiovascular diseases. Animals may also consume microplastics, some will have these particles embedded into their tissue; other problems could include malnutrition, inflammation, reduced fertility, increased toxicity and mortality (Lee et. al 2023). A study released in the *New England Journal of Medicine* in 2024 by a team of physicians and researchers showed that cardiovascular surgical patients are appearing on operating tables with a build-up of micro and nanoplastics in their arterial plaque (Rust 2024). Nanoplastics measure under 1 micrometer in length and pose significant threat to human health.

Trees, and especially forests, are essential for life. They help to cool and moisten our air and they fill it with oxygen to help sustain life. Globally, forests cover about 30 percent of the Earth's land area (Delaney and Madigan 2021). The world's forests have been shrinking at an alarming rapid rate since the last ice age some 10,000 years ago when forests accounted for an estimated 6 billion hectares (57%) of the Earth's habitable land. But, by 2018, forests made up just 4 billion hectares (World Economic Forum 2022). The cause? Deforestation. The primary cause of deforestation is agriculture, resulting in 31 percent of the Earth's habitable land now used for grazing livestock (World Economic Forum 2022). *Deforestation* refers to the clearing, or permanent removal, of a section of the Earth's forests on a large-scale, almost always resulting in damage to the quality of the land, causing soil erosion, poor water quality, reduced food security, impaired flood protection, and an even greater number of people moving to urban areas. Deforestation releases carbon stored in trees and soil. At the current rate of deforestation, the world's rainforests would completely vanish within one hundred years; then again; humans would die off before we reach that point as the lack of oxygen and increased counts of CO_2 would lead to our extinction. Humans would not be the only species to die off as a result of continued deforestation as many living creatures reside in the rainforest and they, like humans and all other living creatures on the planet, are dependent upon oxygen to survive (Delaney and Madigan 2021). So critical are tropical rainforests that they are often called the "lungs of the planet" because they draw in carbon dioxide and breathe out oxygen. The continued destruction of the rainforests will surely doom humanity to a quick and sudden extinction; deforestation is already speeding the sixth ME process.

While there are still other environmental problems that may lead to the extinction of humanity that could be discussed, the final topic to be described here is marine debris. *Marine debris* refers to habitants that are contaminated with man-made items of debris and can be found from the poles to the equator and from shorelines, estuaries and the sea surface to the depths of the ocean, making this problem a global issue (Thompson, La Belle, Bouwman and Neretin 2011). Our marine environments including the oceans and Great Lakes are filled with items that do not belong there including huge amounts of plastics, metals, rubber, paper, textiles, derelict fishing gear, derelict vessels, lost or discarded items and trash of all sorts. This makes marine debris one of the most widespread pollution problems facing the world's ocean and waterways (NOAA Marine Debris Program 2024). Unbeknownst to some people, but certainly known to those who live nearby, there are "dead zones" of marine areas in the United States. The largest one is in the Mexican Gulf Coast region, which extends along the shores of Texas, Louisiana, Mississippi, and Alabama and can extend to nearly 9,000 square miles of ocean (Delaney and Madigan 2021). What is a "dead zone?" This is an area where heavy rains and melting snows wash massive amounts of nutrients—particularly nitrogen and phosphorus—from lawns, sewage treatment plants, farm land and other sources along the Mississippi River into the Gulf of Mexico. Once in the Gulf, these nutrients, which are required for plant and crop growth, trigger algae blooms that choke off oxygen in water and make it difficult, if not impossible, for marine life to survive (The Nature Conservancy 2024). Ocean marine debris is subject to ocean currents and wind. Large amounts of marine debris follow the same ocean and wind currents getting caught in accumulation zones, or "garbage patches." The size of these patches constantly varies depending on the shifts in the currents and winds. There is, however, a notable example of a garbage patch in the North Pacific Ocean known as the "Great Pacific Garbage Patch," or the "Garbage Island." The Great Pacific Garbage Patch is like a floating landfill of trash and marine debris found in the Pacific Ocean north of Hawaii and larger than the size of Texas. It is a loose collection of islands of garbage patches in a close proximity that sometimes link together into large pieces and other times floats apart into smaller islands (many of which are larger than the Hawaiian Islands). Because most of the trash in garbage islands is not biodegradable (a great deal of the garbage is plastics) these islands are destined to float forever in the oceans. As Delaney and Madigan (2021) warn, if the "Great Pacific Garbage Patch" continues to grow, we may have to recognize it as our eighth continent. Tragically, it might someday be the only continent to survive the sixth mass extinction.

Threats to the environment—both by humans and Nature—represent just one possible source of the early extinction of humanity. There are many social and political decisions that may also cause the end of humanity. Let's take a brief look at a couple of them.

Warfare

One of the most devastating and consistent destroyers of life is war. *War* can be defined as a period of collective fighting between large groups or countries through the use of armed combat, usually in an open and declared manner (Delaney and Madigan 2021). War is an inevitable aspect of humanity, we can't seem to help but kill each other, we are very intolerant beings, we are territorial, we fight for scarce resources; we have aggressive tendencies. Most nations across the globe have a long history of war, although often not by choice (e.g., because they were victimized by invasion such as when Russia invaded Ukraine in 2022 without provocation or jus-tification). The United States, for example, has been a warring nation for over 93 percent of its history (realizing that many of these years include wars with indig-enous populations) (Miller Center 2020; Delaney and Madigan 2021). In fact, the United States, overall, is not a very peaceful nation. In 2023, The Institute for Eco-nomics and Peace released its annual "Global Peace Index" and ranking of 163 coun-tries (which comprises 99.7 percent of the world's population) and the U.S. came in the bottom quarter at number 131 on the list. Among the criteria for "positive peace" are well-functioning government; sound business environment; acceptance of the rights of others; good relations with neighbors; free flow of information; high lev-els of human capital; low levels of corruption; and equitable distribution of resources (Harmer 2023; Institute for Economics & Peace 2023). In 2023, the Top Five Most Peaceful Nations are Iceland, Denmark, Ireland, New Zealand and Austria. The Top Five Least Peaceful Nations beginning at #163 are Afghanistan, Yemen, Syria, South Sudan and Democratic Republic of the Congo (Russia and Ukraine came in 158th and 157th, respectively) (Institute for Economics & Peace 2023). At any given time, nearly all nations of the world are *not* at peace. Over the past 15 years, the IEP reports that the world has become less peaceful. In 2023, 122 of the 163 countries were involved in at least one external conflict since 2008, although the majority did so as part of broad coalitions and not committing substantial resources (IEP 2023). Several armed conflicts and warfare include attempts of *genocide*—the deliberate killing of a large number of people from a particular nation or ethnic group with the aim of destroying that nation or group.

War has been waged throughout most of human history dating back to con-flicts between clans of people and entire nation-states. As sociologist C. Wright Mills (1958) states, "To reflect upon war is to reflect upon the human condition" (p. 1). And what does it say about the human condition that war is so commonplace that there exist "laws" of war? In essence, humanity is resigned to the fact that there will always be war and that rules be abided by, rather than having the nations of the world adhere to an agreement not to go to war. In other words, why not have a law that forbids war? In extreme cases, there are world wars—wars (two of them so far) that involve many large nations in all different parts of the world. Another question to ponder is, "Can humanity survive a third World War?"

The very meaning of war involves the willful destruction of people, property and the physical environment. The costs of war go way beyond the financial. Con-sider, for example, ecocide. *Ecocide* refers to the extensive damage to, or destruc-tion of, large areas of the natural environment, leading to the loss of ecosystems as a consequence of human activity. Wars are a major cause of ecocide. With the advent of nuclear and chemical weapons we must worry about warfare dominated by weaponry so extreme that humanity will not only destroy the environment to the point where nothing could survive but most assuredly could destroy all of human-ity within a matter of relative moments. Not even war crimes tribunals will save humanity if nuclear bombs and hydrogen bombs are used in a full-scale world war. Such chemical warfare would kill countless people immediately and the radioactiv-ity of the weapons would continue to kill people, plants, animals and ecosystems.

With all the threats to the environment, continuous warfare and the threat of nuclear warfare, there is little wonder that the famous "Doomsday Clock" is set at 90 seconds to midnight—meaning humanity continues faces an unprecedented level of danger (when the clock reaches midnight, humanity ends) (Mecklin 2024).

There's good reason why nuclear war is an often-predicted cause of the extinction of humankind as the possible full-scale use of nukes and other more dangerous weapons in war as the potential to destroy humanity. Back in the 1980s, I had a friend and neighbor in Los Angeles who had a bumper sticker on his car that read, "One nuclear bomb can ruin your whole day." Well, it sure could!

The Role of Big Business and Politics

Business is a vital aspect in the survival of any society and it is a primary source of employment for most workers. Business, especially "Big Business" has the capacity to make a positive impact on humanity or a negative one. As the discussion of the environment earlier in this chapter revealed, Big Business in the form of the oil industry can have a devastating effect on both the environment and humanity. And, as briefly alluded to in Chapter 10, Big Tech (e.g., AI) can also have a negative impact on energy consumption. This constant consumption of energy and reaping the environment of natural resources will have dire lasting negative consequence. In order to sustain their harmful practices, Big Business leaders turn to political leaders for favorable legislation that will allow them to conduct business without oversight intrusion. They have formed a symbiotic relationship.

In their *Beyond Sustainability: A Thriving Environment (Second Edition)* book, Delaney and Madigan (2021) put forth the notion that residing in an environment where all living species thrive should be the goal of all people, and such a goal should be devoid of political overtones. After all, we should be able to presume that regardless of political affiliations and socio-economic backgrounds, we all want to breathe clean air and drink water and we all want to enjoy a high quality of life. Such notions reflect why common sense is not a viable paradigm of thought, as most people, especially those in a position of power, act in a very self-centered manner. For example, it is political leaders that make decisions on matters of waging war and "Big Business" that supply the war machines to wage destruction. It is also Big Business that make decisions on matters of destroying the environment in order to secure greater profits via the extraction of fossil fuels and the insistence that the populace remain depended on fossil fuels rather than securing safe, renewable forms of energy. Political leaders, influenced by money given to them by business people, attempt to sway public opinion on all sorts of matters of political interest that benefit the symbiotic relationship between politics and big business. Decisions are seldom made on what is best for humanity but rather, what will help to keep politicians in office and increase profits for Big Business. Recall that in Chapter 9, Kaku stated that the key to the future of humanity is wisdom. To reach this goal of wisdom, society must embrace higher education and science. Dictators and those who hate democracy will attack higher education and science and those are the very people we must worry about as they will contribute to the end of humanity. Kaku (2011) said, "The key to a democracy is an educated, informed electorate that can rationally and dispassionately discuss the issues of the day" (p. 406). Our current civilization is drifting away from this ideal more and more every year.

As a general rule, progressive thinkers (including political leaders and business leaders) realize how important an educated populace is for the survival of humanity. They will do whatever it takes to make higher education available for all citizens and that includes making it affordable, even if that means eliminating student loan debt for students. Progressives are left-leaning, they support progress in all spheres of life, and they support equality for all. And, they certainly want to protect the environment and the rights of citizens, especially their right to vote. In the United States, as a general rule, the members of the Democratic Party, among other things, support higher education for all, they promote the use of science and want it taught in the classroom, they want all eligible people to have easy access to vote, and they want protections for the environment including an easing on the reliance of fossil fuels in favor of the development of renewable forms of energy. Somehow, many Republican political leaders still cannot grasp the concept of climate change and this is despite the overwhelming evidence that has existed for decades now. Republicans tend to be very pro fossil fuel industry and support such things as fossil fuel extraction and quasi-green initiatives so long as they are good for business. The brief review in this chapter of the problems confronting the environment should have made it clear just how important is to protect the environment and local ecosystems at all costs. However, at a time when the environment needs help from humanity the most, the conservative Supreme Court (3 conservative judges were appointed while far-right Donald Trump was president) has scaled back the authority of the Environmental Protection Agency (EPA) instead of strengthening it. It is a move that completely defies common sense, logic, enlightened and rational thought. For example, a 2022 Supreme Court decision (6–3, with conservative judges all voting in favor) stated that the Clean Air Act does not give the EPA broad authority to regulate greenhouse gas emissions from power plants that contribute to global warming (Sherman 2022). The conservatives in Congress will not vote in favor of protections for the environment, especially for clean air.

The world has looked toward the United States to be the leader and protector of democracy for a long time. The U.S. could always be counted on to protect the ideals of democracy and guard against populism, tyranny and authoritarianism abroad and at home. However, since the 2016 presidential election, democracy is under threat in the United States. Populist movements led by charismatic leaders that attempt to galvanize people who are angry over certain societal aspects promise the people simple solutions to complex issues even though simple solutions do not exist. All nations, including the United States, must fear extremist political leaders who do not have the best interest of humanity at heart when they run for, and take office. Often, these dangerous, extremist politicians come into power by duping the naïve and undereducated—underscoring once again the need for a highly educated populace. The people of any society must be wary of any political leader that constantly lies and makes false claims, especially when fact-checkers can easily disprove such falsehoods. One of the biggest and most dangerous lies in political circles in the

United States are the false claim that the 2020 U.S. Presidential election was "stolen"—this despite the reality that it was the most secure election in American history. There is not a single sane person who believes that the 2020 presidential election was stolen, an election won by Joseph (Joe) Biden. Consider that the election was confirmed by the Election Infrastructure Government Coordinating Council (GCC) Executive Committee—Cybersecurity and Infrastructure Security Agency (CISA) Assistant Director Bob Kolasky, U.S. Election Assistant Director Benjamin Hovland, National Association of Secretaries of State (NASS) President Maggie Toulouse Oliver, National Association of State Directors (NASED) President Lori Augino and Escambia County (Florida) Supervisor of Elections David Stafford—and members of the Election Infrastructure Sector Coordinating Council (SCC), who released the following statement: "The November 3rd election was the most secure in American history." As a result of Trump's continuing questioning of the results, Christopher Krebs, Trump's most senior cybersecurity official responsible for securing the presidential election also declared the 2020 presidential election "the most secure in American history" (Cybersecurity & Infrastructure Security Agency 2020). Because of that statement, Krebs was fired by then-president Trump. The future of humanity is threatened when the most democratic society in the nation holds secured elections that are challenged by narcissistic losers; especially when such challenges lead to threats to elected officials, the Constitution and democracy itself. In a democracy, leaders should be looking out for the people and they should not be convicted felons and clear threats to democracy; they should be friends with other democratic leaders and not world dictators; they should not be fascists and they should not praise Hitler as a good leader and desire generals just as he had. Every election going forward these are concerns for Americans and who would have thought that? And, these are not just concerns for Americans, but for others across the world who want rights for all people and who want to try and secure the future of humanity. After all, any world leader that threatens to use nuclear weapons is not a good sign for the fate of humanity.

We must worry about any world leader that cares more about assuring profits for Big Business at the expense of small business owners and we must really be concerned about high-power politicians who are in business and lack in ethics and morality. Consider, for example, Donald Trump and all of his legal transgressions, some of which involve his business dealings. In May 2024, in the first of four scheduled trials—the "hush money trial" in Manhattan, New York—a Manhattan jury unanimously found Donald Trump guilty of all 34 counts of falsifying business records, an unprecedented and historic verdict that made him the first former president in U.S. history to be convicted of a felony. Think about that—Trump became the first American president or former president in the nation's 234 year history to become a convicted felon; no other president had ever been indicted.

The preceding pages provided us with just three categorical reasons (mass extinctions and attacks on our environment; warfare; and the role of big business and politics) why humanity is doomed and destined to a premature mass extinction. Is there a chance that the fate of humanity is not fated to an early extinction? Even if you believe that there is a chance that humanity will stop its dependency on fossil fuels, learn to protect the environment, curtail its population, end all warfare and truly unite to help the less fortunate while forgoing corporate profits (something that will never happen) there's still that pesky chance of a mass extinction caused by an outer-worldly source.

So, what possible alternative fate could be in store for humanity if not a guaranteed premature mass extinction? The answers are not overly reassuring.

A Possible Alternative Fate of Humanity

The many realistic scenarios of the fate of humanity described previously in this chapter lead to a conclusion that humanity is facing a premature mass extinction. This leaves us to ponder are there any scenarios wherein humanity could save itself? The foremost alternative involves humans leaving Earth and populating other planets. Consider, for example, that in Chapter 8, Hawking warned that the human race will perish on Earth after we turn it into a sizzling fireball in less than 600 years. He declared that (quoting from "Star Trek") humans must "boldly go where no one has gone before" if we hope to continue our species (Murphy 2017). In other words, humans need to find a way to colonize other planets in order to survive as a species as Hawking worked with the premise that our behavior had already caused irreparable harm to this planet. It is human dependency on fossil fuels that will be the cause of Earth turning into a ball of fire. Kaku also warns that human dependency on fossil fuels will lead to the demise of humanity and insists that we must develop and use alternative sources of inexhaustible power including fusion, breeder reactors and solar energy (see Chapter 9). If we have enough time and if technology can catch up with theoretical technology, antimatter engines are something Kaku believes will help solve our energy needs; but Kaku believes such technology will not be developed until the year 2100.

The problem is—and it is an overwhelming problem—there are no known planets that could host humans. It has certainly not gone unnoticed by those of us who track such things but humans have not traveled very far into space. We have sent probes and satellites into space to gather information but to date humans have only been to the Moon and that was just for a few short days at a time during the six crewed landings between 1969 and 1972. There surely must be life of some sort on some/many of the endless array of planets in the Universe but that does not mean that any of those planets are adequate to support the very specific needs of humans (e.g., oxygen, temperature, water and food supplies). An optimist would say, "There is always hope."

American astrophysicist Frank Drake proposed an equation—the Drake Equation, also called the Green Bank Equation—in 1961 at a conference on the "search for extraterrestrial intelligence" (SETI), held at the National Radio Astronomy Observatory in Green Bank, West Virginia, that purports there are at least 20 detectable civilizations of extraterrestrial intelligence in our galaxy alone (Tikkanen 2024). The Drake Equation does not imply that any of these host planets of extraterrestrial intelligence are suitable for humans. Furthermore, utilizing the Drake Equation, the nearest of these advanced civilizations would be a few hundred light years away (Tikkanen 2024). (Note: One light year is nearly 6 trillion miles.) The public, and assumingly, the scientific community have not been contacted by any of these extra-terrestrial intelligent beings either. If we were to seriously consider the possibility of extraterrestrial intelligence on other planets we would also have to consider them a threat to humanity, as often depicted in sci-fi. However, we will not dwell on something such at that or we would have to also entertain string theory's ideas of multiverses and who knows what could come out of those realms (if such universes existed)!

In 2022, scientists for the first time were able to grow plants in soil from the moon (on Earth) collected by NASA's Apollo astronauts Neil Armstrong and Buzz Aldrin, among other moonwalkers (Associated Press 2022). Our limited knowledge of space has led to a number of recent discoveries that might provide hope for the future of humanity beyond Earth. For example, scientists at the Center for Astrophysics believe that approximately 1.3 percent of known exoplanets in our solar system might have liquid water on their surface (Center for Astrophysics 2023). Among other things, scientists at this Center are developing new models for the spectroscopic signatures that identify the composition of planetary atmospheres, and build new instruments to detect them; they are looking for exoplanets that are most likely to harbor life; and they are designing ways to measure chemical compositions of exoplanets' atmosphere.

There are any number of scientific entities, universities and individual brilliant scientists looking into space trying to learn as much as possible about such things. Is there life on other planets, and if so, where? Is there any place hospitable enough to host humans? It is also impossible to ignore that in addition to governments (i.e., the United States and its NASA program) firing rockets into space, a number of other entities have also entered the space exploration foray including Blue Origin; SpaceX; Bigelow Aerospace; Bellatrix Aerospace; United Launch Alliance (ULA); Arianespace; Axiom; and Ispace. Why are so many companies and wealthy individuals (i.e., Elon Musk, Jeff Bezos, Richard Branson and Paul Allen) looking for ways to leave the planet do you suppose? If the planet is facing an immediate crisis (e.g., turning into a fireball within 600 years) and if humanity is facing a sudden and premature mass extinction, will scientists have enough time to find a suitable planet for humans to move to? And, will there be enough time and resources allocated to develop and build rocket ships to transport humans to these exoplanets or planets? Certainly, all 8+ billion people will not be selected to make such a journey and they will likely leave over 99.9 percent of humanity left here on Earth subject to extinction.

The discussion on AI in Chapter 10 leads us to another possible alternative fate of humanity. Could we transfer human consciousness to robots? This process is known as "mind uploading." *Mind uploading*, also "known as whole brain emulation or substrate-independent minds, is the theoretical process of transferring a person's consciousness, memories, and personality into a non-biological substrate, such as a computer or robot" (Medium 2023). This process would involve scanning a person's brain, mapping it and transferring the information into a machine, creating a digital copy of their mind. The result would be, depending on one's interpretation of what it means to be a human, a quasi-human, or AI-Human. Under such a scenario, the robots or computers might survive an extinction event but are such entities really human? And, how would these AI-Humans survive? Where would the energy come from to operate such entities? And, wouldn't someone/something have to oversee the entire operation (something akin to the operation described in the movie *The Matrix*)?

These alternatives and others do not seem very viable and leads to further support of the original conclusion that the fate of humanity is a premature mass extinction (with no exact date of finality but sooner that it should be because of destructive human behavior).

The Afterlife

Perhaps one of the most daunting questions that confronts humans centers on the socio-philosophical question of, "Is there an afterlife?" And, "If there is an afterlife, what happens in that realm of existence?" An *afterlife* involves a belief in a continued existence in some form after physiological death. While nearly everyone has pondered such basic questions, no one has come up with a definitive answer—even though most have an opinion or strong belief on the topic. One of the simplest and perhaps one of the most plausible explanations as to what happens to us after we die is: nothing. That is to say, we simply cease to exist. End of story.

Most people do not like to even imagine such a scenario as when we die that is the end of it; they want more, they want an afterlife. And not just any afterlife, they want one that is filled with happiness and joy and one that reunites them with their loved ones that predeceased them. When someone dies, think about how many times you have heard comments such as "They are in a better place now"; "They are reunited with their mother and father"; and "They are in happy in Heaven now." A belief in an afterlife has much credence in contemporary society primarily because of religious doctrines and teachings (to be discussed later in this chapter). But, even beyond religion, or in addition to religion, most people are not comfortable with the thought of the "finality" that death implies. They want to think, they want to hope, that there is more to their existence than their time on earth in their physical bodies.

Has this notion of an afterlife always existed? What did prehistoric people think happened after their death? Did they even have time to ponder such thoughts or did their daily battle for basic survival not allow for time to reflect on an afterlife? And, if they did think about an afterlife, would they assume things would simply be better than their current lives, or much the same? Since written records do not exist in the prehistoric period (*prehistoric* refers to the period before written records) we cannot know for sure. Notions of behaviors and thought patterns of early humans during the Paleolithic era (circa 2.5 millions years ago through to 10,000 BC) would be speculative at best and this includes the Neanderthals, the earliest hominins, and Homo sapiens, who first evolved around 350,000 years ago but were barely distinguishable from Neanderthals for the first couple of hundred thousand years (Handwerk 2021a). It appears as though basic rituals such as a burial of the deceased did not occur until humans developed cognitive skills. Cognition allowed for many things, including speculation (e.g., the ability to think about the possibility of an afterlife).

Prehistoric humans seldom bothered with burial rituals, or even burials for that matter, an indication that preparation for an afterlife did not exist. In 2021, scientists discovered the (currently) oldest known human grave in Africa. "The unearthing of a tiny child suggests Africa's Stone Age humans sometimes practiced funerary rites and had symbolic thoughts about death" (Handwerk 2021). This grave is estimated to be 78,000 years old. The scientists found the remains of a dead child curled into the fetal position but one would have to speculate whether the child's family or community connected such a burial with any thoughts of an afterlife (Handwerk 2021).

Ancient civilizations, such as the Egyptians, had a concept of an afterlife wherein those who died must not only have a sin-free heart but must also perform a number of tasks (as articulated in the *Book of the Dead*) in order for their spiritual body to reach the Kingdom of the Dead (the final resting place). In later Ancient Egypt, the practice of mummification was utilized as it was believed that the body must continue to remain intact for the deceased to live in the next world (Baines 2024). Following the mummification process (that included such things as draining the body of fluids, removing organs and wrapping the mummy with hundreds of yards of linen), part of the religious funeral rites at the tomb's entrance was an important ceremony called the "Opening of the Mouth." A priest touched various parts of the mummy with a special instrument to "open" those parts of the body to the senses enjoyed in life and needed in the Afterlife (e.g., the mouth, so that the dead person could speak and eat in the Afterlife) (Smithsonian Institution 2024b).

"Living On" as a Legacy

The Ancient Romans had a variety of ideas about the afterlife. For example, it was believed that some humans were transformed into special, empowered beings after death. These deified dead, known as *manes*, watched over and protected their surviving family members (King 2020). Many Ancient Romans also believed in a type of immortality that comes from a person's presence living in the hearts and minds of those they left behind. The idea of stone tombs with inscribed epitaphs reinforced this idea of prolonging the memory of life after death (Hayward 2020). While this is certainly not the same thing as an afterlife—as the person who dies does not benefit from those left behind thinking about them—it is a thought process shared by many people today as demonstrated by similar funeral procedures (e.g., a eulogy read at one's funeral and epitaph honoring the deceased). The graveside tomb with epitaph is a message about the deceased to all who stop and read such things. In this matter, the person "lives on" but again, not (necessarily) in an afterlife.

Many people today believe that their legacy lives on through the blood (actually the DNA) of their children. While there is some legitimacy in the idea that a legacy can be created through procreation, there comes a time when the living forget about their grandparents and certainly their great grandparents. (Personally, I never met one of my grandmothers as she died long before I was born and two other grandparents died before I graduated from high school. I certainly never met my great-grandparents.) Once again, even if stories are told of ancestors in an attempt to keep their "memories alive" that does not automatically place those deceased in an afterlife.

People without children may try and create a legacy in an attempt to keep their "name alive." Authors, for example, will live on for as long as people discuss their publications, ideas and concepts. As a sociology professor who regularly teaches social theory courses, including classical social theory, I point out how important some social thinkers from the past (often centuries ago) truly are, as we still speak of their contributions and their relevancy on contemporary thought. In this manner, their legacy continues. Artists will live on for as long as their art is displayed and admired. Leonardo da Vinci, for example, has a legacy that most could never dream to attain and it's because of such famous pieces of art as the "Mona Lisa" painting (1503–19) and "The Last Supper" (1495–98). Da Vinci is not alone in establishing centuries-old legacies; there are Michelangelo, Donatello, and Raphael, just to mention a few. There are famous musicians from the past as well that have "lived on" because of their legacies, including: Wolfgang Amadeus Mozart, Johann Sebastian Bach, Ludwig van Beethoven and Frédéric Chopin.

In all the cases of the famous creative people mentioned above who have managed to establish a legacy it is important to point out that none of that guarantees that any of these people exist in an afterlife.

Religion and the Promise of an Afterlife

One of the oldest social institutions of human society is religion. Beginning thousands of years ago, religious leaders were often the ones who attempted to fill the void of the unknown and provide the answers to life's many mysteries. Early religious leaders nearly always provided the wrong answers on important matters such explaining why such phenomenon as lunar and solar eclipses occurred; whereas those trained with scientific knowledge knew that it was simply a matter of planetary alignments. It would take a truly primitive mind not to be able to comprehend that an eclipse is merely the result of planetary alignment and not some sort of nefarious conspiracy or an angry god out for revenge.

Religion is often at odds with science, rationality and reason and the explanation is quite simple, religion is based on beliefs and faith while science is based on empirical research and fact. *Religion* is defined as a system of beliefs and rituals that binds people together into a social category of people while attempting to answer the dilemmas and questions of human existence by making the world more meaningful to adherents (Delaney 2012). Religious answers provided to many of life's dilemmas and questions are not based on reason or science but simply based on doctrines designed to appease a God(s) and to force adherents' compliance to ideological beliefs. Often, these religious words of wisdom (from religious leaders who interpret a holy book written by humans with limited intellect many years ago) provide comfort to adherents as they seek simple solutions to complex questions. Telling a grieving person that their recently deceased loved one is now happy and without pain because they are alongside God does indeed sound comforting. Adherents rarely ask for proof of such a claim. And, it is a good thing because how could a religious leader provide any tangible proof that a recently departed loved one is now with God and living their best afterlife? Religion teaches its followers to have faith and to simply believe what they are being told even in the face of claims that seem quite outrageous to nonbelievers.

In the United States, most Americans believe in God: 63 percent are absolutely certain; 20 percent are fairly certain; and 5 percent are not at all certain. Nine percent of Americans do not believe in God (Pew Research Center 2024). Among those Americans who are absolutely certain there is a God, 87 percent believe in Heaven; of those who are fairly certain there is a God, 70 percent believe that there is a Heaven; and among those who are not too certain/not certain at all there is a God, 40 percent believe there is a Heaven (Pew Research Center 2024). When asked if they believe in the concept of Hell, 72 percent of those who are absolutely certain there is a God believe in Hell; 49 percent of those who are fairly certain there is a God believe in Hell; and 28 percent of those who are not too/not at all certain there is a God believe in Hell (Pew Research Center 2024).

Globally, 62 percent of people self-identify as religious while 72 percent say that there is a God. Just under one in seven (16%) do not believe that any God exists (Gallup International 2023). Just slightly more than half (57%) of respondents to an international Gallup poll reported that they think there is a life after death. One in four (23%) do not believe that anything happens when we die (Gallup International 2023). (Others are not sure.) Globally, people are slightly more likely to believe in Heaven than in Hell.

What do the major world religions teach regarding the afterlife? There is a common link between them all: the social control aspect of religion. Religious teachings instill upon its adherents that the actions of individuals during their lives on earth directly influence their fate in the afterlife. Thus, adherents must follow rules/commandments or face dire consequences (e.g., on Judgment Day). Let's take a quick look at the six major world religions and their basic belief about the afterlife. (This review is purposely brief as to address the primary point—that specific religion's perspective of the afterlife.) We will begin with Hinduism, the world's oldest major religion.

Hinduism (origins dating to 4000–2500 BCE) teaches that the goal in life is to reach enlightenment. One's path, or progress, toward enlightenment is measured by their karma. *Karma* is the concept that a person's behavior in the present life will determine their position in the next life. Good deeds are rewarded and lead the individual to a higher level of enlightenment. Bad deeds are punished and lead the individual to a lower level of social standing in the next life. The idea that individuals have multiple lives is reflected by the Hindu belief in reincarnation. A fundamental concept, *reincarnation* is the belief that the human soul does not die after our biological death but returns (reborn) in a new body that may be human, animal or spiritual depending on the moral quality of the previous life's actions (Nagaraj, Nanjegowda and Purushothama 2013). Thus, in Hinduism, the world's oldest religion, life after death leads to rebirth, it is a cycle (*samsara*) determined by one's karma. One's soul may reach *swarga* (heaven) or *naraka* (hell) for a certain period of cosmic time before they are reborn. Some Hindus, however, may be reincarnated immediately after death. The rebirth cycle continues until the soul achieves *moksha* or salvation and is united with Brahman, the supreme being or the ultimate reality (Harrison 2024).

The second oldest world religion is Judaism (origins dating to 2000–1600 BCE). By the time the Book of Daniel was written, in about 165 BCE, the Jewish belief was that the dead would be resurrected and receive judgment (Encyclopedia.com 2019). Jews believe themselves to be the "chosen" people and await Judgment Day when the Messiah will resurrect the dead and restore Jerusalem. Good deeds will be rewarded in the afterlife. Salvation, then, is attained through action (a way of life) and belief (Delaney 2012).

The third oldest world religion is Buddhism (origins dating to 560–490 BCE) and like Hinduism it originated in India. This religion developed from the teachings of Siddhartha Gautama, who reached enlightenment around 535 BCE and assumed the title of "Buddha" ("the awakened"). Buddhism arose as a rejection of Hinduism, but it retains a belief in reincarnation. Individuals go through a number of life cycles wherein they attempt to detach themselves from all desires in order to reach salvation. When a person dies, their soul (*atman*) is reborn in a different body (*BBC* 2024). Salvation can be attained through knowing and living by "noble truths." Ultimately, Buddhists seek nirvana. *Nirvana* is a state of perfect bliss in which the self is freed from suffering and desire; it represents the final freeing of the soul; it is a state of enlightenment. In this regard, nirvana is a type of supreme happiness that is possible only when the soul relinquishes passion, hatred and delusion (Delaney 2012). With such core beliefs as reincarnation and multiple life cycles, Buddhists clearly believe in life after death.

Confucianism (origin dated to 500 BCE) is the fourth oldest major world religion. It is based on the principles of Confucius (Kong Qiu) who lived from 551 to 470 BCE in the Chinese state of Lu. Confucius traveled across China giving advice to rulers and offering teachings about ethical and philosophical rules for proper conduct. Confucianism emphasizes the importance of many virtues (e.g., wisdom, loyalty, self-control and self-development). As a religious philosophy, Confucianism values proper conduct for its own sake, not to attain some sort of salvation or reward in the afterlife. People are supposed to be good for goodness' sake, not because they will be rewarded for it. Nonetheless, adherents of Confucianism believe that there is an afterlife even it is not outright stated.

Christianity (origin dated to 33 CE) has the largest number of adherents worldwide and began as a sect of Judaism nearly 2,000 years ago. The primary distinction between the two religions is the Christian belief that Jesus Christ is the son of God. Christians believe that the death of the physical body is not the end and that depending on their behaviors on Earth individuals will have eternal life in Heaven in the afterlife. Some Christians, typically Roman Catholics, recognize the existence of purgatory—an intermediate state after death and before final judgment (this is why they offer prayers for the dead). Many Christians also believe in Hell, a place where evildoers are sent to suffer in the furnace of fire through all of eternity. Thus, leading a good life will be rewarded with a place in Heaven while evil deeds will lead people to Hell.

The final major religion formed is Islam (622 CE) and it has the second most adherents. Islam was founded in Arabia in 622 CE by Muhammad (570–632 CE), whom Muslims regard as a Prophet. Islam is linked to Judaism and Christianity, but Muhammad believed that adherents of those faiths misinterpreted the teachings of Abraham, Moses and Jesus. Muslims believe that words of Allah, the one true God, were given to Muhammad in the sacred text the Koran. They believe in a creator who is just and rewards those adhere to the teachings. They also believe that sinners are condemned to Hell. All of this occurs on Judgment Day (Delaney 2012).

With the promise of a happy afterlife (heaven) connected to behaving "properly" here on Earth we can see why most nations of the world embrace religion and why there is a symbiotic relationship between religion and state. The social control aspect of religion (behave a certain way) is rewarded with a righteous, happy and fulfilling afterlife. Violate civil laws and religious doctrines and you can end up in Hell. Either way, the major religions generally teaches us that there is an afterlife. Still, no religion, no religious leader has been able to, or will be able to, provide any factual proof or evidence that an afterlife actually exists. Adherents are told to believe and have faith. That is good enough for those who are easily manipulated but no so good for people who need empirical evidence. Is there an afterlife? No one knows for sure. Maybe we will find out when we die. Then again, maybe we will not.

Physics and Energy

So far, we learned of two possible explanations as to what happens when we die: nothing, or that there is an afterlife that may be either joyous (Heaven) or one filled with damnation (Hell). There is at least one other possibility of what happens to us after we die and that involves the realization that because we are all made up of mass, or energy, and because energy cannot be destroyed, our atoms live on, following our bodily death. As explained by the "law of conservation of mass"—which states that the total mass present before a chemical reaction is the same as the total mass present after the chemical reaction—energy can neither be created nor destroyed; it is converted from one form of energy to another (U.S. Energy Information Administration 2024). The "law of conservation of mass" was formulated by French chemist Antoine Lavoisier's (1743–1794) 1789 combustion experiment and discovery that mass is neither created nor destroyed in chemical reactions (Sterner, Small and Hood 2011). This "law of conservation of mass" is further illustrated by the first law of thermodynamics which states the same thing, that energy cannot be created or destroyed. Consequently, the total energy of a system is constant (Stewart 2024). The law of conservation of mass implies that while the human body may die, the energy particles found within the body continues as mass is conserved.

Preceding the law of conservation of mass are the notions of *atomism* and *atomic theory*. The two founders of ancient atomist theory are Democritus—known in antiquity as the "laughing philosopher" (because of his emphasis on the value of "cheerfulness"—and his teacher Leucippus [Berryman 2023a]). The atomists held that there are small invisible bodies (atoms) from which everything else is composed, and that these particles move about in an infinite void (Berryman 2023a). Democritus (460–370 BCE) argued that everything is made of atoms; atoms are the smallest particles of matter; atoms have existed forever; atoms are indivisible, they can never be cut into smaller particles; atoms are separated from one another by the void; atoms are completely and perfectly solid because no void exists inside an atom (we may cut into an apple only because there are spaces between atoms for the knife to cut into); atoms are not alive; atoms cannot be destroyed; atoms are forever in motion; and a number of other characteristics (Famous Scientists 2024b). Less is known about Leucippus but he is generally referred to as the founder of atomism in ancient Greek philosophy and as a significant influence on Democritus and his ideas on atoms (Berryman 2023b). Modern physicists have found that the atom is indeed divisible and a single atom cannot be a solid or a liquid. It is, therefore, unfortunate that Democritus named the building blocks of matter "atomos" as the term literally means indivisible.

Nonetheless, the atomists gave way to subsequent atomic theories. English chemist and physicist John Dalton converted the atomic philosophy of the Greeks into a scientific theory via experimentation. His *A New System of Chemical Philosophy* (Part 1, 1808; Part II, 1810) provided a full application of atomic theory to chemistry. It offered a physical picture of how elements combine to form compounds and a phenomenological reason for believing that atoms exist (Steward 2023). Dalton proposed: All matter consists of extremely small particles called atoms; atoms are indestructible and resist changes; as per the law of the conservation of mass created in the late 1700s, atoms cannot be created, destroyed, divided into smaller pieces, or transformed into atoms of other elements; elements are characterized by the mass of their atoms; and, when atoms are involved in chemical reactions, they combine in small whole-number ratios to form what are now called molecules (Steward 2023).

There have been other modifications to the atomic theory but the relevant point here is that atoms cannot be created or destroyed. Thus, when someone dies, their atoms continue to exist. Is it their atoms that go to an afterlife, such as Heaven and Hell? What would it be like for atoms to go to a place like Heaven and Hell? Would such small particles experience the emotion of happiness that is promised by going to Heaven? Would it experience the pain that is supposed to be associated with going to Hell? Do atoms possess a consciousness?

Perhaps our atoms go to some sort of other cosmic realm other than Heaven and Hell? Another plane of existence that we don't really understand as of yet but have sometimes seen illustrated in science fiction, such as *Star Wars'* usage of the "Force." In *Star Wars*, the "Force" is what gives a Jedi their power as it is the realm of existence that encompasses all of the energy of all living things; it surrounds us and it penetrates us and it binds the galaxy together. The idea of the "Force" is a central element in the *Star Wars* franchise as it is the energy force that gives the Jedi and the Sith their ability to attain supernatural powers. (The classic "good," God's angels vs. "evil," souls in Hell or devils themselves.) The concept of the "Force" borrows heavily from Hindu theology which also expresses a belief in a unifying Brahman energy that composes and is a composite of the Universe (and by extension, God), and can be used for good or bad. Elements of other religions are also connected to the Fore including the Shinto religion of Japan, Buddhism, Taoism and certain Celtic druidic concepts. The Chinese notion of *qi* or *qigōng* (a system of physical exercises and breathing control), and the splitting of the Force into light side and dark sides, reflect the concepts of yin and yang in Eastern philosophy (Yang 2018; Wookieepedia 2024).

When we die, our energy particles continue to exist. Thus, when contemplating any notion of an afterlife, we are really asking, what happens to our atoms? Will they somehow lie dormant in an abyss (akin to, when we die, nothing happens)? Will they enter some sort of cosmic plane where such places as Heaven and Hell exist; and if so, will our atoms have a sense of consciousness so as to grasp their existence? Or, will our atoms become a part of a cosmic plane that allows us to travel/float across the galaxy (and again, would we have a sense of consciousness as to grasp what was happening)? So, is there life after death? Certainly not as we live it now. Is there some variation of life after death? That depends on what you believe in. One thing is for sure, absolutely no one on earth knows for sure and if they try to tell you otherwise, they are lying.

Summary

In this chapter, two very important aspects of the theory of everything are discussed: the fate of humanity and the afterlife. While humans are capable of acts of generosity toward others, the overall harm we cause to one another and the environment will surely doom humanity to a premature mass extinction. We know humanity is doomed for a number of reasons but especially because of the double threat of the impending reality that we face a sixth mass extinction and that our environment is under constant attack by forces from nature and humans.

The topic of mass extinctions and attacks on our environment was discussed to point out the vulnerability of humanity. The planet has already faced five mass extinctions and we are currently in the sixth mass extinction (ME) period. The first five ME occurred before humans were on the planet but now that we are here, the evidence of the harm caused by our actions is undeniable and fateful. Among the environmental problems that humans are responsible for are reliance on fossil fuels; overpopulation; enviromares (air pollution, water pollution, land pollution, solid waste pollution, noise pollution, celestial pollution, and chemical and nuclear pollution); ocean acidification; plastics; deforestation; and marine debris. Threats to the environment—both by humans and nature—represents just one of the possible sources of the early extinction of humanity.

One of the most devastating and consistent destroyers of life is war. *War* can be defined as a period of collective fighting between large groups or countries through the use of armed combat, usually in an open and declared manner (Delaney and Madigan 2021). War is an inevitable aspect of humanity, we can't seem to help but kill each other, we are very intolerant beings, we are territorial, we fight for scarce resources; we have aggressive tendencies. Most nations across the globe have a long history of war, although often not by choice. War has been waged throughout most of human history dating back to conflicts between clans of people and entire nation-states. As sociologist C. Wright Mills (1958) states, "To reflect upon war is to reflect upon the human condition" (p. 1). The very meaning of war involves the willful destruction of people, property and the physical environment. The costs of war go way beyond the financial. Consider, for example, ecocide. *Ecocide* refers to the extensive damage to, or destruction of, large areas of the natural environment, leading to the loss of ecosystems as a consequence of human activity. Wars are a major cause of ecocide.

Big Business and politics will also play a big role in the ultimate downfall of humanity as these two symbiotic entities work cooperatively in their own best interests that center primarily on making as big as profits as possible. The greater good of humanity is not the top priority. It is political leaders that make decisions on matters of waging war and "Big Business" that make decisions on matters of destroying the environment in order to secure greater profits via the extraction of fossil fuels and the insistence that the populace remain depended on fossil fuels rather than securing safe, renewable forms of energy. Political leaders, influenced by money given to them by business people attempt to sway public opinion on all sorts of matters of political interest that benefit the symbiotic relationship between politics and big business.

The conclusion arrived at in this chapter is that humanity is doomed to a premature mass extinction. However, a possible alternative fate was presented. The foremost alternative involves humans leaving Earth and populating other planets. The problem is—and it is an overwhelming problem—there are no known planets that could host humans. The discussion on AI in Chapter 10 leads us to another possible alternative fate of humanity. Could we transfer human consciousness to robots? This process is known as "mind uploading." *Mind uploading*, also "known as whole brain emulation or substrate-independent minds, is the theoretical process of transferring a person's consciousness, memories, and personality into a non-biological substrate, such as a computer or robot" (Medium 2023). These alternatives and others do not seem very viable and leads to further support of the original conclusion that the fate of humanity is a premature mass extinction (with no exact date of finality but sooner that it should be because of destructive human behavior).

The topic of the afterlife was also discussed. Perhaps one of the most daunting questions that confronts humans centers on the socio-philosophical question of, "Is there an afterlife?" And, "If there is an afterlife, what happens in that realm of existence?" While nearly everyone has pondered such basic questions no one has come up with a definitive answer—even though most have an opinion or strong belief on the topic. Notions of life after death from ancient and past cultures were provided.

Some people think they can "live on" long past their death through their children and their children's children because their DNA is passed on to subsequent generations. People without children believe that they can "live on" by leaving behind some sort of legacy, such as through their book publications, art work or music. Neither of these scenarios, however, equates to the deceased moving on to an afterlife.

There are those who believe that when one dies that it is it, nothing else happens. Life ceases to exist, end of story. A large number of people believe in what various organized religious teachings preach, namely, that people move on to Heaven, if they are good or to Hell if they were bad. The six major religions and their ideas on an afterlife were reviewed in this chapter. We can also turn to physics for an answer regarding the afterlife. Physics, and the sciences, remind us that mass consists of particles of energy and energy can neither be created nor destroyed. Thus, when the human body dies, the atoms that make up that person still exist in the form of energy. But, where does that energy go?

12

The Fate of Earth
and the Fate of the Universe

Introduction

We learned in the previous chapter that humanity is (in all probability) doomed to a premature mass extinction. Most likely, the majority of all the other species on Earth are doomed alongside humanity. That second scenario becomes a reality if anything close to what Hawking warned—that the human race will perish on Earth after we turn it into a sizzling fireball in less than 600 years—comes to fruition. At the current pace that humanity is destroying the planet's environment, there is little doubt it will soon (a matter of generations, maybe a couple of centuries at tops) be inhabitable for humans and many other lifeforms (animals and plants). Make no mistake about it; we are in the sixth mass extinction period. As described in Chapter 11, the previous five mass extinction (ME) periods lasted for hundreds of thousands of years, something that might give us hope. However, all the previous ME took place prior to the introduction of humans to the environment. Humans have sped the 6th ME period tremendously, especially since the Industrial Revolution and the subsequent dependence on fossil fuels for our energy needs.

This chapter is concerned with the fate of the Earth and the fate of the Universe as these two topics round out the final elements of the theory of everything. So, let's think about the impact of a ME on the planet itself. Clearly, because there have already been 5 ME over the course of the past 440 million years or so, the planet has survived and is therefore likely to survive the 6th ME as well. However, the survival of Earth has nothing to do with the survival of all the current living species residing on the planet (especially if it does turn into a sizzling fireball). As in previous cases, Earth will cleanse itself and start all over. Such a scenario is not good for humans and most other species. A planetary cleansing is somewhat like a worse-case electronic reboot situation wherein you lose all your data, programs and apps. The computer is still there but you now have to start fresh and add new programs, apps and files. In the case of Earth, the new uploads would occur through the process of evolution and the formation of new plant and animal (including, perhaps, human) species. As comedian, and de facto social thinker, George Carlin said (*Jamming in New York*, 1992) about people and their attempt to "Save the planet," or "Save the trees," or "Save the bees!" and so on … there is nothing wrong with the planet, Carlin insists,

"The planet is fine…. The people are f*cked. Difference! The planet is fine!" Compared to people, the planet is doing great. It's been here four and half billion years. People have been here 100–200,000 years. The planet has been through a lot worse than us.

Carlin was certainly correct about a number of things, but is he correct about the fate of the planet? Will the planet survive after humans have destroyed themselves? Is Earth invulnerable, or can something destroy it? Let's investigate.

The Fate of Earth

While Earth will likely survive the 6th ME, it is indeed experiencing the ill effects of humanity and nature. The planet's environment is under constant "attack" by forces of nature that include repeated lightning strikes; natural wildfires; volcanic eruptions; superstorms; hurricanes; tornadoes; floods and tsunamis; snowstorms; earthquakes; an influx of invasive species; and it has been attacked by outer-worldly forces such as asteroids, meteorites and comets. In fact, the first 5 ME were caused by such forces of nature: glaciation; global cooling and climate change; volcanism; and asteroids. In each scenario, the Earth survived. Humans harm the planet and its atmosphere through their reliance on burning fossil fuels; extracting fossil fuels (e.g., extracting coal, crude oil, and natural gas) and other natural resources (e.g., copper, iron, aluminum, cobalt, lithium, rare elements); over-extending the Earth's carrying capacity; overpopulation; the creation and utilization of single-use goods; choking marine life and fresh water supplies via pollution and the dumping or discarding of plastic and microplastic products; harmful agricultural practices that strip away limited fertile topsoil; and deforestation, just to mention a few. As far as the Earth is concerned, humans act like an invasive species that take and take and rarely give back. In a study published in *Nature*, an international group of scientists—the Earth Commission—concluded that if the planet Earth just got an annual check-up, similar to a person's physical, the doctor would conclude that the planet is really quite sick right now and is sick in many different ways and that this sickness is also affecting the people living on Earth (Rockström et. al. 2023). The authors of this study believe that the planet can recover, if humans stop using coal, oil and gas and change the way they treat the land and water. But, how plausible is that? There are many people who still refuse to accept the fact that climate change is real and greatly negatively affecting the planet and there are many who do not want to embrace the use of alternative forms of energy. I think we all know the likelihood of humans halting their dependency of fossil fuels.

Earth Will Flourish Without Humans

One thing is certain, Earth is much better off without humans as inhabitants. If common sense and reason alone didn't lead someone to that conclusion then the events of the COVID-19 lockdown surely did. Having its origins in Wuhan, China, the novel Coronavirus (COVID-19), caused by the virus SARS-CoV-2, first appeared in late 2019 and quickly spread worldwide in the early months of 2020 (Delaney 2020). It was declared a pandemic by the World Health Organization in March 2020. The family of Coronaviruses that causes respiratory illness would infect more than fifteen million people and cost the lives of three-quarters of a million people globally prior to August 1, 2020. (Note: According to the Coronavirus Tracker, which stopped updating COVID-19 statistics on April 13, 2024, there were, as of that date, over 704 million Coronavirus cases and more than 7 million deaths [Worldometer 2024].) Nearly all of the governments of the world (sans countries like Taiwan which had prepared for such an outbreak since the 2003 SARS pandemic) were not prepared for the microbes associated with COVID-19. The lack of leadership in a number of countries (especially the United States, Brazil and Great Britain) would contribute to the spread of the disease and high fatality rates. The United States, which boasts brilliant scientists, but was led by an inept president at the time, ended up with the highest number of COVID-19 deaths, over 1.2 million; Brazil had the second most deaths at 711,380 (Worldometer 2024).

In early–April 2020, Brazil's leader Jair Bolsonaro, known uncomplimentarily as "Brazil's Trump," completely discounted warnings from medical experts and continued to mingle with the people sans face mask and shaking hands with his followers at his Trump-like political rallies. Such behavior encouraged Brazil's citizens to also ignore the advice of medical experts. In the United States, President Donald Trump also ignored the warnings and advice from medical experts, refused to wear a mask in public and encouraged his followers to also ignore mask mandates (Delaney 2020). The highly-esteemed Dr. Anthony Fauci, the director of the National Institute of Allergy and Infectious Diseases (NIAD), and White House coronavirus advisor, explained that if everyone wore a mask and practiced social distancing for a minimum of just 20 days, the disease would be mostly under control. The idea that it would be "mostly" under control is a reference to Fauci's dire warning (July 2020) that COVID-19 would likely never be completely eradicated (Delaney 2020).

By March 2020, it was clear to most state governors, especially in those states that were recording high numbers of COVID-19 hospitalizations and deaths that they would have to take charge if there were to be any hope of containing the virus. Most states enacted stay-at-home or shelter-in-place orders which required schools and colleges to end face-to-face classroom meetings and caused most businesses to have their employees work from home; banned large gatherings (e.g., at beaches, ball games and places of worship); required people to wear protective masks in public (some people wore surgical gloves as well); mandated physical distancing of 6 feet in public areas; and closed all but essential businesses (e.g., grocery stores, pharmacies and liquor stores). These drastic measures were deemed necessary in order to "flatten the curve." All of this was done on behalf of the health of citizens. The motto of "We're all in this together" came into vogue and all those who wanted to protect their fellow Americans and the country as a whole freely abided by this. Initially, most people went along with all these flatten the curve requirements (a strategy to slow the spread of a virus during a pandemic by limiting the contact among people in the greater population through such means as "social distancing"). It was easier for many people, especially professionals, as they were able to perform their work duties at home and as a result, continued to receive their paychecks. Eventually, a number of people protested these protective measures and ignored the "We're all in this together" motto and embraced the attitude "F*ck you, I'm going to do whatever I want, even if it kills me and others."

The most relevant aspect of this brief synopsis of the COVID-19 pandemic is to highlight was happened during those few months when most people worked at home, did not travel and stayed indoors. There were far fewer people on the roads and outdoors. Countless ecosystems benefited from this as when people stayed home the Earth turned much cleaner. Consider some of these highlights: smog cleared up in New Delhi; nitrogen dioxide pollution in the northeastern United States was down 30 percent compared to normal (in April 2020); air pollution in Rome from mid–March to mid–April was down 49 percent from the previous year; and wild animals roamed in areas normally occupied by humans. In addition, the air from Boston to Washington was the cleanest since a NASA satellite started measuring nitrogen dioxide, in 2016; air pollution was down 46 percent in Paris, 35 percent in Bengaluru, India, 38 percent in Sydney, 29 percent in Los Angeles, 26 percent in Rio de Janeiro, and 9 percent in Durban, South Africa, NASA measurements indicate; more than 70,000 olive ridley sea turtles were seen nesting on the beaches of eastern Indian state of Odisha, and sea turtles in Costa Rica and Mexico were also able to safely lay eggs on empty beaches as humans were quarantined, leaving the turtles undisturbed; and in Venice, the water in the famed canals became clearer than it had been in recent memory and even fish were visibly swimming around them (Borenstein 2020a; Johnson 2020; Guy and Di Donato 2020; Delaney and Madigan 2021). As for carbon pollution in sum, the world cut its daily carbon dioxide emissions by 17 percent at the peak of the pandemic shutdown in April (2020) (Borenstein 2020b).

Among the lessons learned from the pandemic lockdown is the fact that when humans act collectively, we can help save the planet. Then again, we also learned that many people are not willing to work toward the greater good and even those who are seem to have a limit to just how long they are willing to do the right thing. And, in nearly every case, humans did not do this to save the environment. They did it to stop from getting a deadly virus.

Perhaps you have wondered what the planet would be like if all humans were to die off. This question was posed to Marilyn vos Savant, a national syndicated columnist and author who is listed in the Guinness Book of World Records Hall of Fame as the person with the highest recorded intelligence quotient (IQ), in her weekly "Ask Marilyn" column that used to appear weekly in *Parade Magazine*. (Note: *Parade* issued its final print edition in newspapers on November 13, 2022; its final e-magazine edition on December 31, 2023; and now exists only as a website and emailed newsletter for those who sign up for it.) A reader asked, "If all human life were to disappear from the planet, leaving only animals and plants, how long would it take for the environment to return to a pristine state?" Vos Savant (2015) replied, "Stone building, concrete roads and dams, and steel bridges would be in ruins in just a few centuries, but they'd take thousands of years to disappear entirely. Meanwhile, nuclear waste in long-term storage would gradually become harmless." Savant adds, "Without human attention, civilization's hundreds of active reactors would catch fire or melt down and release radiation, but even that wouldn't stop nature's rapid return: Many plants and animals seem to be flourishing in the contaminated area around Chernobyl, the scene of a nuclear disaster in Ukraine [in 1986]." Vos Savant continues, "Excess carbon dioxide would remain for a long time, but the oceans would cleanse itself over tens of thousands of years. By then, added methane would be long gone. The toxic impact of pollutants such as DDT wouldn't even last a century." In short, the Earth would have forgotten about us in about 50,000 years—far less time than humankind has existed (vos Savant 2015).

Carlton Basmajian, an associate professor of Community and Regional Planning, Urban Design at Iowa State University, points out other aspects of what Earth would be like without the presence of human by answering the question: "What would the world be like if everyone suddenly disappeared?" Basmajian (2023) states, if humans disappeared for a year and if someone returned to Earth a year later, the first thing they would notice is how quiet the world would be. Humans make a great deal of noise. All daily activities of humans involve making noise, especially driving cars and living in urban environments. The sky would be bluer and the air cleaner. The wind and the rain would scrub the surface of the Earth and the smog and dust that humans make would be gone. Inside homes, the water pipes would have frozen and burst after the first winter (in those climates subject to such winters). There would be no electricity and no fuel for your homes or any buildings. Your house would be dark, with no lights, TV, phones or computers and, of course, no social media sites. The grass in your yard would grow and grow until it got so long and floppy it would stop growing. New weeds would appear and they would be everywhere. There would be new plant life as well. Without people spraying to kill bugs, there would bugs everywhere and they would have free reign of the world again. Many animals would grow bigger. With no electric lights, the rhythm of the natural world would return. The only light would be from the Sun, the Moon and the stars. Natural fires would happen frequently (e.g., from lightning strikes and wildfires) and there would be no way of putting them out (no fire departments). Bridges with metal legs would slowly rust, so too would the beams and bolts that hold the bridges up. Dams and levees would eventually erode. The plants that people eat (corn, potatoes and tomatoes) would soon disappear.

Life on Earth would certainly be quite different without humans and the planet would survive just fine.

Potentially Lethal Threats to Earth

It is not just humans that pose the fatal threat to the planet as Earth faces other potentially lethal dangers including giant asteroid strikes; being swallowed into a black hole; the collapse of the Sun; solar flares and superflares; and exploding supernovas to mention a few. Perhaps the most obvious threat to Earth involves the planet being hit by asteroids large enough as to break the planet apart. The fear of asteroids hitting the planet is a topic of many sci-fi stories and films but beyond that as already discussed they were (at least partially) the cause of the previous 3 mass extinctions. [Note: As a point of interest, when asteroids strike one another, or when they strike a planet as depicted in sci-fi films or at your local planetarium, the collision does not create explosive sounds because in the vacuum of space, such events would be silent. What we call sound is the way our brains interpret vibrations that propagate in waves through a medium such as air until it reaches our ears. Without any medium to vibrate, no sound exists. It may also surprise people to learn the vibrant photos we see from the James Webb Space Telescope are artificially colored. This is because the images are so laden with data they need to be scaled down before they can be translated into visible light as the human eye cannot see infrared and near-infrared light (vos Savant 2022; Schultz 2022).] While those strikes were large enough to cause global havoc to the extent that they killed off the vast majority of all life forms on Earth they did not destroy the planet itself. Asteroids or comets can be the size of our planet or larger and if they hit Earth at a sufficient force the planet would be more than vulnerable enough for demise. Essentially, Earth is unprotected against asteroids, comets and meteorites. Until recently, humans were just as defenseless as the dinosaurs were 65 millions ago; that is, until NASA's Double Asteroid Redirection Test (DART) spacecraft proved that humans could, in principle, deflect asteroids from catastrophic collisions with Earth (Hyman 2024).

As explained by NASA (2021), DART was the first-ever mission dedicated to investigating and demonstrating one method of asteroid deflection by changing an asteroid's motion in space through kinetic impact. Launched on November 23, 2021, aboard a SpaceX Falcon 9 rocket from Vandenberg Space Force Base in California with science targets of Asteroid Didymos (a 2,560-foot in diameter) and its moonlet Dimorphos (a small body just 530 feet in diameter), DART impacted the asteroid moonlet Dimorphos by changing its motion in space through kinetic impact (NASA 2021). The DART spacecraft, weighing just over half a ton, smashed into Dimorphos at nearly 14,000 mph (22,500 km/h) generating the energy equivalent of three tons of TNT (Hyman 2024). While DART was able to deflect the asteroid projected path, David Jewitt, a professor of astronomy at the University of California, Los Angeles, provided some perspective by saying, "If you wanted to deflect a bigger asteroid—for example, something 10 times larger—then you'd need 1,000 DARTs to get the same minuscule deflection. This deflection business is very, very tough" (Hyman 2024). Jewitt added, in order to deflect a larger asteroid (one that was the size that could harm the planet and not just kill lifeforms on earth) it would require a far greater shove or need to occur decades ahead of an impending terrestrial collision to have a cumulative effect (Hyman 2024). Then again, a larger impact results in more debris causing other significant problems (mostly for lifeforms on Earth rather than the planet itself). Assuming scientists could build large enough deflectors to modify the path of dangerous asteroids headed our way, they would still have to find said harmful asteroids in time to do something about them. NASA's Center for Near-Earth Object Studies currently lists only a few space rocks of immediate concern, but new ones show up frequently and with little warning. For example, with barely a day of advance notice, asteroids whipped past Earth in 2012, 2019 and 2021, ranging in size from a football field to several city blocks. "The 11,000-ton Chelyabinsk meteor that exploded over the Russian Urals in 2013, damaging thousands of buildings and injuring over 1,000 people was not on anybody's radar" (Hyman 2024). Examining the asteroid impact five years later, it was concluded that the explosion released the energy equivalent of around 440,000 tons of TNT and generated a shock wave that blew out windows over 200 square miles, damaged buildings, and injured over 1,600 people, mostly due to broken glass (Talbert 2018). Leading scientists, especially those at NASA, realized that a defense system must be put into place in order to warn citizens of Earth and that would involve a deflection system placed in space (Talbert 2018).

To further address the need for an early detection system of asteroids headed toward Earth is the forthcoming Vera C. Rubin Observatory in Chile (2025) and the launch of NASA's Nancy Grace Roman Space Telescope in 2026. When both of these systems come to fruition and join forces, both hemispheres of the sky will come under intense scrutiny for everything from asteroids to supernovas (Hyman 2024).

Another possible source of the demise of the planet Earth would be if it were swallowed by a black hole. The world of physics has long described the concept of "black holes" and the ramifications of their existence have discussed in earlier chapters (see Chapters 7, 8 and 9). Hawking's theories, using the ideas of Penrose's theory of space-time singularity led to the development of new set of mathematical techniques for dealing with the origin of the universe using singularity. Their work showed that there was an implied beginning to space and time—the Big Bang—and an end, through black holes (Hawking 1993). Hawking's theory of everything, as any theory of everything should, addresses such big picture questions as "What is the Origin of the Universe?" and "What is the Fate of the Universe?" I have done the same thing in this book. The fate of the Universe will be discussed later in this chapter and, of course, black holes become a variable in that conversation too. Pondering whether or not black holes could engulf the entire Universe is applicable to the idea that a black hole could also lead to the demise, or disappearance, of Earth. Recall that, as described by Hawking (see Chapter 8), black holes are regions of space-time where extremely strong gravity prevents everything, including light from escaping from within them and explains that they form during the collapse of massive stars. Black holes pose no immediate threat to Earth as most of them are a safe distance away. The black hole found in the middle of our galaxy, the Milky Way, is located 26,000 light years away and thus Earth is in no danger of being pulled in (NASA 2019b). Still, as the European Organization for Astronomical Research in the Southern Hemisphere (commonly referred to as the European Southern Observatory, or ESO) states, there might be rogue black holes drifting through space, gobbling up matter as they go, so there is always a very small chance one could endanger Earth in the very distant future (ESO Supernova 2024).

The eventual collapse of the Sun represents another threat to Earth. There is good news and bad news with regard to the Sun's eventual collapse. The good news involves the realization that it will not happen for billions of years, likely 5 billion years. Additional good news, according to NASA, is that the Sun would not become a black hole as it is too small for that. The Sun would need to be about 20 times more massive to end its life as a black hole (NASA 2019a). Now, the bad news. The manner in which the Sun will collapse comes with the awareness that all stars and planets have a limited lifetime, and like most stars, the Sun creates energy by fusing hydrogen atoms in its core. "In about 5 billion years, the Sun will start to run out of hydrogen in its core to fuse and it will begin to collapse" (NASA 2019a). This will start a process wherein the Sun will "start to fuse heavier elements in the core, along with fusing hydrogen in a shell wrapped around the core. When this happens, the Sun's temperature will increase, the outer layers of the Sun's atmosphere will expand so far out into space that they'll engulf Earth" (NASA 2019a). Sutter (2022) adds, "In the final stages of hydrogen fusion, our sun will swell and swell, becoming distorted and bloated—and red. The red giant sun will consume Mercury and Venus for sure. It might or might not spare Earth depending on exactly how large it gets. If the Sun's distended atmosphere does reach our world, Earth will dissolve in less than a day." Sutter (2022) posits that even if the Sun's expansion stops short of Earth "the extreme energies emitted by the Sun will be intense enough to vaporize rocks, leaving behind nothing more than the dense iron core of our planet." In this regard, Earth is not really "Earth," it would be just a core of itself.

Astrophysicist Ethan Siegel, writing for *Forbes*, essentially shared these same sentiments a few years earlier when he said that in five-to-seven billion years as the Sun runs out of hydrogen fuel in its core, the core will contract, heat up, and begin fusing helium to release even more energy than ever before. In this state, the Sun turns into a helium-burning red giant, and no lifeforms on Earth will be able to withstand this. The Sun will swell to almost a hundred times its current diameter, and will become thousands of times as luminous as it is today. Mercury and Venus will be totally devoured. The Sun will later die, being reduced to a white dwarf, while the Earth remains just a roasted remnant, floating through space in its orbit around a stellar corpse (Siegel 2017). Siegel (2017) believes that even though Earth will have been cleared of life, boiled, then charred and evaporated, and finally bombarded with quadrillions of years' worth of cosmic rays, our corpse of a planet will still continue to exist. It will remain intact, until one of the following things happen: (1) An object collides with the Earth, either destroying it or engulfing it, depending on the size and speed of the collision; (2) A massive object passes close by the Earth, gravitationally ejecting it from the Solar System and the galaxy entirely, where it wanders in obscurity throughout the empty cosmos for eternity; (3) Or, it remains bound to the Sun's corpse, and slowly, over countless orbits, spirals into our stellar remnant, where it's swallowed by the black dwarf that dominates whatever's left of our Solar System (Siegel 2017).

Far short of an explosion, the Sun often launches benign solar flares. Solar flares "are outbursts of light and radiation launched from regions of the Sun with intense magnetic fields, whose endpoints are marked on the solar surface by the cooler dark patches known as sunspots" (Hyman 2024). Solar flares stretch out for tens of thousands of miles carrying superheated, magnetically bound plasma that can release huge quantities of plasma, called coronal mass ejections (CMEs). If a CME approaches Earth, its protective magnetosphere generated by its molten iron core is harmlessly deflected. Once in a while, however, a flare hundreds or thousands of times more powerful than normal—a superflare—develops and penetrates Earth's magnetosphere. A superflare is a very large-scale magnetic eruption that expels intense electromagnetic radiation into space. A superflare emerging from the Sun could be potentially catastrophic for Earth, delivering serious damage to our planet's atmosphere and to the lifeforms that depend upon it. Luckily, superflares occur around stars far away from us and we seem to be safe from this potential source of demise (Lea 2024). There is conflicting research, however, that suggests that superflares have hit Earth in the past (from 993 CE and 774 CE to 663, 5259, 5410 and 7176 BCE) (Hyman 2024). Research at the University of Colorado Boulder sums up the confusion over superflares as, until recently, researchers assumed that explosions from superflares occurred mostly on stars that, unlike our Sun, were young and active (Strain 2019). New research shows with more confidence that superflares can occur on older, quieter stars like our own—albeit more rarely, or about once every few thousand years (Strain 2019). Still, the scientists point out that while the wave of high-energy radiation caused by a superflare could disrupt electronics across the globe, causing widespread black outs and shorting out communication satellites in orbit, it would not lead to the demise of the planet (Strain 2019).

One other noteworthy topic to mention when describing the potential causes of the demise of the planet involves supernovas. A supernova is the biggest explosion that humans have ever seen; it is an explosion of a star (NASA Science 2024a). A supernova is a type of "last hurrah" of a dying massive star and it occurs when a star at least five times the mass of our Sun goes out with a fantastic bang. "Massive stars burn huge amounts of nuclear fuel at their cores, or centers. This produces tons of energy, so the center gets very hot. Heat generates pressure, and the pressure created by a star's nuclear burning also keeps that star from collapsing" (NASA Science 2024a). When a massive star runs out of fuel, it cools off, and this causes the pressure to drop and gravity wins out, resulting in the star suddenly collapsing. Usually a very dense core is left behind, along with an expanding cloud of hot gas called a nebula. A supernova of a very large star may leave behind the densest objects in the universe—black holes (NASA Science 2024a). A second type of supernova exists in systems where two stars orbit one another and at least one of those stars is an Earth-sized white dwarf. A white dwarf is what's left after a star the size of our Sun has run out of fuel. If one white dwarf collides with another or pulls too much matter from its nearby star, the white dwarf can explode (NASA Science 2024a).

This completes our brief synopsis of the possible fate of Earth. While it was safe to predict the premature mass extinction of humanity (see Chapter 10), it is also relatively safe to predict that the planet Earth will be around for billions of years. That is to say, so long as it does not get hit by a giant asteroid(s); the Sun and the Universe remain intact; and we are not attacked by intelligent extraterrestrial beings from one of the planets hypothesized by the Drake Equation (see Chapter 11). That last scenario seems quite far-fetched, at least right now, anyway.

The Fate of the Universe

As stated in Chapter 11, we Earthlings have not traveled very far into space. In this regard, we are a primitive species. Other than the six crewed landings (that landed a total of 12 astronauts, all men) on the moon between 1969 and 1972 and humans living in the International Space Station (ISS) orbiting 248 miles (400 kilometers) overhead, our knowledge of the Universe is based on information and data attained from a number of probes and satellites sent into space, giant telescopes on Earth and in space, and a number of brilliant scientists capable of conducting calculations of all this data and employing the scientific method in order to learn more about the Universe.

Not surprisingly, it seems like the more we learn about the Universe the more questions we are left to figure out. However, we have learned a number of things including the fact that just like the Earth and the Sun, the Universe does have a limited shelf life. As established by Max Planck and his team in 2013, the Universe is 13.8 billion years old, give or take a hundred million years or so. Its development followed the Big Bang. But, what do we really know about our Universe? Let's start our discussion on the fate of the Universe by first examining the composition of the Universe.

The Composition of the Universe

Planck also found that the Universe is expanding and consists of 4.9 percent normal matter, 26.8 percent dark matter, and 68.3 percent dark energy (Plait 2013). *Normal matter* is what we call protons, neutrons, and electrons. *Dark matter* is a substance that we know exists but it's invisible; it profoundly alters how galaxies rotate and clusters of galaxies behave. *Dark energy* was only discovered in 1998 and is still very mysterious, but acts like a pressure, increasing the expansion rate of the Universe (Plait 2013). More recently, Chelsea Gohd of NASA's Jet Propulsion Laboratory, echoes Plait's conclusions about both dark matter and dark energy, namely that scientists do not know exactly what either are but agree that they do exist (Gohd 2024). Gohd also agrees that the Universe is made up of approximately 68.3 to 70 percent of dark energy and that dark energy is what makes the Universe expand at an accelerating rate. Dark energy is simply the name that astronomers gave to the mysterious "something" that is causing the Universe to expand at an accelerated rate (much faster than what Planck believed). Astronomers Adam Riess, Saul Perlmutter and Brian Schmidt won the 2011 Nobel Prize in Physics for their work on observing far-off supernovae and discovering that at a certain redshift the stellar explosions were dimmer than expected. Scientists can determine distance (and speed) of a supernovae (or any object in space) using an objects' brightness, and dimmer objects are typically farther away (through surrounding dust and other factors can cause an object to dim). By examining their redshifts, the scientists were able to conclude that these supernovae were much farther away than they expected. Unable to explain their observations as to what could be driving the Universe to stretch out faster over time they came up with the concept of dark energy. Dark energy was essentially being used as a substitute for the mysterious "something" that is causing the Universe to expand at an accelerated rate (Gohd 2024). This explanation for dark matter certainly doesn't sound very scientific, especially for physics; however, as we have learned in this book, physics is not always grounded in sound logic.

Gohd (2024) and CERN (2024b) also agree with the ambiguity with the concept of "dark matter." "Unlike normal matter, dark matter does not interact with the electromagnetic force. This means it does not absorb, reflect or emit light, making it extremely hard to spot. In fact, researchers have been able to infer the existence of dark matter only from the gravitational effect it seems to have on visible matter" (CERN 2024b). Dark matter makes up about 27 percent of the Universe. Combine that with dark energy and that means the matter that we know about (normal matter), the same matter that makes up all the stars and galaxies, accounts for only 5 percent of the content of the Universe (CERN 2024b). CERN works with a theory that dark matter could contain "supersymmetric particles"—hypothesized particles that are partners to those already known in the Standard Model (fundamental structure of matter—that everything in the Universe is found to be made from a few basic building blocks called fundamental particles, governed by four fundamental forces) (CERN 2024b; CERN 2024c). (See Chapter 9 for a discussion on supersymmetry.) Experiments at the Large Hadron Collider (LHC) may provide more direct clues about dark matter (CERN 2024b).

Planck also found that the Universe is just a bit lopsided (Plait 2013). This indicates that the Universe is asymmetrical, suggesting that some force, perhaps in the extremely early moments of its formation, caused it to develop that way. That the Universe is slightly lopsided has profound implications (Plait 2013). The distribution of the fluctuations is quite random and it takes computers, math and statistics to measure the distribution to test for true randomness. While the distribution is random, the amplitudes of the fluctuations are not. "It's hard to see by eye, but in the big map made by Planck, the fluctuations are a wee bit brighter than they should be on one side, and a wee bit dimmer on the other. It's an incredibly small effect, but appears to be real. It was seen in WMAP data and confirmed by Planck" (Plait 2013). Physicists at the University of Oxford, having analyzed the observations of over a million quasars and half a million radio sources to test the "cosmological principle," which underlies modern cosmology present the idea that a "lopsided" Universe could mean the revision of the standard cosmological model (Secrest et. al. 2022). Professor Sarkar (one of the contributing authors and scientists) says, "When the foundations of today's standard cosmological model were laid a hundred years ago, there was no data. We didn't even know then that we live in a galaxy—just one among a hundred billion others. Now that we do have data, we can, and should, test these foundational assumptions since a lot rests on them—in particular the inference that dark energy dominates the Universe" (Secrest et. at. 2022).

The Universe and Its Many Galaxies

There is, of course, a distinction between a universe and a galaxy. The *Universe* is the totality of all that exists, the entire cosmos, and the billions of galaxies; it is believed to be at least 10 billion light years in diameter; and it has been expanding since its creation as the result of the Big Bang. We can think of the Universe as the totality of existence, which includes all stars, all of space, and all the matter and energy that space contains (NASA 2024b). Most people tend to think of space as something beyond Earth as in "out in space" but the reality is, Earth is "out in space" too. We are all out in space at all times as the Earth is a planet, and it's in space and part of the Universe just like the other planets (NASA 2024b). "It just so happens that things live here and the environment near the surface of this particular planet is hospitable for life as we know it. Earth is a tiny, fragile exception in the cosmos. For humans and other things on our planet, practically the entire cosmos is a hostile and merciless environment" (NASA 2024b). We know that the age of the Universe is approximately 13.8 billion years old because scientists measured the ages of the oldest stars and the rate at which the Universe expands. "They also measured the expansion by observing the Doppler shift in light from galaxies, almost all of which are traveling away from us and from each other. The farther the galaxies are, the faster they're traveling away" (NASA 2024b). In the distant future, the galaxies' motion from one another will lead them to be so far away that their light will not be visible from Earth (NASA 2024b). The known composition of the Universe (the 4.9 percent "normal matter" mentioned earlier) contains all the energy and matter there is. "Much of the observable matter in the universe takes the form of individual atoms of hydrogen, which is the simplest atomic element, made of only an electron (if the atom also contains a neutron, it is instead called deuterium). Two or more atoms sharing electrons is a molecule. Many trillions of atoms together is a dust particle. Smoosh a few tons of carbon, silica, oxygen, ice, and some metals together, and you have an asteroid. Or collect 333,000 Earth masses of hydrogen and helium together, and you have a Sun-like star" (NASA 2024b). Scientists categorize clumps of matter based on their attributes. Among the categories used for practically's sake: galaxies, star clusters, planets, dwarf planets, rogue planets, moons, rings, ringlets, comets, and meteorites. All of these categories of matter exhibit different characteristics from one another but obey the same natural laws. It is impossible for most people to fathom the idea of the vastness of the Universe but consider this: Earth is a member of the Milky Way galaxy. The Milky Way contains at least 100 billion stars, and the observable Universe contains at least 100 billion galaxies. If galaxies were all the same size, that would give us 10 thousand billion (or 10 sextillion) stars in the observable Universe (NASA 2024b).

From the above description of the Universe we can ascertain that a galaxy is a subset of the greater whole. A *galaxy* is a huge collection of gas, dust, and billions of stars and their solar systems, all held together by gravity (NASA Science 2024b). Galaxies come in many different sizes. Our galaxy, the Milky Way, is big. Our neighboring galaxy, Andromeda is much larger. The Milky Way is but one of billions of galaxies in the observable Universe. "There are so many, we can't even count them all yet! The *Hubble Space Telescope* looked at a small patch of space for 12 days and found 10,000 galaxies, of all sizes, shapes, and colors" (NASA Science 2024b). All galaxies, including our own, are thought to have supermassive black holes at their centers (NASA 2024e).

Scientists are continually learning new things about our Universe, in general, and our galaxy, specifically. For example, in 2023 scientists using data from the James Webb Space Telescope discovered six very massive galaxies that, according to our current scientific understand of the Universe, should not exist at all (Labbé et al 2023; Feldman 2023). The detection of light emitted by these galaxies allowed the scientists to determine that these galaxies were formed about 13 billion years ago, or to be more precise, 500 to 700 million years after the Big Bang (with the age determined from the redshift of their radiation). By analyzing the light intensity and spectrum, the scientists were able to deduce the masses of the galaxies and conclude that they are almost as large as our Milky Way and therein lies the problem as this contradicts modern cosmology which claims that such massive galaxies should not have formed during the early stages of the evolution of the Universe (Labbé et al 2023; Feldman 2023). Erica Nelson, one of the authors of the study that appeared in *Nature* said of the discovery, "It's bananas. You just don't expect the early Universe to be able to organize itself that quickly. These galaxies should not have had time to form" (Feldman 2023). To put things in perspective, Nelson adds, "The Milky Way forms about one to two new stars every year. Some of these galaxies would have to be forming hundreds of new stars a year for the entire history of the Universe" (Feldman 2023). Joel Leja, another author in this study, calls the six galaxies "universe breakers" because their existence could upend current theories of cosmology. "The revelation that massive galaxy formation began extremely early in the history of the universe upends what many of us had thought was settled in science" (*The Post-Standard* 2023). These findings do indeed contradict past and current theoretical ideas of galaxy formation but also hard data collected by other well-known space observations, such as the Hubble and Spitzer telescopes, which have previously observed galaxies of about the same age, but much less massive. Labbé and his associates caution that before the world of cosmology worries that their theories and knowledge of the existence of the Universe are all incorrect, or at the least, need to be greatly modified, that these newly discovered galaxies might actually be lighter than the preliminary study suggests, which will make their masses consistent with theoretical understanding. Another possible explanation for the contradiction is that these galaxies are not what scientists think they are, but actually new objects that need their own classification; thus, making them consistent with modern cosmological theory (Feldman 2023). "Whatever these objects are, further research is likely to have a serious impact on our theories of the evolution of stars, galaxies, and perhaps the Universe as a whole, requiring a significant change in understanding of the processes occurring shortly after the Big Bang" (Feldman 2023).

In July 2023, photographs from the James Webb Space Telescope revealed the dramatic close-up of dozens of stars at the moment of birth. NASA's Jet Propulsion Laboratory unveiled images of about 50 baby stars in a cloud complex 390 light years away. (Reminder: A light year is nearly 6 trillion miles.) All of the young stars appear to be similar in mass to the Sun, or smaller. "The darkest areas are the densest, where thick dust cocoons still-forming protostars. Huge bipolar jets of molecular hydrogen, represented in red, dominate the image, appearing horizontally across the upper third and vertically on the right. These occur when a star first bursts through its natal envelope of cosmic dust, shooting out a pair of opposing jets into space like a newborn first stretching her arms out into the world" (NASA Jet Propulsion Laboratory 2023). Webb's images allow scientists to witness a very brief period in the stellar lifecycle with new clarity. Our own Sun experienced a phase like this long ago. Now, thanks to the Webb Space Telescope we have the technology to see the beginning of another star's story, says Klaus Pontoppidan, a project scientist at the Space Telescope Institute in Baltimore. Some stars in the image display telltale shadows indicating protoplanetary disks—potential future planetary systems in the making. The James Webb Space Telescope has transformed humanity's view of the cosmos, peering into dust clouds and seeing light from faraway corners of the universe for the very first time. Every new image is a new discovery, empowering scientists around the globe, says NASA Administrator Bill Nelson (NASA Jet Propulsion Laboratory 2023). According to NASA's Jet Propulsion Laboratory, "From its very first deep field image, unveiled by President Joe Biden, Vice President Kamala Harris, and [Bill] Nelson live at the White House, Webb has delivered on its promise to show us more of the universe than ever before" (NASA Jet Propulsion Laboratory 2023). As the world's premier space science observatory, the James Webb Space Telescope is solving mysteries in our solar system, looking beyond to distant worlds around other stars, and probing the mysterious structures and origins of our Universe and our place in it (NASA Jet Propulsion Laboratory 2023).

The discussion of "universe breaker" galaxies and the cosmic photographs of dozens of stars at the moment of birth highlight at least three things: (1) What we think we know about the Universe is subject to change; (2) We are learning more and more about the Universe because of advanced technology; and (3) There are many more mysteries yet to be solved.

We also know that early cosmological thinking that the Universe can be studied by using the mind alone (see Chapter 8) is wrong. Hawking (1993) did not agree with the view that the Universe is a mystery, something that one can have intuition about but never fully analyze or comprehend. And while Hawking was correct that the scientific revolution started more than four hundred years ago by Galileo and carried on by Newton provided early scientists with some precise mathematical laws to study the Universe, it is recent technology that has greatly advanced our knowledge of the Universe.

Potentially Lethal Threats to the Universe

The above paragraph should not lead one to conclude that the findings of Galileo and Newton are no longer relevant. In fact, one of the leading theories on the ultimate fate of the Universe that will lead to its demise involves Newton's second law of thermodynamics which involves the state of entropy of the entire Universe. Defined by *Oxford Dictionary*, *entropy* refers to a thermodynamic quantity representing the unavailability of a system's thermal energy for conversion into mechanical work, often interpreted as the degree of disorder or randomness in the system; the second law of thermodynamics says that entropy always increases with time. *Merriam-Webster* adds, entropy is a scientific concept that is most commonly associated with a state of disorder, randomness or uncertainty; the degradation of the matter and energy in the Universe due to an ultimate state of inert uniformity; and the general trend toward the death of the Universe. A campfire provides a simple example of entropy. The wood used in the campfire will eventually cool and burn out and become ash, smoke and gases. In Chapter 9, we saw how Kaku applied the second law of thermodynamics to the fate of the Universe when he described how the total amount of entropy in the Universe always increases leading to everything eventually aging and running down. Kaku (2005) states, "The stars will exhaust their nuclear fuel, galaxies will cease to illuminate the heavens, the universe will be left as a lifeless collection of dead dwarf stars, neutron stars, and black holes. The universe will be plunged in eternal darkness" (p. 290). (See also Chapter 8 for a discussion on Hawking's discussion of the second law of thermodynamics which states that entropy, or the degree of disorder within an object, should never decrease.)

Among the implications of the second law of thermodynamics and entropy is the realization that hot things always cool unless you do something to stop that process. The concept of *entropy* has been applied to the theory of the Heat Death of the Universe. The "heat death" theory of the Universe is the idea that when the Universe has reached a state of maximum entropy (the time when all available energy has dissipated) no more energy can be extracted from the Universe and when the heat flow ends and the Universe can no longer acquire heat, it will cool, and die. In the 1850s, Hermann von Helmholtz (1821–1894), a German physicist, proposed what became the standard cosmological theory based on the "Law of Entropy," his theory of "heat death." Helmholtz's heat death theory stated that the universe is gradually running down and eventually will reach the point of maximum entropy or heat death where all available energy will have been expanded and no more activity will occur (Rifkin 1980). Rifkin (1980) states, "The heat death of the universe corresponds to a state of eternal rest."

Using hard data from the Wilkinson Microwave Anisotropy (WMAP) satellite that indicates a mysterious antigravity force is accelerating the expansion of the Universe, Kaku (2005) describes how the laws of physics predict a doom and gloom scenario for the Universe (see Chapter 9). If expansion continues for billions or trillions of years, Kaku (2005) states, an inevitable Big Freeze will end all life in the Universe as we know it. "This antigravity force pushing the universe apart is proportional to the volume of the universe. Thus, the larger the universe becomes, the more antigravity there is to push the galaxies apart, which in turn increases the volume of the universe. This vicious cycle repeats itself endlessly, until the universe enters a runaway mode and grows exponentially fast" (Kaku 2005:288). The Big Freeze theory or "Big Chill" has the same scenario as the "Heat Death" theory and shares the same prevailing theoretical construct that the Universe will continue to expand forever until eventually all matter reaches a final uniform state and becomes too cold to sustain life. The basic idea behind these theories holds that, as the Universe stretches thinly across space, nothing will remain warm and as the Law of Entropy states, when the heat flow ends and the Universe can no longer acquire heat, it will cool, and die.

In the 1990s, there was a theory among astronomers of the "Big Crunch" scenario as the ultimate fate of the Universe. The Big Crunch theory put forth the notion that the expansion of the Universe eventually reverses and the Universe recollapses, ultimately causing the cosmic factor to reach zero, and even potentially followed by a reformation of the Universe with another Big Bang. However, this theory has been mostly completely ruled out as evidence indicates that the expansion of the

Universe has not slowed, but is accelerating. As NASA (2024c) explains, the fate of the Universe is determined by a struggle between the momentum of expansion and the pull of gravity. The rate of expansion is expressed by the Hubble Constant (H_o) while the strength of gravity depends on the density and pressure of the matter of the Universe. "If the pressure of the matter is low, as is the case with most forms of which we know, then the fate of the universe is governed by the density. If the density of the universe is less than the 'critical density,' which is proportional to the square of the Hubble constant, then the universe will expand forever. If the density of the universe is greater than the 'critical density,' then gravity will eventually win and universe will collapse back on itself, the so called 'Big Crunch.'" However, as NASA (2024c) explains, "The results of the WMAP mission and observations of distant supernovas have suggested that the expansion of the universe is actually accelerating, which implies the existence of a form of matter with strong negative pressure, such as the cosmological constant." This form of matter is referred to as dark energy. If dark energy (which makes up over 68 percent of the Universe) in fact plays a significant role in the evolution of the Universe, then in all likelihood the Universe will continue to expand forever (NASA 2024c).

It is the uncertainty of dark energy that has this author and other scientists pondering the true properties of the Universe and its ultimate fate. NASA (2024d) admits that observations made by the Hubble Space Telescope and future space telescopes will be needed in order to determine the properties of dark energy. Dark energy is thought to be the driving force behind the expanding universe and its accelerated rate of expansion. But, scientists are not sure why. Recall the discussion on Einstein's "cosmological constant" concept (see Chapter 7) that he applied to the possibility that even empty space has energy and couples to gravity. Einstein originally discarded his own theory but when Edwin Hubble found through his research that the Universe was indeed expanding and not static, validity was given to the cosmological constant idea. The pull of gravity and the push of dark energy have been "trying to outmuscle each other since the beginning of time" but about seven billion years ago, dark energy got the upper hand because the Universe had grown so large and matter (the source of gravity) had expanded and scattered (NASA 2024d). As a possible fate of the Universe, unstable dark energy could cause a "Big Rip" (the universe expands violently, then the stars, planets and atoms come unglued) or a "big crunch" (the Universe implodes or compresses) could occur. The Big Rip hypotheses then, states that the expansion of the Universe accelerates to the point where galaxies, stars and eventually atoms are torn apart. Researchers at Hubble believe it will take about 30 billion years before something like could happen (NASA 2024d).

During the earlier discussion on the possible sources of the demise of Earth, the question of whether or not a black hole could swallow the planet was explored and it was found to be an unlikely source of termination. As stated earlier, all galaxies, including the Milky Way, are thought to have supermassive black holes at their centers (NASA 2024e). Astronomers generally divide black holes into three categories according to their mass: stellar-mass, supermassive, and intermediate-mass. "The mass ranges that define each group are approximate, and scientists are always reassessing where the boundaries should be set. Cosmologists suspect a fourth type, primordial black holes formed during the birth of the universe, may also lurk unde-tected in the cosmos" (NASA 2024e). *Stellar black holes* occur when a star with more than eight times the Sun's mass runs out of fuel, its core collapses, rebounds, and explodes as a supernova (NASA 2024e). *Supermassive black holes* are hundreds of thousands to billions of times the Sun's mass, although some scientists place the lower boundary at tens of thousands. Scientists are not sure how these monster objects came to be. The size of *intermediate black holes* falls in between stellar-mass and supermassive black holes. Scientists believe this category is necessary because, over cosmic time, collisions between stellar and supermassive black holes should lead to the creation of intermediate black holes. While scientists are actively hunting for examples of these so-called missing-link black holes, none have been confirmed to exist (NASA 2024e). Scientists theorize that *primordial black holes* formed in the very first second after the birth of the Universe. "In that moment, pockets of hot material may have been dense enough to form black holes, potentially with masses ranging from 100,000 times less than a paperclip to 100,000 times more than the Sun's. Then as the universe quickly expanded and cooled, the conditions for form-ing black holes this way ended" (NASA 2024e). Disappointingly, scientists have yet to find definitive proof that these primordial black holes ever existed; although, it is theorized that they could have evaporated as the cosmos aged due to quantum mechanical processes occurring at the edges of their event horizons. Very early and small black holes (those with a mass less than a mountain) would evaporate more quickly than larger black holes (NASA 2024e).

The supermassive black hole in the center of the Milky Way, named Sagittar-ius A* (pronounced ey-star), is 4 million times the mass of the Sun—relatively small compared to those found in some other galaxies (NASA 2024e). Roger Penrose, Reinhard Genzel and Andrea Ghez won the 2020 Nobel Prize in Physics for their discovery of one "of the most exotic phenomena in the universe, the black hole" (The Nobel Prize 2020). Penrose showed that the general theory of relativity leads to the formation of black holes while Genzel and Ghez discovered that an invisible and extremely heavy object governs the orbits of stars at the center of our galaxy. "A supermassive black hole is the only currently known explanation" (The Nobel Prize 2020).

As to the primary issue at hand here, can a black hole swallow up the entirety of the Universe? "Black holes are infamous for their immense gravity—they can swal-low stars, planets and even other black holes" (Coffey 2023). But, is it possible for a black hole to swallow the Universe? According to NASA (2019b), "No. There is no way a black hole would eat an entire galaxy. The gravitational reach of supermassive black holes contained in the middle of galaxies is large, but not nearly large enough for eating the whole galaxy."

This completes our brief review of the possible fate of the Universe. Predict-ably, if the Earth is safe for billions of years it is even easier to say that the Universe will continue to exist for many more billions of years. An especially important point when discussing the fate of the Universe is the role of dark energy. Recall that sci-entists believe that dark energy makes up over 68 percent of the Universe. If dark energy in fact plays a significant role in the evolution of the Universe, then in all likelihood the Universe will continue to expand forever (NASA 2024c). The existence of dark energy essentially assures the existence of the Universe for at least 30 billion years, according to Hubble researchers (NASA 2024d).

Summary

This chapter concludes the review of the social physics theory of everything. In Chapter 10 we learned about social physics and its connection to a "theory of everything"; the fourth stage of human progress (Artificial Intelligence); and were warned about AI singularity. Chapter 11 described the fate of humanity and addressed the issue of the afterlife—and whether or not there is one. In this chapter, the final puzzle pieces of the social physics theory of everything were discussed: the fate of Earth and the fate of the Universe.

The chapter begins with a look at the fate of Earth. The planet's environment is under constant "attack" by forces of nature that include constant lightning strikes; natural wildfires; volcanic eruptions; superstorms; hurricanes; tornadoes; floods and tsunamis; snowstorms; earthquakes; an influx of invasive species; and has been attacked by outer-worldly forces such as asteroids, meteorites and comets. In fact, the first 5 ME were caused by such forces of nature: glaciation; global cooling and climate change; volcanism; and asteroids. In each scenario, the Earth survived. Humans are constantly attacking the planet and its atmosphere through their reliance on burning fossil fuels; extracting fossil fuels (e.g., extracting coal, crude oil, and natural gas); over-extending the Earth's carrying capacity; overpopulation; the creation and utilization of single-use goods; choking marine life and fresh water supplies via pollution and the dumping of plastic and microplastic products; harmful agricultural practices that strip away limited fertile topsoil; and deforestation, just to mention a few. The brief 2020 lockdown because of COVID-19 revealed just how quickly Earth can flourish without humans and just how much better off it would be without humans.

A number of potential lethal threats to Earth were explored: giant asteroid strikes; being swallowed into a black hole; the collapse of the Sun; solar flares and superflares; and exploding supernovas. Following the review it is relatively safe to predict that the planet Earth will be around for at least five billion years; that is to say, so long as it does not get hit by a giant asteroid.

While humans have very limited direct knowledge of the Universe, we have attained a great deal of information and data from a number of probes and satellites sent into space, giant telescopes on Earth and in space, and a number of brilliant scientists capable of conducting calculations of all this data and employing the scientific method in order to learn more about the Universe. The composition of the Universe was presented and a distinction between the Universe and Galaxy explained.

A number of potentially lethal threats to the Universe were explored including: the theory of the Heat Death of the Universe; the Big Freeze; the Big Chill; the Big Crunch; the Big Rip; and the question of whether or not a black hole could swallow up the Universe.

Understandably, since the Earth was deemed safe for billions of years (unless hit by a giant asteroid/s) it is even easier to say that the Universe will continue to exist for many more billions of years. The mystery of dark energy makes any one wonder just what is going on with the composition of the Universe but otherwise, the conclusion is that the Universe is safe for at least 30 billion years.

Glossary

Acceleration—The rate at which velocity changes with time, in terms of both speed and direction; acceleration is a vector quantity (because it has both a magnitude and a direction); an object is accelerating if it is changing its velocity.

Acoustics—A branch of physics that examines sound and its way of propagating; vibration; ultrasound; infrasound; mechanical waves passing through different forms (e.g., gases, liquids and solids); and focuses on the production, control, transmission, reception and effects of sound and how it is absorbed.

Afterlife—A belief in a continued existence in some form after physiological death.

Age of Enlightenment—A collective term used to describe the trends and writings in Europe and the American colonies during the eighteenth century that helped to propel societies from centuries of darkness and ignorance into a new age of enlightenment by means of reason, science, and a respect for humanity.

AI Singularity—This refers to the point in time when artificial intelligence becomes more intelligent than humans (they reach Level II consciousness) with the fear that AI systems becomes self-aware and uncontrollable. This point in time also represents a new level of intelligence wherein AI has a reached a level that humans cannot achieve. It would also be the polar extreme in the fourth stage of human progress.

Algorithm—Refers to a process or set of rules with precise steps to take to be followed in calculations or other problem-solving operations written in a computer program. AI systems, for example, contain algorithms for operating and processing.

Amyotrophic lateral sclerosis (ALS)—Sometimes referred to as Lou Gehrig's disease, is a type of progressive neurological degenerative disorder that affects motor neurons, the nerve cells in the brain and spinal cord that control voluntary muscle movement and breathing.

Annus mirabilis—A miracle year, a year in which an unusual number of remarkable things occurred; a term applied to Isaac Newton's discoveries in 1666 and Albert Einstein's papers published in 1905.

Archimedes' Principle of Buoyancy—The Archimedes' Principle states that "the upward buoyant force that is exerted on a body immersed in a fluid, whether partially or fully submerged, is equal to the weight of the fluid that the body displaces and acts in the upward direction at the center of mass of the displaced fluid." This applied force reduces the net weight of the object submerged in a fluid (e.g., a boat in water); from this we have the Law of Buoyancy (see Law of Buoyancy).

Artificial Intelligence (AI)—The ability of a digital computer or computer-controlled robot to perform tasks commonly associated with intelligent beings; AI means that a machine-based system can perform any number of human defined objectives, make predictions, recommendations or decisions and influences real or virtual environments. It is AI that has led to the fourth stage of human development, or the fourth step in the Law of Human Progress as articulated by the social physics perspective.

Astrophysics—The branch of physics that studies the physical nature of the motion of bodies and systems in space, such as stars, quasars, galaxies, radio telescopes and space probes; it also examines the application of the laws and theories of physics in its interpretation of astronomical observations.

Atom—The smallest unit of ordinary matter that forms a chemical identity and consists of a heavy nucleus with positive particles (protons) and neutral particles (neutrons) surrounded by a cloud of negatively charged particles called electrons.

Atomic theory—Ancient philosophical speculation that all things can be accounted for by innumerable combinations of hard, small, indivisible particles—called atoms—of various sizes but of the same basic material. The modern scientific theory version of the theory states that larger elements of matter consist of aggregations of smaller subunits (atoms) possessing nuclear and electron substructure characteristic of each element.

Atomism—A doctrine that the physical or physical and mental universe is composed of simple indivisible minute particles.

Big Bang—The scientific expansion for the origin of the Universe that describes how it started from a primordial state of high density and temperature and led to the expansion of space itself; this starting point of the Universe occurred at a point of infinite density and infinite curvature of space-time—a singularity—exploded outwards and expanded. (This event took place circa 15 billion years ago.)

Big Business—Large companies and commercial enterprises organized and financed on scale large enough to influence social and political policies.

Big Data—Extremely large data sets that contain so much information that no one person could ever process and therefore humans have to turn to AI to process the files to reveal patterns, trends and associations, especially relating to human behavior and interactions.

Black holes—A phenomenon wherein objects of such enormous density have gravity so strong that it traps even light; as explained by Hawking, black holes are regions of space-time where extremely strong gravity presents everything, including light from escaping from within them and explains that they form during the collapse of massive stars.

Bosons—Subatomic particles that carry energy.

Brownian motion—The erratic random movement of microscopic particles (the existence of atoms and molecules) in a medium (fluid or a gas) as they collide.

Calculus—An advanced branch of mathematics that concerns itself mostly with rates of change and with problems such as determining areas or volumes within curved lines or surfaces.

Carrying capacity—Refers to the maximum feasible load the planet can sustain just short of the level that would end the environment's ability to support life.

Casual explanation—When a direct connection between events is established.

Cathetus Principle—In a right triangle, a catheus, commonly known as a leg, is either of the sides that are adjacent to the right angle; the side opposite the right angle is the hypotenuse.

Classical mechanics (often called Newtonian mechanics)—The branch of physics and an area of mathematics that involves the study of motion of macroscopic objects under the action of forces or displacements and the subsequent effects of the physical bodies on their environment; and the examination of bodies that remain at rest.

Cosmology—The scientific study of the large scale properties of the universe as a whole. It endeavors to use the scientific method to understand the origin, evolution and ultimate fate of the entire universe.

Critical thinking—Intellectually disciplined thinking that is clear, rational, open-minded, centered on reason and supported by evidence; it is a mental process of skillful conceptualization, analyzing, synthesizing and/or evaluating information gathered from, or generated by, observation, experience, reflection, questioning what biased others say is the truth, and an overall grounding in empiricism.

Dark energy—A mysterious form of energy that accounts for about 70 percent of the mass-energy content of the Universe.

Deep learning (in AI)—A method of learning in artificial intelligence systems in which neural networks have four or more layers, including the initial input and final input; some networks are able to learn unsupervised.

Deepfakes—The AI manipulation of facial appearance through deep generative methods; they are very realistic and hard to detect and therefore pose a threat to humans in a variety of ways.

Deforestation—Refers to the clearing, or permanent removal, of a section of the Earth's forests on a large-scale, almost always resulting in damage to the quality of the land, causing soil erosion, poor water quality, reduced food security, impaired flood protection, and an even greater number of people moving to urban areas. Deforestation releases carbon stored in trees and soil.

Doomsday Clock—A metaphor and symbolic clock adopted by atomic scientists to show how close humanity is to self-destruction and global catastrophe, due to nuclear weapons and climate change.

Ecocide—The extensive damage to, or destruction of, large areas of the natural environment, leading to the loss of ecosystems as a consequence of human activity.

Electrical Induction—Electrical induction, or just induction, is the result of the process of generating electrical current in a conductor by placing the conductor in a changing magnetic field.

Electromagnetic force—Arises from the interaction between electrically charged particles; it is what holds atoms together; it makes the electrons (with negative charge) orbit around positively charged nucleus of the atom.

Electromagnetic Waves—Electromagnetic (EM) waves are waves that are created as a result of vibrations between an electric field and a magnetic field. In this regard, EM waves are composed of oscillating magnetic and electric fields.

Electromagnetism—The study of the interaction among electrically charged particles in electric and magnetic fields and the propagation of electromagnetic waves through space.

Enviromare—An environmentally produced nightmare which causes great harm to humanity and the physical environment.

Ergodic theory—A branch of mathematics that studies statistical properties of deterministic and commutative dynamical systems.

European Council for Nuclear Research (CERN)—A European atomic physics research facility that operates the largest particle physics laboratory that is designed to uncover the make-up of the Universe and discover how the Universe works; there are 23 member states in the intergovernmental organization.

Fermions—Any member of a group of subatomic particles having off half-integral angular momentum.

Finite pool of worry—This theory states that humans have limited emotional resources for worry and therefore when they are already invested in something that really worries them because of a direct influence on their lives they cannot possibly take on additional worries.

Force—A force may influence the motion of an object in a push or pull manner resulting from the object's interaction with another object; a force can cause an object with mass to change its distance, velocity, acceleration, speed and time.

The four fundamental forces of Nature—A key aspect of Einstein's unified field theory consisting of gravitational force, strong (nucleus) nuclear force, weak (nucleus) force and electromagnetic force.

The Fourth Stage of Human Progress—The modified and expanded version of Comte's Law of Three Stages recognizes that humanity has moved beyond the positive stage (stage 3) and has moved on to the fourth stage of human development, or progress, highlighted by Artificial Intelligence (AI).

General theory of relativity—This theory presumes the validity of the *special theory of relativity* (in Einstein's *theory of relativity*); it is a physical theory about space and time involving gravity with gravity being a curving or warping of space. The general relativity theory predicts that the path of light will follow the curvature of spacetime as it passes near a star.

Gravity—Understandably, gravity is a force of utmost importance in physics and for all objects, including humans and other species.

Homo sapiens—The primate species to which modern humans belong and the only member of the genus Homo that is not extinct. "Homo" is the Latin word for "human" or "man" and "sapiens" is derived from the Latin word that means "wise" or "astute."

Indulgences—A practice utilized by the Catholic Church in the Middle Ages that involved selling forgiveness for a sin in exchange for a monetary payment; making such a payment would supposedly absolve one of past sins and/or release one from purgatory after death.

Intelligence—The ability to acquire and apply knowledge and skills which is characterized by the capability to learn or understand and develop complex cognitive feats.

Kangaroo court—A mock court in which the principles of law and justice are disregarded or perverted and ignores recognized standards of law or justice.

Law of Buoyancy—The buoyant force is equal to the weight of the displaced fluid.

Law of Conservation of Mass—This law states that the total mass present before a chemical reaction is the same as the total mass present after the chemical reaction—energy can neither be created nor destroyed; it is converted from one form of energy to another.

Law of Momentum Conservation—This law states that an object/system will not change unless acted upon by an external force.

Law of Refraction—When light travels from one medium to another, it generally bends, or refracts caused by the change in speed.

Law of Three Stages, or Law of Human Progress—Comte's theory that the human mind, each science, and societies evolve through stages: theological, metaphysical and positivism; each stage of development represents a step in human progress.

Level II consciousness—The point when robots reach the ability to think and because these robots possess artificial intelligence, it is a point in time that many people fear.

Linguistics—The scientific study of language and its structure, including syntax, phonetics and semantics.

Logical reasoning—Involves the discovery of causes for human behavior and social events following a rigorous pursuit of explanations; it is a system of forming conclusions based on a set of premises or factual information.

The Manhattan Project—A United States government research project (1942–45) that, under the guidance of J. Robert Oppenheimer, produced the first atomic bombs.

The Many Worlds Interpretation (MWI)—The MWI of quantum mechanics holds that there are many worlds which exist in a parallel at the same space and time as our own.

Mass extinction (ME)—A ME occurs when the planet loses more than three-quarters of its species in a geologically short interval of time, usually during a few hundred thousand to a couple of million years; although a single major event could cause a ME in a very short period of time.

Maxwell-Boltzmann distribution law—A general law based on a probability distribution that can be characterized in a variety of ways.

Mechanical physics—The branch of physics dealing with the study of motion when subjected to forces or displacements and the subsequent effects of the bodies on their environment; the dominant version of physics prior to the introduction of quantum theory, quantum mechanics and string theory.

Mechanics—The general study of the relationships between motion, forces and energy.

Microplastics—Tiny particles that result from both commercial product development and the breakdown of larger plastics.

Mind uploading—The theoretical process of transferring a person's consciousness, memories, and personality into a non-biological substrate, such as a computer or robot.

Molecule—A group of atoms (two or more) held together by an intricate chemical bonding between their electrons.

Motion—Motion is the action of an object changing its location or position with respect to space and time.

Multiple dimensions—The world we live in consists of multiple dimensions; generally we think of three: length, width and depth. Physicists have long promoted a fourth dimension, time. Sting and superstring physicists promote the idea of ten or even sixteen dimensions even though they have yet to provide any proof of such a concept.

Multiverse—The idea that our Universe is just one of many universes that appeared spontaneously out of nothing, each with different laws of nature and different laws of physics.

Neural network—A method utilized in AI that teaches computers to process data in a way that is inspired by the human brain; it is a type of machine learning process, called deep learning that uses interconnected nodes or neurons in a layered structure that resembles the human brain.

Newtonian mechanics, or Newtonian physics—The system of mechanics which relies on Newton's laws of motion concerning the relations between forces acting and motions occurring.

Objectivity—Refers to the researcher being self-conscious about their values, opinions and biases and making sure it does not interfere with the research process.

Observational research—Involves focusing on a social situation and meticulously recording key characteristics and events found in a specific setting.

Ocean acidification—Comes about as a result of the increased output of CO_2 and climate change; it represents a global threat to the world's oceans, estuaries, and waterways.

Optics—The scientific study of the branch of physical science that deals with the properties and phenomena of sight and the behavior of light and the properties of the transmission and deflection of other forms of radiation.

Overpopulation—An excessive number of people in an area to the point of overcrowding, depletion of natural resources, an impaired quality of life, or environmental deterioration.

Paradigm of thought—A model of thinking and a way of viewing reality for a community of like-minded people and their associated behavioral patterns—especially in connection with social interaction.

Particles—Minute portions of matter (e.g., a molecule, atom or electron) that make up everything in the universe; basic units of matter and energy. All things on Earth are made of particles and are in one of three states of matter: solids, liquids or gases.

Personal troubles—An aspect of the "sociological imagination" that reveals that the personal character of the individual affects their behavior and that they are responsible for any personal shortcoming actions.

Physicist—A scientist who specializes in the field of physics.

Physics—The branch of science that is concerned with elements of Nature and properties of matter and energy with a subject matter that includes mechanics, heat, light and other radiation, sound, electricity, magnetism and the structure of atoms.

Planck's constant—A fundamental, or universal, constant that defines the quantum nature of energy and relates the energy of a photon to its frequency.

Positive philosophy—A theoretical doctrine centered on the idea that the social world can be studied in the same manner as the natural sciences through scientific observation and the establishment of natural laws; it is theory that promotes rationality, logic and mathematical proof (through observation and measurement) and rejects metaphysics and theism.

Positivism—A philosophical and socio-political movement which enjoyed a very wide diffusion in popularity in the second half of the nineteenth century in various parts of the world; it was created by Auguste Comte.

Public Issues—An aspect of the "sociological imagination" that demonstrates that there are issues from the environment that are beyond the control of the individual and yet affect their behavior.

Quantum—Refers to a quantity or an amount, specifically, the smallest discrete unit of a phenomenon (e.g., a quantum of light is a photon; a quantum of electricity is an electron); it is the most basic building block and cannot be broken into smaller parts.

Quantum computing—A multidisciplinary field comprising aspects of computing science, physics and mathematics that utilizes quantum mechanics to solve problems faster than classical computers that will revolutionize computing systems by computing multiple values at the same time via subatomic particles, such as electrons or photons.

Quantum electrodynamics—A theory that describes mathematically how light and matter interact.

Quantum entanglement—The theory that two subatomic particles can be intimately linked to each other even if separated by billions of light-years of space.

Quantum mechanics—The field of physics that explains how extremely small objects simultaneously have the characteristics of both particles (tiny pieces of matter) and waves (a disturbance or variation that transfer energy), what physicists call the "wave-particle duality."

Quantum theory—A branch of theoretical physics that seeks to explain phenomena occurring at an atomic and subatomic scale; a theory of matter and energy based on the concept of quanta, especially with regard to quantum mechanics; it represents a break from mechanical physics.

Quarks—Any number of subatomic particles carrying a fractional electric charge and postulated as building blocks of hadrons (a composite subatomic particle made of two or more quarks held together by the strong interaction).

Qubit—The basic unit of quantum information.

Radioactivity—The release of energy from the decay of the nuclei of certain kinds of atoms and isotopes.

Religion—A system of beliefs and rituals that binds people together into a social category of people while attempting to answer the dilemmas and questions of human existence while trying to make the world more meaningful to adherents; followers generally abide by these tenets without question.

Robots—From a physics standpoint, robots often use electromagnets by channeling electricity through already present magnets to help carry out tasks like navigating and performing tasks. Most current robots view humans as simply a collection of pixels moving on their TV sensors; however, as Kaku states, when AI-enhanced robots reach Level II consciousness they will realize that humans are more than just random pixels, and that they have emotional states.

Science—Having attained knowledge through the scientific method.

Scientific method—The pursuit of knowledge involving the stating of a problem, the collection of facts through observation and (perhaps) experimentation, and the testing of ideas (hypotheses) to determine whether they appear to be "valid" or "invalid."

Snell's Law—Expressed in terms of the ratio of the sine of the angle of incidence to the sine of the angle of refraction is a constant for a given color of light and for a given pair of media; this Law is important for optical devices, such as fiber optics.

Social dynamics—The social forces found in society that lead to change (e.g., inventions, innovations and entrepreneurships).

Social physicist—A scientist that utilizes the social physics perspective—which involves incorporating physics (and the related natural sciences), sociology (and the related social sciences and humanities) and the rejection of metaphysics and theism—in their study of humanity, Nature and the Universe.

Social physics—As first coined by Comte, this term was preferred to describe his positivist science and manner of studying society. As it is used here, social physics is a field of science which incorporates physics (and the related natural sciences), sociology (and the related social sciences and humanities) and the rejection of metaphysics and theism.

Social statics—A term used to described the social processes that hold society together (e.g., the criminal justice system, criminal laws, religion and schools).

Social theory—Involves the use of abstract and often complex theoretical frameworks to describe, explain and analyze the social world; in particular, social events and the actions and behaviors of people; while also attempting to uncover patterns that may lead to the discovery of laws.

Sociological imagination—An aspect of the sociological perspective that highlights the importance of the social environment on human behavior; when studying human behavior the personal biography (life history) of an individual is combined with their current social environment thus providing the sociologist with a more complete understanding of the individual.

Sociology—The scientific study of groups, organizations, societies, cultures and the interactions between people.

Solar flares—Outbursts of light and radiation launched from regions of the Sun with intense magnetic fields, whose endpoints are marked on the solar surface by the cooler dark patches known as sunspots.

Spacetime (or space-time)—In physics, spacetime is a mathematical model that fuses the three dimensions of space and the one dimension of time into a four-dimensional continuum; it is a concept that recognizes the union of space and time.

Special relativity theory—An explanation of how speed affects mass, time and space; a moving object measures shorter in its direction of motion as its velocity increases until, at the speed of light, it disappears.

Spirituality—Involves feelings of awe, contentment, wonderment, peace and tranquility.

String theory—A theoretical framework in physics that posits that the most fundamental particles we observe are not actually particles but tiny strings that only "look" like particles through our scientific instruments because they are so small.

The sum-over-histories approach—A concept in quantum mechanics conceived by Richard Feynman that states that particles do not have one history but rather have every possible path, or history, in space-time, and therefore physicists should sum over all possible shapes of space-time.

Superflare—A very large-scale magnetic eruption that expels intense electromagnetic radiation into space.

Supernova—The colossal explosion of a star; it is the biggest explosion that humans have ever seen.

Superstring theory—Attempts to explain all of the particles and fundamental forces of Nature in one theory by modeling them as vibrations of tiny supersymmetric strings; it is a mathematically-based theory built on the idea that vibrating strings of various shapes and a range of tension exist as tiny vibrating objects.

Supersymmetry—The idea that the fundamental particles of Nature are connected through a deep relationship. Supersymmetry is a complex mathematical framework that was developed to enhance the shortcomings of the symmetry framework.

Symmetry—Balanced and proportionate similarity that is found in two halves of an object. In physics, symmetry is the concept that the properties of particles such as atoms and molecules remain unchanged after being subjected to a variety of symmetry transformations or "operations."

Theoretical physics of cosmology—The scientific study of the large scale properties of the Universe as a whole.

Theory—A statement that proposes to explain or relate observed phenomena or a set of concepts; it involves a set of interrelated arguments that seek to describe and explain cause and effect relationships.

Theory of Relativity—This theory encompasses two interrelated physics theories by Albert Einstein: *special relativity* and *general relativity*; it is based on the idea that massive objects cause a distortion in space-time; the theory is connected with the fact that motion from the point of view of possible experience always appears as the relative motion of one object with respect to another.

Thermal expansion—Refers to the increase of the size (length, area or volume) of a body due to a change in temperature, usually as a result in a rise of temperature.

Thermodynamics—The branch of physics that is concerned with heat, temperature and other forms of energy (such as mechanical, electrical or chemical).

Uncertainty Principle—States that we cannot know both the position and momentum of a particle, such as a photon or electron, with perfect accuracy; it refers to the degree of indeterminateness in the possible present knowledge of the simultaneous values of various quantities with which the quantum theory deals with; it is contrary to Newtonian physics.

Unified field theory—An attempt to describe all four fundamental forces of Nature and the relationships between elementary particles in terms of a single theoretical framework. (To date, this theory has not been successfully accomplished.)

United States Environmental Protection Agency—An independent agency of the U.S. government designed to protect human health, welfare, quality of life and the physical environment

The Universe—The totality of all that exists, the entire cosmos, all of space, the billions of galaxies, and all the matter and energy that space contains; it is believed to be at least 10 billion light years in diameter; and it has been expanding since its creation as the result of the Big Bang.

War—A period of collective fighting between large groups or countries through the use of armed combat, usually in an open and declared manner.

Wave-particle duality—A concept in quantum mechanics that refers to the fundamental property of matter where, at one moment matter can exhibit particle-like properties while particles can exhibit wave-like properties.

Wormholes—A hypothetical connection between widely separated regions of space-time.

Bibliography

Acoustics Research Group. 2022. "What is Acoustics." Brigham Young University, Department of Physics & Astronomy. Retrieved July 15, 2022 (https://acoustics.byu.edu/what-is).

Adams, Bert, and R.A. Sydie. 2001. *Sociological Theory*. Thousand Oaks, CA: Pine Forge Press.

Ajo, Reino. 1953. *Contributions to "Social Physics": A Programme Sketch with Special Regard to National Planning*. Lund, Sweden: Royal University of Lund.

Albert, Mathias. 2019. "Luhmann and Systems Theory." *Oxford Research Encyclopedias*. Retrieved March 2, 2024 (https://oxfordre.com/politics/display/10.1093/acrefore/9780190228637.001.0001/acrefore-9780190228637-e-7).

ALS Association. 2023. "What is ALS?" Retrieved December 27, 2023 (https://www.als.org/understanding-als/what-is-als).

American Museum of Natural History. 2000. "Georges Lemaitre, Father of the Big Bang." *Cosmic Horizons Collections*. Retrieved July 12, 2022 (https://www.amnh.org/learn-teach/curriculum-collections/cosmic-horizons-book/georges-lemaitre-big-bang).

American Museum of Natural History. 2023a. "What is Theory?" Retrieved July 27, 2023 (https://www.amnh.org/exhibitions/darwin/evolution-today/what-is-a-theory).

American Museum of Natural History. 2023b. "Quantum Theory." Retrieved August 19, 2023 (https://www.amnh.org/exhibitions/einstein/legacy/quantum-theory).

American Physical Society. 2022. "Michio Kaku: Theoretical Physicist." Retrieved July 23, 2022 (https://www.aps.org/careers/physicists/profiles/kaku.cfm).

American Physical Society. 2024. "Michio Kaku: Theoretical Physicist, Why Physics?" Retrieved January 12, 2024 (https://www.aps.org/careers/physicists/profiles/kaku.cfm).

Amma, T.A. Sarasvati. 1999. *Geometry in Ancient and Medieval India, second edition*. Delhi: Motilal Banarsidass Publishers.

Amsterdamski, Shaul. 2014. "At CERN, God Particle Research at Crossroads." American Committee for the Weizmann Institute of Science. Retrieved July 13, 2022 (https://www.weizmann-usa.org/news-media/in-the-news/at-cern-god-particle-research-at-crossroads/).

Andryszewski, Tricia. 2008. *Mass Extinctions: Examining the Current Crisis*. Minneapolis, MN: Twenty-First Century Books.

Anyoha, Rockwell. 2017. "The History of Artificial Intelligence." Harvard University, Blog. Special Edition on Artificial Intelligence. Retrieved February 3, 2024 (https://sitn.hms.harvard.edu/flash/2017/history-artificial-intelligence/).

Armstrong, Dave. 2012. "Martin Luther's Devotion to Mary." *Catholic Culture*. Available: https://www.catholicculture.org/culture/library/view.cfm?id=788.

Aron, Jacob. 2013. "Gravity Map Reveals Earth's Extremes." *New Scientist,* August 19. Retrieved July 14, 2022 (https://www.newscientist.com/article/dn24068-gravity-map-reveals-earths-extremes/).

Ashcraft, Richard. 1987. *Locke's Two Treatises of Government*. London: Allen & Unwin.

Ashley, David, and David Orenstein. 1985. *Sociological Theory*. Boston: Allyn & Bacon.

Associated Press. 2022. "'Holy Cow': Plants Grow in Soil from Moon, Scientists Find." *Los Angeles Times,* May 16:A14.

Associated Press. 2023. "In Stark U.N. Report, A Quarter of World Lacks Safe Drinking Water." *Los Angeles Times,* March 23:A2.

Associated Press. 2024. "FCC Outlaws AI Voices in Deceptive Robocalls." *The Citizen,* February 9:A3.

Atomic Heritage Foundation. 2019a. "Niels Bohr." Retrieved July 19, 2022 (https://www.atomicheritage.org/profile/niels-bohr).

Atomic Heritage Foundation. 2019b. "Ernest Rutherford." Retrieved July 19, 2022 (https://www.atomicheritage.org/profile/ernest-rutherford).

Atomic Heritage Foundation. 2019c. "Julian Schwinger." Retrieved July 21, 2022 (https://www.atomicheritage.org/profile/julian-schwinger).

Atomic Heritage Foundation. 2022. "Ernest Rutherford." Retrieved August 25, 2023 (https://ahf. nuclearmuseum.org/ahf/profile/ernest-rutherford/).

Aubin, David. 2014 (May). "'Principles of Mechanics that are Susceptible of Application to Society': An Unpublished Notebook of Adolphe Quetelet at the Root of His Social Physics." *Historia Mathematica,* 41(2):204–223.

Augustyn, Adam. 2021. "Symmetry." *Encyclopedia Britannica.* Retrieved January 14, 2024 (https://www. britannica.com/science/symmetry-physics).

Bachman, Rebecca. 2010. "Ordem e Progresso: Popularity of National Flag Amongst Brazilians Means You'll Never Forget Where You Are." *Independent,* February 11. Retrieved July 17, 2023 (https://www. independent.com/2010/02/11/ordem-e-progresso/).

Baggott, Jim. 2018. "What Einstein Meant By 'God Does Not Play Dice.'" *AEON,* November 21. Retrieved August 21, 2023 (https://aeon.co/ideas/what-einstein-meant-by-god-does-not-play-dice).

Bagley, Mary, and Scott Dutfield. 2021. "The Five States of Matter: Definition and Phases of Change." *Live Science,* December 13. Retrieved July 14, 2022 (https://www.livescience.com/46506-states-of-matter. html).

Baines, John R. 2024. "The World of the Dead." *Encyclopedia Britannica.* Retrieved April 15, 2024 (https:// www.britannica.com/topic/Buchis).

Baird, Christopher S. 2019. "Electromagnetism." Boston, McGraw-Hill: *Access Science.* Retrieved July 16, 2022 (https://www.accessscience.com/content/electromagnetism/223000).

Ball, Philip. 2002. "The Physical Modeling of Society: A Historical Perspective." *Physica A,* 314:1–14.

Barabasi, Albert-Laszlo. 2014. *Linked: How Everything is Connected to Everything Else and What it Means for Business, Science, and Everyday Life.* New York: Basic.

Barnes, Harry Elmer, and Ronald Fletcher. 2023. "Auguste Comte." *Encyclopedia Britannica.* Retrieved July 13, 2023 (https://www.britannica.com/biography/Auguste-Comte).

Barnes, Trevor J., and Matthew W. Wilson. 2014. "Big Data, Social Physics, and Spatial Analysis: The Early Years." *Big Data & Society,* 1(1): 1–14.

Barnosky, Anthony D., Nicholas Matzke, Susumu Tomiya, Guinevere O.U. Wogan, Brian Schwartz, Tiago B. Quental, Charles Marshall, Jenny L. McGuire, Emily L. Lindsey, Kaitlin C. Maguire, Ben Mersey, and Elizabeth A. Ferrer. 2011. "Has the Earth's Sixth Mass Extinction Already Arrived?" *Nature,* 471 (7336):51–57.

Basmajian, Carlton. 2023. "If Humans Went Extinct, What Would the Earth Look Like One Year Later?" Space. com, July 4. Retrieved April 28, 2024 (https://www.space.com/what-would-the-earth-look-like-one-year-after-humans-go-extinct).

BBC. 2024. "Life After Death—CCEA: A Belief in Reincarnation." Retrieved April 22, 2024 (https://www. bbc.co.uk/bitesize/guides/zddbqp3/revision/6).

Becker, Brett. 2017. "Artificial Intelligence in Education: What Is It, Where Is It Now, Where Is It Going," pp. 42–46 in *Ireland's Yearbook of Education 2017–2018.* Education Matters.

Bembenek, Scott. 2017. "Why Nobody Believed Einstein When He Discovered How Light Worked." *Salon,* November 5. Retrieved August 15, 2022 (https://www.salon.com/2017/11/05/why-nobody-believed-einstein-when-he-discovered-how-light-worked/).

Benacquista, Matthew J., and Joseph D. Romano. 2018. *Classical Mechanics.* Cham, Switzerland: Springer.

Berryman, Sylvia. 2023a. "Democritus." *Stanford Encyclopedia of Philosophy.* Retrieved April 26, 2024 (https://plato.stanford.edu/entries/democritus/).

Berryman, Sylvia. 2023b. "Leucippus." Stanford Encyclopedia of Philosophy. Retrieved April 26, 2024 (https://plato.stanford.edu/entries/leucippus/).

Bertram, Christopher. 2012. "Rousseau's Legacy in Two Conceptions of the General Will: Democratic and Transcendent." *The Review of Politics,* 74(3):403–419.

The Big Bang Theory. 2008. "The Tangerine Factor." First aired date: May 19, 2008.

Bird, Alexander. 2018. "Thomas Kuhn." *Stanford Encyclopedia of Philosophy.* Retrieved June 24, 2024 (https://plato.stanford.edu/entries/thomas-kuhn/).

Bivens, Josh, and Jori Kandra. 2022. "CEO Pay has Skyrocketed 1,460% since 1978." Economic Policy Institute, October 4. Retrieved July 31, 2023 (https://www.epi.org/publication/ceo-pay-in-2021/).

Blinder, S.M. 2004. *Introduction to Quantum Mechanics: In Chemistry, Materials Science and Biology.* Burlington, MA: Elsevier.

Borenstein, Seth. 2020a. "As People Stay Home, Earth Turns Cleaner." *The Post-Standard,* April 23: A20.

Borenstein, Seth. 2020b. "Study: Carbon Pollution Plunges." *The Citizen,* May 20:A7.

Bourdeau, Michel. 2022. "Auguste Comte." *Stanford Encyclopedia of Philosophy.* Retrieved July 17, 2023 (https://plato.stanford.edu/entries/comte/).

Brecht, Martin. 1985. Martin Luther: *This Road to Reformation, 1483–1521,* translated by James L. Schaaf. Philadelphia: Fortress.

Buchanan, Mark. 2000. *Ubiquity: Why Catastrophes Happen.* New York: Three Rivers Press.

Buchanan, Mark. 2002. *Nexus: Small Worlds and the Groundbreaking Science of Networks.* New York: W.W. Norton & Company.

Buchanan, Mark. 2007. *The Social Atom: Why The Rich Get Richer, Cheaters Get Caught, and Your Neighbor Usually Looks Like You.* New York: Bloomsbury.

Byrd, Deborah. 2021. "Einstein's Most Famous Equation: E=mc2." Earth Sky, September 26. Retrieved August 16, 2023 (https://earthsky.org/human-world/einsteins-most-famous-equation-emc2/).

Calaprice, Alice, and Trevor Lipscombe. 2005. *Albert Einstein: A Biography.* Westport, CT: Greenwood Press.

Calendar. 2020. "The History of the Calendar." *Calendar.com.* Retrieved July 2, 2022 (https://www.calendar.com/history-of-the-calendar/).

California University of Technology. 2023. "J. Robert Oppenheimer on the Caltech Campus." Retrieved August 15, 2023 (https://calisphere.org/item/be95c85ed27be309cd466d6d51aedb8d/).

Carlin, George. 1992. *Jammin' in New York.* Eardrum/Atlantic Records.

Carroll, Sean. 2011. "Are Many Worlds and the Multiverse the Same Idea?" *Discover Magazine,* May 26. Retrieved July 23, 2022 (https://www.discovermagazine.com/the-sciences/are-many-worlds-and-the-multiverse-the-same-idea).

Catton, William R. 1980. *Overshoot: The Ecological Basis of Revolutionary Change.* Urbana, IL: University of Illinois Press.

CBS News. 2024. "Google is Rebranding its Bard AI Service as Gemini. Here's What it Means," February 8. Retrieved February 10, 2024 (https://www.cbsnews.com/news/google-gemini-ai-bard/).

Centers for Disease Control and Prevention (CDC). 2022. "Global Water, Sanitation, & Hygiene (WASH): Fast Facts." Retrieved March 10, 2024 (https://www.cdc.gov/healthywater/global/wash_statistics.html).

Centers for Disease Control and Prevention, National Center for Health Statistics. 2020. "Life Expectancy in the U.S. Dropped for the Second Year in a Row in 2021." Retrieved March 9, 2024 (https://www.cdc.gov/nchs/pressroom/nchs_press_releases/2022/20220831.htm).

CERN (European Council for Nuclear Research). 2022a. "The Big Bang." *CERN Accelerating Science.* Retrieved July 12, 2022 (https://www.home.cern/science/physics/early-universe).

CERN. 2022b."Who We Are." Retrieved July 13, 2022 (https://home.web.cern.ch/about/who-we-are).

CERN. 2022c. "The Higgs Boson." Retrieved July 13, 2022 (https://home.cern/science/physics/higgs-boson).

CERN. 2024a. "Supersymmetry." Retrieved January 14, 2024. (https://home.cern/science/physics/supersymmetry).

CERN. 2024b. "Dark Matter." Retrieved May 8, 2024 (https://home.web.cern.ch/science/physics/dark-matter).

CERN. 2024c. "The Standard Model." Retrieved May 8, 2024 (https://home.web.cern.ch/science/physics/standard-model).

Chalmers, Matthew. 2018. "The Roots and Fruits of String Theory." *CERN Courier,* October 29. Retrieved July 23, 2022 (https://cerncourier.com/a/the-roots-and-fruits-of-string-theory/).

Chugerman, Samuel. 1965 [1939]. *Lester F. Ward: The American Aristotle.* New York: Octagon Books.

The Citizen. 2024. "Google's Gemini AI App to Land on Smartphones," February 10:C5.

Cockerham, William. 1995. *The Global Society.* New York: McGraw-Hill.

Coffey, Donavyn. 2023. "Could a Black Hole Devour the Universe?" Live Science, August 6. Retrieved May 15, 2024 (https://www.livescience.com/space/black-holes/could-a-black-hole-devour-the-universe).

Collins, Randall. 2004. *Interaction Ritual Chains.* Princeton: Princeton University Press.

Collins, Randall, and Michael Makowsky. 2010. *The Discovery of Society, 8th edition.* Boston: McGraw-Hill.

Colom, Roberto, Sherif Karama, Rex E. Jung, and Richard J. Haier. 2010. "Human Intelligence and Brain Networks." *Dialogues in Clinical Neuroscience,* 12(4):489–501.

Commager, Henry Steele. 1967. *Lester Ward and the Welfare State.* New York: Bobbs-Merrill Company.

Comte, Auguste. 1854. *System of Positive Polity* (or *Treatise on Sociology*): *Instituting the Religion of Humanity, Vol. 4.* 1854. Paris: Carilian-Goeury and Vor Dalmont.

Comte, Auguste. 1856. *Social Physics: From the Positive Philosophy of Auguste Comte.* New York: Calvin Blanchard.

Comte, Auguste. 1857. *A General View of Positivism.* New York: Robert Speller & Sons.

Comte, Auguste. 1896 [1830–1842]. *Course of Positive Philosophy,* translated by Harriet Martineau. London: Bell.

Coolman, Robert. 2014. "What is Classical Mechanics?" *Live Science,* September 12. Retrieved July 18, 2022 (https://www.livescience.com/47814-classical-mechanics.html).

Cope, Kevin L. 1999. *John Locke Revisited.* New York: Twayne.

Copeland, B.J. 2024. "Artificial Intelligence." *Encyclopedia Britannica.* Retrieved January 29, 2024 (https://www.britannica.com/technology/artificial-intelligence).

Coser, Lewis. 1977. *Masters of Sociological Thought, Second Edition.* New York: Harcourt, Brace & Jovanovich.

Cross, Katherine. 2019. "Toward a Formal Sociology of Online Harassment." *Human Technology,* 15(3): 326–346.

Crump, Thomas. 2001. *A Brief History of Science: As Seen Through the Development of Scientific Instruments.* New York: Carroll & Graf Publishers.

Cybersecurity & Infrastructure Security Agency. 2020. "Joint Statement from Elections Infrastructure

Government Coordinating Council & the Election Infrastructure Sector Coordinating Executive Committees." Retrieved May 1, 2024 (https://www.cisa.gov/news/2020/11/12/joint-statement-elections-infrastructure-government-coordinating-council-election).

D'Youville University News. 2024. "D'Youville University Features AI Robot Commencement Speaker." News Release, April 24. Retrieved May 12, 2024 (https://www.dyu.edu/news/2024/04/25/dyouville-university-features-ai-robot-commencement-speaker).

Davidson, Michael W. 2022. "Claudius Ptolemy." *Science, Optics & You: Pioneers in Optics.* Retrieved July 2, 2022 (https://micro.magnet.fsu.edu/optics/timeline/people/ptolemy.html).

de Broglie, Louis. 2021. *Research on the Theory of Quanta,* with a Foreword by Hirokazu Nishimura, translated by Andre Michaud and Fritz Lewertoff. Montreal: Minkowski Institute Press.

de Condorcet, Nicolas. 1795. *Esquisse d'un Tableau Historique des Progres de l'esprit Humain.* Paris: Chez Agasse.

Delaney, Tim. 2004. *Classical Social Theory: Investigation and Application.* Upper Saddle River, NJ: Pearson.

Delaney, Tim. 2005. *Contemporary Social Theory: Investigation and Application.* Upper Saddle River, NJ: Pearson.

Delaney, Tim. 2012. *Connecting Sociology to Our Lives.* Boulder, CO: Paradigm.

Delaney, Tim. 2019. *Common Sense as a Paradigm of Thought: An Analysis of Social Interaction.* London: Routledge.

Delaney, Tim. 2020. "'We're All In This Together': Some, More Than Others." *The New York Sociologist,* Vol. 8.

Delaney, Tim. 2024. *Classical and Contemporary Social Theory: Investigation and Application, Second Edition.* New York: Routledge.

Delaney, Tim, and Tim Madigan. 2021. *Beyond Sustainability: A Thriving Environment, Second Edition.* Jefferson, NC: McFarland.

Delaney, Tim, and Anastasia Malakhova. 2020. "The Need for Renewable Energy Resources and the Reasons Why the United States and Russia Lag Behind." *Journal of Strategic Innovation and Sustainability,* 15(2):45–54.

Dijkgraaf, Robbert. 2020. "Remembering the Unstoppable Freeman Dyson." *Quanta,* April 13. Retrieved July 21, 2022 (https://www.quantamagazine.org/remembering-the-unstoppable-freeman-dyson-20200413/).

Dudas, Emilian. 2006. "Aspects of String Phenomenology," pp. 395–455 in *Particle Physics Beyond the Standard Model, Vol. 84* edited by Les Houches. Amsterdam: Elsevier.

Duggal, Nikita. 2023. "Advantages and Disadvantages of Artificial Intelligence (AI)." Simple Learn, November 24. Retrieved February 4, 2024 (https://www.simplilearn.com/advantages-and-disadvantages-of-artificial-intelligence-article).

Dukas, Helen, and Banes Hoffmann, editors. 1979. *Albert Einstein: The Human Side.* Princeton, NJ: Princeton University Press.

Durkheim, Emile. 1928. *Socialism.* New York: Collier Books.

Durkheim, Emile. 1951 [1897]. *Suicide.* New York: Free Press.

Durrani, Matin. 2018. "Stephen Hawking's Final Book: A Review of Brief Answers to the Big Questions." *Physics World,* October 16. Retrieved December 28, 2023 (https://physicsworld.com/a/stephen-hawkings-final-book-a-review-of-brief-answers-to-the-big-questions/).

The Economic Times. 2022. "What is 'Electromagnetic Waves,'" July 14, 2022. Retrieved July 15, 2022 (https://economictimes.indiatimes.com/definition/electromagnetic-waves).

Edgerton, Anna, and Leah Nylen. 2023. "Feds Open Probe on ChatGPT." *The Citizen,* July 15:C3.

The Editors of Encyclopedia Britannica. 2020. "Law of Three Stages." Retrieved January 29, 2024 (https://www.britannica.com/topic/law-of-three-stages).

The Editors of Encyclopedia Britannica. 2022. "Lars Onsager: American Chemist." Retrieved July 13, 2022 (https://www.britannica.com/biography/Lars-Onsager).

The Editors of Encyclopedia Britannica. 2023a. "Henri de Saint-Simon." Retrieved July 12, 2023 (https://www.britannica.com/biography/Henri-de-Saint-Simon).

The Editors of Encyclopedia Britannica. 2023b. "Special Relativity." Retrieved August 16, 2023 (https://www.britannica.com/science/special-relativity).

The Editors of Encyclopedia Britannica. 2023c. "Lester Frank Ward." Retrieved January 28, 2024 (https://www.britannica.com/biography/Lester-Frank-Ward).

Effoduh, Jake Okechukwu. 2021. "Weapons Powered by Artificial Intelligence Pose a Frontier Risk and Need to Be Regulated." World Economic Forum, June 23. Retrieved February 7, 2024 (https://www.weforum.org/agenda/2021/06/the-accelerating-development-of-weapons-powered-by-artificial-risk-is-a-risk-to-humanity/).

Einstein, Albert. 1923. "Albert Einstein Nobel Lecture: 'Fundamental Ideas and Problems of the Theory of Relativity.'" Lecture delivered to the Nordic Assembly of Naturalists at Gothenburg, July 11. Retrieved August 18, 2023 (https://www.nobelprize.org/uploads/2018/06/einstein-lecture.pdf).

Einstein, Albert. 1987. *The Collected Papers of Albert Einstein, Volume 1: The Early Years, 1879–1902.* Princeton, NJ: Princeton University Press.

Einstein, Albert. 1990. *Volume 2: The Swiss Years: Writings, 1900–1909,* edited by John Stachel, David. C. Cassidy, Jurgen Renn and Robert Schulmann. Princeton, NJ: Princeton University Press.

Einstein, Albert. 2016. *The Albert Einstein Collection, Volume One: Essays in Humanism, The Theory of Relativity, and the World As I See It* (Kindle Edition). 2016. Philosophical Library.

Einstein, Albert, Boris Podolsky, and Nathan Rosen. 1935 (May). "Can Quantum-Mechanical Description of Physical Reality Be Considered Complete?" *Physical Review,* 47, 777.

Eitzen, D. Stanley, and George H. Sage. 1989. *Sociology of North American Sport, 4th ed.* Dubuque, IA: William C. Brown.

Emspak, Jesse, and Kimberly Hickok. 2022. "Quantum Entanglement: A Simple Explanation." Science.com, March 16. Retrieved July 22, 2022 (https://www.space.com/31933-quantum-entanglement-action-at-a-distance.html).

Encyclopedia.com. 2019a. "Kaku, Michio 1947-." Retrieved January 12, 2024 (https://www.encyclopedia.com/arts/educational-magazines/kaku-michio-1947).

Encyclopedia.com. 2019b. "How the Major Religions View the Afterlife." Retrieved April 22, 2024 (https://www.encyclopedia.com/science/encyclopedias-almanacs-transcripts-and-maps/how-major-religions-view-afterlife).

Environmental Protection Agency (EPA). 2023a. "Report on the Environment: Contaminated Land." Retrieved March 11, 2024 (https://www.epa.gov/report-environment/contaminated-land).

Environmental Protection Agency (EPA). 2023b. "Clean Air Act Overview: Clean Air Act Title IV—Noise Pollution." Retrieved March 11, 2024 (https://www.epa.gov/clean-air-act-overview/clean-air-act-title-iv-noise-pollution).

Errico, Gina. 2023. "Humans Exploit Like No Other Species." *Los Angeles Times,* June 30:A5.

ESO Supernova. 2024. "Could the Earth Be Swallowed by a Black Hole?" Retrieved May 7, 2024 (https://supernova.eso.org/exhibition/1219/).

Event Horizon Telescope Collaboration (EHT). 2022. "Astronomers Reveal First Image of the Black Hole at the Heart of Our Galaxy." Retrieved July 13, 2022 (https://eventhorizontelescope.org/blog/astronomers-reveal-first-image-black-hole-heart-our-galaxy).

Famous Scientists. 2022. "Max Planck." Retrieved July 18, 2022 (https://www.famousscientists.org/max-planck/).

Famous Scientists. 2024a. "Michio Kaku." Retrieved January 12, 2024 (https://www.famousscientists.org/michio-kaku/).

Famous Scientists. 2024b. "Democritus." Retrieved April 26, 2024 (https://www.famousscientists.org/democritus/).

Feldman, Andrey. 2023. "Explaining the 'Universe Breaker' Galaxies Discovered by the James Webb Telescope." *Advanced Science News,* February 27. Retrieved May 13, 2024 (https://www.advancedsciencenews.com/explaining-the-universe-breaker-galaxies-discovered-by-the-james-webb-telescope/).

Feldman, Burton. 2007. *112 Mercer Street: Einstein, Russell, Gödel, Pauli, and the End of Innocence in Science.* New York: Arcade Publishing.

Ferguson, Kitty. 2012. *Stephen Hawking: An Unfettered Mind.* New York: Palgrave.

Folger, Tim. 2004. "Einstein's Grand Quest for a Unified Theory." *Discover,* September 29. Retrieved August 22, 2023 (https://www.discovermagazine.com/the-sciences/einsteins-grand-quest-for-a-unified-theory).

Forsee, Aylesa. 1963. *Einstein: Theoretical Physicist.* New York: Macmillan.

Frank, Adam. 2023. "How Einstein Challenge Quantum Mechanics and Lost." *Big Think,* January 19. Retrieved August 19, 2023 (https://bigthink.com/13-8/quantum-mechanics-einstein/).

Frankel, Martin. 1983. "Sampling Theory," pp. 21–67 in *Handbook of Survey Research,* edited by Peter H. Rossi, James D. Wright and Andy B. Anderson. New York: Harcourt Brace Jovanovich.

Frey, William, R., Desmond U. Patton, Michael B. Gaskell, and Kyle McGregor. 2018. "Artificial Intelligence and Inclusion: Formerly Gang-Involved Youth as Domain Experts for Analyzing Unstructured Twitter Data." *Social Science Computer Review,* 38(1):42–56.

Gallup International. 2023. "Survey Result/News Detail." Retrieved April 21, 2024 (https://www.gallup-international.com/survey-results-and-news/survey-result/more-prone-to-believe-in-god-than-identify-as-religious-more-likely-to-believe-in-heaven-than-in-hell).

Garfinkel, Harold. 1967. *Studies in Ethnomethodology.* Englewood Cliffs, NJ: Prentice Hall.

Garner, Roberta (ed.) 2000. *Social Theory.* Orchard Park, NY: Broadview.

George, Gerard, Martine R. Haas, and Alex Pentland. 2014. "Big Data and Management: From the Editors." *Academy of Management Journal,* 57(2):321–326.

Gildin, Hilail. 1983. *Rousseau's Social Contract: The Design of the Argument.* Chicago: University of Chicago Press.

Gleick, James. 2022. "Richard Feynman: American Physicist." *Encyclopedia Britannica.* Retrieved July 13, 2022 (https://www.britannica.com/biography/Richard-Feynman).

Gohd, Chelsea. 2024. "What is Dark Energy? Inside our Accelerating, Expanding Universe." NASA, February 5. Retrieved May 8, 2024 (https://science.nasa.gov/universe/the-universe-is-expanding-faster-these-days-and-dark-energy-is-responsible-so-what-is-dark-energy/).

Goldberg, Amir. 2014 (Spring). "Going with the 'Idea Flow.'" *Stanford Social Innovation Review*. Retrieved January 28, 2024 (https://ssir.org/books/reviews/entry/going_with_the_idea_flow).

Goldstein, David L. 2022. "Mechanics." *Britannica*. Retrieved July 18, 2022 (https://www.britannica.com/science/mechanics#ref618102).

Goldstein, Sheldon. 2001. "Boltzmann's Approach to Statistical Mechanics." Retrieved July 12, 2022 (https://arxiv.org/pdf/cond-mat/0105242.pdf).

Goodwin, Albert. 1970. *The French Revolution*. London: Hutchinson.

Gordon, Eden Arielle. 2019. "From Chinese Origins to Gutenberg's Bible: How the Invention of the Printing Press Changed the World." *MagellanTV*. Retrieved July 8, 2022 (https://www.magellantv.com/articles/from-chinese-origins-to-gutenbergs-bible-how-the-invention-of-the-printing-press-changed-the-world).

Grantham-Philips, Wyatte, and Matt O'Brien. 2023. "'Godfather of AI' Leaves Google to Warn of His Creation." *The Post-Standard*, May 4:A1.

Green, Martin. 2022. "Niccolo Machiavelli." *Philosophy Now*, 153 (December 2022/January 2023):46.

Greene, Brian. 2011. *The Hidden Reality: Parallel Universes and the Deep Laws of the Cosmos*. New York: Vintage.

Greene, Brian. 2022. "String Theory." *Britannica*. Retrieved July 23, 2022 (https://www.britannica.com/science/string-theory).

Greene, Nick. 2019. "Hans Lippershey: Telescope and Microscope Inventor." *ThoughtCo*. Retrieved July 8, 2022 (https://www.thoughtco.com/hans-lippershey-3072382).

Gregersen, Erik. 2022a. "Ludwig Boltzmann." *Encyclopedia Britannica*. Retrieved July 12, 2022 (https://www.britannica.com/biography/Ludwig-Boltzmann).

Gregersen, Erik. 2022b. "Acceleration." *Encyclopedia Britannica*. Retrieved July 14, 2022 (https://www.britannica.com/science/acceleration).

Griffiths, David J., and Darrell F. Schroeter. 2017. *Introduction to Quantum Mechanics, Third Edition*. Cambridge: University Press.

Gross, David. 2007. "Einstein and the Search for Unification," pp. 1–13 in *Legacy of Albert Einstein, The: A Collection of Essays in Celebration of the Year of Physics*, edited by Spenta R. Wadia. Hackensack, NJ: World Scientific Publishing Company.

Grossman, Lev. 2011. "2045: The Year Man Becomes Immortal." *Time*, February 22: 42-49.

Gunn, J. Alexander. 1922 (April). "The Philosophy of Emile Boutroux." *The Monist*, 32(2):164–179.

Guy, Jack, and Valentina Di Donato. 2020. "Venice's Canal Water Looks Clearer as Coronavirus Keeps Visitors Away." *CNN Travel*, March 16 Retrieved April 28, 2024 (https://www.cnn.com/travel/article/venice-canals-clear-water-scli-intl/index.html).

Hadden, Richard W. 1997. *Sociological Theory*. Orchard Park, NY: Broadview.

Hamer, Ashley. 2019. "What's the Story Behind That Wacky Einstein Tongue Photo?" *Discovery*, August 1. Retrieved September 4, 2023 (https://www.discovery.com/science/Story-Behind-That-Wacky-Einstein-Tongue-Photo).

Hampson, Norman. 1963. *The Social History of the French Revolution*. Toronto: University of Toronto Press.

Han, Zhao Hong, and Paul Wiita. 2022. "Social Physics and the Dynamics of Second Language Acquisition." *Frontiers*. Retrieved July 18 (https://www.frontiersin.org/research-topics/45825/social-physics-and-the-dynamics-of-second-language-acquisition).

Handwerk, Brian. 2021a. "An Evolutionary Timeline of Homo Sapiens." *Smithsonian*, February 2. Retrieved June 25, 2022 (https://www.smithsonianmag.com/science-nature/essential-timeline-understanding-evolution-homo-sapiens-180976807/).

Handwerk, Brian. 2021b. "Scientists Discover Oldest Known Human Grave in Africa." *Smithsonian Magazine*, May 5. Retrieved April 17, 2024 (https://www.smithsonianmag.com/science-nature/scientists-discover-oldest-known-human-grave-africa-180977659/).

Harmer, Ariel. 2023. "The 10 Most Peaceful Countries to Visit in 2024." *Desert News*, December 6. Retrieved March 13, 2024 (https://www.deseret.com/2023/12/6/23989740/10-peaceful-countries-2024/).

Harrington, Austin. 2022. "Social Theory." *Oxford Bibliographies*, modified, March 23. Retrieved July 28, 2023 (https://www.oxfordbibliographies.com/display/document/obo-9780199756384/obo-9780199756384-0054.xml).

Harrison, Ross. *Hobbes, Locke, and Confusion's Masterpiece: An Examination of Seventeenth-Century Political Philosophy*. New York: Cambridge University Press.

Harrison, Theo. 2024. "Life After Death In Hinduism? Here's What Hinduism Teaches About the Afterlife." *Mind Journal*. Retrieved April 21, 2024 (https://themindsjournal.com/life-after-death-in-hinduism/#google_vignette).

Hartle, Jim B., and Stephen W. Hawking. "Wave Function of the Universe." *Physical Review D*, 28(12):2960.

Hatfield, Gary. 2014. "Rene Descartes." *Stanford Encyclopedia of Philosophy*. Retrieved July 6, 2022 (https://plato.stanford.edu/entries/descartes/).

Hawking, Stephen. 1993. *Black Holes and Baby Universes and Other Essays*. New York: Bantam Books.

Hawking, Stephen. 1996. *The Illustrated A Brief History of Time Updated and Expanded Edition*. New York: Bantam Books.

Hawking, Stephen. 2001. *The Universe in a Nutshell*. New York: Bantam Books.

Hawking, Stephen. 2002. *The Theory of Everything: The Origin and Fate of the Universe*. New York: New Millennium Entertainment.

Hawking, Stephen, G.F.R. Ellis, P.V. Landshoff, D.R. Nelson, D.W. Sciama, and S. Weinberg. 1973/1975 Reprinted Edition. *The Large Scale Structure of Space-Time*. Cambridge: Cambridge University Press.

Hawking, Stephen, and Leonard Mlodinow. 2012. *The Grand Design*. New York: Bantam Books.

Hawking, Stephen W., and Martin Rocek, editors. 1981. *Superspace and Supergravity: Proceedings of the Nuffield Workshop*. Cambridge: Cambridge University Press.

Hawking, Stephen, editor. 2007. *A Stubbornly Persistent Illusion: The Essential Scientific Writings of Albert Einstein*. Philadelphia: Running Press.

Hayward, Laura. 2020. "Death in Ancient Rome: The Fascinating Relationship Between Life and Death." TheCollector.Com, September 4. Retrieved April 15, 2024 (https://www.thecollector.com/death-in-ancient-rome/).

Heisenberg, Werner. 2013 [1949]. *The Physical Principles of the Quantum Theory*. Mineola, NY: Dover

Hetler, Amanda. 2024. "ChatGPT." TechTarget. Retrieved February 3, 2024 (https://www.techtarget.com/whatis/definition/ChatGPT).

Higham, Tom. 2021. *The World Before Us: The New Science Behind Our Human Origins*. Haven, CT: Yale University Press.

Highfield, Roger, and Paul Carter. 1994. *The Private Lives of Albert Einstein*. London: Faber & Faber.

Hiltzik, Michael. 2023. "Spreading Faster than AI Chat Bots: The Hype." *Los Angeles Times*, July 16:A2.

Hobbes, Thomas. 1994 [1651]. *Leviathan,* edited, with an Introduction by Edwin Curry. Indianapolis: Hackett.

Hodgkin, Luke. 2005. *A History of Mathematics: From Mesopotamia to Modernity*. New York: Oxford Press.

Homeland Security. 2023. "Increasing Threat of Deepfake Identities." Retrieved February 8, 2024 (https://www.dhs.gov/sites/default/files/publications/increasing_threats_of_deepfa ke_identities_0.pdf).

Horgan, John. 2019. "String Theory Does Not Win a Nobel, and I Win a Bet." *Scientific American,* October 8. Retrieved July 23, 2022 (https://blogs.scientificamerican.com/cross-check/string-theory-does-not-win-a-nobel-and-i-win-a-bet/).

Hospital for Special Surgery. 2023. "ALS (Amyotrophic Lateral Sclerosis)." Retrieved December 27, 2023 (https://www.hss.edu/condition-list_amyotrophic-lateral-sclerosis.asp).

Howell, Elizabeth, and Andrew May. 2022. "What is the Big Bang Theory? *Space.com,* January 10. Retrieved July 12, 2022 (https://www.space.com/25126-big-bang-theory.html).

Howgego, Joshua. 2022. "Schrödinger's Cat." *New Scientist*. Retrieved July 19, 2022 (https://www.newscientist.com/definition/schrodingers-cat/).

Hyman, Randall. 2024. "These are the Ways Our World Will End." *Astronomy* (March). Retrieved May 6, 2024 (https://www.astronomy.com/science/these-are-the-ways-our-world-will-end/).

IBM Heritage. 2024. "Deep Blue." Retrieved February 3, 2024 (https://www.ibm.com/history/deep-blue).

Iggers, Georg G. 1958. *The Cult of Authority: The Political Philosophy of the Saint-Simonians a Chapter in the Intellectual History of Totalitarianism*. The Hague: Martinus Nijhoff.

Iggers, Georg G. 1959. "The Cult of Authority: The Political Philosophy of Saint-Simonians a Chapter in the Intellectual History of Totalitarianism." *Les Etudes Philosophiques,* 14(3):374–375.

The Indian Express. 2023. "Unpacking Oppenheimer's Cordial Yet Complicated Relationship with Albert Einstein, Who Once Called Him a 'Fool' for Not Turning His Back on the US Govt." Retrieved August 15, 2023 (https://indianexpress.com/article/entertainment/hollywood/oppenheimer-albert-einstein-real-relationship-christopher-nolan-film-8854094/).

Indrasiene, Valdone, Violeta Jegeleviciene, Odeta Merfeldaite, Daiva Penkauskiene, Jolanta Pivoriene, Asta Railene, Justinas Sadauskas, and Natalija Valaviciene. 2021. "The Value of Critical Thinking in Higher Education and the Labour Market: The Voice of Stakeholders." *Social Sciences,* 10(8): 286–305.

Infeld, Leopold. 1950. *Albert Einstein: His Work and Its Influence On Our World*. London: Charles Scribner's Sons.

Institute for Advanced Study. 2022. "Freeman Dyson." Retrieved July 21, 2022 (https://www.ias.edu/sns/dyson).

Institute for Advanced Study. 2023. "Albert Einstein." Retrieved August 15, 2023 (https://www.ias.edu/idea-tags/albert-einstein).

Institute for Economics & Peace (IEP). 2024. "Global Peace Index 2023." Retrieved March 13, 2024 (https://www.visionofhumanity.org/wp-content/uploads/2023/06/GPI-2023-Web.pdf).

Isi, Maximiliano, Will M. Farr, Matthew Giesler, Mark A. Scheel, and Saul A. Teukolsky. 2021. "Testing the Black-Hole Area Law with GW150914." *Physical Review Letters*, 127: 011103.

Jeewandara, Thamarasee. 2020. "Time-reversal of an Unknown Quantum State." Physics.org, August 10. Retrieved July 22, 2022 (https://phys.org/news/2020-08-time-reversal-unknown-quantum-state.html).

Johnson, Hannah. 2020. "70,000 Sea Turtles Nested on Desert Beaches Due to COVID-19." STN2.tv, April 18. Retrieved April 28, 2024 (https://stn2.tv/2020/04/18/70000-sea-turtles-nested-on-deserted-beaches-due-to-covid-19/).

Kaku, Michio. 1994. *Hyperspace: A Scientific Odyssey Through Parallel Universes, Time Warps, and the Tenth Dimension*. New York: Anchor Books.

Kaku, Michio. 1997. *Visions: How Science Will Revolutionize the 21st Century*. New York: Anchor Books.

Kaku, Michio. 2005. *Parallel Worlds: A Journey Through Creation, Higher Dimensions, and the Future of the Cosmos*. New York: Anchor.

Kaku, Michio. 2011. *Physics for the Future: How Science Will Shape Human Destiny and Our Daily Lives by the Year 2100*. New York: Anchor.

Kaku, Michio. 2014. *The Future of the Mind*. New York: Anchor.

Kaku, Michio. 2021a. A post he made on X, March 21. Retrieved January 15, 2024 (https://twitter.com/michiokaku/status/1373683657500721161?lang=en).

Kaku, Michio. 2021b. *The God Equation: The Quest for a Theory of Everything*. New York: Doubleday.

Kaku, Michio. 2022. "Albert Einstein." *Britannica*. Retrieved July 7, 2022 (https://www.britannica.com/biography/Albert-Einstein/From-graduation-to-the-miracle-year-of-scientific-theories).

Kaku, Michio. 2023. "Albert Einstein: German-American Physicist." *Britannica*. Retrieved August 14, 2023 (https://www.britannica.com/biography/Albert-Einstein).

Kaku, Michio. 2024a. "Conversation with Michio Kaku." LearnOutLoud.com. Retrieved January 12, 2024 (https://www.learnoutloud.com/Free-Audio-Video/Science/Physics/Conversation-with-Michio-Kaku/81703).

Kaku, Michio. 2024b. "Official Website: About." Retrieved January 12, 2024 (https://mkaku.org/home/about/).

Kaku, Michio, and Jennifer Thompson. 1995. *Beyond Einstein: The Cosmic Quest for the Theory of the Universe*. New York: Anchor Books.

Kasler, Dirk. 1988. *Max Weber: An Introduction to His Life and Work*. Chicago: University of Chicago Press.

Kastalskiy, Innokentiy, Evgeniya V. Pankratova, Evgeny M. Mirkes, Victor B. Kazantsev, and Alexander N. Gorban. 2021. "Social Stress Drives the Multi-Wave Dynamics of COVID-19 Outbreaks." *Scientific Reports*, 11. Retrieved July 22, 2023 (https://www.ncbi.nlm.nih.gov/pmc/articles/PMC8602246/).

Kaufmann, Thomas. 2017. *Luther's Jews: A Journey into Anti-Semitism*. Oxford: University Press.

Khan Academy. 2017. "Out of Africa." Retrieved June 25, 2022 (https://www.khanacademy.org/humanities/big-history-project/early-humans/how-did-first-humans-live/a/gallery-how-did-the-first-humans-live).

Khan Academy. 2022a. "Heat and Temperature." Retrieved July 14, 2022 (https://www.khanacademy.org/science/chemistry/thermodynamics-chemistry/internal-energy-sal/a/heat).

Khan Academy. 2022b. "The Quantum Mechanical Model of the Atom." Retrieved July 19, 2022 (https://www.khanacademy.org/science/physics/quantum-physics/quantum-numbers-and-orbitals/a/the-quantum-mechanical-model-of-the-atom).

King, Charles W. 2020. *The Ancient Roman Afterlife*. The University of Texas Press.

Klein, Sanford, and Gregory Nellis. 2012. *Thermodynamics*. Cambridge: University Press.

Kobya, Murat. 2018. "Enlightenment and Metaphysics Conception in Auguste Comte." *Turkish Studies*, 13(26):849–859.

Kornblum, William. 1994. *Sociology, Third Edition*. Fort Worth, TX: Harcourt Brace.

Kuhn, Karl F., and Frank Noschese. 2020. *Basic Physics: A Self-Teaching Guide, Third Edition*. Hoboken, NJ: Wiley & Sons.

Kull, Steven, and J.P. Thomas. 2023. "We've Reached a Real Crossroads for AI and Distorting Democracy. *The Citizen*, December 28:A16.

Kumar, Pradeep. 2017 (April). "Heisenberg's Invention of Matrices." *Resonance*, pp. 399–405. Retrieved July 21, 2022 (https://www.ias.ac.in/article/fulltext/reso/022/04/0399-0405).

Kurtus, Ron. 2022. "Snell's Law for the Refraction of Light." Retrieved July 2, 2022 (https://www.school-for-champions.com/science/light_refraction_snell.htm#.YsCjW6jMKM8).

Labbé, Ivo, Pieter van Dokkum, Erica Nelson, Rachel Bezanson, Katherine A. Suess, Joel Leja, Gabriel Brammer, Katherine Whitaker, Elijah Mathews, Mauro Stefanon, and Bingjie Wang. 2023. "A Population of Red Candidate Massive Galaxies 600 Myr after the Big Bang." *Nature*, 616:266–269.

Lakshmibala, S. 2004 (August). "Heisenberg, Matrix Mechanics, and the Uncertainty Principle." *Resonance*, 46–56. Retrieved July 20, 2022 (https://www.ias.ac.in/article/fulltext/reso/009/08/0046-0056).

Lalli, Roberto. 2013. *Einstein As Founding Father of Quantum Theory: Douglas A. Stone: Einstein and the Quantum: The Search of the Valiant Swabian*. Princeton: Princeton University Press.

Lavinsky, Dave. 2014. "Pareto Principle: How to Use It to Dramatically Grow Your Business." *Forbes*, January 20. Retrieved July 31, 2023 (https://www.forbes.com/sites/davelavinsky/2014/01/20/pareto-principle-how-to-use-it-to-dramatically-grow-your-business/?sh=36169a483901).

Lea, Robert. 2024. "Stellar Detectives Find Suspect for Incredibly Powerful 'Superflares.'" Space.com, April 25. Retrieved May 8, 2024 (https://www.space.com/superflare-star-system-more-powerful-than-solar-flares).

Lee, Yongjin, Jaelim Cho, Jungwoo Sohn, and Changsoo Kim. 2023. "Health Effects of Microplastic Exposures: Current Issues and Perspectives in South Korea." *Yonsei Medical Journal*, 64(5):301–308.

Lents, Nathan H. 2019. "Why Are Symmetrical Faces So Attractive?" *Psychology Today*, July 8.

Retrieved January 14, 2024 (https://www.psychologytoday.com/us/blog/beastly-behavior/201907/why-are-symmetrical-faces-so-attractive).

Lewis, Rick. 2023 (April/May). "Mind and Artificial Intelligence: A Dialogue." *Philosophy Now,* Issue 155:3.

Library of Congress. 2022. "How Does Static Electricity Work?" Retrieved July 14, 2022 (https://www.loc.gov/everyday-mysteries/physics/item/how-does-static-electricity-work/).

Library of Congress. 2023. "Annus Mirabilis of Albert Einstein." Retrieved August 15, 2023 (https://guides.loc.gov/einstein-annus-mirabilis/1905-papers).

Lindsay, Alexander. 1943. *Religion, Science, and Society in the Modern World.* New Haven, CT: Yale University Press.

Liu, Aijun, Rajendra Prasad Mahapatra, and A.V.R. Mayuri. 2021. "Hybrid Design for Sports Data Visualization Using AI and Big Data Analytics." *Complex & Intelligent Systems,* 9:2969–2980.

Lloyd, Noah. 2024. "President Joseph E. Aoun tells Northeastern Graduates: 'No Machine Can Match Your Creativity, Innovation." *Northeastern Global News,* May 5. Retrieved May 12, 2024 (https://news.northeastern.edu/2024/05/05/president-aoun-commencement-speech-2024/).

Locke, John. 1867 [1689]. *Two Treatises of Government: A Critical Edition,* introduction by Peter Laslett. London: Cambridge.

Locke, John. 1975 [1690]. *Essay Concerning Human Understanding,* edited with an Introduction by Peter H. Nidditch. New York: Oxford University Press.

Locke, John. 1991 [1689]. *Letter Concerning Toleration,* translated by William Popple. London: Routledge.

Luhmann, Niklas. 1983. "Insistence on Systems Theory: Perspectives From Germany-An Essay." *Social Forces,* 61 (June): 987–996.

Lukes, Steven. 1972. *Emile Durkheim: His Life and Work.* New York: Harper & Row.

Luskin, Casey. 2023. "Ray Kurzweil Predicts: The 'Singularity' by 2045." *Evolution News,* November 8. Retrieved February 18, 2024 (https://evolutionnews.org/2023/11/ray-kurzweil-predicts-the-singularity-by-2045/).

Machiavelli, Niccolo. 2006 [1532]. *The Prince,* translated by W.K. Marriott. The Project Gutenberg EBook. Available: https://www.gutenberg.org/files/1232/1232-h/1232-h.htm.

Maldcena, Juan. 2011. "Black Holes and the Information Paradox in String Theory." Institute for Advance Study. Retrieved January 3, 2024 (https://www.ias.edu/ideas/2011/maldacena-black-holes-string-theory).

Mann, Adam, and Robert Coolman. 2022. "What is Quantum Mechanics?" *Live Science,* March 4. Retrieved July 21, 2022 (https://www.livescience.com/33816-quantum-mechanics-explanation.html).

Manning, Christopher. 2020. "Artificial Intelligence Definitions." Stanford University Human-Centered Artificial Intelligence. Retrieved February 3, 2024 (https://hai.stanford.edu/sites/default/files/2020-09/AI-Definitions-HAI.pdf).

Maria, Sandra. 2020. "The Millisecond 0.001." *Medium,* June 25. Retrieved March 3, 2024 (https://medium.com/@sandramaria2418/the-millisecond-0-001-555d33455fcc).

Mark, Joshua. 2022. "Aristarchus of Samos." *World History Encyclopedia.* Retried July 2, 2022 (https://www.worldhistory.org/Aristarchus_of_Samos/).

May, Andrew. 2021. "4 Bizarre Stephen Hawking Theories that Turned Out to be Right (and 6 We're Not sure About). *Live.science,* July 22. Retrieved January 3, 2024 (https://www.livescience.com/bizarre-stephen-hawking-theories.html).

McKie, Robin. 2013. "The 10 Best Physicists." *The Guardian,* May 11. Retrieved July 11, 2022 (https://www.theguardian.com/culture/gallery/2013/may/12/the-10-best-physicists).

McNamara, Paul. 2011. "Jennings Explains his Jeopardy Loss to Watson." Network World, February 17. Retrieved January 15, 2024 (https://www.networkworld.com/article/751828/data-center-jennings-explains-his-jeopardy-loss-to-watson.html).

Mecklin, John, editor. 2024. "2024 Doomsday Clock Statement." *Bulletin of the Atomic Scientists,* January 23. Retrieved March 13, 2024 (https://thebulletin.org/doomsday-clock/current-time/).

Merali, Zeeya. 2020. "This Twist on Schrödinger's Cat Paradox Has Major Implications for Quantum Theory." *Scientific American,* August 17. Retrieved July 19, 2022 (https://www.scientificamerican.com/article/this-twist-on-schroedingers-cat-paradox-has-major-implications-for-quantum-theory/).

Merchant, Brian. 2024. "How AI Firms Intend to Skirt Copyrights." *Los Angeles Times,* January 16:A6.

Miller Center. 2020. "The 2020 William and Carol Stevenson Conference: The Presidency and Endless War." Retrieved March 13, 2024 (https://millercenter.org/news-events/events/presidency-and-endless-war).

Mills, C. Wright. 1958. *The Causes of World War Three.* New York: Simon & Schuster.

Mills, C. Wright. 1959. *The Sociological Imagination.* New York: Oxford University Press.

Minkewicz, Sarah. 2024. "'Definitely Different': AI Robot Speaks at D'Youville University Commencement Ceremony." WIVB.com, May 11. Retrieved May 12, 2024 (https://www.wivb.com/news/education/definitely-different-ai-robot-speaks-at-dyouville-university-commencement-ceremony/).

Misner, Charles W., Kip S. Thorne, and John Archibald Wheeler. 1973. *Gravitation.* Princeton: University Press.

Mommsen, Wolfgang, and Jurgen Osterhammel, editors. 1987. *Max Weber and His Contemporaries.* Boston: Allen & Unwin.

Moor, James. 2006. "The Dartmouth College Artificial Intelligence Conference: The Next Fifty Years." *AI Magazine*, 27(4):87–91.

Moore, G.E. 1925. "A Defense of Common Sense." Originally appearing in *Contemporary British Philosophy* (2nd series), edited by J.H. Muirhead. Retrieved July 19, 2017 (www.ditext.com/moore/commonsense.html).

Moskowitz, Clara. 2018. "String Theory May Create Far Fewer Universes Than Thought." *Scientific American,* July 30. Retrieved July 23, 2022 (https://www.scientificamerican.com/article/string-theory-may-create-far-fewer-universes-than-thought/).

Murphy, Margi. 2017. "Stephen Hawking Says the Earth Will Be a Fireball by 2600." *New York Post,* November 7. Retrieved January 3, 2024 (https://nypost.com/2017/11/06/stephen-hawking-says-the-earth-will-be-a-fireball-by-2600/).

Museum of the Bible. 2017. "The Guttenberg Press: An Invention that Changed the World." Retrieved July 8, 2022 (https://www.museumofthebible.org/book-minute/the-gutenberg-press-an-invention-that-changed-the-world?utm_source=google&utm_medium=grant&utm_campaign=274305293&utm_content=68249116760&utm_term=gutenberg%20bible&gclid=EAIaIQobChM Iq6-KjMHk-AIVT ciUCR1eLQyfEAAYASAAEgLQrvD_BwE).

Nadler, Steven. 2020. "Baruch Spinoza." *Stanford Encyclopedia of Philosophy.* Retrieved August 21, 2023 (https://plato.stanford.edu/entries/spinoza/).

Nagaraj, Anil Kumar Mysore, Raveesh Bevinahalli Nanjegowda, and S.M. Purushothama. 2013 (Jan.). "The Mystery of Reincarnation." *Indian Journal Psychiatry,* 55(2): S171-S176.

Narlikar, Jayant V. 2007. "Einstein's Legacy: Relativistic Cosmology," pp. 193–206 in *Legacy of Albert Einstein, The: A Collection of Essays in Celebration of the Year of Physics,* edited by Spenta R. Wadia. Hackensack, NJ: World Scientific Publishing Company.

NASA. 2011. "Big Bang Cosmology." Retrieved August 23, 2023 (https://map.gsfc.nasa.gov/universe/WMAP_Universe.pdf).

NASA. 2019a. "Why the Sun Won't Become a Black Hole." Retrieved May 7, 2024 (https://www.nasa.gov/image-article/why-sun-wont-become-black-hole/).

NASA. 2019b. "10 Questions You Might Have About Black Holes." NASA Science Editorial Team, September 23. Retrieved May 15, 2024 (https://science.nasa.gov/universe/10-questions-you-might-have-about-black-holes/).

NASA. 2021. "Double Asteroid Redirection Test (DART)." Retrieved May 6, 2024 (https://science.nasa.gov/mission/dart/).

NASA. 2022a. "Johannes Kepler: His Life, His Laws and Times." Retrieved July 8, 2022 (https://www.nasa.gov/kepler/education/johannes#anchor784359).

NASA. 2022b. "NASA Reveals Webb Telescope's First Images of Unseen Universe." Press Release, July 12. Retrieved July 13, 2022 (https://www.nasa.gov/press-release/nasa-reveals-webb-telescope-s-first-images-of-unseen-universe).

NASA. 2022c. "Optical Telescope Element (OTE)." Retrieved July 15, 2022. (https://www.jwst.nasa.gov/content/observatory/ote/index.html).

NASA. 2023. "Edwin Hubble." Retrieved December 31, 2023 (https://science.nasa.gov/people/edwin-hubble/).

NASA. 2024a. "Frequently Asked Questions." Retrieved March 10, 2024 (https://orbitaldebris.jsc.nasa.gov/faq/).

NASA. 2024b. "What is the Universe?" Retrieved May 13, 2024 (https://science.nasa.gov/exoplanets/what-is-the-universe/).

NASA. 2024c. "Will the Universe Expand Forever?" Retrieved May 14, 2024 (https://wmap.gsfc.nasa.gov/universe/uni_shape.html).

NASA. 2024d. "Dark Energy Changes the Universe." NASA Hubble Mission Team, February 27. Retrieved May 14, 2024 (https://science.nasa.gov/missions/hubble/dark-energy-changes-the-universe/).

NASA. 2024e. "Black Hole Types." Retrieved March 11, 2024 (https://science.nasa.gov/universe/black-holes/types/).

NASA Jet Propulsion Laboratory. 2023. "Webb Celebrates First Year of Science with Close-Up on Birth of Sun-like Stars," July 12. Retrieved May 14, 2024 (https://www.jpl.nasa.gov/news/webb-celebrates-first-year-of-science-with-close-up-on-birth-of-sun-like-stars).

NASA Science. 2022. "NASA Astrophysics." Retrieved July 16, 2022 (https://science.nasa.gov/astrophysics).

NASA Science. 2024a. "What is a Supernova?" Retrieved May 7, 2024 (https://spaceplace.nasa.gov/supernova/en/).

NASA Science. 2024b. "What is a Galaxy?" Retrieved May 13, 2024 (https://spaceplace.nasa.gov/galaxy/en/).

Nassau, Kurt. 2022. "Color: Optics." *Britannica.* Retrieved July 15, 2022 (https://www.britannica.com/science/color).

Natarajan, Vasant. 2008. "What Einstein Meant When He Said 'god Does not Play Dice…'" *Resonance,* July: 655–661.

National Academy of Sciences. 2023. "Albert Einstein." Retrieved August 11, 2023 (http://www.nasonline.org/member-directory/deceased-members/20001817.html).

National Geographic Society. 2024. "Microplastics." Retrieved March 12, 2024 (https://education. nationalgeographic.org/resource/microplastics/).

National Institute of Environmental Health Sciences. 2023. Safe Water and Your Health. Retrieved March 10, 2024 (https://www.niehs.nih.gov/health/topics/agents/water-poll).

National Oceanic & Atmospheric Administration (NOAA). 2024. "Trends in Atmospheric Carbon Dioxide." Retrieved March 10, 2024 (https://gml.noaa.gov/ccgg/trends/).

Nature. 2022. "Optical Physics." Retrieved July 15, 2022 (https://www.nature.com/subjects/optical-physics).

The Nature Conservancy. 2024. "Gulf of Mexico Dead Zone." Retrieved March 12, 2024 (https://www. nature.org/en-us/about-us/where-we-work/priority-landscapes/gulf-of-mexico/stories-in-the-gulf-of-mexico/gulf-of-mexico-dead-zone/).

New World Encyclopedia. 2022a. "Archimedes." Retrieved July 15, 2022 (https://www.newworld encyclopedia.org/entry/Archimedes).

New World Encyclopedia. 2022b. "Classical Mechanics." Retrieved July 18, 2022 (https://www.newworld encyclopedia.org/entry/Classical_mechanics).

New World Encyclopedia. 2023. "Ibn Khaldun." Retrieved July 10, 2022 (https://www.newworldencyclopedia. org/entry/Ibn_Khaldun).

Newton, Roger G. 2000. *Thinking about Physics.* Princeton, NJ: Princeton University Press.

Nichols, John Benjamin. 1902 (Oct.) "Spencer's Definition of Evolution." *The Monist,* 13(1):136–138.

NOAA Fisheries. 2024. "Understanding Ocean Acidification." Retrieved March 12, 2024 (https://www. fisheries.noaa.gov/insight/understanding-ocean-acidification#:~:text=For%20good%20reason%2C%20 ocean%20acidification,hea lth%20is%20also%20a%20concern.).

NOAA Marine Debris Program. 2024. "What is Marine Debris?" Retrieved March 12, 2024 (https:// marinedebris.noaa.gov/discover-marine-debris/what-marine-debris).

The Nobel Prize 2023b. "The Nobel Prize in Physics 1921." Retrieved August 18, 2023 (https://www. nobelprize.org/prizes/physics/1921/summary/).

The Nobel Prize. 2020. "Press Release: Black Holes and the Milky Way's Darkest Secret." Retrieved May 15, 2024 (https://www.nobelprize.org/prizes/physics/2020/press-release/).

The Nobel Prize. 2021. "Albert Einstein: Facts." Retrieved July 12, 2022 (https://www.nobelprize.org/prizes/ physics/1921/einstein/facts/).

The Nobel Prize. 2022a. "Ernest Rutherford." Retrieved July 12, 2022 (https://www.nobelprize.org/prizes/ chemistry/1908/summary/).

The Nobel Prize. 2022b. "Lars Onsager." Retrieved July 13, 2022 (https://www.nobelprize.org/prizes/ chemistry/1968/summary/).

The Nobel Prize. 2022c. "Max Planck: Biographical." Retrieved July 18, 2022 (https://www.nobelprize.org/ prizes/physics/1918/planck/biographical/).

The Nobel Prize. 2022d. "Erwin Schrödinger." Retrieved July 19, 2022 (https://www.nobelprize.org/prizes/ physics/1933/schrodinger/facts/).

The Nobel Prize. 2022e. "Werner Heisenberg." Retrieved July 20, 2022 (https://www.nobelprize.org/prizes/ physics/1932/heisenberg/biographical/).

The Nobel Prize. 2022f. "Paul A.M. Dirac" Retrieved July 20, 2022 (https://www.nobelprize.org/prizes/ physics/1933/dirac/biographical/).

The Nobel Prize. 2022g. "John Clauser: Facts." Retrieved July 22, 2022 (https://www.nobelprize.org/prizes/ physics/2022/clauser/facts/).

The Nobel Prize. 2023a. "Albert Einstein: Biographical." Retrieved August 11, 2023 (https://www.nobelprize. org/prizes/physics/1921/einstein/biographical/).

Olson, Eric. 2024. "Despite Warnings of Potential Injury, Fans Keep Storming Courts After Wins." *The Post-Standard,* January 30:B5.

Omnes, Roland. 1999. *Understanding Quantum Mechanics.* Princeton: University Press.

Online Encyclopedia of Human Thermodynamics (EoHT). 2011. "Social Physics: Generations." Retrieved July 19, 2023 (https://www.eoht.info/page/Social%20physics).

Oppenheimer, J. Robert, and Hartland Snyder. 1939. "On Continued Gravitational Contraction." *Physical Review,* 56(5): 455–459.

Osborne, Hannah. 2019. "Scientists Have Reversed Time in a Quantum Computer." *Newsweek,* March 13. Retrieved July 23, 2022 (https://www.newsweek.com/time-reversed-quantum-computer-1361215).

Overbye, Dennis. 2022. "Scientists Marvel at NASA Webb Telescope's New Views of the Cosmos." *The New York Times,* July 12. Retrieved July 13, 2022 (https://www.nytimes.com/live/2022/07/12/ science/webb-telescope-images-nasa).

Paine, Thomas. 1997 [1776]. *Common Sense.* Mineola, NY: Dover.

Pal, Palash B. 2021. "The Incredibly Strange Story of Einstein's Nobel Prize." ARXIV Archives. Retrieved August 18, 2023 (https://arxiv.org/pdf/2112.13519.pdf).

Parsons, Talcott. 1949 [1937]. *The Structure of Social Action.* Glencoe, IL: Dorsey Press.

Pedrotti, Frank L., Leno M. Pedrotti, and Leno S. Pedrotti. 2018. *Introduction to Optics, Third Edition.* Cambridge: University Press.

Pentland, Alex. 2014. *Social Physics: How Good Ideas Spread—The Lessons from a New Science.* New York: Penguin Book.

Pentland, Alex. 2015. *Social Physics: How Social Networks Can Make Us Smarter.* New York: Penguin Books.

Perelman, Michael. 1978. "Karl Marx's Theory of Science." *Journal of Economic Issues,* 12(4):859=870.

Perkins, Sid. 2023. "Humans Exploit About One-Third of Wild Vertebrate Species." *Science News,* June 29. Retrieved March 11, 2024 (https://www.sciencenews.org/article/humans-exploit-third-wild-vertebrate-species-animals).

Petruzzello, Melissa. 2022. "Isaac Newton's Achievements." *Britannica.* Retrieved July 6, 2022 (https://www.britannica.com/summary/Isaac-Newtons-Achievements).

Pew Research Center. 2024. "Belief in God." Retrieved April 21, 2024 (https://www.pewresearch.org/religious-landscape-study/database/belief-in-god/).

Phys.org. 2022. "Three Scientists Share Nobel Prize in Physics for Work in Quantum Mechanics." Retrieved June 1, 2023 (https://phys.org/news/2022-10-scientists-nobel-prize-physics-quantum.html).

The Physics Hypertextbook. 2022a. "Motion." Retrieved July 13, 2022 (https://physics.info/motion/).

The Physics Hypertextbook. 2022b. "The Nature of Light." Retrieved July 15, 2022 (https://physics.info/light/).

The Physics Hypertextbook. 2022c. "Color." Retrieved July 15, 2022 (https://physics.info/color/).

The Physics of the Universe. 2023. "Special Theory of Relativity." Retrieved August 16, 2023 (https://www.physicsoftheuniverse.com/topics_relativity_special.html).

Physics World. 1999. "Physics: Past, Present, Future." Retrieved August 13, 2023 (https://physicsworld.com/a/physics-past-present-future/).

Pickering, Mary. 1993. *Auguste Comte: An Intellectual Biography, Vol. 1.* Cambridge: University Press.

Pickrell, John. 2006. "Introduction: Human Evolution." *New Scientist,* September 4. Retrieved March 9, 2024 (https://www.newscientist.com/article/dn9990-introduction-human-evolution/).

Plait, Phil. 2013. "The Universe is 13.82 Billion Years Old." *Slate,* March 21. Retrieved May 8, 2024 (https://slate.com/technology/2013/03/age-of-the-universe-planck-results-show-universe-is-13-82-billion-years-old.html).

Planck, Max. 1949. *Scientific Autobiography and Other Papers.* New York: Philosophical Library.

Ple, Bernhard. 2000. "Auguste Comte on Positivism and Happiness." *Journal of Happiness,* 1:423–445.

Population Council. 2011. "Auguste Comte on the Natural Progress of Human Society." *Population and Development Review,* 37(2):389–394.

Pössel, Markus. 2006. "The Sum Over All Possibilities: The Path Integral Formulation of Quantum Theory." *Einstein.online.* Retrieved December 29, 2034 (https://www.einstein-online.info/en/spotlight/path_integrals/#author).

The Post-Standard. 2023. "Galaxies Appear So Massive and Old, They Could be 'Universe Breakers,'" February 23:A19.

Powers, Anna. 2018. "The Theory of Everything: Remembering Stephen Hawking's Greatest Contribution." *Forbes,* March 14. Retrieved December 28, 2023 (https://www.forbes.com/sites/annapowers/2018/03/14/the-theory-of-everything-remembering-stephen-hawkings-greatest-contribution/?sh=4111edbb23ed).

Prakash, Prarthana. 2023. "'The Godfather of A.I.' Just Quit Google and Says He Regrets His Life's Work Because It Can Be Hard to Stop 'Bad Actors from Using It for Bad Things.'" *Fortune,* May 1. Retrieved February 9. Retrieved February 9, 2024 (https://fortune.com/2023/05/01/godfather-ai-geoffrey-hinton-quit-google-regrets-lifes-work-bad-actors/).

Pratt, Carl J. 2021. *Quantum Physics for Beginners: From Wave Theory to Quantum Computing.* Columbia, MD: Ippoceronte Publishing.

Randall, Robert H. 2005. *An Introduction to Acoustics.* Mineola, NY: Dover.

Reid, Thomas. 1764. *An Inquiry Into the Human Mind: On the Principles of Common Sense,* 4th ed. Edinburgh: Edinburgh University Press.

Rickless, Samuel C. 2014. *Locke.* Malden, MA: Wiley-Blackwell.

Rifkin, Jeremy. 1980. *Entropy: A New World View.* New York: Viking.

Rigden, John S. 2005. *Einstein 1905: The Standard of Greatness.* Cambridge, MA: Harvard University Press.

Ritzer, George. 2000. *Classical Social Theory, Third Edition.* Boston: McGraw-Hill.

Ritzer, George, and Jeffrey Stepnisky. 2018. *Sociological Theory, Tenth Edition.* Los Angeles: Sage.

Robinson, Marilynne. 2017. "The Luther Legend." *New Republic,* December 12. Available: https://newrepublic.com/article/145925/luther-legend.

Rockström, Johan, Joyeeta Gupta, Dahe Qin, Steven J. Lade, Jesse F. Abrams, Lauren S. Andersen, David J. Armstrong McKay, Xuemei Bai, Govindasamy Bala, Stuart E. Bunn, Daniel Ciobanu, Fabrics DeClerck, Kristie Ebi, Lauren Gifford, Christopher Gordon, Syezlin Hasan, Norichika Kanie, Timothy M. Lenton, Sina Loriani, Diana M. Liverman, Awaz Mohamed, Nebojsa Nakicenovic, David Obura, Daniel Ospina, and Xin Zhang. 2023 (May). "Safe and Just Earth System Boundaries." *Nature,* 619: 102–111.

Rogers, Leo. "The History of Negative Numbers." *NRICH.* Cambridge: University of Cambridge. Retrieved July 2, 2022 (https://nrich.maths.org/5961).

Rousseau, Jean-Jacques. 2009 [1755]. *Discourse on the Origin of Inequality.* Oxford: University Press.

Rouzé, Michel. 2023. "J. Robert Oppenheimer." *Encyclopedia Britannica.* Retrieved August 3, 2023 (https://www.britannica.com/biography/J-Robert-Oppenheimer).

Rude, George. 1988. *The French Revolution.* New York: Weidenfeld & Nicholson.

Sack, Harald. 2018. "Sir Fred Hoyle—How Big Bang Theory's Eager Opponent was Responsible for its Popularity." *SciHi Blog,* August 20. Retrieved January 2, 2024 (http://scihi.org/fred-hoyle-big-bang-theory/).

Sacristan, Manuel. 2014. "Karl Marx as a Sociologist of Science," pp. 67–120 in *Marxism of Manuel Sacristan* translated and edited by Renzo Llorente. Chicago: Haymarket Books.

Sawhill, Isabel V., and Christopher Pulliam. 2019. "Six Facts about Wealth in the United States." Brookings, June 25. Retrieved July 31, 2023 (https://www.brookings.edu/articles/six-facts-about-wealth-in-the-united-states/).

Scharff, Robert. 1995. *Comte After Positivism.* New York: Cambridge.

Schilpp, Paul Arthur, editor. 1970. *Albert Einstein: Philosopher-Scientist.* London: Cambridge University Press.

Schultz, Isaac. 2022. "Are the Colors in Webb Telescope Images 'Fake'?" Gizmodo, August 6. Retrieved May 9, 2024 (https://gizmodo.com/webb-space-telescope-image-colorization-1849320633).

Schutz, Alfred. 1967 [1932]. *The Phenomenology of the Social World,* introduction by George Walsh. Evanston, IL: Northwestern University Press.

Schweber, Silvan. 2022. "Julian Seymour Schwinger." *Britannica.* Retrieved July 21, 2022 (https://www.britannica.com/biography/Max-Planck).

Science Alert. 2022. "What is the General Theory of Relativity?" Retrieved July 16, 2022 (https://www.sciencealert.com/general-relativity).

Science Alert. 2023. "Who is Stephen Hawking?" Retrieved September 4, 2023 (https://www.sciencealert.com/stephen-hawking).

Science Council. 2023. "Our Definition of Science." Retrieved July 26, 2023 (https://sciencecouncil.org/about-science/our-definition-of-science/).

Scott, Steve. 2019. "Spirituality vs. Religion: 3BIG Differences Between Each." *Happier Human,* July 8. Retrieved June 25, 2022 (https://www.happierhuman.com/difference-religion-spirituality/).

Secrest, Nathan J., Sebastian von Hausegger, Mohamed Rameez, Roya Mohayaee, and Subir Sarkar. 2022. "A Challenge to the Standard Cosmological Model." *American Astronomical Society,* 937(2). Retrieved May 8, 2024 (https://www.physics.ox.ac.uk/news/lopsided-universe-could-mean-revision-standard-cosmological-model).

Seidman, Steven. 1983. *Liberalism and the Origins of European Social Theory.* Los Angeles: University Press.

Sellers, Mortimer N.S. 2015. "Niccolo Machiavelli: Father of Modern Constitutionalism." *Ratio Juirs,* 28(2):216–225.

Sherman, Mark. 2022. "Authority Scaled Back." *The Citizen,* July 1: B8.

Siegel, Ethan. 2017. "The Four Ways the Earth Will Actually End." *Forbes,* September 27. Retrieved May 8, 2024 (https://www.forbes.com/sites/startswithabang/2017/09/27/the-four-ways-the-earth-will-actually-end/?sh=4c4c45454f0f).

Siegel, Ethan. 2023. "How Einstein Made the Biggest Blunder of His Life." Big Think, June 7. Retrieved August 23, 2023 (https://bigthink.com/starts-with-a-bang/einstein-biggest-blunder/).

Simmons, Leigh W., Gillian Rhodes, Marianne Peters, and Nicole Koehler. 2004. "Are Human Preferences for Facial Symmetry Focused on Signals of Developmental Instability?" *Behavioral Ecology,* 15(5):864–871.

Simon, Walter M. 1963. *European Positivism in the Nineteenth Century.* Ithaca, NY: Cornell University Press.

Simpson, David. 2022. "Blaise Pascal (1623–1662)." *Internet Encyclopedia of Philosophy.* Retrieved July 6, 2022 (https://iep.utm.edu/pascal-b/).

Simpson, George. 1969. *Auguste Comte: Sire of Sociology.* New York: Crowell.

Singh, Simon. 2004. *Big Bang: The Origin of the Universe.* New York: Harper Perennial.

Singh, Virendra. 2006. "Einstein and the Quantum," pp. 165–191 in *Legacy of Albert Einstein, The: A Collection of Essays in Celebration of the Year of Physics,* edited by Spenta R. Wadia. Hackensack, NJ: World Scientific Publishing Company.

Singleton, John D. 2011. "Money Is a Sterile Thing: Martin Luther on the Immorality of Usury Reconsidered." *History of Political Economy,* 43(4): 683–693.

Smeenk, Christopher. 2017. "Philosophy of Cosmology." *Stanford Encyclopedia of Philosophy.* Retrieved December 28, 2023 (https://plato.stanford.edu/entries/cosmology/).

Smith, Walter Fox. 2020. *Experimental Physics: Principles and Practice for the Laboratory.* Boca Raton, FL: Taylor & Francis.

Smithsonian Institution. 2018. "Ocean Acidification." Retrieved March 12, 2024 (https://ocean.si.edu/ocean-life/invertebrates/ocean-acidification).

Smithsonian Institution. 2024a. "Introduction to Human Evolution." Retrieved March 9, 2024 (https://humanorigins.si.edu/education/introduction-human-evolution#:~:text=Human%20evolution%20is%20the%20lengthy,of%20approximately%20six%20million%20years).

Smithsonian Institution. 2024b. "Egyptian Mummies." Retrieved April 17, 2024 (https://www.si.edu/spotlight/ancient-egypt/mummies).

Snell, Melissa. 2019. "Profile of Ibn Khaldun, Philosopher and Historian." *Thought.Co.* Retrieved July 10, 2023 (https://www.thoughtco.com/ibn-khaldun-profile-1789066).

Sonmez, Felicia. 2022. "Senate Candidate Herschel Walker Questions Evolution, Asking, 'Why are There Still Apes?'" *The Washington Post,* March 16. Retrieved July 28, 2023 (https://www.washingtonpost.com/politics/2022/03/15/georgia-senate-candidate-herschel-walker-questions-evolution-asking-why-are-there-still-apes/).

Soukup, Paul A. 2017. "A Shifting Media Ecology: What the Age of Luther can Teach Us." *Media Development,* 64)2): 5–10.

Spencer, Herbert. 1862. *First Principles.* London: Williams and Norgate.

Standley, Arline Reilein. 1981. *Auguste Comte.* Boston: Twayne.

Stanford Encyclopedia of Philosophy. 2018. "John Philoponus." Retrieved July 2, 2022 (https://plato.stanford.edu/entries/philoponus/).

Stanford Encyclopedia of Philosophy. 2021. "Many-Worlds Interpretation of Quantum Mechanics." Retrieved July 23, 2022 (https://plato.stanford.edu/entries/qm-manyworlds/).

Stangor, Charles. 2004. *Research Methods for the Behavioral Sciences, 2nd ed.* New York: Houghton Mifflin.

Stayer, James M. 2000. *Martin Luther, German Saviour: German Evangelical Theological Factions and the Interpretations of Luther, 1917–1933.* Montreal: McGill-Queen's University Press.

Stein, Vicky. 2023. "What is the Speed of Light?" Space.com, May 17. Retrieved August 16, 2023 (https://www.space.com/15830-light-speed.html).

Stein, Vicky, and Charlie Wood. 2023. "What is String Theory?" Space.com, May 18. Retrieved January 16, 2024 (https://www.space.com/17594-string-theory.html)

Steinbauer, Anja. 2023 (Dec)/2024 (Jan). "News: AI for Grief." *Philosophy Now,* Issue 159:6.

Sterner, R.W., G.E. Small, and J.M. Hood. 2011. "The Conservation of Mass." *Nature Education Knowledge,* 3(10):20.

Stewart, Ken. 2023. "Atomic Model." *Encyclopedia Britannica.* Retrieved April 26, 2024 (https://www.britannica.com/science/atomic-model).

Stewart, Ken. 2024. "Laws of Thermodynamics." *Encyclopedia Britannica.* Retrieved April 24, 2024 (https://www.britannica.com/science/laws-of-thermodynamics).

Strain, Daniel. 2019. "Rare 'Superflares' Could One Day Threaten Earth." *CU Boulder Today,*" June 10. Retrieved May 7, 2024 (https://www.colorado.edu/today/2019/06/05/superflares).

Stromberg, Joseph. 2015. "Some Physicists Believe We're Living in a Giant Hologram—and It's Not that Far-fetched." *Vox,* Jun 29. Retrieved July 24, 2022 (https://www.vox.com/2015/6/29/8847863/holographic-principle-universe-theory-physics).

Sullivan, Kate. 2024. "Trump Says He Would Encourage Russia to 'Do Whatever the Hell They Want' To Any NATO Country That Doesn't Pay Enough." *CNN Politics,* February 11. Retrieved March 14 (https://www.cnn.com/2024/02/10/politics/trump-russia-nato/index.html).

Susskind, Leonard, and Art Friedman. 2014. *Quantum Mechanics: The Theoretical Minimum.* New York: Basic.

Sutter, Paul. 2021. "What is Quantum Entanglement?" *Live Science,* May 26. Retrieved July 22, 2022 (https://www.livescience.com/what-is-quantum-entanglement.html).

Sutter, Paul. 2021b. "From Quarks to Gluinos: It's Not Looking Good for Supersymmetry." Space.com, January 7. Retrieved January 14, 2024 (https://www.space.com/no-signs-supersymmetry-large-hadron-collider).

Sutter, Paul. 2022. "Will Our Solar System Survive the Death of Our Sun?" Space.com, March 23. Retrieved May 8, 2024 (https://www.space.com/solar-system-fate-when-sun-dies).

Sutton, Christine. 2023. "Unified Field Theory." *Encyclopedia Britannica.* Retrieved August 20, 2023 (https://www.britannica.com/science/unified-field-theory).

Talagala, Nisha. 2021. "Don't Worry About the AI Singularity: The Tipping Point Is Already Here." *Forbes,* June 21. Retrieved February 9, 2024 (https://www.forbes.com/sites/nishatalagala/2021/06/21/dont-worry-about-the-ai-singularity-the-tipping-point-is-already-here/).

Talbert, Tricia. 2018. "Five Years After the Chelyabinsk Meteor: NASA Leads Efforts in Planetary Defense." NASA, February 15. Retrieved May 6, 2024 (https://www.nasa.gov/solar-system/five-years-after-the-chelyabinsk-meteor-nasa-leads-efforts-in-planetary-defense/).

Thomas, Mike. 2023. "12 Risks and Dangers of Artificial Intelligence (AI)." BuiltIn. Retrieved February 5, 2024 (https://builtin.com/artificial-intelligence/risks-of-artificial-intelligence).

Thompson, Kenneth. 1975. *Auguste Comte: The Foundation of Sociology.* New York: Wiley & Sons.

Thompson, Richard C., Bruce La Belle, Hindrik Bouwman, and Lev Neretin. 2011. "Marine Debris as a Global Environmental Problem: Introducing a Solutions Based Framework Focused on Plastics. *STAP Advisory.* Retrieved March 13, 2024 (https://www.thegef.org/sites/default/files/publications/STAP_MarineDebris_-_website_1.pdf).

Thomson, Garret. 1993. *Descartes to Kant.* Prospect Heights, IL: Waveland Press.

Tikkanen, Amy. 2022. "Bohr Model." *Encyclopedia Britannica.* Retrieved July 11, 2022 (https://www.britannica.com/science/atomic-theory).

Tikkanen, Amy. 2023. "Stephen Hawking." *Encyclopedia Britannica,* November 23. Retrieved January 2, 2024 (https://www.britannica.com/science/space-time).

Tikkanen, Amy. 2024. "Drake Equation." *Encyclopedia Britannica,* April 2. Retrieved May 9, 2024 (https://www.britannica.com/science/Drake-equation).

Tilley, David, and Stephen Pumfrey. 2003. "William Gilbert: Forgotten Genius." *Physics World.* Retrieved July 8 (https://physicsworld.com/a/william-gilbert-forgotten-genius/).

Tillman, Nola Taylor, Meghan Bartels, and Scott Dutfield. 2022. "Einstein's Theory of General Relativity." Space.com, January 5. Retrieved July 16, 2022 (https://www.space.com/17661-theory-general-relativity.html).

Tillman, Nola Taylor, and Ailsa Harvey. 2022. "What is Cosmology? Definition & History." Space.com, February 21. Retrieved August 23, 2023 (https://www.space.com/16042-cosmology.html).

Torretti, Roberto. 1999. *The Philosophy of Physics.* Cambridge: University Press.

True, June Audrey. 1989. *Finding Out: Conducting and Evaluating Social Research, 2nd ed.* Belmont, CA: Wadsworth.

Tucker, Robert C. 1978. *The Marx-Engels Reader,* Second Edition. New York: Norton.

Turner, Jonathan. H. 2003. *The Structure of Sociological Theory, 7th ed.* Belmont, CA: Wadsworth.

United Nations (UN). 2023. "Peace, Dignity and Equality on a Healthy Planet." Retrieved March 10, 2024 (https://www.un.org/en/global-issues/food).

United Nations Environment Programme. 2024. "Plastic Pollution. Retrieved March 12, 2024 (https://www.unep.org/plastic-pollution).

United States Department of Energy. 2022. "Nuclear Physics." Retrieved July 16, 2022 (https://www.energy.gov/science/np/nuclear-physics).

United States Department of Energy. 2024. "DOE Explains… Quantum Mechanics." Retrieved June 24, 2024 (https://www.energy.gov/science/doe-explainsquantum-mechanics).

United States Department of State. 2020. "Artificial Intelligence (AI)." Retrieved February 2, 2024 (https://www.state.gov/artificial-intelligence/).

University of Birmingham. 2013. "The Beginning of Time? World's Oldest 'Calendar' Discovered." *Phys.org.* Retrieved July 1, 2022 (https://phys.org/news/2013-07-world-oldest-calendar.html).

University of Bristol. 2021. "Time-Reversal Phenomenon: In the Quantum Realm, Not Even Time Flows As You Might Expect." *Science Tech Daily,* November 26. Retrieved July 23, 2022 (https://scitechdaily.com/time-reversal-phenomenon-in-the-quantum-realm-not-even-time-flows-as-you-might-expect/).

University of Washington. 2021. "Dr. Stephen Hawking: A Case Study on Using Technology to Communicate with the World." Retrieved December 27, 2023 (https://www.washington.edu/doit/dr-stephen-hawking-case-study-using-technology-communicate-world).

U.S. Energy Information Administration. 2024. "Laws of Energy: Energy Transformations." Retrieved April 24, 2024 (https://www.eia.gov/kids/what-is-energy/laws-of-energy.php#:~:text=Energy%20is%20neither%20created%20nor%20destroyed&t ext=To%20scientists%2C%20conservation%20of%20energy,into%20another%2 0form%20of%20energy.).

Van Helden, Albert. 2022. "Galileo: Italian Philosopher, Astronomer and Mathematician." *Britannica.* Retrieved July 8, 2022 (https://www.britannica.com/biography/Galileo-Galilei).

Van Ness, H.C. 1969. *Understanding Thermodynamics.* New York: Dover.

Veblen, Thorstein. 1899. *The Theory of the Leisure Class: An Economic Study of Institutions.* New York: Macmillan.

Veblen, Thorstein. 1921. *The Engineers and the Price System.* New York: Viking.

Violatti, Cristian. 2013. "Ancient Greek Science." *World History Encyclopedia.* Retrieved July 1, 2022 (https://www.worldhistory.org/Greek_Science/).

vos Savant, Marilyn. 2015. "Back to Nature—All the Way Back." *Parade Magazine,* February 14. Retrieved April 28, 2024 (https://parade.com/373513/marilynvossavant/back-to-nature-all-the-way-back/).

Voss, David. 2017. "Virgo & LIGO: Joint Detection of Gravitational Waves." *APS News.* Retrieved July 13, 2022 (https://www.aps.org/publications/apsnews/201710/virgo.cfm).

Wadia, Spenta R. 2007. "Preface: The Legacy of Albert Einstein (1879–1955)," pp. pp. ix-xv in *Legacy of Albert Einstein, The: A Collection of Essays in Celebration of the Year of Physics,* edited by Spenta R. Wadia. Hackensack, NJ: World Scientific Publishing Company.

Wake, David B., and Vance T. Vredenburg. 2008. "Are We in the Midst of the Sixth Mass Extinction? A View from the World of Amphibians." *Proceedings of the National Academy of Sciences,* 105(1): 11466–11473.

Wald, Robert. 2022. *Advanced Classical Electromagnetism.* Princeton: University Press.

Walecka, John Dirk. 2008. *Introduction to Modern Physics: Theoretical Foundations.* Hackensack, NJ: World Scientific.

Ward, Lester Frank. 1883. *Dynamic Sociology, or Applied Social Science, Vol. 1 and Vol. 2.* New York: D. Appleton and Company.

Weinberg, Steven. 2015. *To Explain the World: The Discovery of Modern Science.* New York: Harper Perennial.

West, Darrell M. 2018. "What is Artificial Intelligence?" The Brookings Institute. Retrieved February 2, 2024 (https://www.brookings.edu/articles/what-is-artificial-intelligence/).

White, Matthew. 2018. "The Enlightenment." *The British Library.* Retrieved July 11, 2023 (https://www.bl.uk/restoration-18th-century-literature/articles/the-enlightenment).

White, Michael, and John Gribbin. 1992. *Stephen Hawking: A Life in Science.* New York: Dutton Books.

Whitrow, G.J., editor. 1967. *Einstein: The Man and His Achievement.* New York: Dover.

Williams, L. Pearce. 2022. "History of Science." *Britannica.* Retrieved July 1, 2022 (https://www.britannica.com/science/history-of-science).

Williams, Matt. 2014. "A Universe of 10 Dimensions." Phys.org, December 11. Retrieved January 14, 2024 (https://phys.org/news/2014-12-universe-dimensions.html).

Williams, Matt. 2021. "60 Years Later, Is It Time to Update the Drake Equation?" Phys.org. Retrieved July 16, 2022 (https://phys.org/news/2021-05-years-drake-equation.html).

Wilson, Edward O. 2002. *The Future of Life.* New York: Knopf.

Wolchover, Natalie. 2017. "A Physicist's Physicist Ponders the Nature of Reality." *Quanta Magazine,* November 28. Retrieved January 14, 2024 (https://www.quantamagazine.org/edward-witten-ponders-the-nature-of-reality-20171128/).

Wolchover, Natalie. 2019. "Physicists Debate Hawking's Idea That the Universe Had No Beginning." *Quanta Magazine,* June 6. Retrieved December 31, 2023 (https://www.quantamagazine.org/physicists-debate-hawkings-idea-that-the-universe-had-no-beginning-20190606/).

Wookieepedia. 2024. "The Force." Retrieved April 26, 2024 (https://starwars.fandom.com/wiki/The_Force/Legends).

The World Bank. 2019."Fossil Fuel Energy Consumption (% of total). https://data.worldbank.org/indicator/EG.USE.COMM.FO.ZS.

World Economic Forum. 2022. "Here's How the Earth's Forests Have Changed Since the Last Ice Age." Retrieved March 12, 2024 (https://www.weforum.org/agenda/2022/04/forests-ice-age/).

World Economic Forum. 2024. "AI and Energy: Will AI Help Reduce Emission or Increase Demand? Here's What to Know." Retrieved October 26, 2024 (https://www.weforum.org/agenda/2024/07/generative-ai-energy-emissions/)..

World Health Organization (WHO). 2024. "Guidance on Chemicals and Health." Retrieved March 11, 2024 (https://www.who.int/tools/compendium-on-health-and-environment/chemicals).

Worldometer. 2024. "Coronavirus Tracker." Retrieved April 28, 2024 (https://www.worldometers.info/coronavirus/).

Wüthrich, Urs. 2015. "Die Liebesbriefe des Untreuen Einstein" [The Love Letters of the Unfaithful Einstein]. *BZ Bemer Zeitung.* Bern, Switzerland.

Xia, Rosanna. 2019. "As the Seas Rise, Cities Face Climate Change Cost." *Los Angeles Times,* December 5: B1, B4.

Yang, Jwing-Ming. 2018. "An Introduction to Qi and Qigong." *YMAA,* January, 29. Retrieved May 17, 2024 https://ymaa.com/articles/2014/01/an-introduction-to-qi-and-qigong).

Yates, Emma. 2002. "Hawking's Universe wins Aventis Prize." *The Guardian,* June 26. Retrieved January 1, 2024 (https://www.theguardian.com/books/2002/jun/26/scienceprizes.awardsandprizes).

Zerubavel, Eviatar. 2007. "Generally Speaking: The Logic and Mechanics of Social Pattern Analysis." *Sociological Forum,* 22(2): 131–145.

Zik, Yaakov, and Giora Hon. 2019. "Claudius Ptolemy (ca. AD 100—ca 170) and Giambattista Della Porta (ca 1535–1615): Two Contrasting Conceptions of Optics." *Arxiv.org.* Retrieved July 2, 2022 (https://arxiv.org/ftp/arxiv/papers/1902/1902.03627.pdf).

Index